Richard, Thanks so much for being one of my experts! Sincerely, Carolyn Bennett

The Killingham Matter

by

Carolyn Bennett-Hunter

Copyright 2018 by Carolyn Bennett-Hunter

INDEX

1. Reunion 1

2. Wedding Gift 31

3. Rodeo Queen...69

4. The Other Wife 116

5. Jack 165

6. Lady Elleanor..218

7. Expedition 251

8. Chance Encounter 303

9. Happy Acres..337

10. Artifact 387

Other Books by Carolyn Bennett-Hunter:

City Beyond the Deep

The Widow's Four

The Oceanview Matter

The Powell Mountain Matter

ACKNOWLEDGMENTS

My heartfelt thanks to the family and friends who carefully proofed the pages of this book, including, but not limited to paralegal friends Julie Cohen and Jacky Withem for their extraordinary efforts, unique insights and many helpful suggestions!

Great appreciation to attorney friend Robert Sullivan for his wealth of knowledge pertaining to all things military and for his unique suggestions. Among other things, he has served as an active duty Judge Advocate General for the United States Air Force in civil and criminal law, as well as General Counsel to the State of Nevada for the Air National Guard.

Thanks to attorney friend Rachel Bertoni, to my mother Charlene Bennett, and to friend Jonell Bissonette, for their many hours spent proofing and making it possible for this book to be its best.

Of special mention is the moral support and encouragement from long-time dear friend and film producer Sherry Collins as this project progressed on an almost daily basis. I am particularly grateful for her assistance in arranging for the filming and production of my recent YouTube video interview where all three volumes of The Matter Series were featured – *The Oceanview Matter*, *The Powell Mountain Matter* and *The Killingham Matter*. My heartfelt thanks to videographer Liz Rogers, who is well known for her meticulously researched documentaries, including *On Sacred Ground* and *Hot Water*, which addresses one of the most important stories of our time. Is your drinking water safe? I was astonished by what I saw. Both are films that everyone will want their family and friends to see!

I am particularly indebted to my wonderful husband David for his tireless hours of proofing, advice regarding all things mechanical and equestrian, and his unique perspective on how some of the male characters in this book might have reacted under similar circumstances.

Thank you to friends Susan "Rives" and Janette "Manza" (whose real last names must be kept confidential) for volunteering again to be characters in this book along with Sherry "Collingsworth" and several others whose real names I am not at liberty to disclose.

Many thanks to former classmate and email friend Bert Higa for again sharing his aeronautic expertise, and for looking over the flight sequences included in this book. Bert was a chief inspector at an aircraft repair station for commercial airliners, inspected propulsion systems for orbiting spacecraft, and worked for many years as an airplane mechanic. Bert is now semi-retired but actively participates in piloting small planes on humanitarian aid missions of mercy to third world countries.

Special thanks to church friend Kent Garrett for confirming the factual accuracy of the flight sequences herein. Kent is a retired Air Traffic Controller and commercial pilot with experience flying many different types of airplanes.

Unlike the old days when it was necessary for writers to make repeated trips to the local library while researching various topics, a vast realm of knowledge is literally at one's fingertips in today's modern electronic age. I am especially grateful for the marvelous "Wikipedia" feature on my computer.

My appreciation to Mazda Mokalla and Bryan Ball from The Shutterbug for all their hard work photoshopping and typesetting the cover of this book.

Thanks to Richard Hilts, owner and manager of the City View Funeral Home & Cemetery for taking time from his busy schedule to visit with me and explain the finer points of exhumation. Not only did Rick describe the legalities involved, but also the physical aspects of an actual dig and removal. I had no idea so much was involved.

Finally, my great appreciation to proofers Rachel Bertoni and Jacky Withem for suggesting that I include a *Killingham Family Tree*. Nothing too elaborate, just something basic that lays out the direct family line, and a helpful tool to make the book more enjoyable for the reader.

FOREWORD

Will Kevin and Linda Killingham finally manage to unravel the remaining mystery behind Kevin's real father? Or will Kevin's desire to finally find and meet his real father prove to be his downfall?

Will the Priest and Krain Detective Agency discover who the *black widow* is in time to stop her from striking again? Or will Mark Killingham finally get his just reward for bilking innocent women of their life savings and become the *black widow's* next victim?

What will Kevin do when he finds out his wife has been married before? An emotional rollercoaster of romance between the most unlikely people will keep you intrigued. Mystery and suspense will keep you turning the pages.

Killingham Family Tree
(Quick Reference Guide)

Jeremy Killingham, 1848-1922, from Dingle, Ireland
(spouse Bonnie – all progeny raised at the Killingham Lighthouse)
        Daisy Killingham, born 1869[1]
        Rose Killingham, born 1870
        Violet Killingham, born 1871
        Lilly Killingham, born 1872
        Rosemary Killingham, born 1874
        Heather Killingham, born 1875
        Petunia Killingham, born 1878

[1]Daisy Killingham, 1869-1892
(abandoned by the sailor who fathered her boys)
        Jed Killingham, born 1890[2]
        Bill Killingham, born1891

[2]Jed Killingham, born 1890
(never married mothers of his children)
        Jack Killingham, Sr., born 1910[3]
        James Killingham, born 1911[4]
        Ellie Mae Killingham, born 1912[5]

[3]Jack Killingham, Sr., born 1910
[5]Ellie Mae Killingham, born 1912
        Mark Killingham, born 1930[6]
        Jack Killingham, Jr., 1930-2009
        Vivian (Killingham) Lamont, born 1932

[4]James Killingham, born 1911
 Bell Sanderson
        James Killingham, Jr., 1930-2005

[6]Mark Killingham, born 1930
 Linda Dixon *(Mark's first wife and stepsister)*
        Ray Dixon Killingham (Roth)
 Maria Santori *(one of Mark's wives)*
        Michael (Killingham) Santori, born 1949
        Justin (Killingham) Santori, born 1950
        Phillip (Killingham) Santori, born 1951
        Evan (Killingham) Santori, born 1954
        Eric (Killingham) Santori, born 1956
 Bobby Sue Johnson *(another of Mark's wives)*
        Kevin (Smith) Killingham, born 1956

1. Reunion

Quickly winding its way along the blufftop highway, the white Dodge Dart rental car that Kevin Killingham was driving that day narrowly avoided going off the road.

"Slow down!" yelled Linda as she grabbed the handgrip on her side. "It would be nice to get there in once piece!"

"Oh, quit complaining," countered Kevin. "At least you're getting to go."

"Would you *please* slow down?" persisted his wife as she shot him an angry glance.

"Shut up and enjoy the scenery or I'm turning back right now!" hollered Kevin. *They had been driving for nearly four hours already and should be there by now!* He was tired, hungry and very irritable. The last thing he wanted to do was spend his weekend with a group of complete strangers. Kevin much preferred to spend his free time hunting and fishing in the wilderness, as far from most people and city life as possible.

Linda folded her arms and scowled as she glared out the passenger side window at the row of windswept eucalyptus trees beside them, and at the sprawling ocean beyond. *Had it really been 49 years since her graduation from Oceanview Academy in 1974?*

"Hey, look, I'm sorry," Kevin apologized. He had no desire to continue their argument in front of her friends – none of whom he had ever met – and they were almost there.

Linda merely pouted and refused to answer. His apology just did *not* sound sincere.

Spying a rest stop along the way, Kevin pulled in and brought the vehicle to a stop. After getting out long enough to use the restroom, Kevin returned and slowly climbed back in. "It is beautiful here."

Linda could tell he was about to apologize again, so decided to maintain her silence.

Kevin reached over and tenderly put a hand on Linda's shoulder. "Do you want to drive the rest of the way?"

"I thought you'd never ask," Linda suddenly smiled as she leaned over and gave her husband a kiss on the cheek. "Apology accepted."

After changing places with him, Linda started up the engine and leisurely resumed their journey. Just then, a seagull flew by overhead, unexpectedly dropping its "present" onto the hood of the car.

"Nice!" laughed Kevin. He knew how important it was to Linda that the car they arrived in be clean and presentable. In fact, she was so concerned about it that she had insisted upon using a rental car rather than their own older-model Subaru. "I'll clean it off before we get there, at the next turnout. Be sure to remind me."

"Thanks, I'd appreciate that," responded Linda as she flirted with her handsome husband. Thankfully, she had persuaded him to use some beard dye on his graying facial hair that morning. "Your beard looks great, by the way. You look at least 15 years younger now."

"Yeah, yeah," chuckled Kevin. "You're just saying that cause it's true."

"Well, it is. And thank you for coming," added Linda. "It means a lot to me."

"I know," sighed Kevin. "It's just too bad your hair color can't be an affordable over-the-counter brand like mine."

"Well, I've considered it," answered Linda as she slowed for a hairpin turn, "but matching the exact shade to the hair sample I had from high school is not exactly something you can find in a box."

"But, over two hundred dollars at the hair dresser?" Kevin furrowed his brows and shook his head. "Just to color your hair?"

"That included the cut, too," elaborated Linda. "Not only that, they waxed my eyebrows. You know how important this is to me."

"I doubt that many of your classmates fared as well as you did, especially after all these years," predicted Kevin.

Linda was six feet tall with curved shapely legs, alabaster skin, penetrating blue eyes and dark brown shoulder length hair. She flashed Kevin one of her beautiful smiles and her eyes twinkled with delight at his compliment. She did yoga exercises each day and worked diligently at maintaining her physique.

"I suppose that didn't include the nail job?" razzed Kevin.

"Nope," grinned Linda as she flexed the fingers on her lovely hands where they rested on the steering wheel. "They don't do acrylic nails where I get my hair done."

"So, how much did that cost me?" teased Kevin.

"Only about $70," advised Linda. The royal blue acrylic nails were an exact match to the lowcut sweater top she wore with her formfitting black leather pants. The high heeled black leather boots she had on exactly matched the black leather dress jacket on the back seat beside her new overnight bag.

Kevin's aging camouflage-patterned duffel bag sat next to it. He had also brought along a long narrow tube containing his fly rod – just in case there might be some free time for him to do some fly fishing while he was there.

"How much is the room where we're staying?" pressed Kevin.

"More than too little, and less than too much," bantered Linda as she slowed to read the sign ahead.

"The *Killingham Lighthouse Bed and Breakfast?*" Kevin was surprised and suddenly frowned. His real father, Mark Killingham, had never mentioned anything about a lighthouse or a bed and breakfast in the family, at least not during the short time they had been in contact with one another. Kevin's mother had remarried when he was quite young to a man named Peter Smith, the father figure Kevin had grown up with. It was not until adulthood that he had finally found and met his birth father. Ironically, things had gone badly – very badly – and the relationship had ended abruptly.

"I wasn't sure you'd come if you knew," admitted Linda.

"And if *he* is here, then what?" demanded Kevin.

Kevin was well aware of the threats Mark Killingham had made against Linda during the brief time they had known him in 1981, and how upset Linda had been after their other encounter with Mark in 2016. Frankly, Kevin had no desire to see the man again. *Why was Linda willing to risk an encounter with him now?*

"Aren't you sick and tired of worrying whether or not we will run into him again?" questioned Linda as she turned onto Silver Creek Road. She would never forget Mark Killingham telling her that she should plan to look over her shoulder for the rest of her life.

Kevin took that opportunity to remove his handgun from its concealed holster and pulled back the action just enough to check for a live round in the chamber.

"Seriously?" scoffed Linda. "Are you planning to shoot him?"

"A man's gotta be ready for anything," replied Kevin. "Always be prepared."

"I was just hoping to finally find him and get the police to arrest him," Linda advised. "After everything he's done – and not just to us – he should be put away. And frankly, I'm sick and tired of feeling like I have to look over my shoulder all the time."

"You're always safe with me," promised Kevin as he carefully tucked his handgun back into its holster.

"You know I don't approve of that thing," reminded Linda as they emerged from the dense section of coastal forest and passed by a well-kept golf course before stopping at a wrought iron security gate.

"We can always find another place to stay," suggested Kevin.

"It's probably not even him. Still, Killingham is an unusual name," mumbled Linda as she pressed the "guest" button on a kiosk beside the gate, immediately causing it to swing open so they could drive through without getting out.

"Nice," admired Kevin.

A short but sturdy brick wall bordered the cliff-side edge of the steep road ahead of them leading to the lighthouse above.

Shimmering rays of afternoon sun reflected off the water of the vast but peaceful ocean beside them as they made their way up the narrow road. The smell of eucalyptus and cypress trees hung heavily in the air. Seagulls cawed loudly as they circled overhead, searching for unsuspecting prey along the beach below. The hypnotic sound of ocean waves licking the shoreline echoed up the mountainside next to them.

"Oh, no! The hood!" Kevin suddenly realized that he had not yet cleaned the seagull poop from the hood of the car. "When we get there, wait while I take care of it, before we go inside."

"Thanks." Linda grinned with amusement as she abruptly reached the top of the hill, pulled into a parking spot, and handed her husband a small pack of tissues from the dashboard. She then got out of the car to admire the view while she waited, but her attention was immediately drawn to the lighthouse.

The unusually shaped white structure was trimmed all in bright red. The building itself was octagonal in shape and approximately thirty feet in diameter. A long, pointed tower projected upward at least sixty feet from its center that was only about fifteen feet in diameter at the very top, but entirely round. Randomly placed windows could be seen spiraling their way up its exterior, obviously to provide natural lighting to as many interior locations as possible. An octagonal shaped lookout tower at the very top had large picture windows on all sides, except for a single arched exit door that led to an exterior catwalk which encircled the entire upper tower at that level. The catwalk was about three feet wide, could only be accessed through the arched exit door, and was protected by a sturdy wrought iron railing that had been painted white. The tower's conical shaped roof came to a perfect point on top and was covered entirely with bright red ceramic tiles. At ground level there was a covered entryway, also covered with bright red ceramic tiles. The cement porch and steps leading up to it were painted bright red, to match the ceramic tiles, and a large brass bell mounted beside the front door was graced with a long brass chain with which to ring it.

In front of the lighthouse was a well-lit freestanding sign that read, "Killingham Lighthouse Bed and Breakfast."

"What are those other buildings over there?" wondered Linda aloud as she and Kevin finally started toward the front door.

"Those are for the generators and yard maintenance stuff," advised a vaguely familiar voice from behind her.

Linda turned around and stared with disbelief. "Jim Otterman?"

"None other," smirked Jim as he and Linda embraced. "I saw your name on the guest register."

"I can't believe it's you!" marveled Linda.

"You are signed up to stay in the Daisy Room," reminded Jim with a wry grin.

"This is *your* place?" questioned Kevin.

"You could say that," replied Jim as he turned his attention to the man beside Linda.

"Forgive me," apologized Linda. "This is my husband Kevin."

"Kevin *Killingham*," added Kevin as he and Jim shook hands.

"Nice to meet you, sir. I'm an old friend of your better half," grinned Jim as he nodded towards Linda, causing her to blush.

Kevin narrowed his eyes at Jim, not sure what to make of his remark.

"Killingham is an unusual name," added Jim as he motioned toward the front door. "Any relation to a Mark Killingham?"

Linda became serious. "He's not *here* right now, is he?"

"Not for a while now," answered Jim.

"You don't expect him this weekend, do you?" pressed Kevin, concerned about the possibility of an unpleasant encounter between Linda and his estranged father.

"I'm sure we'll have plenty of time to talk after you get settled," promised Jim as he opened and held the front door open for them. "The reunion's not until tonight."

"You didn't answer my question," pointed out Kevin as he stood there with his arms folded. He was not about to budge until Jim gave him a straight answer.

Kevin reminded most people who met him of an actor from the 1980s who starred as a vice detective on a popular TV series filmed in Miami. So much so, in fact, that he had been asked on more than one occasion for his autograph, back in the day. Kevin was an intimidating presence toward most strangers. To the few who really knew him, Kevin was a devoted friend who would do just about anything for them, especially his lovely wife Linda. He loved her with all his heart and could refuse her nothing.

"Very well, then," Jim finally relented. "Mark Killingham is buried in the Ocean Bluff Cemetery, up on the hill by The Ocean Bluff Mental Institution."

"You don't say?" Linda was clearly relieved by the news.

"Any relation?" frowned Jim.

"My father," answered Kevin, who was surprisingly undisturbed by the news.

"I'm sorry for your loss," apologized Jim.

"We're not!" blurted out Linda. "He was an awful man."

"Are we talking about the same Mark Killingham who owned and ran the ice cream shop over in Ocean Bluff for all those years?" scowled Jim. "The old guy was almost 80 years old when his stepson Ray found him dead on the floor there one morning. Everybody loved Mark Killingham."

"He can't possibly have been the same man who used to bring ice cream over to the school, *could* he?" Linda was flabbergasted. "Oh, my God! I always wondered where I'd seen Kevin's father before. Now that I think of it, that was it! It had to be him. I'm pretty sure."

"An ice cream shop?" questioned Kevin. "I didn't realize he actually had a shop somewhere."

"He ran the shop for years," added Jim as he began walking into the lighthouse, hoping that Linda and her husband would follow.

"When did he die?" questioned Linda.

"Well, let's see." Jim paused to fold his arms and put one hand on his chin as he thought about it. "It would have been around 2009. I can look it up if you like. It would also be on his headstone up there at the cemetery."

"That's just not possible," differed Linda. "The last time we saw Mark Killingham was in 2016."

"That's right," corroborated Kevin. "We were at the Saturday market up in Seattle on vacation."

"And you had just bought that 40-pound Chinook salmon at the fish place there, right before we ran into him," remembered Linda.

"Well, it obviously was a different Mark Killingham then," reasoned Jim as Kevin and Linda followed him inside to register.

"Then he could still be out there somewhere," worried Linda.

Kevin sighed deeply and shook his head with frustration.

"There's a photo of Mark Killingham on the wall of the ice cream shop down there at the golf course, put there in his memory," recalled Jim as he handed keycards to each of his guests. "These can be synchronized with your smartwatches if you wish to use them instead."

"Hey, thanks, sorry for overreacting," apologized Linda. She suddenly felt foolish.

"You know, I do seem to remember something about a twin brother or something," remembered Jim. "My daughter Ann has done the genealogy for that side of the family and would know. Perhaps it was his long-lost twin brother."

"No, it was definitely him," maintained Kevin. "We spoke."

"Humph," snorted Jim as he began ascending the spiral staircase but paused about a third of the way up by two tandem crescent-shaped guest rooms that had been built just off the staircase at that level. "This is The Daisy Room. The other room on this level is The Violet Room."

"I can see that," advised Kevin. He was losing his patience. "The names are on the doors."

"As are the other rooms above us," advised Jim. "There are two rooms on each of the four levels as you make your way to the top. The rooms are actually named after their original occupants."

7

"That's neat," admired Linda. "Hey, look at the beautiful hardwood floors and the Queen Anne furniture in those rooms."

Kevin merely nodded. As the adopted son of a general contractor, Kevin had worked extensively with wood himself and had an eye for quality craftsmanship. He was just not much for useless chitchat.

"The bed quilts and matching throw rugs were all made by hand," informed Jim. "And so were the wooden rocking chairs and seat cushions. All made by the original Killinghams who lived here."

"Where are the restrooms located?" asked Linda, suddenly realizing the need to use one.

"There's one toilet at each level, shared by the two guest rooms on that level," revealed Jim. "Each room has its own sink, but the showers are all downstairs."

Kevin shot Linda a look of displeasure. "And I suppose there's no television?"

"No," smirked Jim. It was obvious that Kevin was not as enthusiastic about being there as Linda was.

"Where are the door scanners for the keycards?" questioned Linda.

"The keycards are for the main entrance door downstairs," laughed Jim. "There are no locks on the inside rooms, but we've never had any complaints before. And, we ask that anyone going out for the day please straighten their room and leave the door open for when other guests come on a tour of the lighthouse."

"I'm not comfortable with that," replied Kevin.

"We do have state-of-the-art security cameras both inside and outside the front door, as well as in the common areas and everywhere else besides the actual rooms," bragged Jim. "Not only that, visitors on tours always have a staff member with them."

"If Linda's happy with it, then fine," Kevin finally acceded.

"Great. Let me just show you the tower room," continued Jim, "where breakfast will be served each morning from 6:30 until 8:30."

"I need to use the facilities first," advised Linda as she headed into the small restroom on that floor. "I'll be right up."

"This way, sir," Jim motioned for Kevin to follow.

As Kevin followed Jim up the spiral staircase, afternoon sunlight streamed in from above. "Anyplace to get lunch around here? I don't think I can wait until tonight to eat again."

"You haven't had lunch yet?" Jim seemed surprised, since it was already 1:30 in the afternoon.

"No," grunted Kevin. *Why would he ask about it if he had?*

"The only place around here is the school cafeteria, but I'm afraid they have it shut down at the moment," apologized Jim. "They are busy getting everything ready for the reunion tonight."

"Cafeteria food?" questioned Kevin. "For a reunion?"

"I'm sure it will be a step up from what they normally serve," laughed Jim as they reached the tower room.

Kevin carefully studied the highly shellacked, natural wood siding that covered all eight of the octagonal room's four-foot high surrounding walls and the interior of its conical shaped ceiling above them. Resting above each four-foot wall was a large viewing window made of bullet-proof glass that extended upward to the room's fifteen-foot high ceiling above. "Nice job on the finish work," remarked Kevin.

"Right here is where the main lighthouse lamp used to be, when this was used as a lighthouse," informed Jim as he motioned toward the perfectly round wooden table in the center of the room. The table was surrounded entirely by a perfectly round wooden bench, both of them made from the same highly shellacked yellow pinewood that covered the inner ceiling and walls.

"What happened to the lamp?" frowned Kevin.

"It was Mark Killingham's idea to have the table put here to fill up this space after the lighthouse was decommissioned by the military at the end of World War II," explained Jim.

"That still doesn't explain what happened to the lamp," pointed out Kevin as he glanced up at the expensive looking Tiffany chandelier hanging above the round table, right where the lighthouse lamp would normally be.

"Nice use of space," commented Linda from the doorway to the tower room as she entered. "I like it."

"Jim was just about to tell us what happened to the lamp that was originally here," reported Kevin.

"It was confiscated by the military and taken to another lighthouse somewhere else," revealed Jim.

"But, why?" pressed Kevin.

"Because you can't have a functioning lighthouse without proper approval," explained Jim. "You must have a valid permit to be

9

in compliance with federal regulations, and since it was the military who voided the Killinghams' permit and decommissioned the lighthouse in the first place, it hardly seemed likely they would change their minds."

"How sad," remarked Linda.

"Not only that, there's a complete set of installation, validation and operational protocols, as well as on-site inspection requirements that are necessary to be sure the system complies both electronically and procedurally with federal code. Besides, you'd need the right kind of lamp, and those were pretty hard to come by in those days. Still are, in fact," described Jim. "The special type of compound lens used by a lighthouse lamp is also extremely expensive. It's not like you can just go pick one up at the hardware store. They have to be custom made."

Kevin suddenly became intrigued by the ingenious use of space in the lookout tower room. Beneath the counter and sink, was a series of wooden cupboards and some open shelves filled with dishes and various cooking tools in small wooden boxes with handles on them. On the next wall was a small red refrigerator. Beside it was a bright red, hard plastic trash receptacle with swinging lid, where the very edge of a trash can liner could barely be seen protruding. *Perhaps something like this might be just the thing for a custom-built motor home someday,* considered Kevin. *If only he could get Linda to travel more!*

Two more of the eight four-foot walls were filled entirely with shelves of rare and valuable looking old books. The catwalk access door faced due west on the ocean-side wall. The final two walls were located on either side of the catwalk access door's wall, and had bench seats built right into them from the same highly shellacked knotty pinewood veneer that adorned the rest of the lookout tower room. Bright red seat cushions placed on the bench seats bore a striking resemblance to the chaise lounge cushions once manufactured at a nearby lumber mill to accompany its popular patio furniture kits.

"I remember sewing on chaise lounge cushions like that when I worked at the lumber mill," reminisced Linda.

"You worked in a lumber mill?" chuckled Kevin.

"She did," corroborated Jim. "In fact, that's where those cushions are from."

10

"Just about all the kids who went to school at Oceanview Academy had jobs," added Linda. "We would go to classes half a day and then work the other half."

"They still have the kids doing that," informed Jim.

Kevin leaned close to Linda and whispered, "We really do need to go get some lunch."

"Yeah, we do," agreed Linda.

"How 'bout here?" suggested Jim, whose hearing was excellent. He then walked over to the small red refrigerator and began taking out jars of mustard and mayonnaise and a package of thinly sliced lunch meat. "There's a loaf of bread in that bread keeper on the counter."

Kevin shrugged and nodded. "Sure, why not? What do I owe you for it?"

"It's on the house," offered Jim. "It will give Linda and me a chance to visit and catch up. Who knows, we might not have that opportunity later at the reunion."

"Sounds good to me," beamed Linda as she walked over to the window to admire the view while her husband helped Jim make the sandwiches. She was accustomed to having Kevin make their meals at home, anyway.

The sound of ocean waves could be heard crashing against the craggy shoreline below, interrupted occasionally by cries from a lone seagull as it circled overhead in search of small prey below, near the shoreline. It was almost mesmerizing to watch the panoramic scene sprawled out below and around them, complete with brilliant tentacles of light moving across the water's surface while the bright afternoon sun slowly made its way toward the ocean horizon.

"Just how many are expected to show up for the reunion?" quizzed Kevin.

"Maybe 40 or 50," guessed Jim. "Several class members are no longer with us, you know."

"Like who?" asked Linda as she approached and sat down at the table. She had waited for years to finally see Lenny Owens again, and fervently hoped he was still around to see her now. If nothing else, Lenny would be able to see how great she still looked, and what he'd missed out on all those years ago by choosing to focus his attentions on Carolyn Bennett instead of her.

11

Jim became somber and remained silent for several moments as he and Kevin finished making the sandwiches, but did not answer her question. Jim was well aware of the feelings Linda once had for Lenny when they were in high school together. *Should he tell her yet?*

"I thought you ate already," Linda razzed Jim, in an attempt to get him to say something.

"Actually, no," admitted Jim. "Things have been pretty busy around here with Susan and Ann both gone."

"Your family?" assumed Kevin as he started to take a bite from his sandwich.

"Can we bless the food first before we eat?" requested Linda.

Kevin sighed deeply and suddenly began, "Dear Lord, thank you for safe travels and for this food we are about to eat. We thank you also for Jim and his hospitality. Amen."

"Amen," chorused Linda and Jim.

"Ann is actually my stepdaughter," described Jim. "Her mother Sheree and I were married in 2016."

"So, who is Susan, then?" questioned Kevin as he proceeded to devour his sandwich.

"Susan Rives was Ray Killingham's wife," continued Jim as he grabbed three bottles of mineral water from the small refrigerator and handed one to Linda and another one to Kevin.

"Ray Killingham?" repeated Kevin, with his mouth still partly full of food. "The stepson of the same Mark Killingham who used to live here?"

"The man who allegedly died in the ice cream shop?" asked Linda rather skeptically.

"When they were both alive, yes. You knew him as Ray Dixon when you went to school here," advised Jim. "He was the handyman and fix-it guy who worked for the Dean over at the girls' dormitory."

Linda looked as if she had been hit by a bolt of lightning. "You're kidding me, right?"

"Why?" interjected Kevin. "Was there something wrong with Ray Dixon?"

"Well," replied Linda, "for one thing, he was about 20 years older than Susan – if we are talking about the same Susan Rives who was Carolyn Bennett's roommate. For another, it was common knowledge that he was an ex-convict, though no one was really sure what he'd been in prison for. Still, the guy was just plain creepy."

12

"Seems to me you thought I was pretty creepy myself, back in the day," reminded Jim with a mischievous grin. "I never was sure whether it was the bright red hair or the greasy men's hair tonic that turned girls off the most."

Linda blushed with embarrassment. "You'd never know it now that you had a severe acne problem or Coke-bottle glasses back then, either."

"Or that I was thin as a rail," added Jim with amusement.

"Why would your friend Susan marry someone like Ray?" Kevin suddenly asked.

"First of all," elaborated Jim, "Ray was never in prison. His mother died in childbirth, so his stepfather raised him alone."

"Mark Killingham?" grilled Kevin.

"Yes," replied Jim. "It was in the 1960s when Ray served in Vietnam. He was honorably discharged with a Medal of Honor just before coming to Oceanview Academy to stay and work for his aunt."

"So, that was why he had a crewcut like that," realized Linda with a nod of understanding.

"Back then, most guys with crewcuts were either ex-cons or ex-military," added Kevin as he unscrewed the cap on his bottle of mineral water and took a drink.

"Except here," smiled Linda, feeling foolish for having assumed that Ray had been an ex-convict.

"When Susan ran into Ray again in 2016," continued Jim, "she was in the middle of going through an ugly divorce from her first husband. Alcoholic."

"How sad," acknowledged Linda. True, she had never liked Susan much when they were in school, but no one deserved to go through something like that.

"Where is Ray now?" pressed Kevin. "I'd like to talk with him while we're here."

"I'm afraid that won't be possible," responded Jim with his mouth full.

"I suppose he's dead, too?" Kevin was being flip.

"Just last month," responded Jim with a serious expression on his face. "Heart attack on March 23rd followed by an unsuccessful transplant surgery. He died the following day."

"How horrible!" exclaimed Linda as she set down her sandwich. She was no longer hungry.

"Where is Susan?" questioned Kevin.

"She and Ann are down in South America right now," revealed Jim. "Remember Carolyn Bennett?"

Linda merely glared at Jim in return. *Of course, she remembered Carolyn Bennett!*

"Well, Carolyn won the Powerball last week," described Jim. "She had always wanted to visit Machu Picchu. So, she took Susan, Ann and another lady named Sherry with her, who spells her name with a *y* instead of two *e*'s like my wife Sheree does."

"Carolyn won the $43 million-dollar jackpot?" Linda could not help but feel jealous about it.

"Why there?" frowned Kevin. "That's not exactly a safe place for women to be traveling alone, even if they are in a group."

"Susan's new husband – a guy named Rupert – is with them," revealed Jim. "They'll be alright."

"Why there?" Kevin asked again. *Was Jim trying to hide something? Why couldn't the man simply answer a direct question?*

"Susan's previous husband died last month and she already has a new one?" questioned Linda with obvious disapproval.

"That's about the size of it," replied Jim. He did not want to get into the particulars of it with Kevin and Linda just then.

Jim's mind began to wander as he thought about the tragic death of Ray Killingham, right when *The Powell Mountain Matter* was being solved.

"You never answered my question," reminded Kevin.

"What question?" frowned Jim.

"Why, of all the places in the world there are to go, would Carolyn want to visit Machu Picchu?" reminded Kevin.

Jim suddenly got up and walked over to the book shelf, grabbed a hollow faux book, and pulled out a recent color photograph for them to see. The small round object pictured was roughly three inches in diameter, half an inch wide, covered with ancient markings, and appeared to be solid gold!

"Where is it now?" questioned Kevin.

"In a safe place," assured Jim. "This faux book is where we first found it, though. Right here in this room, just last month."

"What does it say?" Linda suddenly wanted to know.

"Susan's husband – *Professor* Rupert Williams – confirmed it to be Sumerian," replied Jim with a sly smile. "Cuneiform began as a

14

system of pictographs but was eventually replaced by the Phoenician alphabet around the time of the Neo-Assyrian Empire. These are also the same type of characters used on the Code of Hammurabi. Anyway, the writing continues on the back." Jim then pulled out a second color photo for them to see.

"So, this is why they went to Machu Picchu?" scowled Kevin.

"We believe it's a treasure map," clarified Jim.

"Maybe this is how the Killinghams were able to afford this lighthouse in the first place?" guessed Linda.

"Who knows?" Jim merely shrugged his shoulders as he took a big drink of water.

"And, perhaps there's even more treasure where that came from," pointed out Linda, rather excitedly as she began to look more closely at the other books in the bookshelf.

"We've already checked out the other books," smiled Jim. "*All* of them."

"What numbers did she play?" pressed Linda.

"Well," began Jim. "It was on March 23, 1973, that the tragedy involving Steve Fredrickson, Veronica Jensen and Joyce Troglite took place – I'm sure you remember that. Anyway, 3 and 23 were two of the numbers she used."

"That seems like it would be bad luck," opined Kevin.

"Apparently not for her!" snapped Linda. "What else?"

"I believe she also used the number 16," continued Jim, "since that's how old she was when all that happened."

"And?" encouraged Linda.

"It was 43 years later when she and Susan came back here and finally found out what had happened to them," revealed Jim. "So, 43 was another one of her numbers."

"They found out what happened to Joyce and Veronica?" Linda became excited. She had been one of the volunteers who had originally combed the beach looking for them in 1973 but had never heard anything about the case being solved.

"Yes indeed. They were murdered by Jon Roth," replied Jim rather sadly.

"Jon Roth?" scowled Linda.

"Birdboy," clarified Jim.

"No way!" Linda could hardly believe it.

"Never let my wife Sheree hear you call him that."

"Why not?" questioned Linda.

"Because he was her first husband," replied Jim. "And, Jon Roth aka Birdboy was Ann's real father."

"Sheree Wilkins ended up marrying Birdboy?" Linda gasped with surprise. *Still, Sheree had been Birdboy's date at the Harvest Festival Prom when they were in high school together.*

"It was on March 23, 2016, when Jon Roth committed suicide right in front of his wife Sheree. Carolyn and Ray were there, too," volunteered Jim. "But, that is a long and horrible story and I don't want to get into it right now."

After an awkward silence while everyone finished eating their sandwiches, Kevin finally recounted, "3, 23, 16 and 43. That makes four. What other numbers did Carolyn use?"

"Well, she was 66 years old when she finally returned here for a subsequent visit this last month – still is, in fact – so that was the fifth number," answered Jim.

"What about the Powerball?" urged Kevin.

Jim hesitated before responding. "1979 was the last time Carolyn ever saw Lenny Owens, so 79 was the Powerball."

"You seem pretty certain about that," noted Linda as she exchanged a meaningful glance with Jim.

"Yes, ma'am," smirked Jim. He was not about to tell her just yet how he was so certain about the last time Carolyn had seen Lenny, or that the final number he had just mentioned was inaccurate.

"Tell me again how the Powerball works," requested Linda. She hoped that the expression on her face had not been noticed by Kevin when Jim mentioned Lenny Owens.

"Well, drawings include five winning numbers drawn from a pool of balls, as well as one extra ball called the Powerball. If you're lucky enough to match five numbers and the Powerball, then you'll hit the jackpot. The odds are about 1 in 292,201,338 of winning a jackpot per play," recounted Jim.

"Hold it!" interjected Kevin. "There are only 69 balls to choose from in the Powerball pool. There is no 79."

"You got me," laughed Jim.

"I think he's making this whole thing up," accused Kevin with a sarcastic grin.

"Alright," relented Jim. "The numbers Carolyn played were 3, 23, 16, 43, 66 and 59 – not 79."

"Why 59?" questioned Linda. *Did the number still have something to do with Lenny Owens? What wasn't Jim telling her?*

"Who knows," lied Jim as he shrugged his shoulders. He and Linda locked eyes at that moment, and it did not go unnoticed by Kevin. Jim did know why, and Linda knew it!

While it was true that Carolyn had funded the expedition to Machu Picchu with her lottery winnings, doing so had been totally unnecessary, at least as far as Jim was concerned. Jim's financial worth far exceeded anything imaginable and it was difficult for him to understand her refusal to accept his help. Nevertheless, Carolyn had finally agreed to allow Jim to fly her and her group down to South America in his Learjet. Jim then managed to convince them to keep in touch by skyping him each afternoon at 3:00, and to let him know when they were ready for him to come pick them up and bring them back. Despite his best efforts to conceal the fact that he still had feelings for Carolyn – even after all these years – it was rather obvious, particularly to his wife Sheree.

"I take it you and Carolyn have kept in touch?" pressed Linda with an accusing smirk.

"You could say that," responded Jim, rather evasively.

The red-headed, freckle-faced man had been hopelessly in love with Carolyn Bennett during their junior year of high school, relentlessly attempting in vain to win her affections. Linda Shaver had been just as hopelessly in love with Lenny Owens. Acting together, Linda and Jim had hatched one unsuccessful plan after another to try to keep Lenny and Carolyn apart.

Still barely five feet eight inches tall, skinny and gangly looking, with slouched bony shoulders, Jim's fair complexioned skin was continuously sunburned, especially around his freckled ears and face. Jim had once switched from glasses to contact lenses in an attempt to make himself more appealing to Carolyn, but finally reverted back to wearing glasses again. Jim had also quit wearing greasy looking hair tonic in high school, again in a useless attempt to make himself more desirable to Carolyn. Jim's curly but well-trimmed red hair still continued to have its own mind without the use of hair tonic.

"I thought you were going to start that last load of laundry," chastised Sheree as she entered the tower room, surprised to see Linda and Kevin. "Oh, I'm sorry! I didn't realize anyone was here yet."

"You know Linda Shaver, dear," motioned Jim.

"Oh, yes, hello," smiled Sheree, still embarrassed that Linda had seen her in her work clothes.

"This is my husband Kevin," introduced Linda. "Kevin *Killingham.*"

"Killingham?" questioned Sheree. "For some reason, I figured that was a mistake in the guest register."

"He's got a father named Mark Killingham," advised Jim.

Sheree merely stared at Kevin with disbelief as she slowly came over and sat down beside her husband.

"You look great!" Linda complimented Sheree as she gaped at Sheree with awe. Sheree looked absolutely amazing now and nothing like she had in high school!

In high school, Sheree had worn horn-rimmed glasses. Not only that, the Coke-bottle eyeglasses Sheree had worn were so thick that her eyes had resembled large insect eyes. Sheree's acne problem had been quite noticeable back then, as well, with her buck teeth firmly attached to an unsightly orthodontic headgear device that had wrapped around her head. Sheree had also been extremely flat chested, knock-kneed, and had worn flat shoes with thick braces on them. To top that off, she had worn a special brace on her back after surgery to correct damage from a serious car accident her family had been involved in.

Sheree now had clear alabaster skin, piercing blue eyes, beautiful straight teeth, and healthy shoulder length dark hair with no trace of gray in it. Corrective eye surgery had eliminated any need for eyeglasses, and her trim but shapely body was stunning. Linda suddenly felt a twinge of jealousy as she noticed her husband flirting with Sheree.

"Very pleased to meet you," acknowledged Kevin as he reached out to shake Sheree's hand and held it for a moment longer than Linda felt was necessary. "For some reason, I was under the impression you were in South America at the moment and that Jim was running the place here by himself."

Neither Linda or Jim were amused by Kevin's remark.

"I'm Sheree – with two *e*'s. The other Sherry – with a *y* like in the drink – is a friend of Carolyn's from Ashton."

"Dear, we need to ask Ann about Mark Killingham's twin brother when she skypes us again," mentioned Jim.

"Okay, sure," agreed Sheree rather guardedly. "Ann is the genealogist in our family, so that's probably a good idea." *Just who was this Kevin Killingham, anyway? Was he here to try and claim some sort of ownership in the lighthouse? And if he was, what would happen to their bed and breakfast?*

It had been at Carolyn's suggestion seven years ago that Jim had decided to marry Sheree, so that she would have someone to care for her following the untimely suicide of her former husband Jon Roth. Sheree had secretly managed over time to learn of her new husband Jim's sizable fortune, inherited following his parents' demise during an avalanche over in Switzerland when they were skiing in the Alps back in 2004. Not only had Jim Otterman inherited their fortune, but also his dad's multi-million-dollar brokerage firm. Though employees had been hired to run it for him, it still was necessary for Jim to show up once or twice a year for board meetings.

Jim still maintained his aging Cessna as a patrol plane for occasional flights over the beach as he had done when previously serving as the town Sheriff, and would take up guests wishing to participate in occasional skydiving adventures. Jim's plane of choice was now a Learjet. Not only did this make Jim's periodic trips to the home office of his mortgage brokerage firm more enjoyable, but also made it more convenient for him to commute back and forth from the Priest and Krain Detective Agency up in Ocean Bay where he was a silent partner. Naturally, his Learjet featured the best-in-class ease of mobility available with ample leg and headroom, and seating for up to eight passengers.

"How long have you two been married?" asked Kevin.

"Seven years," replied Jim. "Sheree, would you like a sandwich, while I have this stuff out?"

"Sure," accepted Sheree as she grabbed a plate from the cupboard and began making herself a sandwich. "Can I make another one for anyone else?"

"We're good until tonight," assured Kevin as he flashed one of his winning smiles at Sheree. A woman Sheree's age needed to know she was admired by someone else once in a while. It might bolster her confidence. He knew it would bother Jim but really didn't care. What he didn't realize was how much it bothered Linda.

Sheree blushed deeply but said nothing as she resumed making her sandwich. Clearly, she was pleased by the attention. Linda merely glared at her.

"How old is your daughter Ann?" questioned Kevin.

"She's 23," replied Sheree.

"No kidding," responded Kevin. "You don't look old enough to have a daughter that age. Neither of you."

"Ann's father was Jon Roth," informed Sheree with a pointed glance at Linda. "You knew him as Birdboy, I believe."

Linda suddenly looked as if the pit of her stomach had fallen out. *Was the subject of Birdboy now open for general conversation?* A warning stare from Jim answered her question in the negative.

"What's Ann like?" probed Kevin.

"She is rather thin and pale complexioned," described Sheree. "She also has my straight dark hair and facial features." *Not to mention my large hooked nose!* thought Sheree, though too self-conscious to mention it out loud.

"Then she must be a beauty indeed," flirted Kevin.

Sheree blushed again. "I'm afraid Ann spends most of her time helping Marine Biology Professor John Murray and his wife Jeon maintain and operate the Killingham Wildlife Center on campus near the dairy where her colony of feral cats still lives," elaborated Sheree. "At least when she's here."

"Her husband Ted Jensen is the nephew of Veronica Jensen," added Jim as he glanced at Linda.

"*The* Veronica Jensen who went missing in 1973?" asked Linda, being careful not to mention in front of Sheree that she was aware of the murders.

"The same," verified Jim. "Ted spends most of his time maintaining the Silver Creek Golf Course next door, when he's not out surfing and boogie boarding. He and Ann live over in Ms. Eggersol's old house, right by the Roth House."

Linda was shocked. "I thought they outlawed all surfing and boogie boarding along here, especially after what happened to Steve Fredrickson! What a needless way for some to die."

"People forget, or just don't think it can happen to them," replied Jim. "It actually was outlawed, for a while. Now they have a surfboard factory on campus, right where the lumber mill used to be. That's one of the campus jobs."

20

"Making surfboards?" doubted Linda. "You're kidding?"

"They even allow the kids to wear blue jeans on campus now," informed Jim. "They also let the guys and girls hold hands these days, as long as it is in public and they aren't doing anything else."

"Sounds like it was pretty strict before," chuckled Kevin.

"It was," promised Linda as she thought of Lenny Owens. Hopefully, he would be at the reunion that night so she might have a chance to visit with him. *Since he wasn't with Carolyn, was he married to someone else? Was he happy? Had he finally become a doctor?*

"The Roth House, by the way, is where Jon and I lived when he was alive," volunteered Sheree. "It's nothing more than a tourist attraction now. Be sure and go through it if you get a chance while you're here. I think you'll find it quite interesting."

"Kevin, you might enjoy the arsenal of weapons down in the bunker tunnel beneath it," suggested Jim. "I notice you carry."

"Concealed," replied Kevin, rather guardedly.

"Me, too," responded Jim with an even grin. "Boot holster."

"That's a little too far for me," replied Kevin as he palmed his hip. "I like to keep my waist holster at a 15-degree forward cant where I can get at it in a hurry if I need it."

"Touché!" exclaimed Jim.

After bringing in their suitcases, Kevin and Linda headed for the ice cream shop at the golf course. Fluffy white clouds danced against the azure sky as a brisk ocean breeze suddenly hit them from the side.

"My hair!" fretted Linda.

"You'll be fine," assured Kevin. He found the crisp air to be refreshing.

"I hope they have vanilla," mentioned Linda as she struggled to negotiate the downhill road in her high heeled boots.

"And black walnut," grinned Kevin as he gently grasped Linda's arm to assist her.

"I think that golf course used to be a trailer park," commented Linda as they finally approached the level area where it was located. "Golf actually sounds like fun – with the right shoes, of course."

"You know I don't play golf," cautioned Kevin. "I mainly want to see that picture of Mark Killingham they have on the wall there."

"And make it back before they skype with Ann at 3:00?" doubted Linda. "It's already 2:45."

"Then we'd best hurry."

"We close at 3:00 today," informed a handsome, well-built Polynesian man as they entered the tiny shop. "Because of the reunion."

"You must be Ted Jensen," assumed Linda.

"Who wants to know?" frowned the long-haired young man.

"I was Linda Shaver, a former classmate of Jim's. He mentioned that you might be over here."

"Sure," nodded Ted. "Strawberry, chocolate or vanilla?"

"No black walnut?" scowled Kevin.

"Sorry, everything else is already over at the cafeteria for the reunion," apologized Ted. "There's probably some over there."

"I'll have some vanilla," advised Linda.

As Ted began scooping some of the delicious smelling vanilla ice cream onto a cone for her, Linda mentioned, "I was one of the volunteers who helped search for Joyce and Veronica when they first went missing in 1973."

"Really?" Ted seemed surprised.

"I understand Veronica was your aunt," added Linda as she took the vanilla ice cream cone from Ted and quickly licked a drip from the side.

"Yes, she was," confirmed Ted as he studied Linda more closely.

"Chocolate," selected Kevin as he glanced at the old black and white photo of Mark Killingham hanging on the wall behind Ted.

"Coming up," agreed Ted as he proceeded to scoop some onto a cone for him.

"What can you tell me about the man in that photo?" asked Kevin when Ted finally handed him the ice cream cone.

"Mark Killingham was his name," advised Ted. "That was before my time, though, so I really don't know much about him. He was Ray Killingham's stepdad, and this was his ice cream recipe. They used to serve it regularly at the school, from what I understand."

22

"I remember this ice cream!" exclaimed Linda. "I'd forgotten how good it was."

"May I get a closer look at the photo?" pressed Kevin.

Ted obligingly removed the framed picture from the wall and handed it to Kevin.

"How much do I owe you for the ice cream?"

"On the house," replied Ted. "I'm already closed out for the day, anyway. No charge."

"Thank you!" beamed Linda as she moved closer to her husband to study the picture of Mark Killingham. "Sure looks like him."

"It does," scowled Kevin as he turned the picture frame over to see if anything was written on the back.

"Mark Killingham," read Linda. "Born 23 March 1930."

"That's his birthdate, alright," acknowledged Kevin.

"There's no death date," observed Linda with a worried expression on her face.

"They probably just never got around to adding it," assumed Ted as he took the picture from Kevin to hang back up again.

"Something doesn't add up," mumbled Kevin as he and Linda each grabbed a handful of napkins and quickly exited the small pro golf and deli shop with their unfinished ice cream cones. "We'd better hurry if we're gonna make it."

"Thanks, Ted!" called Linda as they left.

"Are we late?" questioned Kevin as he burst into the tower room of the lighthouse where Sheree was still cleaning up from lunch. Jim had already left.

"Late for what?" asked Sheree.

"It's 3:02 already," pointed out Linda as she entered the room after him, out of breath from running. "Has Ann skyped you yet?"

"Skyped us?" laughed Sheree. "I think Jim meant tomorrow. Ann is on PET time."

"PET time?" repeated Kevin as he leaned over and put his hands on his knees while trying to catch his breath.

"Machu Picchu is on Peru time," clarified Sheree. "It's 5:02 p.m. where Ann is right now. We had just finished our daily skype session with her at 1:15 today – our time – right before your arrival. You did get here at 1:30, didn't you? That's what Jim put in the register." Sheree then glanced at her new smartwatch to double check their arrival time.

"You've got to be kidding!" exclaimed Linda as she gasped for air and exchanged a disappointed look with Kevin. She had stumbled in her high-heeled boots and nearly twisted her ankle on the way back, due to their unbridled haste to try and make it in time.

"Sorry if you misunderstood," apologized Sheree, "but you are welcome to join us tomorrow. That would be 1:00 p.m. our time, here."

"Thanks, we will," promised Kevin. He was obviously disappointed, and so was Linda.

"Good thing I brought another pair of pants," muttered Linda as she surveyed the damage to her black leather pants.

"All I see is vanilla ice cream dripping down one leg," Kevin suddenly smiled.

"Like I said!" snapped Linda as she turned and stormed off to their room to change.

"It is beautiful here," noted Kevin as he paused to admire the freshly mowed lawn on either side of the steep, winding walkway he and Linda were ascending toward the cafeteria for her 49th class reunion dinner.

Vaguely familiar faces of other people in the crowd with them left Linda unsure who most of them were. They, too, were making their way toward the cafeteria. *What if she greeted someone by the wrong name?* Linda searched the crowd in vain for any sign of Lenny Owens. *Was he already inside the cafeteria?* Thankfully, her extra pair of black leather pants looked as enticing on her as the ones that she had scuffed and spilled ice cream on earlier.

The cafeteria at Oceanview Academy was a flurry of activity as last-minute details were still being put into place for the reunion that night, even as the guests arrived. The sound of disco music from the 1970s wafted from the building. Clearly heard above it, noisy seagulls circled overhead as they made their way toward the beach below.

Cypress and eucalyptus trees grew in abundance along the windswept cliffs nearby, their pungent odors distinct upon the balmy ocean breeze as evening fog began to roll in for the night.

A hearty mat of creeping succulent ice plants with hot pink blooms lined the walkway, accented along the outer edge by golden yellow coreopsis, lavender and sedum plants where they met the edges of the expansive but well-kept lawn. Many of the plants which did well here in the cooler coastal environment would never have survived back in the valley Kevin and Linda called home four hours away. Especially lovely were the colorful flowers planted around the cafeteria and dormitories. Red Salvia flowers grew intermingled with bright yellow Shasta Daisies, Lamb's Ears and Lavender Cotton. Juniper, hydrangea and creeping cypress shrubs stood out in relief against many of the freshly white washed military style buildings still being used by the school.

"They would never have allowed us to listen to music like that when I went to school here," Linda informed Kevin. "Even transistor radios were considered to be contraband and were strictly forbidden."

"I'm sure glad I didn't go to school here!" exclaimed Kevin.

"At least they're not playing military marching music like they did at the Harvest Festival Prom my junior year!"

Kevin merely smiled and shook his head.

"After vesper service each morning," elaborated Linda, "we would come straight over here for breakfast. They would serve food from 6:15 until 7:00."

"What if you were late?" questioned Kevin.

"You weren't," replied Linda. "Not if you wanted to eat. Besides, people's work shifts at the lumber mill – or wherever they were assigned – usually began right after that."

"As I said," repeated Kevin, "I'm *really* glad I didn't go to school here!"

"At least it gave us good work experience," countered Linda. "Most of us soon realized how important it was to stay in school and get a decent college education. That way, we would never end up doing something like this for the rest of our lives."

Behind the school and farthest from the cliff lined beach was a towering stand of old growth trees, mostly spruce, cedar and various varieties of fir. Off to either side of the main campus area sprawled endless fields of crops and various other white washed military style buildings. Some were used for farming or dairy equipment, while other buildings served as facilities for physical education, woodshop, auto mechanics, photography, equestrian stables, an aviation hangar, and of course the laundry, bakery and candle making factory. Beyond them was the old lumber mill where surf and boogie boards were now being manufactured.

"There you are!" It was Jim Otterman. "Sheree and I are seated over there by the galley, if you'd like to join us."

"We'd love to," accepted Kevin. He was not anxious to be forced into yet another social encounter with someone else. At least with Jim, he knew he could talk about weapons, if nothing else. He also wanted to find out more about Mark Killingham.

"That's fine," agreed Linda as she surveyed the crowd again for any sign of Lenny. *Where was he? Why wasn't he here?* She had hoped to sit at his table.

Kevin glanced at the vegetarian food selections behind the clear acrylic safety glass on the stainless steel serving galley with trepidation. "No meat?"

"Not here, I'm afraid," sympathized Jim as he gently slapped Kevin on the shoulder. "But, let's plan on having a real barbecue up at the lighthouse tomorrow, when we skype with Ann."

"Deal!" promised Kevin as he stared with disbelief at the old fashioned, single nozzle, stainless steel milk dispenser on one end of the food serving galley, and then at the stainless steel cash register on the opposite end of it. Then, leaning close to Linda, he whispered, "I thought you paid for our dinner already."

"That's just for parents or visitors during regular school hours," advised Jim, who had easily overheard. "They would have a cashier there already, if they were expecting us to pay tonight."

"Don't we want to go ahead and get in line?" questioned Linda.

"They will be serving us at the tables tonight," responded Jim as he motioned again toward the table where Sheree was already seated. "The food is just there to keep it warm until they dish it up."

"I'll be right back," promised Linda. "I see someone I need to say hello to." She had just spotted Lenny's cousin Pete. His black afro was now gone, replaced by a clean-shaven head; Pete had also put on a few pounds, but it definitely was him! Linda made her way past faces she knew she should have recognized but didn't bother to stop until reaching Pete's table.

"Linda!" greeted Pete as he stood and gave her a quick hug. He then pulled out a chair beside his and motioned for Linda to sit down.

After glancing toward the table where her husband Kevin was seated and busy chatting with the Ottermans, Linda cautiously sat down. "You're here alone?"

"I am. My family was unable to get away," replied Pete as he took a sip of water from his glass and rewarded Linda with one of his irrepressible grins.

"Now that's the Pete I remember," grinned Linda. She wanted to just come out and ask him about Lenny, but decided it would be best to engage in some polite conversation first.

"Is that your husband over there?" questioned Pete.

"Since 1979," revealed Linda.

"Wow!" marveled Pete. "That would be ..."

"Forty-four years," interrupted Linda. "No kids. How 'bout you?"

"Well, I'm an IT guy at Ocean Bay Hospital by day and a cab driver by night," described Pete.

"Family?" pressed Linda.

"Four kids, eleven grandkids, and a huge mortgage on the house. That's why I'm working two jobs, just to pay for it all," answered Pete. "What about you?

"Retired receptionist from a doctor's office," replied Linda. "Kevin still works, though."

"Hey, you two." It was Jim Otterman. "Why don't you come over and join us?"

"Jim Otterman," chuckled Pete as he grinned and shook his head. "Here we are again."

It had been 49 years since the time Pete fully intended to beat the living tar out of Jim – right at this very table – but had been stopped only by his cousin Lenny's intervention.

"You don't plan on beating me up, do you?" laughed Jim.

"I hear you're the Sheriff these days," responded Pete. "I wouldn't want to get arrested."

"You're the Sheriff?" Linda was surprised.

"Technically, I'm the Mayor now," answered Jim. "When I'm not busy running the bed and breakfast, doing detective work, or looking after some of my other business interests."

"You're quite the busy guy, aren't you?" Pete tried not to sound snide about it. He had never cared for Jim.

27

"Most of the time, yes," verified Jim with a confident air about him that did not set well with Pete.

"I hear you met my nephew last month," mentioned Pete as he studied Jim with disapproval.

"Oh yes, Lenny, Jr.," confirmed Jim. "He and his wife Lila were staying at the new annex. That's where the overflow rooms are for the Killingham Lighthouse Bed and Breakfast. It used to be the old servants' quarters for the lighthouse staff."

"I understand he was having a private conversation with Carolyn Bennett down on the beach when you interrupted them," added Pete.

"Wait just a minute!" commanded Linda. "What was Carolyn doing on the beach last month with Lenny's son?"

Jim sighed deeply and shook his head. "Later."

"And why in the world would you think Pete would want to beat you up?" probed Linda. "Though I must admit, I'm starting to feel the urge myself!"

"*You* wanna tell her?" smirked Pete.

"Not particularly," replied Jim as he folded his arms.

After a long and uncomfortable pause, Pete advised, "It had to do with how the two of *you* were always trying to keep Lenny and Carolyn apart, among other things. But, since you're both happily married to other people now, I'm sure that's ancient history."

"Indeed," agreed Jim.

"In that case, Pete, why don't you come over and join us?" challenged Linda.

Perhaps she still might be able to find out from Pete what Lenny was up to these days, though she would need to be careful what was said in front of Kevin.

"Okay, sure, why not?" Pete finally agreed and got up to follow them to their table. "I know I should know who half of these people are, but most of them have changed so much that there's just no way to tell."

"That's for sure!" agreed Linda as she and Pete accompanied Jim over to where Kevin and Sheree were seated.

Linda gently tapped Kevin on the shoulder to get his attention. Kevin had been so engrossed in his conversation with Sheree that he had not noticed their approach.

"Honey, this is Pete."

"Pete," acknowledged Kevin as he shook his hand but then studied him with disapproval. *Why would Linda bring him to their table?* Kevin was basically a red-neck at heart, and his upbringing had not included socializing with minorities.

"Pleased to meet you," replied Pete, who was keenly aware of the all-too-familiar reaction from Linda's husband.

"Pete is an IT guy," mentioned Linda as she sat down beside her husband. "Perhaps he can help you with your laptop."

"I'm sure the man has better things to do," assumed Kevin.

"Hey, I'm obviously intruding," guessed Pete as he turned to leave.

"Nonsense!" insisted Jim as he pulled out a chair, grabbed Pete by the arm, and shoved him into it.

"Fellow classmates," came a loud voice from the far end of the room, near the front entrance. It was Nanci Zipper. "Welcome!" Reverberation from the microphone was quickly corrected by a large man nearby who looked somewhat familiar but was just as unrecognizable as most of the other former classmates.

"She looks great!" admired Linda.

"She does," agreed Sheree. "She must do yoga or something."

"Shh!" insisted Jim as he seated himself beside Pete and Kevin, across from Sheree and Linda.

"Before we begin bringing the food to your tables," announced Nanci, "there will be a brief memorial to those who have passed on and could not be here with us tonight."

The lights were quickly dimmed; the disco music immediately ceased, and a 1973 song titled *The Way We Were* began playing in the background while a video collage of old photographs displayed on a freestanding projection screen. Each person pictured was accompanied by a subtitle including their name, and the years of their birth and death.

Silent tears streamed down many cheeks as the sad reality sunk in that these former classmates had really died before their time. Linda silently wrung her cloth table napkin back and forth with her hands on her lap as she watched the memorial presentation. A dire feeling descended upon her. *Would Lenny be in this film?* Then, just as she had feared, there he was! Lenny Owens, 1956-2016. Linda felt as if she had been punched in the gut. The tears already flowing down her cheeks suddenly increased tenfold. Hopefully, Kevin would not notice. Along with each decedent's former yearbook photo, a few other select photos from their life were also displayed. Without warning, a larger-than-life photo of Linda and Lenny at the Harvest Festival Prom was displayed on the screen!

"Is that *you?*" whispered Kevin with disbelief. He could not believe that his wife actually dated a black guy and had never bothered to mention it!

Linda merely nodded her head without looking at him.

There she was, in her bright red prom dress, wearing the baby blue corsage that had been intended for Carolyn Bennett. Linda's face blanched as she thought of how she had managed to convince Lenny that Carolyn would not be coming to the prom, and of the look on Carolyn's face when she had arrived in her baby blue dress and saw Linda wearing the corsage intended for her.

Though Linda had ordered another baby blue corsage for delivery to Carolyn Bennett the following day with a note that simply said, "I'm sorry" – it was not one of her prouder moments. She had hurt Carolyn deeply, and Lenny, too. In her mind's eye, Linda could see Lenny leaving her alone at the prom to run after Carolyn when he saw her rush out upon seeing them together. Even after 49 years, the memory was still painful.

"Lenny was 59 years old when he died," remarked Jim when the film was finally over. "That was why Carolyn chose that as her Powerball number."

Linda's nostrils flared with rage as she glared at Jim. *He had known that Lenny was gone and hadn't even bothered to tell her!*

Kevin then informed her, "I've hired Jim to help us find out what really happened to Mark Killingham."

"I'm not sure we can afford something like that right now," muttered Linda. She was obviously shaken.

"No charge," advised Jim from across the table as his eyes locked with Linda's. "Ray's dad was a dear friend of ours. If there was something suspicious about his death, we would all like to know."

"If anyone can figure it out, Jim can," assured Sheree. "He's quite the detective. Trust me!"

30

2. Wedding Gift

Kevin nervously paced the floor as he waited for the music to begin. It was February 14, 1979. He and Linda Shaver had decided to get married on Valentine's Day.

The country ranch house where Kevin and Linda were having their ceremony belonged to a family friend. Kevin's stepfather, Peter Smith, was the general contractor who had overseen its design and creation. Kevin had worked on the construction crew and was familiar with every detail of the extravagant home.

Views of the cattle covered hillside surrounding it and the mountains beyond were visible from the formal living room where the guests were seated in padded folding chairs, waiting for the ceremony to begin. About 30 close family friends and relatives were there in all.

"Nervous?" questioned Kevin's half-brother Greg. He was Kevin's best man and dressed in a royal blue tuxedo and white puffy shirt. Kevin's tuxedo was entirely white.

"What do *you* think?" countered Kevin. He felt as if he had a knot in his stomach that wouldn't quit and he could hardly breathe.

"You'll be okay, old man," teased Greg as he slapped Kevin on the back. He was five years younger than him and could call him that.

"You just wait," replied Kevin. "Someday it will be your turn."

"But not today," grinned Greg as the wedding march began to play. A friend of Linda's was seated at the organ, expertly playing the familiar tune. The guests suddenly stood.

Kevin felt as if he were glued to the spot, frozen with trepidation and uncertainty.

"Go!" urged Greg as he gave him a gentle shove from behind.

Linda was breathtaking in her beautiful white wedding dress as she stood at the front of the room holding a bouquet of white roses. Inviting flames from the large rock fireplace behind her gave the entire room a cozy warmth. Gentle fingers of light streamed in through a sky window and focused themselves on the bride. Her alabaster skin and piercing blue eyes were inescapable as Kevin made his way towards her. Just enough of the cleavage on her bosom was showing to entice him. The jeweled tiara she wore reflected against the gossamer rays, causing tiny specks of light to dance against the walls.

Linda's maid of honor was a church friend of hers named Lilly Souza. She and Kevin had discussed whether or not to have additional bridesmaids and groomsmen, but financial concerns had caused them to decide against it. Lilly and the other members of the small bridal party were dressed in royal blue.

Kevin's half-sisters Nichole and Yvette had made the wedding cake themselves, as well as the bridal bouquets, corsages and boutonnieres. Kevin's younger half-sister Deena was the flower girl, and his youngest half-brother Daniel was the ring bearer. Though simple, the ceremony was beautiful and elegant. The minister who conducted the ceremony was also a family friend from their church.

To Kevin and Linda, the ceremony flew by and seemed as if it were over before it had even begun. Before they knew it, they could hear the minister announcing them as Mr. and Mrs. Kevin Killingham. Linda beamed with excitement and anticipation as she and Kevin kissed again and locked arms before heading toward the other end of the large ranch house.

The weather outside was sunny but brisk, so the reception would be held indoors, as well. The wedding supper was a potluck brought by the various guests in attendance. A small table of gifts awaited them in the reception room, at a table near the homemade cake.

Once the main festivities were over and most of the guests had left, Kevin's and Linda's parents settled down to watch their children open the various gifts.

"A toaster," nodded Kevin as he set it by the other two toasters they had already unwrapped.

"I think this one might be a popcorn maker," guessed Linda with a deep sigh.

"You can probably exchange it," mentioned her mother. Arlene Shaver was a practical woman, and not the least bit offended that her daughter might need to trade in the duplicate gift for something else.

"Yes, it's a popcorn maker," acknowledged Linda as she carefully placed it by the other one.

"At least you can always use lots of towels," reminded Kevin's mother. Bobby Sue had made it a point to get them something they would need.

"Open this one," directed Bill Shaver as he handed an envelope to his new son-in-law.

"Now, that's something we can use," grinned Kevin. "The kind of gift that folds!"

"It might not be what you think," cautioned Arlene with a devious grin.

After slicing open the envelope with his pocketknife, Kevin removed the card and stared at what was inside.

"Well?" urged Linda. "Let me see."

Linda then studied the paper and slowly started to smile. "Kevin, do you know what this means?"

"Care to fill us in?" requested Peter.

"It's a gift certificate," advised Mr. Shaver.

"Oh, thank you!" exclaimed Linda as she came over and gave each of her parents a hug.

"Yes, thank you!" beamed Kevin as he, too, came over and embraced his new in-laws.

"What kind of a gift certificate?" pressed Bobby Sue.

"My parents have hired a private detective to try and locate Kevin's real father," blurted out Linda.

Bobby Sue suddenly looked as if she were going to be ill. *Should she have tried to warn her son about the dangers of finding his real father?* It obviously was too late now!

She had known for years that it was Kevin's dream to find and finally meet the man, ever since learning of his adoption when he was in his first year of high school. That had been five years earlier. While milking the cows one morning before school, Kevin had gotten into a serious argument with his stepfather. In an unguarded moment of anger, Peter Smith had blurted out the words, "if you were my son ...."

Peter regretted it immediately, of course, but could not take it back. Worse still, Kevin had *not* known until that moment that Peter Smith was not his real father or that he had been adopted. But, it had been said, and things changed forever between them after that. Not only that, it had altered Kevin's relationship with his mother. *Didn't he have a right to know his real father and decide for himself if he wanted him to be a part of his life?* Still, no urging on his part would convince Bobby Sue to tell him what he wanted to know.

33

Then, when learning that Kevin had chosen to take on the name of Killingham – despite the fact that Peter Smith had legally adopted him at the age of two – Bobby Sue had suffered a nervous breakdown. Kevin, who had formerly been known as Kevin Smith, was now Kevin Killingham and there was nothing she could do about it.

"Are you alright?" questioned Peter as he put a comforting arm around his wife.

"No," muttered Bobby Sue, but only so Peter could hear.

Their other wedding gifts virtually forgotten, Kevin and Linda beamed with delight as they continued to study the gift certificate from her parents with awe.

"It's for the services of Floyd Shoeman," advised Arlene rather proudly.

"*The* Floyd Shoeman?" doubted Bobby Sue. She had finally forced herself to join in the conversation again.

"The same," corroborated Mr. Shaver. "And it wasn't cheap."

"Isn't he the man whose case files are featured on that television show?" questioned Linda with excitement.

"Yes, of course, *Finder of Lost Relatives*," recognized Kevin. "I've seen that show!"

"Impressive," remarked Peter, without the same enthusiasm the Shavers seemed to have. His wife Bobby Sue merely shook her head with trepidation.

Two entire years had passed since Floyd Shoeman started his search to try and locate Mark Killingham. It was now March 23, 1981.

Kevin and Linda barely made ends meet, each working fulltime jobs just to pay the few bills they had. Their tiny, two-bedroom apartment was located upstairs in a rather large complex beside the airport. The sound of planes overhead would often prevent them from hearing what was said when they were on the phone with someone. Even watching television was a challenge under such circumstances.

Linda had come home early that day with a migraine headache and was preparing to put some ice on her head. Suddenly, the phone rang. Linda thought of just letting the answering machine get it, but decided at the last moment to go ahead and pick up the call.

"Hello?" answered Linda.

"Linda Killingham?" questioned the man at the other end of the line.

"Who is this?" demanded Linda.

"This is Floyd Shoeman. I believe we have located your husband's father."

"Is this some kind of a joke?" demanded Linda. "Who is this, really?" She felt certain that the money her parents had spent on Floyd Shoeman had been wasted, as they would have heard from him before now if he was legitimate.

"It took us quite some time to find him," continued the man, "but we believe it's him."

"Why would it have taken you so long?" questioned Linda.

Just then a jet zoomed by overhead, drowning out what the voice on the other end of the phone was trying to say.

"I can hardly hear you!" shouted Linda.

"I'll just send you a brief synopsis of what I have," advised the man. "Then have your husband call me when he gets a chance."

"If you could just tell me again ...," began Linda, but then a dial tone could be heard. *The man had hung up! How dare he!*

Right then, Kevin came inside. "You're home early."

"I've got a migraine," replied Linda. "But, before I lay down, I need to let you know that Floyd Shoeman just called."

"Floyd Shoeman?" doubted Kevin.

"Yes," confirmed Linda. "He is sending you a synopsis of what he found out about your dad and wants you to call him after you've looked it over."

"Did you get his number?" demanded Kevin.

"No, I didn't," informed Linda.

"I told you we should have gotten caller ID," chastised Kevin. "Hey, don't we still have that gift certificate?"

"I'll see if I can find it," offered Linda, though she was pretty certain they had finally thrown it out when not hearing back for so long.

Kevin then picked up the phone and dialed for directory assistance. If they were unable to help, he would call the Shavers. Perhaps they might still have the man's number.

Over a week had passed before the synopsis from Floyd Shoeman arrived in the mail.

"That's it?" scowled Kevin. "They believe they have found him! He already told you that much on the phone!"

35

"Call him," urged Linda.

Kevin anxiously dialed the number on the stationery, only to reach a recording that indicated the office was closed for the day.

"I'm going to have to call him tomorrow, they're closed right now," advised Kevin as he shook his head and hung up the phone.

"Don't they have an answering machine?" asked Linda.

"I let it ring eight times and there was no message machine," answered Kevin.

"Well, he sure better have something for us," responded Linda, "especially after all that money my parents spent!"

"We can only hope," agreed Kevin.

The following day, Kevin was successful in reaching Floyd Shoeman's secretary, only to learn that her boss was out for "the rest of the week on business."

After playing phone tag for two additional weeks, it was Linda who happened to pick up the phone when Floyd Shoeman finally called again.

"Please don't hang up!" entreated Linda. "We live by an airport and often we can't hear what is being said by the other party, so please – if that happens – don't hang up!"

"I won't," promised Mr. Shoeman. "Sorry it has taken me so long to get back to you, but we had another lead on Mark Killingham."

"Another lead?" frowned Linda.

"Please keep in mind that he has no idea we were looking for him," mentioned Mr. Shoeman. "The man seems to move around quite a bit, too, and at first we thought perhaps he was involved in some type of criminal activity."

"You're kidding?" Linda could not believe what she was hearing.

"But," continued Mr. Shoeman, "I believe we were mistaken. From what we've found, he appears to be a businessman of some sort who travels rather frequently."

"Doing what?" questioned Linda.

"It would appear that he deals in selling antiquities," elaborated the detective.

"Antiquities?" repeated Linda.

"Anyway," added Mr. Shoeman, "he's living in Colorado right now with a woman named Flo. They do not appear to be married."

"Do you have a phone number or an address for him?" pressed Linda. "So, we can call him?"

"I just wanted to be sure that's what you still want before giving you the information," advised Mr. Shoeman. "Sometimes folks change their minds about things like this."

"We still want to meet him," assured Linda.

"Very well, here's the address," related the detective. He then gave Linda the information.

"Oh, thank you!" replied Linda as she carefully wrote it down. "Kevin will be thrilled."

"Just be mindful that this man has no idea anyone was looking for him," cautioned Mr. Shoeman again. "If you would like me to make the initial contact, I'd be happy to do so."

"I think we can handle it," insisted Linda.

"Very well," replied the detective. "I'm officially closing my file on this one."

"What if we do need anything else?" Linda suddenly asked.

"Then just call."

"Okay, that sounds reasonable," agreed Linda. "Thank you again, sir."

"Good luck," bid Floyd Shoeman before hanging up the phone.

Kevin had been the one to call Mark Killingham while Linda listened in on the extension. They talked for hours, each excited to finally find one another. Unfortunately, due to prearranged travel plans pertaining to a business trip to Europe, Mark would not be available to personally meet with Kevin until November. But, they would keep in contact by phone and mail, if possible.

"What about Thanksgiving?" suggested Kevin.

"That sounds great!" agreed Mark. "Would you have any objection if I bring my friend Flo?"

"Absolutely not!" assured Kevin.

"You don't know what this means to me, son," advised Mark. "I've been looking for you for a long time, and had almost given up hope of ever seeing you again."

"When did we see each other last?" pressed Kevin.

"Oh, I think you were about six months old," guessed Mark. "But, we can talk more about that when we see each other. I'm just grateful to be a part of your life again."

"Me, too," replied Kevin. His lip quivered with emotion, though Kevin had been raised in an environment where it was considered unmanly to cry or openly express his feelings.

"I'll call you soon," promised Mark after exchanging contact information with his newfound son.

"I'll look forward to it," responded Kevin before ending the call.

Linda slowly hung up the receiver on the bedroom phone and rushed into the living room where Kevin was seated at the couch.

"Congratulations!" beamed Linda as she rushed over to embrace her husband. "I can't wait to meet him! He sounds very nice."

Kevin then frowned.

"What is it?" pressed Linda.

"We were so busy getting caught up, that we never discussed where he would be staying when he comes out," explained Kevin.

"Why here, of course," smiled Linda.

"But how?" asked Kevin. "We don't even have a bed in the extra bedroom."

"He can sleep in our bed," suggested Linda. "We can always sleep on those camping cots in the extra room. It won't hurt us to do that for a night or two."

"That works," agreed Kevin. "But, what about our sheets? They are pretty worn out."

"We've still got some credit left on the Visa card," pointed out Linda. "We need some new sheets anyway. And, probably some towels, too."

"Don't go overboard," cautioned Kevin. The last time Linda had gone on a shopping spree, she had managed to max out their other credit card, and they were still having trouble keeping up on the payments.

"I won't," promised Linda with a mischievous grin.

"I mean it," warned Kevin.

"I'll keep it reasonable," assured Linda. "Trust me!"

The months dragged by as Kevin and Linda anxiously awaited the Thanksgiving holiday. Kevin had considered mentioning to his mother that he had finally located Mark Killingham, but something inside held him back. *What if it caused her to have another nervous breakdown?*

"Perhaps your sister Carrie and her family might like to join us," suggested Linda, only two days before Thanksgiving. "I'm sure she would like to meet him, too."

"I don't know," hesitated Kevin.

"She's not going to say anything to your mom," predicted Linda. "We can trust her."

"I hope you're right," replied Kevin.

"She never even told your mom about the time you totaled her car," grinned Linda.

"That's true," acknowledged Kevin. "Okay, fine. Let's call Carrie tonight and see if she wants to come."

It was finally Thanksgiving Day, Thursday, November 26, 1981. Carrie and Fred Orange arrived with their four children at ten o'clock that morning, bringing with them a huge potato salad and a large platter of homemade whole wheat rolls.

Their oldest son Brent had already found his way to the apartment complex playground area. He was 5 and full of energy. His sisters China and Beatriz – ages 4 and 3 – were there with him, already playing on the merry-go-round. Their younger brother Jake was only 18 months and forced to remain at Kevin's and Linda's apartment with his parents. He tightly clutched Carrie's hand as she sat watching Linda set everything up for the non-traditional meal.

"What if he doesn't like Japanese food?" questioned Fred.

"It does kind of clash with the potato salad," commented Carrie. She was the oldest of Kevin's half-siblings.

"I guess that's why they call it pot *luck*," quipped Linda as she studied the place settings to be sure there were enough.

"That must be them!" exclaimed Kevin as the doorbell buzzed.

"It's just us," chuckled Arlene Shaver as she and her husband Bill entered without waiting for the door to be answered.

"I wonder where *he* is?" asked Linda, suddenly concerned that their guest of honor had not yet made an appearance.

"I saw a red Honda pulling in while we were coming up the stairs," advised Bill. "Maybe he's just having trouble finding a place to park."

39

"You'd think they would have come earlier than this," muttered Linda. "I'm sure they won't want to leave their suitcases in the car."

"Especially around here," added Kevin, who was also becoming worried and anxious about his first encounter with his real father.

"Hello!" greeted a male voice from the open doorway behind them. *It was Mark Killingham!*

"Dad?" questioned Kevin as he approached the stranger.

"That's my boy!" beamed the man as he stepped forward and tightly embraced Kevin before gently slapping him on the back in acknowledgment. *The resemblance between them was astonishing!*

The room became silent enough to hear a pin drop as the others stared with amazement at the reunion.

"And this must be the lovely Linda!" exclaimed the man as he gallantly bowed in greeting before taking Linda's hand in his and kissing the back of it.

Mark Killingham was about six-foot three, trim for his age, well dressed in a casual but expensive looking business suit, and was charming. He seemed to be everything they had hoped for. It was almost as if he were too good to be true. Linda, Arlene and Carrie each blushed as he flirted with them. *He was obviously a ladies' man!* Mark's neatly trimmed mustache and slightly graying sideburns gave him an added air of distinction. If he did have any gray in his deep red hair, it was most likely covered by the miracle of hair dye.

"And this is Flo," introduced Mark as he motioned toward a stunning redhead standing in the doorway behind him.

"Flowing Waters," clarified the woman in a rather seductive voice. "But you can call me Flo."

Flo looked as if she had stepped from the front page of a high-class fashion magazine. She was at least ten years younger than Mark, if not more. The red dress she wore was lowcut and provocative, leaving little to the imagination. Her black stilettos were graced by red leather roses on top, which perfectly matched the red and black handbag that she had tucked under one arm. Every man in the room was drawn to her, including Kevin.

Flo was also holding a rather heavy looking gift bag on the other arm, and tried not to appear too anxious to rid herself of it.

"Let me help you with that," offered Bill, who was the closest.

"Actually, this is for Kevin," smiled Flo as she handed it directly to him. Her bright red fingernails were stunning.

"From both of us," added Mark with a crooked grin.

"May I open it after dinner?" asked Kevin.

"Absolutely!" beamed Mark.

Her makeup is perfect! thought Linda with envy as she glanced in a nearby mirror to be sure hers was acceptable.

Unexpectedly, another woman appeared at the doorway, wearing a raggedy pair of blue jeans, worn tennis shoes, but with a clean white blouse and black leather blazer. She was short and stubby with a haggard-looking face. Her short auburn hair was badly windblown. With her were two children, ages 8 and 10.

"And this is my sister Jodean," added Mark, with far less enthusiasm.

"Sorry," apologized the woman. The fumes of alcohol emanated from her breath as she spoke.

"She's your aunt," mentioned Mark, obviously embarrassed by his sister's appearance and behavior.

"I just had to meet my nephew," stammered Jodean as she staggered toward Kevin to give him a hug.

The expression on Kevin's face was telling, though he did a remarkable job of maintaining his composure throughout the encounter.

"And those are my children," mentioned Flo from behind them. It was her intention to draw as much attention away from Jodean as possible.

"I'm Windy Waters," announced the girl. "Age 8."

"And I'm Stormy Waters, age 10," declared her brother.

Both children were unusually well behaved and unnaturally serious for their age. It was almost as if childhood had escaped them entirely.

"Perhaps you might like to join our other nieces and nephew, down in the play area," suggested Linda. Her tiny apartment was becoming smaller by the moment. *Where in the world would all these people sit for the meal? Or sleep that night?*

"Are you trying to get rid of us?" Windy asked bluntly.

"Oh, sweetie, of course not!" replied Linda. "I just thought ...."

"Is there anything we can do to help?" interrupted Stormy. "Looks like you might need another table."

41

"We can just sit on the couch," differed Windy.

"Actually, sitting on the couch is not such a bad idea," replied Linda. "And, everything is ready. Let me just get a few more plates."

"I'll get the TV trays," volunteered Kevin as he headed for the hall closet to retrieve them.

"It smells delicious," flirted Mark.

"Thanks," blushed Linda.

"I'll go get the kids," offered Fred.

"We'll be here," smiled Carrie as she hurried to help Linda set up the extra place settings, with Jake at her heels.

"Before we eat, let's go around the room and introduce ourselves, shall we?" suggested Mark. It was his hope to put everyone else in the room at ease, and he was surprisingly comfortable in front of perfect strangers.

"I'm Bill Shaver and this is my wife Arlene. We're Linda's parents."

"My parents were unable to be here today," lied Kevin. He did *not* want his father to know that he had purposely failed to tell them about their reunion.

Mark did appear disappointed, but merely nodded.

Had he wanted to see Bobby Sue again? wondered Linda. *And, would he tell them what Kevin's mother hadn't?*

"I'm Kevin's half-sister, Carrie Orange, and this is my son Jake. He's 18 months."

"And I'm her husband Fred," announced the tall burly man coming through the front door with their three other children in tow. "This is Brent, age 5."

"I can introduce myself!" advised Brent.

"And his sisters China and Beatriz are ages 4 and 3," continued Fred as he sat down on the couch with them.

"Japanese food is my favorite," smiled Mark as he finally sat down at the table.

Windy merely made a face and rolled her eyes as she and her brother Stormy sat down beside him.

"Everything is lovely," assured Flo as she sat down on the other side of them.

"Works for me," slurred Jodean.

"Yes, everything does look delicious," praised Arlene as she and Bill sat down across from Mark's group.

"Son, why don't you sit down here so we can have a chance to chat some more?" requested Mark as he motioned toward the head of the table beside him. "I won't bite."

Kevin quickly seated himself at the head of the table by Mark while Linda and Carrie sat at the opposite end of the long table with Brent. The *table* was actually two card tables set up end-to-end with a clean white bedsheet spread over them.

"Card tables," realized Flo as she casually picked up the edge of the bedsheet to glance beneath it while she sat down. "How sweet. Thank you for going to so much trouble for us."

"Good thing we're staying at the Luxury Seven," blurted out Jodean.

"You're staying at a hotel?" questioned Kevin. *Had Linda purchased all those new towels and bed sheets for nothing? Perhaps she should have invested in a nice tablecloth!*

"We didn't want to be an imposition," explained Mark.

"We just want you to be comfortable," added Linda, actually relieved by the news. She was becoming less fond of Flowing Waters and Jodean by the moment.

After a brief prayer to bless the food, it was devoured rather rapidly – much more so than Linda had anticipated. *Should she have prepared more? How could she have foreseen so many extra guests?*

The others at the table listened intently while Mark and Kevin chatted to try and catch up. Once the food was gone, however, the Shaver and Orange families soon made their excuses and left.

"I'm waiting in the car," announced Jodean. She was anxious to have another drink from the flask she had hidden there.

"I'll go with her," offered Flo, for reasons of her own.

"Do you have any coloring books?" asked Windy.

"I do have an old Lego set," offered Linda.

"I like Legos," nodded Stormy.

"Very well," smiled Linda as she rushed off to get the set for them to play with.

"Mind if I smoke?" questioned Mark. "I always like a good cigar after dinner."

"Not in here!" advised Linda as she returned with the Lego set and handed it to the children.

"My wife has asthma," explained Kevin.

43

"I suppose I can do without for once," agreed Mark, though clearly unhappy about it. The cigar he was holding was a Cuban cigar.

"We can go out onto the patio," suggested Kevin.

Mark frowned as he studied the small uncovered cement patio on the other side of the sliding glass doors. There were two folding lawn chairs out there now, and not much room for anything else. Worse still, it was overcast and beginning to rain. Just then, the sound of a jet from the airport next door roared by overhead.

"Hey, I'm good," assured Mark as he put the Cuban cigar back into his inside jacket pocket. The controlled smile was for Kevin's benefit, though Linda astutely noticed a coldness in Mark's eyes when Kevin wasn't looking.

"You're probably better off," interjected Linda as she finished clearing off one of the card tables for Windy and Stormy to use as they played with the Legos. Besides, she had hoped to sit in on the conversation. She wanted to learn as much as she could about her newfound father-in-law, but was starting to have an uncomfortable feeling about the man. It was nothing definitive, so she reasoned with herself that it was just nerves. After all, it had been a long day for everyone.

"Perhaps you'd like to open this now," smiled Mark as he retrieved the gift bag that Flo had handed to Kevin upon their arrival.

"Oh, absolutely!" beamed Kevin. He had been so caught up with meeting his real father for the first time that he had forgotten all about it. "What is it?" Kevin suddenly realized that he did not have anything earmarked to give his father.

"Open it up," instructed Mark. "It's actually for both of you."

Linda came over and sat down beside them. "Won't your lady friend want to be here when we do?"

"Flo is actually more of a business partner," clarified Mark. "Besides, she already knows what it is. And, someone needs to keep an eye on Jodean."

Linda nodded with understanding.

Kevin carefully removed the mysterious box from the gift bag. It was unusually heavy, and wrapped entirely in gold foil paper with a fancy gold bow on top.

"Just rip 'er open," laughed Mark.

After quickly freeing the box from its gold wrapping, Kevin slowly opened it. Inside was an expensive-looking ice cream machine.

44

"A belated wedding gift for the two of you," grinned Mark.

"Hey, maybe we can make some ice cream while you're here," realized Kevin. "This is great! Thank you so much!"

"Yes, thanks," added Linda. *Where would they get the ingredients to make ice cream from before payday?*

"Making ice cream just happens to be one of my specialties," revealed Mark. "I took the liberty of bringing most of the ingredients with me. The perishables are in an ice chest, out in the car."

"What about rock salt?" questioned Linda.

"That's in the trunk," flirted Mark, though it seemed insincere.

"How long does it take to make ice cream?" asked Kevin.

"Well," sighed Mark, "I figured that tomorrow we could get a batch started while we visit a local art gallery I saw in the paper."

"A local art gallery?" frowned Linda.

"The one with the bronze exhibit on display," described Mark. "It's not too far from here. They even have life-sized reproductions of *The Thinker* and *The Kiss* on display."

"Rodin?" asked Linda.

"Just reproductions," answered Mark. "But, amazing ones."

"Don't you deal in antiquities?" queried Linda.

"I do."

"Are any of them yours?"

"I wish!" exclaimed Mark. "Even reproductions like that are absolutely priceless."

"What about Jodean?" Linda suddenly asked.

Kevin shot her a warning glance but remained silent.

"Flo will be taking her and the children to the zoo while we're at the art gallery," described Mark.

"I'd rather go to the art gallery," informed Windy, who was easily able to hear them.

"Me, too," advised Stormy. "We don't want to hang out with that old drunk klepto!"

"Jodean also happens to be a kleptomaniac," admitted Mark, "which is another reason we chose to stay at a hotel."

Kevin and Linda exchanged a concerned look.

"But, you'll probably never see her again after this, anyway," assured Mark.

Mark and Kevin then visited late into the night. Linda tried ever so hard to stay awake but began nodding off. The children had already spread out on the couch and were sound asleep. Flo and Jodean were dozing outside in the car.

Mark described his childhood in great detail, about how he grew up on an Indian reservation in Arizona where he was taught herbal remedies and ancient secrets by a tribal medicine man. He then went on to describe what his life was like after the move to Chicago, where his mobster father had him running numbers by the time he was nine. Linda had drifted off to sleep at that point but awoke when Mark was describing his stint in Korea and how he had rescued several prisoners of war from a concentration camp, accompanied them through the jungle at night, and single-handedly loaded them into a helicopter before flying them to safety. Mark then lifted his shirt to show Kevin the scars from his bullet wounds to prove it.

When the subject of fishing finally came up, Linda excused herself and went to bed. One fish Mark bragged of catching had weighed over a hundred pounds and been taller than a man. *Yeah, right!* thought Linda. It was obvious to her already that Mark was not entirely truthful and tended to exaggerate greatly.

The Ashton Community Art Gallery was open from 10:00 a.m. until 4:00 p.m., manned mostly by volunteers. The aging overweight security guard by its front door was seated in a padded folding chair but did not appear to be armed. It was Black Friday, November 27, 1981. In addition to the traveling bronze exhibit currently on display at the gallery, some of its more permanent artifacts included turn-of-the century items displayed in lifelike scenarios depicting pioneer life in Ashton. The first train station, the first agricultural endeavors, the first winery, the first schoolhouse, and a rather controversial exhibit showing a local Madame with her girls at a house of ill repute were among them. Nearby was a reproduction of a realistic Native American family sitting around a campfire and having supper inside their teepee.

"They look so real," marveled Linda.

"Definitely a step up from the mannequins you see in department store windows," agreed Mark, "but they probably didn't leave the flap to their teepee open like that in real life."

"Unless it was hot outside," interjected Kevin with a smile.

Whenever Kevin was nearby or within hearing range, Mark was unbelievably polite and charming to Linda. When Kevin excused himself to use the men's room, however, Mark's demeanor toward Linda was much different. *What had she done to get on his bad side?* wondered Linda. She was beginning to be most uncomfortable around the man. *What was he hiding?*

When Kevin rejoined them, the charming personality returned. Mark then motioned for Kevin to sit on a nearby marble bench, next to *The Thinker.* Linda hadn't been specifically invited to join them, but did. Windy and Stormy were over by the Native American exhibit. Flo and Jodean had remained at the hotel to sleep off their hangovers.

"I want you to know that I tried for several months to visit you after your mother and I parted ways," informed Mark. "I would bring you gifts, cards and letters."

"And?" prompted Kevin, who was extremely interested in learning more about Mark's efforts to see him.

"No luck at all," replied Mark. "Even when she would open the door, it was only long enough to tell me to leave or she would call the police. Bobby Sue would not even let me leave my gifts for you."

"What kind of gifts?" frowned Kevin.

"This, for one," replied Mark as he pulled out a folding pocket knife with an elaborately carved handle made of walrus tusk. It had the design of a stalking lynx on the side that was showing.

"Oh, wow!" marveled Kevin as he reached for the knife.

"What do you think is on the other side?" questioned Mark with a sly grin as he maintained his grasp on it.

"I have no idea," replied Kevin.

"A rabbit smoking a pipe," interjected Linda with a smile of satisfaction. She had studied Inuit Eskimo and other Native American Indian legends in college and was quite familiar with this one.

Mark's nostrils flared slightly as he shot Linda an irritated look. "And just why would you say that?" he challenged.

"Because he's smarter than the lynx," advised Linda as she met Mark's even gaze with one of her own.

"She's right," sighed Mark as he shook his head. "The rabbit already knows the lynx is there, and just how much time he has to smoke his pipe before he needs to make a run for it."

Mark then flipped the knife over to reveal the side with the pipe-smoking rabbit. "This is yours, son."

"Thanks!" responded Kevin as he took the gift from his newfound father. "It's beautiful!"

47

"What other gifts?" pressed Linda with a distrustful frown. *Why in the world would anyone give a knife like that to a small child? Or was Mark just saying that now?*

"None that I have with me after all this time," said Mark, "but I'd certainly like to make it up to you, son." *It was as if Linda had not been the one to ask him the question!*

"Just why did you and mom split up, anyway?" Kevin came out and asked.

Mark stared off into space for a few serious moments before responding. *He would need to bend the truth, quite a bit.* "I'm not really sure, son. I came home one day after work and all her things were gone. Worst of all, she had taken you with her, and hadn't even bothered to leave me a note! I called everyone we knew, searched the area for weeks, and even called the local authorities, the hospital, and her family, but both of you were gone without a trace. It was some time before I found you again, but nothing I did or said would convince your mother to let me see you."

Mark then shed a few tears for effect.

Kevin was quite touched and put a comforting hand on his dad's shoulder. Linda, however, was not convinced of the veracity of Mark's story. *If Bobby Sue had left like he said she did, there would have to have been a reason! What was it?*

Four months later, Kevin and Linda unexpectedly moved to Seattle. A new job opportunity had presented itself – the kind that was too good to refuse. Kevin had always dreamed of specializing in custom interior carpentry design rather than working on a construction crew. If things went well enough, perhaps in time he could open his own shop!

Not only that, Kevin viewed it as an opportunity to be closer to Mark Killingham, who now lived in the Seattle area. If Kevin was ever to find out what had really happened between his parents, Mark was his last best hope. Bobby Sue was certainly not going to tell him.

Linda, however, was apprehensive about relocating to a new place and starting over. She was also concerned about being so far away from her parents. In particular, she was uncomfortable about being so close to Mark Killingham. She just did not trust him and was *not* anxious to have the man worm his way further into Kevin's affections, or possibly end up disappointing him in some way.

The 26-foot rental truck containing Kevin's and Linda's worldly possessions crept along the freeway at less than five miles per hour in Seattle's infamous five o'clock traffic. Six lanes of gridlocked traffic in each direction stretched as far as the eye could see. Linda desperately needed to use the restroom. Rain poured down relentlessly upon the sea of vehicles. Their white Dodge Dart was in tow behind the truck, with its two front wheels propped up onto a car dolly.

"We need to take the next turnoff," advised Linda, concerned that it would involve working their way across two other lanes of traffic.

"Thank you!" snapped Kevin. He was well aware of that fact.

"I need to use the restroom, too!" complained Linda.

"There's nothing I can do about that right now," pointed out Kevin, also feeling the need himself.

"Perhaps this was a mistake," muttered Linda.

"What?" questioned Kevin. "Moving to Seattle?"

"What if I can't find a job up here?" worried Linda. "We are nearly on the verge of bankruptcy now."

"Everything will be okay," assured Kevin as he adjusted the defogger so the windows would clear. "Trust me."

Though it rarely snowed in March in Seattle, more than a foot and a half of snow found its way onto the ground on Tuesday, March 23, 1982, turning the already gridlocked freeway traffic into a white nightmare. Neither Kevin nor Linda had ever driven in snow before, and especially not with a 26-foot truck. It was after midnight when they finally managed to locate their new apartment. Kevin had rented it ahead of time, sight unseen, over the phone.

Their new apartment manager was nice enough, though not overly pleased about being awakened in the middle of the night.

"This is only half the size of our other apartment," muttered Linda as she studied their new dwelling with dismay.

"We're obviously going to have to get rid of some of the furniture," pointed out Kevin.

"I don't think so!" snapped Linda. "We've worked hard for everything we have."

"Just what do you propose we do with it?" demanded Kevin as he unrolled a sleeping bag onto the living room floor of their new apartment. Aside from the sleeping bag and two small suitcases, the remainder of their belongings would be spending the night in the illegally parked rental truck outside. Hopefully, it wouldn't be towed.

"Perhaps we can put some of it into storage," suggested Linda as she sat down on the floor beside him and began to sob. "You know, I really hate it here!"

"Everything will seem better in the morning," comforted Kevin. "We're both tired and could use some rest."

"Some food wouldn't hurt anything either," sniveled Linda. Their plans of stopping at a grocery store for food had been foiled by the snowstorm, and the small ice chest that had contained their traveling food was now empty.

"I couldn't find the other sleeping bag," mentioned Kevin with a sly grin. "Perhaps we could share?"

"Yeah, whatever," answered Linda. Being intimate was the last thing on her mind at that moment.

"I wasn't going to tell you this," added Kevin, "because it was going to be a surprise, but ...."

"Tell me what?" demanded Linda as she cut him off.

"That my dad and his new friend Verna are coming over tomorrow to help us unload and unpack," revealed Kevin with a big grin. "They are bringing us some groceries, too!"

Linda stared at Kevin with disbelief. *How dare he not tell her that he had been in touch with Mark Killingham!*

"Say something," urged Kevin as he sat down on the sleeping bag and pulled Linda close to give her a hug.

"Whatever happened to Ms. Flowing Waters?" asked Linda with a note of disdain in her voice.

"I don't know and I don't care," answered Kevin. "It's none of my business. That's between Mark and Flo."

"Does Verna have a last name?" pressed Linda.

"Newhart," revealed Kevin. "They live just a few blocks away."

Linda sighed deeply and shook her head.

"What?" scowled Kevin.

"I know how much it means to you to have Mark back in your life again," prefaced Linda, "but there is something about him that I just don't trust. I can't explain why, but I have a bad feeling about the man."

"Even in a court of law, people are considered innocent until proven guilty," reminded Kevin.

"Let's just take it a little slow, shall we?" requested Linda.

"There's no hurry," assured Kevin. "Just keep in mind that this may be my only chance to find out the truth about my childhood."

"I know," sniffed Linda as she hugged him back. "We just need to be careful. We hardly know anything about him."

"We will," promised Kevin.

Verna Newhart was a cheerful woman in her late forties with long, straight brown hair that she usually kept pulled back into a ponytail. She was slightly plump but well-proportioned and wore little or no makeup at all. Down-to-earth and practical in her appearance and attitude, Verna was a breath of fresh air. She seemed genuinely interested in the welfare of those around her, and gazed at Mark Killingham with admiration and awe. Her big toothy smile was cheerful and pleasant. In fact, she reminded Linda of an aging but lovesick flower child from the 1960s. Like many Pacific Northwesterners, Verna wore her open toed earth shoes rain or shine, and only with socks in the coldest of weather. There was nothing flashy or ostentatious about her. Everything about Verna's demeanor was in such stark contrast to that of her predecessor – Ms. Flowing Waters – that it was truly surprising.

Linda was grateful for Verna's help during the past few days and felt certain she could not have managed all the unpacking alone. In fact, she and Verna had hit it off quite well, though she still could not fathom what the woman saw in Mark Killingham.

Kevin and Linda had just arrived at Verna's home for lunch. It was Saturday, March 27, 1982. The two-story Victorian home Verna lived in had been in her family for generations, but was well maintained and in a more exclusive part of town. The antique furniture and expensive artwork were clearly worth quite a bit. From her front window, a docked cruise ship and several fishing boats could be seen in the distance below. Rays of afternoon sunlight reflected off the ocean water beyond.

How had Mark managed to lure this one in? wondered Linda.

"Oh, Linda!" beamed Verna as she approached and gave her a warm hug. "I'm so glad you could come!"

"Thank you for having us," replied Linda. "Your home is lovely."

"Thank you," beamed Verna. "And Kevin!" Verna embraced him much more tightly than he was comfortable with.

"Smells wonderful," acknowledged Kevin, who was quite hungry and anxious to eat.

"Hey, son," greeted Mark as he momentarily embraced and gave him a friendly slap on the back. Then – almost as an afterthought – Mark cordially nodded at Linda but did not give her a hug. Linda was relieved but at the same time concerned by his behavior.

"It does smell wonderful," praised Linda as she followed Kevin to the elaborately set table.

"Verna is not only an excellent cook," bragged Mark, "but has also published her own cookbook. It includes over 300 color photos."

"Very impressive," commented Linda, though not surprised at the lack of response from Mark.

"Thanks again for having us over," mentioned Kevin as he stared with desire at the tempting meal.

"The duck à l'orange was done overnight in a slow cooker," advised Verna as she motioned for them to sit down.

Linda stared at the place settings. *Expensive china and real silverware. The woman must not be hurting for money, either,* thought Linda. *Could that be the attraction for Mark? Verna just didn't seem like his type.*

After a long, leisurely meal, Kevin joined Mark in the parlor to listen to more of his tall tales. Obviously feeling at home there, Mark lit up and proceeded to smoke his Cuban cigar.

Anxious to escape the vicinity, Linda hurried to the kitchen to help Verna wash and put away the dishes and leftover food.

"How long have you two been together?" questioned Linda.

"For two years now," informed Verna with a forced smile.

Linda then wondered to herself whether Verna knew that Mark had come to their home only four months earlier with "Ms. Flowing Waters." *Should she say something to the woman?*

"I've been a widow for eight years now," continued Verna, "and had all but given up hope of finding the perfect man to spend the rest of my life with – that is, until Mark came along."

"So, you're engaged?" pressed Linda.

"Yes, ma'am," confirmed Verna as she showed off her engagement ring, though she didn't seem as enthused about it as Linda would have expected. "Five carats."

"It's beautiful," admired Linda as she paused to gaze at it.

"And expensive," remarked Verna as she resumed washing the dishes that were in the sink.

"So, just what does Mark do?" delved Linda.

"He buys and sells rare art pieces," replied Verna, "so it takes him out on the road more often that I would like."

"You don't go with him?" asked Linda.

"I wish I could, but I'm a full-time interior decorator," explained Verna. "It's not often that I get to go anywhere."

"Do you have any children?" questioned Linda as she dried off and stacked yet another plate.

"Just a son," revealed Verna. "Jared is 28 years old."

"How do he and Mark get along?" queried Linda.

"Actually, not all that well," frowned Verna as she paused to place another clean, wet plate in the dish rack. "But, he has his own place now, so it's not that much of an issue."

"Humph," muttered Linda as she reached for the plate to dry it.

"I'm just so glad that he and Kevin get along," remarked Verna. "He talked about little else for weeks before their reunion."

"Little else?" doubted Linda.

"You should have seen him," reminisced Verna. "He was so excited about finally seeing Kevin again after all these years. I'm just sorry I couldn't have been there to see it."

"It was interesting meeting Jodean," replied Linda.

"I hear she was sloshed again." Verna shook her head apologetically.

"Windy and Stormy were pretty nice, though," added Linda, almost as an afterthought.

"Windy and Stormy?" frowned Verna.

"Flo's children," clarified Linda.

"Flowing Waters?" scowled Verna as she paused from her dishwashing duties to gain her composure.

"Hey, I'm sorry," apologized Linda. "I thought you knew they were with him."

"Flo and her children were with Mark when he came out to Ashton to see you?" pressed Verna.

"Please don't mention to Mark that I told you," begged Linda.

"Oh, you can be certain of that," fumed Verna.

"I take it you and his business partner do not get along," surmised Linda as she cautiously reached for another wet plate.

"Business partner, my butt!" exclaimed Verna.

"But, he told us ...." began Linda.

"I know what he told you," interjected Verna. Then, more softly, "Mark tells everyone that Flo is his business partner."

"His ex?" guessed Linda.

Verna sadly shook her head. "Not to worry, Linda. When I do confront him about it, he will have no idea where I heard it from."

"I hope you're right," replied Linda. She was fearful of what Mark might do or say if he found out she had been the source.

"I'm going to tell you something else in confidence," whispered Verna as she motioned for Linda to come closer.

Linda glanced furtively at the kitchen door, to make sure Mark was not standing there listening. Her bad feelings about the man were growing worse by the minute.

"Mark and Flo were allegedly married once," revealed Verna, "but learned afterwards that their marriage was invalid because his supposed divorce from the wife before that had never come through."

"From Bobby Sue?" Linda was shocked.

"Bobby Sue?" laughed Verna. "Heavens, no! Mark has been married at least four times that I know of, but I didn't find out about any of it until *after* he convinced me to invest $30,000 into his antique business."

"Then why are you still with him?" asked Linda.

"I'm not about to lose my entire life savings if he should decide to bolt," replied Verna. "I'm afraid I'm stuck seeing this one through to the end. He's even got his name on my bank account."

"That can't be good," agreed Linda as she finally dried the last plate and stacked it with the others.

"You two be very careful," warned Verna.

"What about you?" feared Linda.

"I'll bide my time," assured Verna. "I was stupid enough to get myself into this mess. Now, it's just a matter of time until I find a way out. I just hope you don't think too poorly of me."

"Quite the contrary," assured Linda. "You're a brave woman. And, if you ever need to talk – woman to woman – you know where to find me."

"I'm so glad we had this little chat." Verna smiled weakly as she gave Linda a warm hug.

"I'll be sure and tell Kevin about this tonight," informed Linda.

"I wouldn't do that just yet," cautioned Verna. "He might very well decide to confront Mark about it, and the whole thing could blow up on all of us. Let's just give it some time."

"I hope you're right," whispered Linda.

"Things will work out," promised Verna. "Trust me."

Several months had sailed by without incident, and the weekend picnics and other social activities with Mark Killingham were thankfully limited. Linda had come close to sharing Verna's secrets with Kevin on more than one occasion, but was too fearful of what might happen if she did. After all, she had given her word.

It was Wednesday, September 8, 1982. Linda had come home early from work with an unusually bad migraine that day. She desperately missed working as a receptionist for the Ashton Valley Ophthalmology Group. She missed her parents, too! Her new job in Seattle was for a stingy old accountant who had little concept of time, paid her far less than her time was actually worth, and often expected her to work late without notice. She was considering whether or not to find another job.

Linda had just put an icepack on her head and was trying to relax when there was a sudden knock on the apartment door. *Kevin must have come home early, too,* assumed Linda, *but why would he knock? Kevin has a key.* The knock sounded again – like a sledgehammer to Linda's aching head. It sounded urgent.

Irritated by the intrusion, Linda got up and headed for the front door. Through the peephole she could see the face of Mark Killingham. *Oh, no!* mouthed Linda. *What is he doing here?*

Should I open the door, or just pretend like no one's here? Linda wondered. Mark Killingham was the last person in the world she wanted to see right then. At least she hadn't yet put on her pajamas.

"I know you're in there," advised Mark from the other side of the door. "I saw you come home."

Had he been sitting there in the parking lot waiting for her? What in the world did he want?

"Is Kevin home?" questioned Mark, through the door. "I need to speak with him right away."

Realizing there was no way out of it, Linda finally opened the door a crack, but left the security chain in place. "I'm sorry, but Kevin's not home yet."

"May I come in?" requested Mark. He was doing his best to be pleasant and charming.

"I've got a really bad migraine right now," explained Linda. "I'm afraid I wouldn't be very good company. Kevin should be home around 5:30, if you'd like to come back then."

"I'll be back," promised Mark, though it sounded like a threat of some sort.

"I'll let Kevin know you stopped by," called Linda, swallowing hard as she watched him leave.

After closing and relocking the door, Linda cautiously peered again through the curtains – which she had deliberately closed to keep out the extra light because of her migraine. She watched with curiosity as Mark Killingham returned to his car and climbed inside to wait.

Leave already! wished Linda, though the man remained where he was. He obviously planned to wait in his car. *Doggonit!*

Linda was too upset to try and rest now, so decided to make herself a cup of herbal tea to calm her nerves. Just as the whistle on the teapot sounded, the phone began to ring.

After quickly turning off the burner on the teapot, Linda glanced through the front curtains again. *Mark Killingham's car was still there, but where was he? Was it him calling from a nearby payphone, or was it Kevin? If only they still had an answering machine!* Not wanting to speak with Mark – should it be him – Linda finally decided to just let it ring. Kevin would be home soon enough, anyway.

Just two hours earlier, Verna had finally decided to confront Mark about the discrepancies in her bank statement. All but $1,500 of the $30,000 in assets from the antique business had been liquidated. Worse still, only $500 remained of the $20,000 in her personal savings account! *How could he do such a thing? At least she still had the diamond ring – assuming it wasn't a fake!*

"I'm starved," announced Mark Killingham as he entered her home, obviously expecting one of her usual gourmet meals.

"Well, I'm broke!" snapped Verna. "How could you do this to me? Where is all our money?"

"In a safe place." Mark became cold and calculating. "I guess the game is up."

"I really thought we had something special together," sniveled Verna as the tears began to flow down her cheeks.

"You certainly didn't think I was serious about you," laughed Mark in a condescending manner. "Just look at you!"

"You will return what you took from me!" advised Verna.

"Or what?" snickered Mark. "My name is on the bank account, that you willingly put there. You don't have a legal leg to stand on."

"I'm having the locks changed today!" snapped Verna.

"Better change the locks on that warehouse of yours, too!" sneered Mark as he grabbed Verna by the arm, shoved her across the room, and caused her to fall. "At least you've got plenty of padding."

"Oh!" screamed Verna as she started to pick herself up from the floor. "How dare you!"

"No," corrected Mark in a menacing tone as he sauntered toward the front door. "How dare *you* underestimate me."

"A mistake I will not make again!" screamed Verna as she picked up a valuable vase and hoisted it toward him.

Mark laughed with glee as he watched it smash to bits against the wall and land on the floor beside him.

"Not a very good shot, either."

"You will regret this!" hollered Verna.

"No, it is *you* who will regret this," promised Mark as he exited the front door and slammed it shut behind him.

After calling the bank and having a hold put on her savings and checking accounts, Verna quickly called a locksmith, requesting that he meet her at the warehouse. She had one credit card left without Mark's name on it, and would need to use it to pay the man. Once he finished at the warehouse, she would have the locksmith change the locks at her home. She would also need to get a restraining order to keep Mark Killingham away, though that was not as high on her list of priorities at the moment as checking on her merchandise.

Angry, humiliated and frustrated, Verna drove to the warehouse where she knew her son Jared was busy cataloging items for an upcoming art show. Hopefully, she would get there before Mark!

Located at the lower end of the Duwamish Waterway by the First Avenue South Bridge, the warehouse where Verna Newhart kept her rare art pieces was allegedly guarded by a security guard who kept an eye on all the buildings in that complex.

Verna gasped as she saw a plume of smoke rising from one of the buildings. *Why was there smoke?* When realizing that it was her building, Verna noticed a red Honda zooming away from the scene. *It had to be Mark!*

The security guard had already called the Fire Department and the wail of sirens could be heard approaching in the distance.

What about Jared? Was he okay? Verna sped toward the warehouse, hurriedly parked her vehicle, and ran toward the open door of her warehouse.

"Wait, lady!" called the security guard. "You can't go in there!"

"My son's in there!" hollered Verna as she raced inside anyway.

There on the floor lay Jared, unconscious but still alive. A small trickle of blood could be seen oozing from his head. The security guard raced inside to assist, and together they managed to drag Jared to safety.

"I'll call an ambulance!" shouted the elderly guard as he hobbled toward the payphone nearby. *If only there were a phone in his office.*

"Oh, Jared!" moaned Verna as she sat holding her sweater against his forehead to try and stop the bleeding. *Would he regain consciousness and be able to confirm that Mark had done this?*

Just then the locksmith pulled up and approached. "What's going on here?"

"Oh, Mr. Jones," greeted Verna. "I had no idea any of this was happening when I called you."

"Do you still want me to change the locks?"

58

"If you can change the locks at my home first," requested Verna, "here is my card. My address is on the back."

"I'm going to have to charge for the extra time and mileage," cautioned the man.

"That's okay," sniffed Verna. "Just come back here when you're done to do this one. Here's my house key. The police and firemen should be finished here at the warehouse by the time you return."

"Hey, lady, I'm really sorry about whatever has happened here," remarked the man. "I'll tell you what. I won't charge for the extra trip. Clearly, it wasn't your fault."

"Thanks so much!" Verna tried to smile.

Just then an ambulance arrived. All she could do was stand by helplessly and watch as the medics bandaged up Jared's headwound and loaded him into the ambulance.

"Where are you taking him?" questioned Verna.

"The Duwamish Hospital is closest," advised the ambulance driver as he opened the door to climb in.

"I'm coming with you," informed Verna as she opened the back and hopped inside.

"There's not much room in here," advised the medic working on Jared, "but you can sit on the other side of him if you like."

"I'll just send you a bill, lady," called the locksmith. "Where would you like me to leave your new key?"

"Under the sundial in my back yard, if you don't mind," called Verna as the ambulance started up and sped away.

"Sure, lady," mumbled the locksmith as he watched the ambulance disappear. "Hope your son's okay."

Just then, a police car could be seen pulling up.

"Please answer!" wailed Verna. She was calling from a payphone on the wall at the hospital while she waited for her son to get out of surgery. It was her hope to reach Kevin or Linda, to warn them that she and Mark Killingham had parted ways after a horrible falling out, and that they could be in danger. *Why don't those kids have an answering machine?*

Linda paced the floor while waiting for Kevin to get home from work. Perhaps then, she would answer the phone – once she knew it wasn't Mark Killingham! She had hoped to speak with her husband first, before Mark showed up again, to fill him in on what had happened earlier. *If only her head did not hurt so badly!*

Unexpectedly, the front door opened. It was Kevin, but Mark Killingham was *with* him. Kevin appeared troubled by what Mark was saying. Without so much as a hello to Linda, Kevin followed Mark over to the couch and sat down where he continued listening to his tale.

"Welcome home," interrupted Linda as she approached, leaned over, and gave her husband a hug.

"Oh, hi sweetheart," acknowledged Kevin as he handed Linda his coat and lunchbox.

"Sorry I wasn't feeling well earlier," added Linda for Mark's benefit, though she honestly felt no need to apologize.

"No problem," smiled Mark, being overly nice in front of Kevin.

"I came home earlier with a migraine," added Linda, to let Kevin know about it, just in case Mark had mentioned to him that she wouldn't let him in.

"Why don't we get some takeout?" suggested Mark. "On me. How about some pizza? Could you please call that in, hon?"

Hon? Linda felt as if she were going to be sicker than she already was. *Hon? Really?* "Oh, sure. What kind?"

"Hawaiian sounds good, if they have it," decided Mark. "Ham and pineapple."

"Pepperoni on the other half," mentioned Kevin.

"Yes, sir," replied Linda with a mocking hand salute that neither of them saw as she walked away. "I'll just call that in right now."

Linda headed for the bedroom where the phonebook was located and began searching it for a local pizza delivery place. Finally finding one, she called and placed the order. Before she made it out of the bedroom, however, the phone suddenly rang. "I'll get it. It might be them. Maybe they're just calling to confirm the order."

"That's fine," called Kevin, who was still busy listening to Mark's rendition of what had happened earlier that day.

"Hello?" answered Linda.

"Linda? Thank God!" It was Verna.

"Is everything okay?" asked Linda. The panic in Verna's voice was evident.

60

"I have reason to believe the two of you are in danger," blurted out Verna. "It's Mark."

"Hold on just a moment," requested Linda as she set down the phone, whose cord was not long enough to reach to the bedroom door. "Kevin, it's my mom," lied Linda. "The pizza should be on its way."

"Thanks!" came the voices of both men from the living room.

Linda then closed the bedroom door so she could speak freely with Verna, and hurried back to the phone. "I'm alone in the bedroom now, so we can talk."

"Was that Mark I heard in the background?" questioned Verna.

"Yes, he's here with Kevin," replied Linda. "Something sure seems to be up. They're out there in the living room talking about it."

"You bet it is!" fumed Verna. "That monster just got done cleaning nearly everything out my bank accounts, to the tune of $28,500 from our business, and $19,500 from my personal bank account!"

"Oh, my God!" exclaimed Linda. "Why would he do such a thing to you?"

"I was nothing more than a con job to him," answered Verna, who was sobbing again. "And if I hadn't caught onto it when I did, I have no doubt that he would have liquidated the rest of it, too!"

"Have you called the police?" pressed Linda.

"You bet I have," assured Verna. "I'm just sorry I didn't do it before confronting him."

"What happened?"

"He just laughed in my face and reminded me that I'd willingly put his name on my accounts," sniffed Verna. "And he's right, I was an idiot to ever trust him like that. But, I really thought he and I had something special together. I guess there's no fool like an old fool. Heck, this stupid ring's probably a fake, too!"

"Isn't there anything you can do?" Linda was shocked.

"Not about that," confirmed Verna. "But, he also started a fire in my warehouse today."

"A fire?" Linda was deathly afraid of fires. Her grandparents' cabin had been destroyed by fire when she was three years old, and memories of flames shooting 30 feet high on either side of the road as her family made its escape still haunted her. They had lost everything.

"Thankfully, Jared was there to stop him from doing anything else," added Verna, "but he may have paid the ultimate price for it."

61

Linda was speechless. *Was Jared dead? Had Mark murdered him? What would happen now?*

"Jared's in surgery right now," clarified Verna before Linda could ask. "Hopefully, when he wakes up, he can confirm that it was Mark who hit him. The police should be here by then. I'm at a payphone in the waiting room by the lobby at the hospital."

"I'm so sorry," consoled Linda. "Please let us know how he does."

"I will," promised Verna. "And, you need to shake that rat from your back just as soon as humanly possible, young lady. Don't let him bamboozle you. I threw him out, so now he has no place to stay."

"He's certainly not staying here!" assured Linda. She had heard enough to convince her the man was dangerous, and wanted no part of having him in their lives.

"They think you're talking to your mom, huh?" chuckled Verna.

"You heard me?" Linda could not believe it.

"You'd better hope they didn't hear you say Verna!"

Just then, Kevin came into the bedroom. "The pizza's here."

"Okay, mom," replied Linda. "Well, guess I'd better go now. Give dad my love."

"You be careful!"

"Count on it," assured Linda as she hung up.

"Count on what?" questioned Kevin.

"That I would write more often," lied Linda. She wanted to pull Kevin aside right then and share with him what Verna had just told her, but knew she needed to wait until Mark had left.

"Hey, we were about to start without you," flirted Mark, unconvincingly, as Kevin and Linda returned to the living room.

"I'll get some plates," muttered Linda.

"I have a bottle of wine in the car," offered Mark. "I'll be right back. I think Kevin has something he needs to tell you, too."

Linda was apprehensive as she waited for Kevin to tell her whatever it was. *This couldn't be good!*

"Okay then," added Mark as he left, letting the door slam shut on his way out.

"What's this all about?" demanded Linda.

"Mark needs a place to stay," informed Kevin.

"He's not staying here!" exclaimed Linda, instantly enraged by the very thought of it.

"He's my father," added Kevin, quite seriously. "He and Verna had a falling out today, and she threw him out. He needs somewhere to stay for a couple of days, just until he can get back on his feet."

"No!" shouted Linda. "Absolutely not!"

"The matter is not up for debate," replied Kevin. "I already told him he could stay here. He'll be sleeping on the couch, and I've already made it clear to him that he cannot be here when I'm not. You won't ever be left here alone with him, since you apparently do not feel comfortable around the man."

"What makes you say that?" asked Linda, more softly.

"It's obvious by your behavior," answered Kevin. "If there's something else that's happened between you and my father that I don't know about, I suggest you tell me about it right now."

Just then the door opened, and in walked Mark Killingham with a large suitcase in one hand and a bottle of wine in the other.

"Like I'm sure Kevin just told you," advised Mark with a wink at Linda, "it'll just be for a couple of weeks."

"A couple of weeks?" repeated Linda as her mouth dropped open. The prospect of a couple of days had been bad enough!

"Whatever it takes," remarked Kevin. "It'll be okay." He then put an arm around Linda to reassure her.

Later that night, once Linda could hear Mark Killingham loudly snoring from the couch in the living room, she gently shook Kevin to wake him. "We need to talk."

"Later, I'm exhausted," mumbled Kevin as he turned over on his other side to try and go back to sleep.

"We need to talk *now*!" persisted Linda as she shook him again.

Kevin then turned back toward her to listen to what she had to say. "This better be good."

Linda then told him of the phone call from Verna and everything that had been said. "We just can't let him stay here, don't you see?"

Kevin slowly sat up and shook his head. "If the man is as dangerous as Verna says he is, then to turn him away now might be worse than letting him stay here."

"Look, I know how important it is to you to find out about your childhood," continued Linda, "but right now you need to think about your safety and that of your wife – that would be *me!*"

"As long as he believes we know nothing about what Verna told you, we're probably safe," believed Kevin. "Besides, even if it is a couple of weeks, it will be over soon. Perhaps I can find out what I want to know from him about my childhood while he's here."

"I hope you know what you're doing," fretted Linda. "I'm completely against it."

"I think I'd like to call Verna myself, and see how her son Jared is doing," added Kevin. "I'll do it tomorrow, from work. That way Dad will be none the wiser."

"Please don't call him that," frowned Linda.

"Everything will be alright," promised Kevin as he pulled Linda close and gave her a kiss on the cheek. "Trust me."

Two weeks soon became two months, and still Mark Killingham remained as an unwanted house guest in Kevin's and Linda's apartment. Not only had he managed to make himself quite at home, but many personal boundaries had been disregarded.

"What happened to you?" questioned Kevin as he came into the bedroom and noticed that Linda had red welts on her face and arms.

"I'm allergic to strawberries, remember?" snapped Linda.

"Then why would you eat them?" asked Kevin. "Do we need to take you to the hospital?"

"I didn't *eat* them! Just coming into contact with my skin did this! That monster dumped some cheap, leftover strawberry shampoo into my expensive bottle of unscented shampoo that I bought for $25 at the hair salon!" screamed Linda.

"Hey, I'm sorry," apologized Mark from the doorway. "I had no idea you would be allergic to it."

"So, you just go ahead and dump a 99¢ bottle of strawberry shampoo into a $25 bottle of fragrance free shampoo without asking, and in someone else's home?" fumed Linda. *And how dare Mark*

Killingham come into their bedroom like that while she and her husband were having a private conversation!

"I'll buy you a new bottle of the unscented brand," promised Mark, seeming quite sorry for it. "Which hair dresser is it?"

"How about you give me the $25 and I'll just go get some more?" proposed Linda. *Why did he really want to know who her hair dresser was? So he could go burn down their shop?*

"Okay, sure," nodded Mark as he pulled out his wallet, removed two $20-dollar bills, and left them on the dresser. "I'll go make dinner."

"And that's another thing!" fumed Linda as she watched Mark leave and head toward the kitchen. "Perhaps we might want something else to eat once in a while. Why do we always have to eat whatever he seems to think we need to be eating now?"

"He's only trying to help out," assured Kevin.

"Until *when*?" growled Linda. "When is he ever going to leave? I just cannot go on like this!"

"I will talk to him tonight," promised Kevin. "Okay?"

"You need to give him a deadline," pressed Linda.

"He's trying to start up his own business right now," reminded Kevin. "And, the sooner he succeeds, the sooner he will be able to move out and be on his own again."

"I hope you're right," sighed Linda. She was sick and tired of hearing Mark's empty promises about leaving.

"I cosigned for him to get a pocket pager today," informed Kevin. "For his new business."

"You cosigned for him?" Linda felt as if she might have an aneurism. "After what happened to Verna?"

"He *will* pay the bill for it," guaranteed Kevin. "The moment he's out of here, I will contact the company and make sure my name is no longer on the account. Trust me."

Two months soon became four months. It was Tuesday, January 11, 1983. Linda had become clinically depressed, rarely eating and never smiling anymore. She had called in sick again that day, just so she could have some time alone. *When would they ever be rid of Mark Killingham?* That was one wedding gift she would gladly have returned, if only it were possible! Debating on whether to go ahead and call her parents to come and get her, Linda suddenly noticed

65

that the key to her personal file cabinet had been moved from the right side of her dresser to the left. *Kevin would never do that! Had Mark Killingham been into their personal papers?*

Kevin and Mark were at the grocery store, due to return any moment. Linda seized the opportunity to search Mark Killingham's suitcase. She needed to be sure none of their personal papers or information had been stolen.

Linda scowled at the filthy underwear and dirty socks inside the overstuffed suitcase. How odd that there was anything dirty inside at all, since the man usually just tossed his dirty laundry right into their laundry hamper!

The red Honda was just pulling up outside when Linda suddenly discovered a notebook with names and Social Security numbers on it. *Why would Mark have this information? Who were these people?* Linda then noticed a small plastic container with white powder in it. *Was Mark bringing drugs into their home?*

Linda decided to stand her ground and waited for the door to open. Kevin would be with him, anyway, so it was time to finally confront the man. *Kevin would be furious about the drugs!*

Just as the door opened, Linda lost her nerve, quickly closed the suitcase, and sat down on the couch. At least when the man wasn't sleeping on it, it was allegedly still theirs.

"How does Chinese sound?" asked Mark as he and Kevin entered the apartment with a bag containing several containers of Chinese food.

"Sure, why not?" shrugged Linda, trying to appear nonchalant.

"I've been worried about you," mentioned Kevin as he and Mark set out plates and opened the containers of takeout.

Then, realizing that she still had the small plastic container in her hand, Linda regained her courage. "Please explain this."

"Oh, you found my baking soda," grinned Mark. "I was wondering where I had left that."

"Baking soda?" questioned Linda as she opened the container to get a closer look.

"I brush my teeth with it," explained Mark with an amused look on his face as he took it from her.

"May I see that?" requested Kevin.

"Sure," laughed Mark as he handed Kevin the container.

Kevin carefully wetted the end of his little finger, stuck it into the white powder, and then tasted it. "It's baking soda, alright."

Linda's nostrils flared with anger as she looked up in time to see Mark's triumphant smirk.

Later that night, Kevin pulled Linda close and whispered, "I finally did speak with Verna today."

Linda sat up like a bolt of lightning. "And? How's Jared?"

"Verna and Jared have pressed charges against Mark, but want the police to arrest him when he's someplace else besides here," explained Kevin. "Otherwise, Mark will know we gave him up and then we could be in serious danger."

"So, the police have been looking for him, then?" Linda was hopeful for the first time in four months.

"Yes," whispered Kevin. "But, we can't let on like anything's up. And, while that was a very brave thing that you did, confronting him about the baking soda, what if it had been drugs?"

"I don't like the fact that he always has that gun in his boot, either," added Linda.

"Then, that's all the more reason not to antagonize the man," cautioned Kevin. "Besides, he told me tonight when we were out getting the Chinese food that he plans to fly out to Maine this weekend, on business. Things are finally picking up with his new company."

"Won't that be out of the Seattle Police Department's jurisdiction?" questioned Linda, trying not to sound snide about it.

"Not if they catch him at the airport," replied Kevin.

"So, what happens if they don't get him?" worried Linda.

"It won't matter," answered Kevin. "Because when Mark gets back from his trip, either way, we'll be long gone."

"We will?" beamed Linda.

"How would you like to move back to Ashton?"

Tears began to well up in Linda's eyes as she tightly embraced her husband. "How fast can you pack?"

"Verna said she will come down to help us while he's away," revealed Kevin. "But, we must wait until he leaves on Friday night to get started. We don't want him to suspect anything."

67

"I'll quit my job tomorrow," decided Linda. "That way, I can secretly pack boxes and store them in our closet until then. He'll never be any the wiser."

"Just be careful, and don't pack too much," warned Kevin. "The man's no dummy."

"He shouldn't try to come here during the daytime on a week day, though," assumed Linda, "especially if he thinks I've called in sick or something."

"I just hope you're right," worried Kevin. "He has threatened you at least twice that I know of."

"He sure was surprised the time he realized you were standing right there, behind him," recalled Linda.

"Was that when he reminded you that women have their place in the home, and that if you knew what was good for you that you'd keep that in mind?"

"Actually," differed Linda, "I'm pretty sure it was the time he said that if I ever crossed him again that I might just find myself looking over my shoulder for the rest of my life, just like Bobby Sue."

Kevin had not wanted to believe any of it when Linda first told him how things were falling apart with his real father, but knew in his heart that it must be true, especially after overhearing the remark about Bobby Sue. *Just what had Mark Killingham really done to his mother, anyway?*

Kevin had finally come to terms with the fact that Mark would never tell him what he wanted to know about his childhood. Not only that, the man was dangerous, and it was time to cut all ties with him. There would be no going back after that, but it was definitely time.

Would Kevin and Linda really be able to pack everything up and be gone without a trace in a single weekend? Or, would Mark Killingham return early and catch them in the act of trying to leave?

3. Rodeo Queen

Jim Otterman paced the floor while he listened to Kevin and Linda tell their story. *How could this possibly be the same Mark Killingham he had come to know and respect for so many years?*

"Hey, you guys," interrupted Sheree as she entered the tower room of the lighthouse with a platter of tuna sandwiches. "It's lunchtime already. You'd better stop and eat something now if you plan to be finished before 3:00 p.m. Peru time."

"That would be 1:00 p.m. our time," added Jim, for Kevin's and Linda's benefit. He was unaware of their unsuccessful attempt to make it back in time for their skype session with Ann the previous day.

"Yeah, we found that out the hard way yesterday," Kevin smiled at Sheree from where he was seated next to Linda at the round wooden table.

"We would love to be in on your session for today," nodded Linda. "We need to find Mark Killingham – if he is still alive – and have him arrested for anything we can find on him, starting with what he did to us. Hopefully, Ann might have some ideas."

"I know what he did to you was unfair," acknowledged Jim, "but from what you've just told me, it doesn't sound like anything to merit being arrested for. Verna, on the other hand, may have very well done just that, especially after what he did to her warehouse and to her son. There would be a record of it if she did. I'll do a cross check after the skype, to see if Mark Killingham was arrested for anything in 1982. But, as far as Verna's bank accounts, if she did willingly put his name on her accounts, Mark was correct, there's little she could do about something like that – a very hard lesson, for sure."

"Let's bless the food, shall we?" prompted Sheree as she set down the platter of sandwiches and then grabbed four bottles of water from the small red refrigerator nearby and handed one to each of them.

"Yes, ma'am," grinned Jim, and began, "Dear Lord, thank you for this food, and bless it that it will give us nourishment. We pray that you will help us find out what we can about Mark Killingham so that all of us can have our minds put at ease regarding him once and for all. Amen."

"Amen!" exclaimed the others.

"Thanks!" nodded Kevin as he took one of the sandwiches and began to devour it. He hadn't realized how famished he was.

Linda merely smiled and nodded as she took one of the sandwiches, to be polite, but really wasn't hungry. The very thought of Mark Killingham had dampened her appetite.

"Good sandwich," mentioned Kevin as he winked at Sheree.

"It was only one month after our return to Ashton that we received our final utility and other bills from the Seattle apartment," advised Linda as she stared absently out the huge viewing window beside them at the ocean beyond.

"Oh, that's right!" exclaimed Kevin, with his mouth full.

"Our phone bill was for over $800 that last month," fumed Linda, still angry about it even after so many years. "The calls were to Colorado, Wyoming, Maine, Washington DC, and even one to Peru!"

"Peru?" frowned Jim. She definitely had his attention.

"We explained to the telephone carrier that the bills were not ours," added Linda, "so they finally removed all but $500 of them from our account."

"The $300 was for the call to Peru," elaborated Kevin.

"You still had to pay the $500, then?" questioned Jim.

"Yes," answered Linda. "But, we were the lucky ones."

"Compared to Verna, I'd say so," acknowledged Jim.

"That's not even the half of it," interjected Kevin.

"That's right!" exclaimed Linda. "Five years later when we were involved in a rather serious car accident – and totaled the car – we went in for a loan to try and get a new one."

"He didn't try and run you off the road, did he?" Jim suddenly asked.

"I sure wish he'd try!" growled Kevin as he fingered the butt of his concealed weapon. "No, it was just some jerk who ran a stop sign. There wasn't time to stop, so I t-boned him."

"I was the only injury," volunteered Linda. "When the two vehicles slid sideways into each other at the time of impact, it was my side that took the brunt of it."

"You were the passenger?" grilled Jim.

"That was me," confirmed Linda. "The one with the slightly torn rotator cuff. But, after several weeks of physical therapy, I was finally able to avoid surgery to repair it."

"It's 20 minutes until 1:00," pointed out Sheree. "I'll set up the laptop."

"Thanks," replied Jim as he took another bite of sandwich.

"Anyway," continued Kevin, "the guy at the auto dealership where we were trying to get the loan turned us down flat, but then he told us that we had better check out our credit report."

"And, so we did," added Linda, "only to learn that *someone* claiming to be Kevin had set up utility and other accounts in his name up in Vancouver, Washington. There were even debt collectors after Kevin, but we had known nothing about it before that!"

"And I've never even been to Vancouver," mentioned Kevin.

"That certain *someone* even had Kevin's Social Security number!" fumed Linda.

"So, that's why you found the keys to your file cabinet moved to the other side of your dresser," remembered Jim. "No doubt that's when he accessed your personal information."

Linda shook her head with disgust.

"It took us about two years to finally get those bogus charges and debt collectors off our backs," sighed Kevin. "The worst part of it was, some of it was my own fault."

"How do you figure?" frowned Jim.

"Remember the pager I cosigned for?" asked Kevin.

"You forgot to have your name taken off the account?" guessed Jim as he shook his head.

"Oh, I had my name taken off the account, alright," advised Kevin. "But, Mark apparently went back in, forged my signature, and had my name put back on, where it remained for five years. In fact, if we hadn't had that car accident when we did, who knows how many more years' worth of debt plus interest might have resulted."

"Definitely not good," muttered Jim.

"We were forced to pay the pager company for the entire five years – which came to just over $1,200 – before we could get them off our backs so we could get our car loan," explained Linda. "They were the most relentless creditor of all."

"So much for our down payment and the vehicle we really wanted to get," added Kevin as he rolled his eyes. "Instead, we got stuck with some old used car and really high payments, to boot."

"I take it you finally managed to get those items removed from your credit report?" asked Jim before taking a big drink of water.

"Yes," answered Linda.

"Unfortunately, there's a statute of limitations for some things," explained Jim. "And, even though you were able to get the charges removed from your credit report – regardless of the fact that you did end up having to pay the $500 phone bill and the $1,200 pager charges – there still might have been nothing you could have done about it."

"What about all the time and trouble we went through to clear Kevin's name?" demanded Linda. "Taking care of all that wasn't exactly free, you know!"

"I'm sure it wasn't," agreed Jim.

"It was right after that when I called and reconnected with Verna," mentioned Kevin, "just to let her know what had happened to us and to see how she was doing. Also, I wanted to make sure nothing like that had happened to her – you know, her identity being stolen."

"It's 10 minutes until 1:00 and the laptop is ready," advised Sheree as she began cleaning up the mess from the sandwiches.

"What'd Verna say?" grilled Jim, ignoring Sheree completely.

"Apparently, Verna hired a private investigator of her own," revealed Kevin. "After leaving Seattle, Mark went back to Colorado for a while, with Flo."

"Really?" Jim raised an eyebrow.

"The two of them were involved in conning another woman from Montana out of her entire life savings after that," related Kevin.

Jim immediately began making notes on his smartwatch. "I hate this thing, it's so small you can't see a thing! I need the laptop."

"The laptop is already set up for our skype with Ann in five minutes," cautioned Sheree. "You'll have to wait until afterwards."

"Verna also mentioned that there were at least eight more victims after that – that we know of," added Kevin. "All of them were wealthy widows – until they met Mark Killingham, that is."

"He even stole the identity of his own sister's dead husband!" advised Linda.

"Oh, that's right," nodded Kevin. "When Mark flew out to Maine to stay with his sister Jodean, he allegedly found the man's Social Security card and driver's license in a drawer."

"Then, when Jodean realized that her brother Mark had taken the last $700 she had in this world, the poor woman drank herself into a coma and died," elaborated Linda.

"Or, it might have been made to look that way," speculated Kevin. "But, Jodean did have a serious drinking problem, so perhaps in her case it was a blessing."

"And that monster is still out there!" spat Linda. "So, whoever it was that died in that ice cream shop, it wasn't Mark Killingham!"

"She's right," agreed Kevin. "It was definitely him that we ran into when we were at the Saturday market up in Seattle in 2016."

"I'm surprised you'd even go back there for a vacation, after everything that happened before," commented Jim. "What was said between you and Mark Killingham that day, if you don't mind my asking?"

"After his fake apology," described Kevin, "I advised him to stay away from us."

"And then Mark just walked away?" quizzed Jim.

"Actually, we did," interjected Linda, "but not before he gave me that look of his – the one that said I'd better keep looking over my shoulder for the rest of my life."

"You know, I should have just whacked him over the head with that 40-pound Chinook we had with us," added Kevin.

"Did Mark ask you where you live now, or anything like that?" pressed Jim.

"Of course, he did," responded Kevin, "but we didn't tell him. I also mentioned to him that there are some bridges that just cannot be rebuilt."

Jim nodded with approval.

"Ann?" questioned Sheree. "Can you see us?"

"Hi, how are you?" beamed Ann, whose face could be seen on Jim's laptop. "I see you're in the tower room."

"We miss you, sweetheart," smiled Sheree as she adjusted the camera to encompass the entire room behind her. Ann did likewise at her end.

"Hey," acknowledged Carolyn, who was sitting beside Ann.

"Find any treasure yet?" razzed Jim.

"You might be surprised," grinned Susan, who was sitting beside Carolyn.

"Hello!" greeted Sherry, who was on the other side of Ann. "We've got quite an adventure to share with you when we get back!"

"And, of course, we miss you all very much," commented Rupert, who was standing behind them, leaning forward with his hands

73

on the back of Susan's chair. Even Linda could not help but admire Rupert's handsome dark features. *Who was that man?*

"Linda Shaver?" gasped Carolyn, when finally recognizing her. There was something about the way Linda had looked at Rupert that Carolyn recognized. It was the same way Linda had once gazed at Lenny Owens when they were in high school together.

"It's been 49 years, but you look just the same," replied Linda.

"Likewise," complimented Carolyn, in an effort to be polite. *Why in the world was Linda Shaver there? Of all people!*

As if able to read Carolyn's thoughts, Jim suddenly spoke up. "Linda and her husband – Kevin Killingham – have hired me to find out what really happened to his father Mark."

"Mark?" repeated Ann with surprise. "Not Ray's dad?"

"I'm afraid so," confirmed Jim.

"Didn't you tell them yet?" questioned Ann.

"We have reason to believe that the man whose body was found at the ice cream shop might not have been Mark Killingham," elaborated Jim. "After we finish this skype, I'm going to see what can be done about getting his body exhumed."

"Don't you need probable cause?" challenged Susan. She was not sure she wanted the body of her dead husband's father to be put through something like that.

"Oh, we've got plenty of it," assured Jim. "Trust me!"

Susan merely grinned at hearing the words "trust me" and then rewarded Jim with a crooked smile. "Sure, why not, go ahead. He ain't going anywhere, anyway."

The others merely chuckled at Susan's quip.

"You better tell me all about it when we get back, though," added Susan as she blew Jim a kiss.

"Before you close out, Ann, can you please share with us absolutely everything you know about the genealogy on the Killingham side of the family? It's very important."

"Really?" Ann seemed surprised. "You've never had much interest in the family's history before."

"Well, I'm very interested in it now," assured Jim. "Kevin and Linda would also like to know whatever you can tell us, and I'll be recording this."

74

"Hang on," instructed Ann as she dashed off screen to retrieve her Notepad – a separate electronic device on which she kept her genealogy. "I'm pulling it up now," advised Ann as she reappeared.

"Good thing she took the Notepad with her," commented Sheree. "Sometimes an extra device can come in handy."

"Especially if it's big enough to see," agreed Jim as he glanced with contempt at his smartwatch.

"Okay," began Ann. "As we all know, the lighthouse where you are now was originally built in 1872 by the first Killinghams to come here from Ireland."

"That would have been fifteen years before the Ocean Bluff Mental Institution was built in 1887," mentioned Jim, for Kevin's and Linda's benefit.

"The builder's name was Jeremy Killingham, born in 1848 in Dingle, Ireland," indicated Ann as she pointed to the graph pulled up on her Notepad.

"Can you please hold it a little closer to the camera?" requested Jim as he studied the chart.

"He and his wife Bonnie, whose last name we don't know, had several daughters," continued Ann. "Each of them was named after a different flower."

"Aren't those the ones the rooms here at the lighthouse are named after?" questioned Linda, amazed by the connection.

"Yes," replied Ann, "but I would have to bring up the individual family group sheet to display the names of that couple's children. The pedigree chart you are looking at now only displays the direct line of parent to child for each generation."

"I notice you have Daisy listed as Jeremy's oldest daughter," observed Jim, "but no husband for her?"

"There's no record of his name," confirmed Ann, "but we do know that Daisy was born in 1869, three years before the lighthouse was built. Unfortunately, the sailor who fathered her children abandoned them when the boys were quite young, and was never seen or heard from again."

"Daisy eventually became so depressed from the constant howling of the wind at the lighthouse that she flung herself from the blufftops onto the rocks below," elaborated Susan, who was also familiar with the story.

"How sad!" exclaimed Linda.

75

"Jed was one of her sons?" questioned Kevin.

"Yes," replied Ann. "Jed Killingham was born in 1890, right there at the lighthouse. He was Jack Killingham's father, and Mark Killingham's grandfather."

"So, that would make Jack my grandfather, then?" frowned Kevin.

"I guess so," smiled Ann. "And this is where the story gets interesting. Jed Killingham had three children, two by one woman he never married, and the third by yet another one-night stand."

"How do you know all this?" pressed Jim.

"It's right here in Ellie Mae's diary," grinned Ann. "That is one of the things we still have to share with you. Anyway, Jed's oldest son Jack was born in 1910. His brother James was born in 1911. Their half-sister Ellie Mae was born in 1912, and all three of them there at the lighthouse. In fact, they are the ones in that old black and white photograph we found last month."

Jim's eyes opened wide with surprise. "The picture that was in that faux book with the gold disc?"

"That's the one," beamed Ann.

Jim suddenly raced over to the book shelf and pulled the faux book back out, which now housed color photographs of not only the gold disc, but also the two black and white photographs.

"This picture?" pressed Jim, as he held one of them up for the camera to see. "The people down there on the beach?"

"That's them," confirmed Ann. "The tall man on the right is Jed's oldest son Jack, the one who came here to Peru and found the gold disc. The other man on the left is his younger brother James, who was killed in a tragic accident while they were down here."

Jim then pulled out the other picture of Jack from the faux book. It showed Jack wearing a safari outfit and holding a long rifle in one hand and an old-fashioned canteen in the other.

"Wow, he sure was tall!" muttered Kevin as he studied the photo of his grandfather wearing a pith helmet.

"About 7 feet," mentioned Ann.

"And who are the twin boys they are holding?" questioned Linda, suddenly quite interested. *Were these the twins Jim had mentioned earlier?*

"The one being held by Jack is Mark Killingham," replied Ann. "It shows here that he was born on March 23, 1930."

"Of course, he was," chuckled Jim. "March 23rd."

"And the other one?" urged Linda, anxious to find out.

"His name was Jack Killingham, Jr.," related Ann, "and no record of him exists after 2009 that I can find."

Jim exchanged a surprised look with Kevin and Linda.

"That's the year that Mark Killingham allegedly died in his ice cream shop," added Ann. "You don't think Mark killed his identical twin brother and then stole his identity, do you?"

Her question seemed to hit everyone like a ton of bricks. *Could that be what really happened?*

After an uncomfortable pause, Jim spoke up first. "That is something we are definitely going to find out! I know that Mark had a broken arm at one point in his life, so the skeleton in that grave would definitely show it, if it's him."

"I'm betting it doesn't," volunteered Kevin.

"Me, too," nodded Jim, rather sadly.

"It gets even better," enticed Ann. "Jack, Sr. actually married his half-sister Ellie Mae in 1929, right before the stock market crashed, but she was only 17 at the time so they were forced to travel to Alabama where the legal age for marriage was lower."

"Oh, my God!" exclaimed Linda. "The twin sons were *theirs?*"

"You got it," acknowledged Ann. "But, Ellie Mae decided to leave Jack, Sr. when he and his brother James went on safari to Peru in 1932. That was the year James was killed after a cave-in when recovering that gold disc."

"What happened to Ellie Mae after that?" asked Linda.

"No one knows," answered Ann. "But, at least she left her diary behind. We do know that Jack, Sr. eventually married again, but not until several years later. Care to guess to whom?"

Jim strained to get a better look at Ann's Notepad, but she was moving it again. "Can you please hold that thing still?"

"Kate Dixon," advised Ann. "That was when he legally adopted her two girls – Cathy and Linda Dixon. Of course, Linda was already pregnant with Ray by then, so she was showing when her mother married Jack, Sr."

"Linda's sister was Cathy Dixon?" Jim's mouth dropped open, as did Sheree's and Linda's. "*The* Cathy Dixon who was dean of girls over at Oceanview Academy when we were students there?"

"The same," grinned Ann. "Small world, isn't it?"

"And, of course, we already know that her sister Linda died giving birth to my late husband Ray Dixon Killingham back in 1944," interjected Susan. "After confessing on her deathbed to her midwife Edith Roth about the affair she'd had with Edith's husband Jon Roth, Sr., who was actually Ray's real father."

"In other words," interpreted Ann, "Ray Dixon Killingham's real name was Ray Roth, though he never knew about it until later in life, long after his mother had already taken the secret with her to her grave."

"Hold it!" instructed Kevin. "I'm not following any of this."

"Let me put it another way," tried Ann. "Mark Killingham fell in love with his older stepsister Linda Dixon the day he met her, at their parents' wedding. It was love at first sight. Linda was six months pregnant with Jon Roth, Sr.'s child, but that made no difference to Mark. Unfortunately, Mark was only 14 years old at the time so he lied about his age in order to get the marriage certificate."

"No doubt that was the beginning of his life as a con artist," snickered Linda.

"Most likely," agreed Jim.

"Anyway," continued Ann, "we all know the Lizzie Borden story, and how Edith was descended from her."

Kevin and Linda exchanged a look of concern.

"Edith's son Jon Roth, Jr. was my father," explained Ann. "That makes me a direct descendent of Lizzie Andrew Borden."

"And when you get back, I'm sure you can tell them all about that side of your family," suggested Jim.

"Hey, thanks for telling us what you know about Mark Killingham," mentioned Kevin. "We appreciate it."

"Have a good evening," bid Jim.

"Thanks, you too," replied Ann. "And, just so you know, we're headed into the jungle tomorrow and might not be able to skype you for a couple of days."

"So, if you don't hear from us, don't worry," grinned Carolyn. "We'll be fine. Hopefully."

March 23, 1955

Bobby Sue gazed wistfully at the handsome ranch hand her father had just hired to help with the cows. Tomorrow was her big day at the county fair when she would be showing her prized Herford bull named Moose. Perhaps her father would agree to let the new ranch hand help her.

Unusually gentle and good natured, especially after having been bottle-fed by her from the time he was a small calf, Moose followed her nearly everywhere. Unknown to her father, Bobby Sue had even ridden Moose on more than one occasion, trying to imagine herself as a rodeo queen. Thankfully, Moose was too even tempered to be used as a rodeo bull and had never been known to charge at anyone.

"Howdy, ma'am," greeted the stranger as he strutted over to Moose's stall. "Need any help with that guy? I'm Mark, by the way. Mark Killingham."

"Mark?" repeated Bobby Sue as she blushed with shyness. Her experience with members of the opposite sex was extremely limited, due to the strict regulations set down by her father.

"Nice animal," added Mark as he flashed Bobby Sue a charming smile that caused her to blush even more. "Didn't catch the name."

"Moose," stammered Bobby Sue. "His name is Moose."

"Not him," laughed Mark as he gently stroked the bull's withers. "You! What's *your* name?"

"Oh," chuckled Bobby Sue. "I'm Bobby Sue Johnson."

"The boss's daughter," grinned Mark. "Are you allowed to fraternize with the help?"

"I don't see why not," replied Bobby Sue as she studied Mark more closely. She felt herself drawn to him in a way that she could not explain. His charming smile and alluring eyes captivated her. His dark red hair was neatly combed back with men's hair tonic. His well-fitting jeans seemed almost new, as did his boots, but that was the furthest thing from her mind right then. He was mysterious and exciting.

"How old are you?" questioned Mark as he continued to flirt with her. He was more than intrigued by the quality of innocence she possessed. *If she was still a virgin, he would definitely need to do something about it, and soon,* Mark thought as he undressed her with his eyes.

Bobby Sue was quite mature for her age, very well rounded in all the right places, and completely unaware of her stunning beauty. Her silky auburn hair was worn parted on one side, about shoulder length. Her hazel eyes offset her clear alabaster complexion nicely. The western shirt and tight fitting blue jeans she wore were enticing. Her steel-tipped western boots were worn with use, but did not detract from *the package.*

"Sixteen," lied Bobby Sue. Having been born in 1940, she was only 15, but her birthday was next month. "How 'bout you?"

"I was born in 1930," answered Mark, actually being honest about it. "I guess that would make me about ten years older than you."

Bobby Sue felt her heart race for a moment. *Would her father be upset if he knew the thoughts she was having about this stranger?*

"Hey, if you need any help with Moose at the show tomorrow, just let me know," offered Mark with an irresistible smile.

"I'll need to make sure that's okay with my father," replied Bobby Sue. "I think he might have someone else lined up to help me already."

"Never hurts to ask," flirted Mark.

"I may do just that," beamed Bobby Sue as she returned his even gaze. "Yes, I think I will ask him."

"Well, alright, then," smiled Mark as he gently patted Moose on the shoulder. "I'll look forward to it."

Bobby Sue then gawked as Mark sauntered back over to the hay barn to continue unloading bales of hay from the back of her father's bright red 1954 Dodge Ram pickup truck. She continued to watch as Mark used two hay hooks to accomplish the job.

For a moment, Bobby Sue daydreamed of what it would be like to go on a hayride with Mark. *Would someone that much older even want to get involved in a serious relationship with her?*

"You all ready for tomorrow?" asked her father, who had managed to sneak up on her unnoticed. *Why was his only daughter staring at the new ranch hand like that? Was there going to be a problem with this?*

"Oh, father!" exclaimed Bobby Sue as she turned around and gave him a hug. "Moose is ready. Hey, do you think it would be okay if Mark Killingham came along to give me a hand tomorrow?"

John Walter Johnson smiled with amusement at his little girl. She obviously had a crush on the new ranch hand. John was sober at the moment, and in one of his better moods. "Sure, why not?"

"Thank you!" grinned Bobby Sue as she gave her father another hug. "Moose likes him, too."

"You'd better hope so," chuckled John as he tried to visualize Mark being charged by the animal. "Guess we'll find out."

The following day started as any other, with Bobby Sue hurrying to the barn to do her morning chores. Moose would receive special grooming that day, to make sure he looked his best.

The competition went as hoped, with Moose winning the coveted blue ribbon as grand champion in his division. After proudly leading Moose back to his pen, Bobby Sue spontaneously hugged Mark Killingham. "Thanks for your help today."

"Better hurry up and get him back out there," instructed her father from behind them. "The auction's next."

"What auction?" demanded Bobby Sue, suddenly feeling as if she had been betrayed. "He's not for sale!"

"I'm afraid we just can't afford to keep him any longer, baby girl," replied Mr. Johnson. "But, it was fun while it lasted, right?"

"Moose is not for sale!" screamed Bobby Sue as she angrily pounded her fists against her father's chest when he tried to hug her. "Get away from me!"

"Let me talk to her," suggested Mark as they watched Bobby Sue race toward the ladies' restroom with tears of anger streaming down her cheeks.

"Be my guest," invited Mr. Johnson, "but you'd better make it snappy. It would be nice to have her there when we sell him, but either way, it has to be done."

"Wait!" hollered Mark as he raced after Bobby Sue. "Hold up! Hang on a minute!"

Realizing that Mark was coming after her, Bobby Sue hesitated and finally waited for him to catch up.

"Are you okay?" questioned Mark when he caught up, though out of breath from running.

"How could my father do such a thing?" demanded Bobby Sue. Her eyes flashed with anger and defiance. While it was true that her

81

father was the legal owner of the animal, she never would have dreamed that Moose would be sold. She loved Moose!

"I wish there were something I could do," answered Mark, "but your father's mind is made up. He was hoping you could be there for the sale, but either way he plans to do it. Wouldn't you at least like to say goodbye to Moose while you can?"

"No!" snapped Bobby Sue as she headed for an empty barn nearby where several bales of hay were neatly stacked inside.

"You can't go in there alone," reminded Mark. "That's where some of the bulls are put after the auction."

"Well, they're not in there now," pointed out Bobby Sue as she pressed on. She wanted to be alone.

"Oh, heck," muttered Mark as he watched her dash into the barn and climb up to the loft.

"Just go away!" yelled Bobby Sue as she sat down on a bale of hay and proceeded to sob uncontrollably. She did not want Mark to see her like this.

"Sorry, but you're stuck with me," advised Mark as he climbed up to where she was and then sat down beside her.

The moment he put a comforting arm around her, Bobby Sue suddenly hugged him back and cried on his shoulder for nearly an hour. The reassurance she felt in his strong, muscular arms would give her the courage to defy her father in the worst possible way. She would give herself to Mark, body and soul, and there was nothing her father could do to stop it!

It was July 4, 1955, when Bobby Sue made her decision to elope with Mark Killingham. There was no question about it now – she was with child and starting to show. If her father were to find out about it, there was no telling what he might do.

"Perhaps you should talk to your mother first," suggested Mark. "Just to say goodbye."

"I can't talk to either one of them about this and you know it," advised Bobby Sue. "You aren't having second thoughts, are you? I'm *not* putting our child up for adoption!"

"It could be worse," replied Mark, to try and lighten the mood.

"Yeah, I could be *you*!" pointed out Bobby Sue. "You've never seen my father truly angry before, have you?"

"Can't say that I'd want to," answered Mark rather pensively.

82

"He'd *kill* you," advised Bobby Sue most seriously. "Especially if he's been drinking when he finds out."

"Then there's only one thing we can do," decided Mark. "Let's go get married, just like we talked about."

"You mean it?" smiled Bobby Sue.

"Sure," replied Mark, though not as convincingly as she would have hoped. "But we will have to travel to Alabama for it, since you're only 16."

"That's okay," agreed Bobby Sue.

"Meet me in Moose's old stall at midnight. Pack light."

"I'll be there," beamed Bobby Sue as she passionately kissed Mark on the lips.

Midnight arrived like a bolt of lightning. Bobby Sue gazed sadly at Moose's empty stall. *How dare her father sell him like that!*

"Are you ready?" whispered Mark, who seemed to appear out of nowhere from the shadows behind her.

"You bet I am," replied Bobby Sue. "I want nothing more to do with my father ever again after this."

"As you wish," smiled Mark as he picked up her suitcase with one hand and extended his other arm for her to hang onto. "Madam, your chariot awaits."

Bobby Sue had never actually seen Mark's personal vehicle before and was surprised by the dilapidated green 1948 DeSoto. "This is yours?"

"I'm afraid so," apologized Mark as he gingerly tossed her suitcase into the trunk, quietly closed the lid, and then opened the passenger door for her.

The two-day drive to Alabama had been arduous and difficult to endure, especially during the daytime when it was hot and humid. Even with a block of ice sitting in an open ice chest on the floor in front of her, Bobby Sue struggled to stay lucid. Her hair was a mess from the wind, but in this heat the windows needed to remain open.

"There's a diner up ahead," noticed Bobby Sue. "Can we stop?"

"Again?" Mark was becoming impatient with the frequent interruptions in their travel time. "We'll never make it there by nightfall at this rate."

"I don't think you want me peeing on the seat," rebutted Bobby Sue. "Besides, it's almost lunchtime. Let's get something to eat while we're here."

"We need to be careful with what cash we have," cautioned Mark. "If we don't have enough to rent a decent place once we get there, things could get pretty rough, especially for you."

"How much do we have?" questioned Bobby Sue, suddenly concerned.

"We'll be okay," assured Mark. "Just be thrifty in what you order. That's all I'm saying."

"Sure," promised Bobby Sue. He still had not answered her question, but she could tell he was in no mood to be pressed right now.

"Another thing you need to keep in mind," added Mark, "is the fact that we're not out of the woods yet."

"What's that supposed to mean?" frowned Bobby Sue as Mark steered the old DeSoto into the parking lot of the diner.

"You're still jail bait, young lady," spelled out Mark, hopefully so she could understand.

"Jail bait?" Bobby Sue had not considered that possibility.

"The fewer people who actually see us together, the better," continued Mark. "Just in case your father has an all-points bulletin out for my arrest."

"For what?" questioned Bobby Sue. "We are going to be married, aren't we?"

"Yes, but we ain't married yet, princess," reminded Mark. "And right now, you're nothing more than a pregnant minor that I've kidnapped and taken across state lines – at least that's how your father will look at it. Let's just hope we can find someone who will marry us, no questions asked."

"That's ridiculous!" exclaimed Bobby Sue. "I came with you of my own free will, and if anyone asks, I'll tell 'em so, too!"

"I have a better idea," proposed Mark. "Why don't you go use the ladies' room while I place an order to go. I can walk in just a few moments after you. That way, no one will suspect we're together."

Bobby Sue crossed her arms and began to pout.

"Just as a precaution," added Mark with one of his winning smiles as he pulled Bobby Sue close and began to kiss her passionately on the lips. "I'll make it up to you later, I promise."

84

Overcome by his charms, Bobby Sue finally nodded her head in agreement. "Okay."

"Atta girl," nodded Mark with a deep sigh of relief as he watched her get out of the vehicle and head for the ladies' room.

Then, an unbidden thought came to him. *He could just drive away right now and leave her here. No one would ever be any the wiser. He could return to her father's ranch as if nothing had happened, and make up some story about having had the stomach flu for the past couple of days. Then, if Bobby Sue ever did show up again or try to tell her parents he had been with her, he could deny it. Besides, it would be just her word against his.*

"What am I worried about?" Mark suddenly laughed out loud. "Her parents are the last people on earth Bobby Sue would call. Oh, heck!" muttered Mark as he finally climbed from the vehicle to go order some food. He was hungry himself, anyway.

Bobby Sue smiled at him with that lovesick look on her face as they passed one another in the parking lot.

"We don't know each other, remember?" chided Mark in whispered tones as he passed her.

"Oh, okay! Don't forget, I'm eating for two now," whispered Bobby Sue as she played along, quickly looked away, and walked past without looking directly at him.

"I'll be back."

Arriving in Mobile too late the previous night to do anything else, he and Bobby Sue had slept in the DeSoto. He had parked it right at the pump of a gas station, since they were already running on fumes. Bobby Sue sprawled out on the back seat while Mark took the front.

"Hey!" nudged Mark. "They're open now. Go clean yourself up while I get some gas."

Bobby Sue stretched and yawned, surprised that it was morning already. "What time is it?"

"Time to go make yourself presentable," replied Mark.

"Okay, sure," agreed Bobby Sue as she got out of the vehicle and made her way to the restroom with her overnight bag.

Mark again considered the possibility of leaving her behind, but the gas station attendant had already seen them together.

"Where you headed?" asked the young man.

"Mobile," Mark answered. *Should he have said so?*

85

"You been here before?" pressed the gas station attendant.

"Yes, I have an aunt who lives on the other side of town," lied Mark. Hopefully, that explanation would stop the barrage of questions.

"That'll be $5.12," advised the man as he topped off the tank and hung up the nozzle.

"Why so much?" frowned Mark. "Yesterday I filled her up for only $4.64. It was 29¢ a gallon."

"Well, we're 32¢ a gallon out here, sorry," apologized the man. "Sixteen-gallon tank?"

"Yep," sighed Mark as he pulled out his wallet and handed the man a $5-dollar bill before digging through the change in his pocket for 12¢.

"Your daughter?" asked the attendant as he watched Bobby Sue return from the restroom and climb into the passenger side with her bag.

"You sure ask a lot of questions," commented Mark as he gave the young man a mistrustful look while handing him the 12¢.

"Just being friendly," answered the lad, keenly aware that he had somehow overstepped. "Safe travels to you."

"Thanks," nodded Mark as he returned the wallet to his back pocket before getting into the car.

"Can we stop somewhere to eat?" grilled Bobby Sue.

"There are two extra sandwiches in the ice chest," advised Mark. "We can eat 'em while we drive."

"What about coffee?" pressed Bobby Sue. She was exhausted.

"Not in your condition," smirked Mark as he started the engine and drove away from the gas station.

"I'm pregnant, not sick," reminded Bobby Sue. "Don't you have some in a thermos?"

"It's for the driver – that would be me – to make sure I stay awake," maintained Mark. "Besides, we're almost there, and then you can get all the rest you want for the next couple of days, okay?"

"What about the wedding?" asked Bobby Sue. "Won't our new apartment manager need to see a marriage license first before they'll rent to us?"

"After that, of course," Mark forced a smile. *That's right! There would be the cost of the license for $1.25 and at least that much* *more for a preacher. Then, there would be parking. There goes another $5 down the hole!*

"Sure," muttered Bobby Sue as she folded her arms and began to pout while she absently gazed out the window.

God, he hated that thing she did with her lower lip when she pouted! "Okay, you can have a sip of coffee. Will that make you happy? After that, hand it over."

Yes, sir! thought Bobby Sue as she imagined herself giving him a mocking salute – something she would never have dared to really do. Instead, she just smiled sweetly at him as she removed the lid, took a drink, and then handed him the thermos.

The next 24 hours were like a blur. The quick marriage ceremony with two witnesses neither of them had ever seen before, the crotchety old judge who sounded like he had previously had a stroke and could barely pronounce the words of the ceremony, and the fruitless search for a decent apartment in town. That was when Mark had spotted a newspaper ad for help at a local ranch, only five miles outside of town. Included in the deal was private lodging in a single wide trailer – or for only $75 per month to rent the trailer without the job.

They were currently having lunch at a greasy diner in town. Mark had the newspaper spread out on the table in front of him.

"What about the apartment in town?" questioned Bobby Sue. "$125 per month is a fair price, and it is near the hospital."

"You paying for it?" demanded Mark as he finished off the hamburger he had splurged and bought for lunch.

"I just don't know how much more of this I can take," admitted Bobby Sue. She looked as if she was ready to cry again. She had already eaten her hamburger but was still working on the strawberry milkshake she had ordered to go with it.

"Are you planning to finish that?" questioned Mark. He had not bothered to order one for himself, in an effort to save on funds.

Bobby Sue merely shook her head in the negative.

"Fine, I'll finish it," advised Mark as he reached over and grabbed the tall glass containing the thick strawberry milkshake, and took a long slurp from it. "Not bad!"

Was this the same man she had wanted to marry and spend the rest of her life with? wondered Bobby Sue. *Had she made a mistake?*

Worst of all, he did not seem in any hurry to look for a job! What would they do if he couldn't find one?

"Wait here," instructed Mark. "I'm calling about the ad, to see if the trailer is still for rent."

Silent tears of worry escaped onto her cheeks as she watched Mark head for the payphone in the lobby by the cash register. After what seemed like an eternity, he returned with a satisfied smile on his face. "It's ours. The owner is meeting us there."

"What if I need to go to town while you're working during the day?" grilled Bobby Sue as she got up to leave. *Assuming they decide to hire you,* she thought.

"I'm sure it will all work out," assured Mark as he laid a $5-dollar bill on the table and nodded at the waitress. "Keep the change."

The change was only 5¢, though it was more of a tip than Mark normally left for anything.

Little was said during the half hour drive out to the Circle K Ranch. Fields of grazing cattle as well as wheat, corn, soybean, cotton, peanut crops, and citrus orchards, reached as far as the eye could see in every direction. Relieved to see a bus stop near the entrance to the Circle K Ranch, Bobby Sue wondered whether she would ever need to avail herself of it.

"Here we are," announced Mark as he turned onto a rather bumpy gravel road with huge ruts in it. A rickety sign by the entrance read, "Circle K Ranch." It was white with faded red letters.

"Easy!" objected Bobby Sue. "Are you trying to make me lose the baby?"

That was a thought! considered Mark, who slowed down only slightly. *How would she react when it was time for him to leave her here and return to work at her father's ranch? It was the only logical way to make it appear as if he'd had nothing to do with her "disappearance." Besides, she'd get over it – eventually.*

"This must be the main residence where the owner lives," presumed Mark as he pulled up in front of the older, two-story home.

It was most likely built around the turn of the century. Its sprawling porch extended the entire length of the house. Adirondack chairs with overstuffed seat cushions on them looked inviting. The house was painted entirely white but could have used a new coat of paint. Well-manicured red roses climbed the porch railing on the outside. Some tall weeds grew in the flowerbed below them. A single large oak tree provided shade to the circular dirt driveway in front.

"Too bad we're not renting this place!" admired Bobby Sue.

"Just let me do the talking," instructed Mark.

"What if I have a question?" asked Bobby Sue.

Mark sighed deeply with frustration as he got out of the DeSoto and came around to open her door, but smiled anyway. Appearances were important, and their new landlord was probably watching them from the front window now. He had seen the drapes move.

"Why, thank you, sir," beamed Bobby Sue. *It's about time you started opening the car door for me again!* "What a shame I don't have my ring yet."

Mark fought the urge to roll his eyes at that, but was well aware of the additional expense that lay ahead.

Jill Anderson was a devout Protestant who faithfully went to church each week, rain or shine, harvest or not. Only the birth of a new baby calf or foal would have kept her at home on a Sunday. It was July 10, 1955. She also sang in the church choir on Wednesday nights after prayer meeting. Today, however, she had made an exception and was patiently waiting for her prospective new tenants to arrive. Dressed in her Sunday best – with the intention of making it in time for Sunday School after meeting the Killinghams – Jill wore a modest pleated skirt and matching gray shoes with short stubby heels. Like all her clothes, it was handmade and had no frills. The plain white blouse she had on was buttoned all the way to the top. Sitting on the table nearby was her aging black leather purse, a pair of white gloves, and her well-used Bible. Jill glanced at the picture of her late husband on the wall beside her as she adjusted her gray church hat, carefully pulling the netting over to one side for now.

Not only was Jill a God-fearing woman who paid her tithe, but also volunteered to work in the food line at a local homeless shelter on Tuesdays. Between her church activities and running the ranch mostly by herself, there was no room for shenanigans in her life. Jill had a kind face, smiled often, and was well loved by everyone in the community.

Thankfully, she had two dependable ranch hands who were normally there, except on Sundays. Drinking, smoking or anything else that might be unfit for human consumption, was not allowed on the premises, though that was more than likely what her third ranch hand was doing right now. Perhaps if she could persuade Mark Killingham to work for her, in time he could replace the third man.

In particular, Jill had no use for men who were unfaithful to their wives or who caroused. Such sinners were most certainly bound for perdition's gates. In her 45 years of life, she had seen quite a bit and was far more perceptive than most folks gave her credit for.

Jill glanced through the white lace curtains by her door and noticed a delipidated DeSoto that had pulled up out front. The man was helping his wife from the car. She nodded with approval.

Leaving her Bible, purse and gloves on the table inside, Jill quickly opened the front door before the young couple could knock. "You must be the Killinghams?" Her pleasant smile caught Mark off guard. Her dress and appearance would normally have belonged to someone of sterner temperament.

"Oh, it's Sunday, isn't it?" apologized Bobby Sue, realizing immediately that the woman must be on her way to church.

"Not a problem," smiled the woman. "I'm Jill Anderson, and this is my ranch. I'm sure I can catch the next meeting."

"I'm Mark Killingham – we spoke on the phone – and this is my wife, Bobby Sue."

"Kind of young, ain't she?" questioned Jill as she shook hands with each of them.

"We're newlyweds," interjected Bobby Sue. She knew that Mark was probably unhappy with her for speaking – even though he had instructed her not to – but Mrs. Anderson was so nice that she just couldn't help it. She felt drawn to the woman and was certain they could become friends.

"We would normally ride the horses out to where the trailer is, but as you can see I'm not dressed for it," explained Jill.

"We could take the DeSoto," offered Mark, trying his very best to be charming. "If you don't mind, of course."

"That's just what I was going to suggest," agreed Jill, "especially since my car's already washed up for church. Besides, I wouldn't dream of taking it on the road we're about to drive on."

Mark glanced at the baby blue 1952 Plymouth convertible parked nearby. It was spotlessly clean. Clearly, the woman drove it nowhere but to the store and church each week. "She's a beauty!"

"Belonged to my husband when he was alive," revealed Jill. "I've since learned how to drive out of necessity. Hope your vehicle is up to this. The last prospective tenant chose not to live here because of the road."

"Not a problem," assured Mark as he opened the front passenger door and held it open for Mrs. Anderson to get inside.

"Oh, the little Missus should sit up front," insisted Jill.

"Very well," nodded Mark as he opened the back door on the passenger side.

Once both women were inside the vehicle, Mark gingerly closed the doors, took a deep breath, and went back over to the driver's side to get in. *There would be no pulling the wool over that woman's eyes!*

"How long have you two been married?" began Jill as they made their way across her 1,400-acre parcel of land in the DeSoto.

"Since this morning," answered Bobby Sue, again speaking out of turn. Mark shot her a sideways glance of warning that did not go unnoticed by Mrs. Anderson.

"So, Bobby Sue was it?" asked Jill.

"Yes, ma'am."

"Just how old are you, young lady?"

Bobby Sue looked at Mark for approval to answer.

"She's 16," advised Mark as he narrowly missed hitting a large boulder in the road.

"Came here to avoid the age limit, did you?" perceived Jill. "Where you from?"

"Out west," responded Mark.

And what's a guy your age doing marrying a young girl like this, anyway? thought Jill as she studied his face in the rearview mirror.

"Her father owns a cattle ranch in Washington," added Mark rather coldly. "I was one of his hands."

'Til you knocked her up, assumed Jill as she shook her head with disapproval.

As if able to read her mind, Mark glowered at Jill in the rearview mirror.

91

"I do need to know who I'm renting to," Jill smiled at him and tried her best to appear completely unfazed. "Reckon you'll be starting a family soon?"

"We're already expecting," blurted out Bobby Sue.

"Yes, indeed, we are," admitted Mark as he slowed down at a narrow bridge that continued over a swift moving stream and shot Bobby Sue an irritated glance.

"Congratulations to you! Say, that's where the longhorns usually graze, over there on the other side," Jill suddenly pointed out. "Except on Sundays, of course."

"I suppose they go to church, too?" Mark's ridiculous question sounded snider than he intended it to.

"That's when we put 'em in the lower pasture, since the hands are off on Sundays and there's no one up here to keep an eye on 'em," explained Jill. *Rude and sarcastic. Poor girl.*

"I'm sorry," apologized Mark. "It's just that this has been a rather difficult trip, for both of us."

Jill merely nodded. *Especially for her!*

After crossing the bridge, a fork in the road presented itself. "Go left," instructed Jill. The road on the left led into an old growth bayou overgrown with just about everything. Though hauntingly beautiful, it was also just downright creepy.

"Are there any alligators out here?" Bobby Sue suddenly asked with concern.

"Yes, there are," smiled Jill as she glanced at Mark. "You'll want to be sure and stay indoors after a good rain. And at night."

"Do the 'gators ever bother your longhorns?" asked Mark with a smirk on his face.

"On occasion, if they wander too close," answered Jill as she narrowed her eyes at him.

"This just can't be it," frowned Bobby Sue as they approached and pulled to a stop in front of a ramshackle single wide trailer on stilts. The crooked wooden steps in front of it had seen better days and a good-sized slough was only a few yards away!

"I'm told the fishing's pretty good in there, at times," advised Jill through the open window as she waited for Mark to come around and open her door.

"So, this is it, then?" Mark raised his eyebrows and shook his head with disbelief. "I trust the utilities are included in the $75?"

92

"Absolutely," assured Jill.

"Including a phone?" grilled Mark.

"No, not that," relented Jill. "Just the basics – water, plumbing and electricity. Until five years ago, all it had was an outhouse."

Bobby Sue glanced at the surrounding bayou with trepidation, especially the slough, as they followed Jill toward the trailer. "Not much light gets in here, does it?"

"Not much," confirmed Jill as she reached under the mat for a key, unlocked the front door, and held it open for the Killinghams.

"I'll go first," offered Mark.

Occasionally, rays of light did penetrate the dense canopy overhead, like the one that unexpectedly lit up Mark Killingham's left hand. The indentation of where a wedding band had recently been could clearly be seen on his ring finger! Jill sadly shook her head. *It would be a shame to turn them away, but what choice did she have now?* She had absolutely no use for carousers!

"Home sweet home," smiled Mark as he came back outside, trying again to be suave and charming. "Let me carry you across the threshold, my dear."

Jill's mouth fell open with disbelief as she watched him pick Bobby Sue up and gallantly carry her inside. By the lovesick look on the girl's face, it was obvious she had no idea that her new husband had lately been married to someone else. Jill realized at that moment that she could not turn Bobby Sue away, even if it meant renting to the likes of Mark Killingham. *Someone would need to be there for Bobby Sue to turn to when the time came, and it would.*

Inside the kitchen at one end was a wood burning stove, an electric refrigerator, and a sink. Beside it was a small counter and wall cupboard above it. Mark sashayed over to it and looked inside.

"The last tenant left those canned goods behind, if you want them," offered Jill. There were five cans of baked beans, and two glass jars of peaches in all.

"Thanks," nodded Mark as he glanced inside the empty refrigerator. "At least we won't starve."

At the other end of the small trailer was a restroom with an antique tub, a freestanding sink with a wall mirror above it, and a toilet. It was relatively new compared to the other fixtures.

"No door on the restroom?" noticed Bobby Sue.

"Just curtains," indicated Jill as she demonstrated by pulling the door-length curtains shut and then opening them again.

In the middle of the room was a small round table with two chairs, but no bed.

"Where will we sleep?" questioned Mark.

"It's a Murphy bed," smiled Jill. "When you're done eating, all you do is push the table up into the wall and latch it in place like this. Then, on the opposite wall, you just unhook it here and pull down the bed – after you push the two chairs out of the way, of course." She then demonstrated.

"What will we do for sheets?" worried Bobby Sue upon seeing the bare mattress.

"I probably have an extra set up at the house you can have," offered Jill. "Consider it a wedding gift."

"Oh, thank you!" beamed Bobby Sue as she gave Jill a hug.

"Here's $100," offered Mark as he handed two $50-dollar bills to Jill.

"It's only $75," reminded Jill, confused by his generosity.

"The other $25 is for food," clarified Mark. "I'll need to be leaving first thing in the morning and will be gone for a few days. Can you look in on Bobby Sue and make sure she has what she needs?"

"You're leaving in the morning?" Bobby Sue looked as if she was thunderstruck.

"I have some unfinished business with your father," advised Mark. "He still owes me two weeks' pay."

"You're not going back?" gasped Bobby Sue.

"Gotta get my sweetie a wedding ring," flirted Mark as he pulled Bobby Sue close and gave her a passionate kiss, right in front of Jill.

"Alrighty, then," muttered Jill as she cleared her throat to get their attention. "If you'll just take me back up to the house, I can get the sheets for you before I head over to Sunday School."

"Do you mind waiting here?" asked Mark as he smiled at Bobby Sue. "I'll be right back."

"I can probably send a few food items back with you, too," offered Jill. *It was obvious the girl was eating for two now and needed proper nutrition. Just what had she gotten herself into?*

"That would be great!" beamed Bobby Sue. "Thank you so much! We appreciate your generosity."

Bobby Sue then watched as Mark and Jill left, got back into the DeSoto and drove away. *What would she do if she ever needed help with anything while he was away? She had no phone or car and would be stranded in a bayou. And what if an alligator tried to attack while she was outside?*

Jill sat in the white clapboard church on the hard, wooden pew, listening to a pulpit-pounding sermon that should have kept anyone's attention, but all she could think of was Bobby Sue. *Would the child be okay out there by herself?* The bayou site on her property was one she normally rented to single men who hired on as hands to work the longhorns.

Deep in thought as she shook hands with her friends in the foyer after the meeting, Jill decided to skip the after-meeting potluck and head directly for home. She could get her casserole dish later. The five-mile drive seemed to take forever. She almost felt a sense of urgency about it. *Oh, I'm just being silly,* Jill chastised herself.

After reaching home, Jill carefully parked and made sure the top was up on her late husband's baby blue Plymouth convertible. Jill then hurried inside to change into her work jeans, riding boots, and a red plaid flannel shirt. She tossed a loaf of homemade bread, a jar of peanut butter, and some strawberry preserves into a satchel before heading for the barn.

Walter was a faithful old quarter horse, whom Jill had ridden for almost six years now. He had been purchased at an auction as a yearling and trained by her most dependable hand, Peter Smith. Jill saddled Walter up, attached the satchel to his saddle horn, and climbed into the saddle. "Looks like we're headed out to the bayou, Walter."

Hopefully, there would be no alligators, since it was mid-day when they normally slept. Jill made it a point never to take Walter or any of her other animals anywhere near the bayou at dawn or dusk, and particularly at night when the nocturnal predators were out.

"Giddy up, Walter!" directed Jill as she tapped Walter in the flanks with her heels, causing him to start out in the direction indicated by where she turned his head. "Good boy!"

Wheat and alfalfa grew and thrived in abundance on the northerly end of her property where Peter Smith's cabin was situated, and parts of it could be seen from where she was riding. The Circle K Ranch endeavored to be self-sustaining, and harvest would be coming soon. It was also on the northerly end of her property where the cattle pen, the barns and other out buildings were located, as far as possible from the bayou.

Jill's own vegetable garden also did quite well in the rich loamy soil near her residence, but the southern portion of her property where the bayou was located was good for just about nothing. Thankfully, the pasture near it was relatively safe during the daylight hours and provided excellent grazing for the longhorns, thus reducing feed costs. Only one animal had been lost the previous year to an alligator.

"Why am I not surprised?" muttered Jill upon reaching the bayou and noticing that the DeSoto was not there. *Perhaps they had driven into town for lunch while she was at church, since he wasn't leaving until morning.*

After quickly scouting the area to make sure it was free of alligators or snakes, Jill climbed down from Walter's back and tied him to a nearby tree. She untied the satchel from the saddle and approached the front door. "Bobby Sue? You home? Yoo-hoo, Bobby Sue?"

Slowly, the front door of the trailer opened. Bobby Sue had been crying and had a fresh red mark on her cheek that was the size of a man's hand.

"Oh, child, what happened?" demanded Jill. "Did that man hit you?"

"He's gone!" wailed Bobby Sue as she sat down in one of the two wooden chairs and continued to sob. "And it's all my fault!"

"Nonsense!" exclaimed Jill. "Stop crying this instant and tell me what happened. I'm going to make some sandwiches for us to eat while I listen."

"I'm not hungry," sniffed Bobby Sue as she dabbed her eyes with the hem of her dress before wiping her nose on her sleeve.

"You are eating for two now," reminded Jill, "and you *are* going to eat!"

"Yes, ma'am," Bobby Sue finally agreed as she watched Jill remove the items from the satchel.

"Are there any plates in this place?"

"No."

Jill then spread her satchel onto the table and made the sandwiches right on top of it, using her fingers. "Bon appétit."

96

"We don't have any milk, either," advised Bobby Sue. "Mark threw the bottle you sent out and broke it. I just got done cleaning it up before you got here."

"He threw a glass bottle of milk at you?" Jill was enraged.

"No, he threw it at the Murphy bed," clarified Bobby Sue. "Guess he was pretty mad when I told him I just wasn't up to it right now. After all, it is supposed to be our wedding night, so he was expecting us to be intimate."

"How far along are you?" asked Jill as she got up and poured each of them a glass of water.

"A little over three months," replied Bobby Sue.

"When do you expect him back?"

"Probably not for at least a week, if then." Bobby Sue's lip quivered when she pouted.

"Well, that settles it, then," informed Jill. "You will be staying in the guest room at my house."

"What if he comes back here and sees that I'm gone?" worried Bobby Sue.

"Then he'll no doubt come up to the house to ask if I've seen you," predicted Jill. "I can't allow you to stay out here by yourself in your condition, not alone."

"How much more will it be to stay at your house?"

"Not a dime," smiled Jill. "Perhaps you can help out in the kitchen. We could use a good cook around here."

An entire week had passed before Mark Killingham finally called on the phone. It was his intention to ask Jill Anderson if she could get a message to Bobby Sue for him. As fate would have it, however, Jill had taken Bobby Sue with her to help in the food line at a local homeless shelter where she usually volunteered each Tuesday. Mark Killingham continued trying to call for most of the afternoon, so was quite anxious by the time Jill finally returned home to answer the phone.

"Circle K, may I help you?"

"Mrs. Anderson? This is Mark Killingham. Please don't hang up. I was hoping you could get a message to Bobby Sue for me."

After a deafening silence, Jill finally responded. "Go ahead."

"No doubt you are aware that Bobby Sue and I had a disagreement the other day," began Mark, rather cautiously.

97

"A disagreement?" scoffed Jill. "Is that what you call it?"

"I would like to tell Bobby Sue how sorry I am for what happened," continued Mark.

"Well, she's right here," replied Jill. "You can tell her yourself."

Bobby Sue, who had come in with Jill when the phone first rang, had overheard the entire conversation and was emphatically shaking her head *NO!*

"You need to speak with him," whispered Jill as she handed Bobby Sue the phone. "I'll be in the kitchen if you need me, dear."

Bobby Sue's hand began to tremble as she took the phone from Jill and put the headset to her ear. "Hello?"

"Bobby Sue? This is Mark. Please don't hang up!"

After a long period of silence, Mark finally asked, "Bobby Sue, are you there?"

"I'm still here," responded Bobby Sue.

"Please forgive me for what happened?" pleaded Mark. "I had no right to slap you like that."

"I still have a bruise on my cheek," informed Bobby Sue, rather coldly. "And, in case you were wondering, I have a room at the house now. I've been working here as a cook to pay my way, just in case I never heard from you again!"

"Oh, Bobby Sue, I'm so sorry! I love you with all my heart," claimed Mark. "I don't know what came over me that day, but if you'll give me a chance, I'd like to make it up to you."

Tears began to stream down her cheeks. *Should she trust him? After all, he was the father of her unborn child.*

"I'm still working for your father," informed Mark, "and they have reported you as a runaway."

"How did *you* explain being gone that week?"

"Stomach flu."

"And my dad bought it?"

"Absolutely."

"Just how are my parents doing, anyway?"

"They're beside themselves with worry, of course."

"Oh Mark, what are we going to do?"

"Just let me save up enough money to get you that ring," stipulated Mark, "and I'll be back with it before you know it."

"What about your job with my dad?"

"I do have some vacation time coming," continued Mark. "Besides, this way they'll never suspect a thing. I can just come out to Alabama for a short visit this time and be back before I'm missed."

"You've only got so much vacation time," reasoned Bobby Sue. "What then? Will you keep coming out for short *visits*?"

"Look, we may not get to see one another as often as we would like for a while," clarified Mark, "but by the time the baby is born we should have enough saved up to bring you back out here permanently. One look at his new baby grandson, and your father's heart will absolutely melt."

"What makes you so sure it's going to be a boy?" Bobby Sue had finally begun to soften. She could not help herself.

"We can call him Kevin if it's a boy," described Mark, "or Kevana if it's a girl. What do you think?"

"Kevin," approved Bobby Sue. "I like that."

"I'll be there at the end of the month, on payday," promised Mark. "Just two more weeks."

"Not until August?" frowned Bobby Sue.

"I love you," assured Mark. "Wish I were there so I could hold you in my arms and show you how much you mean to me."

"I love you, too!" beamed Bobby Sue. "I'll look forward to seeing you in August."

Jill had not meant to eavesdrop but could not help but overhear Bobby Sue's last statement. *Not until August? Really? After what he had done to the poor child?*

Maria Killingham was beside herself with worry. Why was Mark always so late coming home? She was a beautiful young Italian woman with four young boys already and another one on the way. Not that she minded cooking and cleaning for so many, but was constantly lonely for her husband. His frequent business trips would take him out of town for days at a time, leaving her to fend for herself.

Living in the desert of eastern Washington with no phone and no car had proven to be a challenge on more than one occasion during her husband's many absences, especially being 11 miles from the nearest town.

"Mama!" shouted little Michael. "He's here!"

"Pick up your toy truck," instructed Maria. "We don't want your daddy tripping on it."

"Yes, mama," agreed little Michael, who was 6 years old.

"Daddy! Daddy!" shouted Justin as he threw open the front door, ran outside and into his father's arms. Justin was 5 years old.

"How's my boy?" beamed Mark Killingham as he scooped up little Justin and gave him a hug before setting him down.

"Daddy!" hollered Michael as he ran outside, too.

"Something sure smells good in there," approved Mark as he picked Michael up, and spun around in a circle while holding him.

"Lasagna, salad and garlic bread," informed Philip, who was age 4. "And we helped."

"Come here," grinned Mark as he put Michael down and picked up Philip. "I missed you guys all so much."

"What about *us*?" questioned Maria from the doorway where she stood holding their one-year old son.

Mark then placed Philip on the porch and reached over to hug Maria and little Evan.

"Careful!" cautioned Maria as she carefully handed Evan to Michael to hold for her before embracing her husband again. Mark then pulled Maria close and passionately kissed her on the lips as he sensuously ran his hands across her backside.

Maria suddenly tried to stop him. "Mark, the children!"

"Sorry, but I just can't help myself," flirted Mark as he followed his wife inside, closely followed by the children.

"Oh, Mark, I just felt the baby move!" Maria was excited. "Feel this, right here."

Mark gently placed a hand on Maria's belly and waited until he felt a small kick. "Wow! Looks like little Eric missed me, too."

"And just what makes you so sure it will be a boy this time?" teased Maria as she took Mark's coat from him and carefully hung it up in the hall closet.

"Just a feeling," grinned Mark.

"Oh, sweetheart, where's your wedding ring?" Maria suddenly noticed he was not wearing it.

"Right here," advised Mark as he removed it from the small coin pocket of his blue jeans. "I had to do some really dirty work at the barn yesterday, so I didn't want to mess it up – or worse, end up losing it."

"I don't blame you," smiled Maria, relieved to see he still had it.

"Hear from your mother yet?" asked Mark as he sat down and began heaping salad onto his plate. "How's your dad doing?"

"Sometimes the mail gets delayed out here," reminded Maria as she passed him a bottle of salad dressing which Mark generously applied to his salad.

"What will your mother do when he's gone?" pressed Mark. "There's no way she can run that restaurant by herself."

"Perhaps papa will improve," hoped Maria.

"If not, she may need to sell the business," reminded Mark.

Maria's parents owned and operated an exclusive Italian Restaurant up near Bellevue, Washington. Her home with Mark, however, was located just outside of Sprague, nearly 240 miles away. Thankfully, it was only 37 miles to the Johnson Ranch near Spokane where her husband had worked for the past few months.

"I wish you could get a job closer to home," mentioned Maria as she put a large square of lasagna onto Mark's plate. "We miss you so much when you're gone. It seems like the only time we ever see you anymore is on the weekends."

"Yeah!" exclaimed Michael. "It seems like you're always gone! Even on weekends, sometimes."

"It won't be that way forever," promised Mark as he grabbed a large hunk of warm garlic bread and took a bite.

"We need to bless the food," reminded Maria.

Mark merely nodded for her to go ahead, as he continued to chew his food.

"Let us hold hands," instructed Maria. Baby Evan was in a high chair beside her. "Dear God, thank you for the safe return of my husband tonight, we are so grateful to have him home. Please bless this food that it will strengthen us so that we can do good in the world around us and remember those who are less fortunate and do not have such bounty to enjoy. Amen."

"Amen!" chorused everyone at the table as Mark grabbed and began gulping down a large glass of water.

"Say, did they ever find that Johnson girl you were telling us about last time you were here?" questioned Maria as she put some food on each of the younger children's plates.

"Bobby Sue?" frowned Mark uncomfortably. "No, I don't believe they did. I should ask Mr. Johnson about it on Monday.

Perhaps he might want some of the hands to do another sweep of the area. I'm sure the police must be looking for her already."

"That's really a shame how he just went ahead and sold that prized bull of hers," opined Maria. "You'd think her papa would have consulted her first."

"One would think," agreed Mark as he shoveled a fork load of lasagna into his mouth and began to chew.

Weeks turned into months and in no time Bobby Sue was 8½ months pregnant. Mark had only come out to visit her twice the entire time, though he did manage to faithfully mail $75 cash to Jill Anderson each month like clockwork. Both times, he had forgotten to bring the new wedding band for Bobby Sue, but had faithfully promised to bring it *next time*.

It was Sunday morning, January 29, 1956. Bobby Sue was busy washing up the morning dishes from breakfast. Morning sunlight streamed through the white lace kitchen curtains in front of her, causing floral patterns from its delicate weave to dance across the red linoleum floor and onto the pale, yellow walls behind her.

"I told your husband that it wasn't necessary to keep sending me rent each month," advised Jill upon checking the previous day's mail that was still on the kitchen counter. "As far as I'm concerned, the work you do right here in the kitchen more than covers your expenses."

"I'm sure he just wants to do what's right," assured Bobby Sue. "Besides, I'm not sure how much longer I can do all this kitchen work in my condition." She was not yet dressed for church.

"Aren't you coming to church today?" questioned Jill. As of late, Peter Smith had made it a habit to drive Jill and Bobby Sue to church on Sundays in Jill's baby blue Plymouth convertible.

"I wish I could," apologized Bobby Sue, "but I probably need to just go lay down and take it easy for a while. My back is killing me."

"Will you be okay until we get back?" grilled Jill. "You probably shouldn't be left alone right now. What if the baby comes early?"

"I suppose I could always take the bus into town," joked Bobby Sue. "Seriously, I'll be fine, trust me."

102

"Only if you're sure," stipulated Jill before making her final decision to go ahead and leave Bobby Sue alone for two hours. She had become dear friends with Bobby Sue and had come to think of her as a daughter. The very thought of Mark Killingham returning to take her away was disconcerting. *Perhaps Bobby Sue might somehow change her mind and have the marriage annulled? Can't she see how taken Peter Smith is with her? He would make a perfect husband for the girl.*

"You ladies ready?" asked Peter Smith as he poked his head inside. "The Plymouth is all saddled up and ready to go."

Peter Smith was a well built, handsome man in his early twenties, single, and also a former rodeo clown. Working on a ranch suited him better than constantly putting his life in danger for a few fast bucks. His reddish blonde hair was neatly combed back with hair tonic and he had on his Sunday suit and bolo tie. The pendant on it was something he had won for bull riding, the first time he had actually dared to try it. Unfortunately, a subsequent attempt had resulted in several broken bones and an extensive stay in the hospital. Peter had been cured of any desire to try it again, or to return to the rodeo circuit as a clown. He was clean shaven and his Sunday boots were so shiny that they glistened in the morning sun. The dimple in his chin deepened considerably whenever he smiled, which was often.

"Bobby Sue is staying here," Jill advised Peter as she grabbed her purse and gloves.

The dimple in Peter's chin seemed to fade with his smile.

"We'll be back soon, dear," she called to Bobby Sue.

"See you then," replied Bobby Sue from the top of the staircase. She was headed towards her room.

Just as Bobby Sue sat down on the bed, her water suddenly broke. "Jill!" she screamed as she waddled over to the window, just in time to see the baby blue Plymouth drive away. "Oh, no! Come back!"

Bobby Sue headed back downstairs and began to search for the phonebook. *How could she afford an ambulance, even if she called one? What was she going to do?*

Then it hit her. *The bus! I can take the bus into town. It goes right by the hospital.*

103

Knowing that time was of the essence, Bobby Sue grabbed a blanket to sit on – so she wouldn't soil the places she sat more than necessary – and a small handful of change. Hopefully, she would have enough for bus fare. If not, perhaps the driver would have mercy on her, given the circumstances.

Stopping several times to wait for the waves of pain to subside, Bobby Sue made her way on foot as fast as she dared down the long, circular drive and out onto the main road where the bus stop was located. *I should have brought a hat,* realized Bobby Sue as she held one hand over her eyes to shield them from the sun. Thankfully, she had remembered to put on her coat. Whether it could be washed later was anyone's guess.

Finally reaching the roadside bus stop, Bobby Sue carefully lowered herself onto the bench there. *If only it were covered.* Her belly was huge and maneuvering from one position to another was a challenge, even as young and strong as she was.

What if the bus had already come? worried Bobby Sue. *Surely it must come on Sundays, too! Did it?* Panic set in as her contractions came closer together. *Was her baby going to be born on the side of the road at a bus stop?*

A cold gust of wind caused her to shiver in her damp clothing. A grove of orange trees on the other side of the road seemed to stretch into infinity. Bobby Sue suddenly glanced around to make sure no snakes or alligators were nearby, but she was at least two miles from the bayou and most likely had nothing to worry about.

The wheat fields at the northern end of Jill's property lay barren now, waiting to be replanted in spring. *At least she didn't have to worry about anything lurking in there.*

"Ooooh!" screamed Bobby Sue as another hard contraction hit.

Just then, a bus began to slow down, but didn't look at first like it was going to stop. Bobby Sue forced herself to her feet and waved at the driver. The rundown bus finally stopped and opened its doors.

"There'll be a white bus along in another 45 minutes," advised the driver, who was an elderly black gentleman in his freshly ironed blue bus driver uniform and matching hat.

"Help me!" screamed Bobby Sue, nearly falling down as she tried to climb onto the first step of the bus.

"Land sakes alive, Joe!" chastised a middle-aged black woman in a brilliant white nurse's uniform who sprang to her feet from the seat behind him. "Help the poor child!"

"I don't care what color the bus is," mumbled Bobby Sue. "I need to get to the hospital. Right away!"

Jamima and her friend Freeta hurried to help Bobby Sue up the steps. Both women were nurses at the black hospital in town. It was the closest medical facility.

"Let's get her to the back," instructed Jamima as she and Freeta half carried Bobby Sue to the only seat on the bus that was long enough for her to lay down.

Bobby Sue gazed with a puzzled expression at the other passengers on the bus as they made their way past them. It was entirely filled with black women in white nurse's uniforms. *Black bus, I get it,* chuckled Bobby Sue.

"I forgot to pay my fare," apologized Bobby Sue as she attempted to give her handful of change to Jamima. "Can you please give this to him for me?"

"Your money's no good here, young lady," advised Jamima. "Joe, floor it! Next stop's the hospital."

Bobby Sue screamed again as the contractions became imminent. Jamima grabbed her blanket from her and spread it down between her legs where the baby would emerge.

"You can do it, sweetheart," encouraged Jamima in a comforting voice. "What's your name, honey?"

"Bobby Sue," grunted Bobby Sue before letting out another horrific scream.

"My name's Jamima," advised the woman. "I'm the head nurse at the Mobile General Black Hospital."

"And I'm Freeta, her assistant. We's all nurses, by de way."

"Look at me, Bobby Sue," directed Jamima. "I want you to breathe deeply. Long, slow breaths. Then, when you feel the next contraction, you need to push with everything you got."

Bobby Sue merely nodded and then complied.

"What you doin' out here all by yerself, child?" asked Freeta.

"Later!" Jamima gave Freeta a stern glance. Then turning to Bobby Sue again, she could see that she was having another contraction. "Push, child! Push with all yer might! Push!!"

105

Bobby Sue let out a blood curdling howl as she struggled to push the baby out.

"I sees his head!" shouted Freeta. "He's a comin' fast now."

"I got him," assured Jamima. "The head is out. Just one more good push oughta do it."

Tears were streaming down Bobby Sue's cheeks. The pain was like nothing she had ever felt. It was as if all her insides were coming out at once and there would be nothing left. *What if she were to die, right here in the back of a black bus?* Bobby Sue could not help but smile at the very thought of what her father would say upon learning about it.

"Go get Joe's pocket knife," Jamima directed Freeta.

"Yes, 'um," nodded her friend as she raced to the front of the bus to get the driver's pocket knife. "We needs yer knife."

"What ya'll need dat for?" frowned Joe, who was already driving over the speed limit and worried that he might get pulled over. "It wuz a gift from da wife."

"Fer de baby, stupid!" snapped Freeta. "Hand it over."

"In de glove box," replied Joe.

"Thanks!" nodded Freeta as she retrieved it and hurried back to the back of the bus where Jamima could be seen holding up a newborn baby by his feet and gently slapping his little butt.

"Kevin," muttered Bobby Sue. "His name is Kevin."

"Waaaaaaah!" screamed Kevin as he took his first breath.

The entire bus began clapping and cheering at that point. Several "praise the Lords" and "hallelujahs" could be heard.

"Get Joe's flask, too," beamed Jamima as she held baby Kevin for his mother to see. "And de first aid kit."

Freeta hurried again to the front of the bus and retrieved the items requested, without asking. Joe nodded his head in agreement and smiled from ear to ear upon seeing the new white baby in his rearview mirror. *Imagine that! A white child born in de back of a black bus.*

Freeta was out of breath from running as she opened the first aid kit and set it on the seat beside Bobby Sue.

"Hydrogen peroxide on the cord," instructed Jamima.

Freeta poured way too much, but it didn't seem to matter.

"Pour some on Joe's knife, if there's any left."

Freeta swiftly complied.

"Now cut, right there," pointed Jamima.

"I ain't cuttin' no baby's cord," objected Freeta.

"Would you care to hold baby Kevin while I cut it?" grinned Jamima.

"Yes, 'um!" smiled Freeta as she took the baby in her arms.

"Here goes," remarked Jamima as she expertly sliced the cord and then grabbed a gauze pad from the first aid kit, carefully taping it in place over the fresh cut with some sterile paper tape.

Kevin was most unhappy at that and shouted at the top of his little lungs in protest, loud and long.

"There, there, little guy," comforted Jamima as she took him back from Freeta and carefully handed him to Bobby Sue. "Little Kevin just saved his new mama a great big hospital bill."

"He did, didn't he?" beamed Bobby Sue as she held Kevin in her arms to admire him. "Maybe now, your daddy will come back to stay."

Poor child, thought Jamima.

"What about de flask?" questioned Freeta.

"That's for me," explained Jamima as she took it from her and guzzled half of it down.

As fate would have it, Eric Killingham was born on January 18, 1956, just 11 days before his illegitimate half-brother Kevin was born. Too ill to be left alone, Maria had convinced Mark to stay home and take care of her – at least until her mother could get there to take over.

Maria's father was not doing well and could not be left alone, so her mother would need to find someone to stay with him first before she dared leave to make the journey by bus. Mrs. Santori had never learned to drive.

After a week of faithfully tending to Maria's every need, Mark called in to ask for additional time off from his job.

"Some lady named Jill Anderson called and says you need to call her right away," advised Mr. Johnson over the phone. "And, take as much time as you need for the wife and new baby. Congratulations, by the way."

"Thank you, sir," replied. Mark. "Hey, have you heard anything more about your daughter? Did they find her yet?"

"No, I'm afraid not," answered Mr. Johnson, rather sadly.

"Sorry, sir," consoled Mark. "Hope they hear something soon."

"At least no news is good news," mumbled his boss. "There's always hope she's alive and well somewhere, unless we hear otherwise."

"That's the spirit," agreed Mark. "Guess I'd better go call my Aunt Jill and see what she needs."

"Hope everything's okay," bid Mr. Johnson.

"Me, too," replied Mark. "I'll keep you posted on when I can return to work."

"Give Maria and little Eric my best," answered his boss before hanging up the phone.

If only he knew! worried Mark. *Had Bobby Sue given birth to the baby yet?*

After making a quick trip to the store to get some groceries for Maria and the boys, Mark Killingham pulled up beside a pay phone located in the store's parking lot. *I'd better call Bobby Sue first.*

Rotary dial payphones in 1956 required a nickel for local calls, and dimes and quarters for long distance calls, which required operator assistance.

"Operator?" questioned Mark after jiggling the receiver.

"Would you like to make a call, sir?"

"How much for a call from Sprague, Washington to Mobile, Alabama?" grilled Mark.

"That'll be 35¢ for the first three minutes, and then an additional quarter for every three minutes after that," advised the operator.

"Thank you, ma'am, I'll do that now."

After inserting 35¢, Mark nervously twisted the headset's cord while the phone at Jill Anderson's home began to ring. After only two rings, someone answered.

"Hello?" *It was Bobby Sue!*

"Hey, how's my girl?" greeted Mark. "Is everything okay?"

"Oh, Mark!" exclaimed Bobby Sue. "Little Kevin was born on January 29 and its already February 11 – I can't believe you're not here! Jill left a message with my father for you to call her."

"She didn't tell him what it was about, did she?"

"Of course not, silly," chuckled Bobby Sue.

108

"Or where *you* are?" pressed Mark.

"Absolutely not," assured Bobby Sue. "I just wanted to let you know about our son, and to find out when we will see you again."

"Something terrible has happened," Mark suddenly lied. "I was arrested for being under the influence on my way home the other day."

"You were *arrested?*" Bobby Sue could not believe what she was hearing. *How could this be happening?*

"It was just a few beers with the guys after work, out in the barn," added Mark, to make it sound convincing.

"Where are you now?"

"Out on bail," advised Mark. "But, they've suspended my license for six months."

Bobby Sue was silent and her lip began to quiver. The sound of Kevin crying could be heard in the background. He was upstairs in his crib, waiting to be fed.

"Your father said I could stay in the barn for now," continued Mark. "Just until I get my license back."

"It will be another 25¢ if you plan to continue this call," interrupted the operator.

"Yes, I plan to continue this call!" snapped Mark as he fumbled for the needed quarter and quickly inserted it.

"Go ahead," instructed the operator.

"Mark?"

"Sorry about that," apologized Mark. "Anyway, until I get my license back, there's just no way I can drive out there. You wouldn't want me driving without a license, would you?"

"No, of course not," sniffed Bobby Sue. "I suppose Kevin will just have to wait until then to meet his daddy."

"Six months will come and go before you know it."

"I didn't realize there were any payphones out at the ranch," mentioned Bobby Sue, suddenly curious about it.

"Oh, I'm at the feed store in town," lied Mark. "I rode in with Jerry and am waiting for him to come out now."

As long as he was going to tell a whopper, it might as well be a good one, thought Mark. *Besides, there was no way Bobby Sue would dare to call her parents so she could confirm his story, so he had nothing to worry about.*

"I love you!" sniveled Bobby Sue.

"I love you, too, sweetheart," replied Mark, but not as warmly as Bobby Sue would have liked.

"Do you?" pressed Bobby Sue.

"Of course I do!" assured Mark, trying his best to sound sincere. "Hey, is that Kevin I hear in the background?"

"I'm afraid it's time to feed him again," apologized Bobby Sue.

"Then you'd better get to it. Don't worry, I'll call you again soon," promised Mark. "Give Kevin a big hug and a kiss for me."

"I will," agreed Bobby Sue. "I love you."

"Yeah, yeah, me, too," bid Mark as he hung up the phone, just in time to avoid being interrupted by the operator again.

The next six months went by quickly, but not quickly enough for Bobby Sue. It was Tuesday, August 7, 1956.

Jill had come to the arena by the barn to watch while Bobby Sue practiced for the upcoming barrel racing competition at the annual rodeo in Mobile on Saturday. The grand prize would be $50.

"She's a natural," remarked Peter, who stood beside Jill at the railing, holding little Kevin. "I can't believe how well she's doing."

"What if she wins?" questioned Jill.

"All she talks about is going back to Washington, to be with Mark," described Peter, rather sadly as he brushed a stray hair away from Kevin's eyes. He had come to care deeply for both Bobby Sue and Kevin, though mentioning it was out of the question, especially in light of the fact that she was already married to someone else.

"She could still get her marriage annulled," Jill suddenly said. "It hasn't been a year yet."

"I wish," sighed Peter.

Jill was well aware of his feelings for Bobby Sue. "That Mark is nothing but trouble, I can just feel it. He's the last thing Bobby Sue or little Kevin needs in their lives."

Peter wished with all his heart that he could just marry Bobby Sue, adopt Kevin, and start a happy life with them. He had spent countless hours teaching her all the finer points of riding. *Couldn't she tell how he felt about her?* Twice, he had taken Bobby Sue and little Kevin out for a picnic, tempted both times to just go ahead and let her know that he was in love with her.

"Have you told her how you feel?" pressed Jill.

"Is it that obvious?" asked Peter.

"You need to try harder," urged Jill. "Before it's too late."

Peter tightened his lips as he watched Bobby Sue complete the barrel circuit in just 13 seconds flat. Most likely she would win, at that rate. Then there would be nothing to stop her from leaving.

"I've never seen anyone take up barrel racing so quickly," observed Jill. "And she rides old Marco like they've been together for years."

"Yes, she does," agreed Peter, rather sadly. "I suppose Marco will be missing her when she goes."

"We all will," added Jill. "And we'll miss little Kevin, too!" Jill smiled at Kevin as she gently pinched his cheeks and asked him, "Wouldn't you like Peter to be your daddy?"

"He can't talk yet," chuckled Peter as he adjusted Kevin's weight in his arms.

"Dada!" blurted out Kevin as he reached up and put one of his little hands on Peter's clean-shaven chin and gazed at the dimple in it.

Bobby Sue had climbed down from Marco's back and was leading him over to where Jill and Peter were standing. Her mouth fell open with astonishment upon hearing Kevin's first word: *dada.*

"He's trying to call you *daddy,*" realized Bobby Sue.

"The kid has good taste," grinned Jill. "Maybe his mother should listen to him."

There it was, out in the open, the very subject that Bobby Sue had tried so hard to avoid.

"Come with me, Kevin," smiled Jill as she took him from Peter. "Kevin has a date with a clean diaper, don't you little man? We'll be up at the house if you need us for anything."

"Thanks," nodded Bobby Sue. *This was awkward!*

"I think you did that last run in 13 seconds," informed Peter. "Just a little tighter on the first barrel, and you could win this thing."

"I'd better get Marco into the barn and curry him down," mentioned Bobby Sue rather nervously.

"May I help?"

"I think I can handle it."

"Bobby Sue, we need to talk," blurted out Peter as he gently grabbed her upper right arm to stop her.

"Do we have to?" Bobby Sue's face took on a worried expression. Peter had become her best friend, and she wanted nothing to jeopardize that, especially now.

"Yes, we do," answered Peter as he took the reins from Bobby Sue and began walking toward the barn with Marco.

Realizing she had no choice, Bobby Sue followed. *What would she say if he asked her a direct question about her feelings for him?*

After reaching the tack room, Peter removed Marco's saddle and blanket while Bobby Sue removed his bridle and bit. She quickly slipped a halter onto the horse's head and led him to his stall, where she tied him to a stall ring at its entrance. Peter then grabbed an extra grooming brush and handed it to Bobby Sue. "I can do this side if you'd like to do the other."

"Hey, old boy," Bobby Sue spoke in soothing tones to Marco as she began brushing him.

After an uncomfortable silence, Peter finally began. "You're not going to make this easy for me, are you?"

She swallowed hard.

"Why in the world did you have to go and marry a guy like Mark Killingham?"

"Because my parents would have put my baby up for adoption!" blurted out Bobby Sue as a tear escaped onto her cheek.

"Well, I guess if he hadn't brought you here, we never would have met," continued Peter. "Oh, that's not how I wanted to say this."

"Just what are you trying to say, Peter Smith?"

"That I'm in love with you!" There, it was said, and there was no taking it back.

Bobby Sue stopped brushing Marco for a moment and looked across his back at Peter, who had also stopped brushing the horse. The longing and desire they both felt for one another was overwhelming.

"I've been in love with you since the moment I saw you," added Peter. "I know it's wrong, you being a married woman and all, but I just thought you should know. I love little Kevin, too."

Bobby Sue's lower lip began to quiver as she resumed brushing the horse for several minutes without speaking.

"Say something," pleaded Peter. "I'm also a decent Christian, and would never do anything inappropriate toward you, I hope you know that. I only wanted you to know how I feel before you leave and I never see you again. I just wish things had been different."

"What kind of things?" pressed Bobby Sue.

"Like you being available, for one. Then, I could marry you and adopt Kevin as my own," clarified Peter. "The two of you deserve a decent life with someone who will love, cherish and take care of you."

"Even if I were to split up with Mark," replied Bobby Sue, "I wouldn't be free to marry someone else unless it was because he committed adultery or something like that."

"I know," nodded Peter. "It says that in the scriptures, I agree."

He thought for a moment of mentioning what he and Jill had both noticed – the fact that Mark Killingham's ring finger had the indentation of a recently worn wedding band. *Should he tell her, or let her find out for herself? It was inevitable.*

"And?" prompted Bobby Sue. "What else?"

"If things ever do change for you in the future," described Peter, "you'll know where to find me. I'll always be here for you."

The evening of Saturday, August 11, 1956, arrived like a bolt of lightning for Peter Smith. He had little to say as he drove Bobby Sue to the Greyhound Bus depot in Mobile. The baby blue Plymouth convertible seemed to compel them all toward an uncertain future.

Bobby Sue was seated in the front seat beside him but also had little to say. *Was leaving a mistake? Would Mark be happy to see her and little Kevin?*

"You did us all proud at the rodeo today," praised Jill from the back seat where she sat holding Kevin. She had come along to help Peter see Bobby Sue and Kevin off. "That's a mighty fine trophy you won, too."

"The $50 didn't hurt anything, either," added Bobby Sue, though she was not as excited about it as one might expect.

"Just under 12 seconds flat is a new record, at least around these parts," continued Jill. "Marco will certainly miss you."

"I'll miss him, too," sniffed Bobby Sue as she fought against the tears that were threatening to erupt.

"Are you sure we shouldn't at least call and let Mark know you're coming?" questioned Jill. "What if he's out running errands when you show up? What if you run into your father or mother when you get there? Do you know what you plan to say?"

Bobby Sue swallowed hard. "I can't keep running for the rest of my life. I've got to face my parents sometime."

"What if they try and put little Kevin up for adoption?" asked Peter, who was actually as worried about it as she was.

"Well, I'm married now," reminded Bobby Sue. "There's nothing they can do about it. Mark would never let them take Kevin away from us, no matter what."

"Are you sure about that?" challenged Peter. He was not so sure.

"I read in the paper today that Martin Luther King, Jr. was scheduled to testify before the platform committee of the Democratic National Convention in Chicago, recommending a strong civil rights plank in the party platform," mentioned Jill, to change the subject.

"Who's King?" frowned Bobby Sue. She had never heard of the man.

"He's some black reverend, campaigning for equal rights for negroes," explained Peter. "I can't believe you've never heard of him."

"I'm done reading today's paper," added Jill. "Here, you take this along with you, for something to read during your trip."

Bobby Sue opened the paper and began to read out loud, "*The Birth of a New Age* address will be delivered tonight at the Fiftieth Anniversary of Alpha Phi Alpha fraternity in Buffalo by Dr. Martin Luther King, Jr. He will be presented with the Alpha Award of Honor for Christian leadership in the cause of first class citizenship for all mankind."

"Humph," grunted Peter. "Wonder if news of little Kevin being born on a black bus has traveled very far yet?"

"I haven't seen anything in the paper about it," assured Jill.

"That old driver was probably afraid of losing his job," chuckled Bobby Sue, "especially since he had that flask of whiskey on him."

The three of them chuckled at that as Peter pulled into the Greyhound Bus parking lot.

"Last chance to change your mind," offered Jill.

"I wish I could," replied Bobby Sue, "but this is something we must do."

Peter got out and came around to open the door for her. As she stood, their eyes locked for an eternal moment, neither knowing what to say. Then, deciding to throw caution to the wind, Peter tenderly pulled her close and gave Bobby Sue a hug before kissing her on the cheek.

"Be safe." He then tenderly brushed her cheek with the back of his hand, to wipe away a stray tear.

Bobby Sue broke down crying at that point and hugged Peter back, hard. She then turned to hug Jill as she took Kevin from her. "Thank you so much for everything!"

"Just let us know when you get there and how everything goes," requested Jill. "If it doesn't work out, you know where we are."

Peter then bent close to Bobby Sue from behind and whispered, "I'll always love you, my little rodeo queen."

"Me, too," whispered Bobby Sue as she suddenly grabbed her suitcase with her free hand and ran toward the bus station holding Kevin with the other arm.

"She'll be back," predicted Jill. "Trust me."

4. The Other Wife

Jim Otterman continued to listen for hours as Kevin told his mother's story.

How did he know all of this? wondered Linda.

Unknown to Linda just yet, Kevin's mother had opened up to him 20 years later and revealed the sad tale of why she had left Mark Killingham.

It was nearly midnight, on Sunday, April 23, 2023. Sheree had already retired for the night, and Linda was sound asleep on the bench seat near the catwalk entrance. Out beyond the lighthouse, ocean waves could easily be seen silhouetted across the undulating surface of the water in the full moonlight. The crashing of surf against the bluffs below was almost hypnotic.

"Can we pick this up in the morning?" interrupted Jim. "I definitely want to hear more."

"Sounds good to me," yawned Kevin as he got up and went over to where Linda was and gently shook her. "Come on, sweetheart, let's go to bed."

"A black bus, huh?" grinned Linda as she stretched and sat up.

"You heard that part?" chuckled Kevin.

"How come you never said anything?"

Kevin then shrugged his shoulders. "It wasn't until sometime later that mom finally told me about it."

"Let's resume this where we left off at breakfast tomorrow," suggested Jim.

"How early?" questioned Kevin.

"Let's say 9:00, in view of what time it is now," replied Jim.

"That works for me," agreed Linda as she got up to follow Kevin to their room. *Why hadn't Kevin mentioned any of this until now?*

"Oh yes," reminded Jim. "Checkout time is at 11:00."

"Is it too late to extend our stay?" asked Kevin.

Linda gave him a surprised look but then finally smiled and nodded in agreement.

"No, not at all," grinned Jim. "For how long?"

"At least a couple more days," proposed Kevin.

116

"Maybe just one night?" stipulated Linda. "There might not be enough left on the credit card for two."

"It's on the house," insisted Jim. "I'll write off your entire stay as a business expense while handling *The Killingham Matter*. Stay as long as you like."

"Seriously?" questioned both Kevin and Linda with surprise.

"Like a heart attack," smiled Jim as he shook hands with Kevin and gently slapped him on the shoulder with the palm of his other hand.

"Wow, thanks!" exclaimed Linda as she gave Jim a brief hug, causing him to blush slightly.

"Hey, I want to find out what happened to Mark Killingham as much as both of you do," added Jim. "His adopted son Ray was a very big part of our lives, and I'm certain Ray would have wanted to know the truth about this whole thing."

"I still can't believe that Mark Killingham and the ice cream man were one and the same person," muttered Linda.

You and everyone else who knew him, thought Jim as he watched them leave the tower room of the lighthouse to head to the Daisy Room.

Morning sunlight streamed through the tower room windows as Sheree set the table for breakfast. The smell of bacon, eggs, waffles, coffee and freshly squeezed orange juice wafted through the lighthouse. Ocean breeze laced with eucalyptus and cypress from the forest behind the lighthouse also hung in the air.

"Where's Linda?" questioned Jim as he arrived and sat down beside Kevin at the round wooden table.

They were both quite hungry and anxious to eat.

"She's downstairs taking a shower," shrugged Kevin.

"That figures." Jim shook his head knowingly.

"Oh, look!" exclaimed Sheree as she pointed toward the horizon. "There's an orca out there."

"Guess that rules out surfing," chuckled Kevin.

"That's no joke," replied Jim as he devoured a slice of bacon, without waiting for the food to be blessed. "There are sharks out there, too, especially at high tide."

"Looks like the tide's going out right now," assessed Kevin.

117

"Actually, it's still headed in," advised Jim as he consulted his smartwatch. "Low tide was at 4:37 this morning, and high tide will be at 10:38. Then, of course, it will go back out again at 16:46 this afternoon and be back in again at 23:11 tonight."

"You don't plan to do any surfing while you're here, do you?" Sheree was quite serious. "If you are, Ann's husband Ted would be the best one to take with you. He surfs nearly every day, though I can't imagine why, especially after everything that has happened out there."

"Like when Steve Fredrickson was attacked in '73, and died right there on the beach," interjected Linda from the doorway. "I still remember the funeral they had for Steve, Joyce and Veronica. You couldn't get me out there for anything in the world!"

"Didn't you say that Joyce and Veronica died in a cave or something?" questioned Kevin.

Jim and Sheree both were silent for a few moments as they thought of the tragedy.

"The funeral was for Steve," Linda explained to Kevin as she seated herself beside him, "but also in memory of Joyce and Veronica because at that time they had gone missing and no one knew exactly what had happened to them."

"That's right," corroborated Jim. "They were presumed dead."

"And actually were," added Sheree, "as was finally confirmed in 2016 when Carolyn, Ray and I were trapped at high tide in the cave where their skeletal remains had been hidden for 43 years. It was the earthquake that day that exposed them to us."

"How horrible!" exclaimed Linda.

"Not as horrible as finally remembering that it was my then-husband Jon who had originally killed them. That was when he decided to shoot himself in the head – right in front of us!" snapped Sheree. "Excuse me, but I've lost my appetite."

"Oh, Sheree, I'm terribly sorry," apologized Linda.

"Hey, it is what it is," assured Jim. "She'll be okay. She just needs some space right now. Jon Roth was mentally ill, and I think he wanted to make sure he wouldn't end up doing anything to Sheree or Ann later on that they would all regret."

"Isn't Jon Roth the guy you mentioned earlier that was called Birdboy?" questioned Kevin with raised eyebrows.

"Yes," confirmed Jim as he took a sip of coffee. "Hey, let's bless the food, shall we?"

"Go ahead," Kevin motioned with his hands.

"Dear God, thank you for this food. Amen."

"Okay, then," remarked Linda, truly surprised by the brevity of Jim's prayer.

"After breakfast," advised Jim, "I'm headed out to the Ocean Bluff Cemetery. I think you two will want to join me. We'll be exhuming the body of the Mark Killingham that died in the ice cream shop."

Kevin and Linda exchanged a surprised glance.

"And, I'd like to hear more of your story while we drive," added Jim. "Especially what happened when Bobby Sue showed up unannounced in Washington with *you!*"

"I'd like to hear more about that myself," nodded Linda.

"I'll tell you what I can," agreed Kevin. "Remind me again what you expect to find when they exhume the body?"

"As I mentioned previously, Mark had a broken arm at one point in his life. So, the skeleton in that grave will show it, if it's him."

"And if it's not?" pressed Kevin.

"Then we'll go from there."

Jim Otterman's bright red 2023 Jeep Cherokee carefully wound its way along the narrow blufftop highway leading from Oceanview Academy and the lighthouse over to the Ocean Bluff Cemetery.

Intermittent views of the ocean beside them could be seen in between the never-ending row of cypress and eucalyptus trees growing along the precipice edge. Seagulls and other birds could be seen flying around overhead, in search of some unsuspecting prey below. Memories of her school days at Oceanview Academy filled Linda's mind as they made their way.

"So," began Jim as he glanced at Kevin in his rearview mirror, "exactly when was it that your mother finally decided to share all this information with you about her past?"

"That's what I'd like to know," interjected Linda as she folded her arms.

"It was at our 20-year wedding anniversary party," replied Kevin. "And, once mother began talking, it was such a flood of information that I could barely take it all in."

Jim nodded with understanding. "Sometimes, that's how things are. Kind of like pulling off a Band-Aid."

"Hey, I'm really sorry that I upset Sheree earlier," added Linda. "I was way out of line."

"Nonsense," differed Jim. "Talking about things once in a while can be cathartic for the soul. You're fine."

"Guess it's time for me to get cathartic again," chuckled Kevin. "Where was I? Oh yes, when my mother and I first arrived at the Johnson Ranch that day, you'd never believe who we came across first. Or, I should say, who came across us."

August 16, 1956

Bobby Sue and little Kevin had arrived late the previous evening at the Greyhound Bus depot in Sprague and had spent the rest of that night on one of its hard, wooden benches at the terminal. Spending three days and two nights on a moving bus had been nothing compared to the two-day layover in Mt. Vernon while the bus was being repaired after an unexpected breakdown. Even in the summer, South Dakota was surprisingly cold at night. They had slept in the bus terminal there, too. Bobby Sue had eaten all her meals from a vending machine. Thankfully for little Kevin, he was still nursing.

After debating upon whether or not to pick up the payphone and call her parents, Bobby Sue decided against it. She could hitchhike to the ranch instead. If only there were a way to call Mark without having to talk to *them*, as they most certainly would recognize her voice! *Maybe this way, I'll run into Mark first, and then we can face them together*, reasoned Bobby Sue.

She wasn't sure exactly why her suitcase seemed so heavy – perhaps it was the bronze barrel racing trophy, though it was only a belt buckle. Still, it was worth bringing it along. Mark would no doubt wear it proudly, once she presented it to him. *It can be kind of like a wedding ring, but even better*, smiled Bobby Sue to herself as she reached the main road and set down her suitcase.

"Are you ready for this, Kevin?" smiled Bobby Sue as she adjusted him in her arms. The skirt of her baby blue gingham dress gently flapped in the breeze where it protruded from beneath her navy blue wool coat. Thankfully, Jill had taken the coat to the cleaners for her following Kevin's birth, as it had been covered in afterbirth. Once the morning sun made its way over the tree line, however, it would quickly become too hot to wear it and it would be necessary to tie the heavy coat around her waist. Her brown riding boots and thick wool socks had also been gifts from Jill, but the boots were way too big to fit in her suitcase. So, she wore them, despite the fact that they looked peculiar with a dress. They were now covered with dust, as was the bottom of her suitcase.

Kevin was an amazingly good baby, and rarely fussed. She had put a clean diaper on him in the restroom at the bus station. She had rinsed out the dirty one as thoroughly as possible and stashed it inside an awkward Tupperware container that Jill had given her. *Maybe that's why the suitcase is so heavy!*

If only there were a plastic bag, or something like that I could use instead, wished Bobby Sue.

"Here goes," sighed Bobby Sue as she transferred Kevin's entire weight to her left arm and stuck out the thumb on her right hand.

It was less than five minutes before the first vehicle happened along. It was a rickety old flatbed truck with swaying wooden slatted sides on the back. The farmer driving it was at least 80 years old. Upon seeing Bobby Sue, he brought the vehicle to a stop.

"What in the world are you two doing way out here like this, young lady?" demanded the man.

"I'm trying to get to the Johnson Ranch," explained Bobby Sue. "You headed that way?"

"Well, now, that's a silly question," replied the old man. "You can see that I'm going that direction. I'll be going right past it. Would you like a ride?"

"Oh, yes, thank you!" grinned Bobby Sue as she struggled to pick up her suitcase with her free hand.

The farmer climbed from his truck and approached. "You shouldn't be lifting something like that with a baby in your arms."

"I was hoping to put it in the back," explained Bobby Sue.

"You two get on inside the truck," directed the man as he grabbed and hoisted the suitcase onto the flatbed with amazing alacrity for a man of his age. "What you got in there, anyway? Rocks?"

121

"A few wet diapers," apologized Bobby Sue. She had only one clean diaper left and was hopeful of reaching the ranch before it was needed. The others were all either wet or in various stages of dryness inside the Tupperware container. She had done her best to try and dry as many of them out as possible during the layover at Mt. Vernon, but had finally been asked by the attendant at the bus depot to please remove them from the ladies' restroom.

"Name's Job," advised the man as he climbed back into the truck. The rusty hinges on which the vehicle's doors had once hung stood as a lasting reminder of their absence.

"Like in the Old Testament?" asked Bobby Sue as she adjusted Kevin on the seat between them – just to make sure he wouldn't accidentally slide out of the open door.

"Yes, ma'am," smiled Job as he restarted the clunky sounding engine and shifted into drive.

The sudden jolt caused Kevin to begin crying.

"This is Kevin and I'm Bobby Sue," shouted Bobby Sue to be heard above the noise. "I'm the Johnson girl."

"You don't say?" Job raised an eyebrow and studied her more closely. "Word was, you'd gone missing a while back. They had the police, the fire department, and even the dogs out looking for you!"

"I don't doubt it."

"I reckon your folks will be mighty glad to see you."

"I hope so," nodded Bobby Sue.

"My granddaughter and her husband have been looking for a baby to adopt," mentioned Job. "How soon will Kevin be on the market?"

Bobby Sue's mouth fell open with abhorrence. "Kevin will <u>not</u> be on the market, or up for adoption, or anything else of the kind!"

"I don't see your folks taking on something like that," opined Job. "They're on the verge of foreclosure as it is. If it hadn't been for that old bull your daddy was able to auction off last year, they wouldn't be there now."

"Moose was his name," advised Bobby Sue, more indignantly than she intended.

"That's right, Moose *was* his name," nodded Job. "He sure was a beautiful animal."

122

"Was?" pressed Bobby Sue. Her lower lip had begun to quiver. *Had something happened to Moose?* It was her plan to find and buy him back with what was left of her prize money if she could.

Job seemed to realize that he had overstepped and was quiet for several moments before responding. "Before your daddy sold him, of course."

"That was the reason I ran away, you know," blurted out Bobby Sue. "He had no right to sell Moose like that without asking me!"

"I think I'll leave that up to you and him to hash out," answered Job, "along with whatever else you might be needing to discuss." Job then nodded toward Kevin with a knowing look.

"My husband works at the ranch, I'll have you know!" informed Bobby Sue. "And *no one* will be taking our child away from us!"

"Really?" Job seemed puzzled. "Well, whatever. We're here. Would you two like a ride up to the farmhouse?"

"You can just let me off here at the gate," decided Bobby Sue. "I think I need to stretch my legs first before I get there. It's only half a mile, anyway."

Job climbed from the truck and gingerly unloaded her suitcase. "You *sure* you don't want a ride up to the house? It's no trouble."

"This is fine," persisted Bobby Sue as she adjusted Kevin in one arm and snatched up her suitcase with the other. "Much obliged."

"Good luck to you, young lady," bid Job as he climbed back inside his truck and slowly drove away.

Maria Killingham was rarely allowed to drive her husband's dilapidated green 1948 DeSoto, but today it had been necessary. Her husband Mark had finally given in and shown her how to drive when Eric was six months old. Maria had obtained her driver's license only last week.

After dropping Mark off at work that morning, Maria had driven the DeSoto into town to take little Eric to a doctor's appointment, as he had not been feeling well. Her other four boys had come with them, screaming and making a commotion in the waiting room at the doctor's office. Understandably, Mark had no desire to take off work to join them. Maria hoped she would make it back to the Johnson Ranch in time to pick him up for lunch. Mark did not like to be kept waiting. It was the plan for him to take her and the children home during the lunch hour and then head back to work.

The temperature was starting to climb, even though it was only 11:30. Michael sat in the front seat with her, holding little Eric. Justin, Philip and Evan were in the back, screaming and making quite a raucous. Tired of listening to them, Maria turned on the radio and began listening to *Singing the Blues* by Marty Robbins.

It was still playing when she suddenly swerved to avoid hitting a young woman who was carrying a baby down the dusty road. "Oh, my God! What in the world is she doing out here with a baby like that?"

After bringing the DeSoto to a stop, Maria got out. "I'm so sorry, I almost didn't see you. Are you okay?"

Bobby Sue merely nodded. "I'm fine, thanks."

"Please, let me give you a ride to the ranch," offered Maria. "I assume that's where you're headed?"

"Uh, sure," agreed Bobby Sue. "I think I'll take you up on that."

Maria quickly put Bobby Sue's suitcase into the trunk, along with her coat, and then came and opened the passenger door for her.

"Thanks!" nodded Bobby Sue as she climbed inside, holding little Kevin.

Maria carefully closed the passenger door and then came around to get back into the driver's seat. "This is Michael and little Eric, and I'm Maria."

"Hello!" greeted Michael.

"Evan, Philip and Justin are in the back," added Maria.

"Hello!" chorused the boys.

"Nice to meet you," smiled Bobby Sue.

"They seem to be about the same age," noticed Maria as she nodded at the two young baby boys.

"Kevin was born on January 29," revealed Bobby Sue as Maria started the engine.

"Eric was born on January 18," advised Maria as she shifted the DeSoto into gear and began to drive again.

"This is incredible," mentioned Bobby Sue. "You know, my husband has a car just like this. It's a '48."

"This one is, too," corroborated Maria. "Just what does your husband do?"

"He works at the ranch," advised Bobby Sue. For some unexplainable reason, she was beginning to feel most uncomfortable.

"Mine, too," frowned Maria. "Oh, my God! It can't be! You're not Bobby Sue Johnson, are you?"

"I was," answered Bobby Sue. "It's Killingham now."

"Killingham?" Maria took her foot off the gas pedal and allowed the vehicle to slow down on its own. "His first name wouldn't happen to be Mark, would it?"

"Why yes, it is," confirmed Bobby Sue. "Why?"

Maria suddenly slammed on the brakes and turned off the engine. She looked as if she didn't know whether to laugh or cry, and just sat there with her hands on the steering wheel, shaking her head. Finally, she screamed, "Get out!"

Bobby Sue quickly fumbled for the door handle.

"Not you!" clarified Maria. "Boys, get out! All of you! Bobby Sue and I need to talk. Alone."

The boys sat staring at their mother with disbelief.

"Now!" hollered Maria.

Maria reached over and took Eric from Michael and then instructed him, "You, too! I'll keep Eric here."

"Excuse me, lady," apologized Michael as he climbed past her and Kevin to get out of the car.

"Keep an eye on the others," cautioned Maria. "Don't let them wander off. Especially, do not let them go up to the barn just yet. Keep them here. Do you understand me?"

"Yes, mama," agreed Michael, who was the oldest.

"How old is he?" asked Bobby Sue with concern.

"Six," answered Maria. "He'll keep an eye on 'em."

Once the boys were outside of the vehicle and the doors had been shut, Maria muttered, "There is only one explanation for this."

Not knowing what else to do, Bobby Sue carefully opened her purse and removed a folded piece of paper.

"What's that?" asked Maria. She was trying to gather her thoughts and not yet sure what she wanted to say.

Bobby Sue merely handed it to Maria, who carefully unfolded it. It was the marriage license between Mark Killingham and Bobby Sue. The date on it corresponded exactly with the time period he had been in Alabama "visiting his aunt."

"Just how often has he been back to visit you?" questioned Maria.

"Only twice," admitted Bobby Sue, "but after being arrested and having his license suspended for being under the influence for six months ...."

"Hold it!" interrupted Maria. "He pulled that one on me when Michael was little. It was just an excuse to keep from coming out to see you. I can't believe he would do this again!"

Tears began to stream down Bobby Sue's cheeks. The reality of her situation was beginning to sink in.

"How old are you, child?" questioned Maria.

"Sixteen," answered Bobby Sue. "That was why we had to go to Alabama to get married."

Maria continued to shake her head. "When Mark and I were first married, he kept disappearing for days at a time. It was by chance that I learned he was already married to someone else."

"What?" frowned Bobby Sue.

"Oh, yes," assured Maria. "Then, when Gina found out, she committed suicide. It was horrible!"

"Did he and Gina have any children?" asked Bobby Sue.

"Thankfully, no," replied Maria, "but Michael and Justin were already born by then, and I was pregnant with Philip."

Bobby Sue absently stared at the dashboard of the car.

"Mark *promised* me that nothing like this would ever happen again!" sobbed Maria as she rocked little Eric in her arms.

"My parents will put Kevin up for adoption!" blurted out Bobby Sue. "I just know it! And if my father ever finds out that Mark is the father, there's no telling what he might do."

"Your parents don't know about any of this?" grilled Maria.

"Even Mark has no idea I'm out here now," confirmed Bobby Sue. "I was going to surprise him. After he meets Kevin for the first time, I thought that together we could confront my parents."

"Your marriage isn't even valid," pointed out Maria. "Neither was mine, at first, until I made him marry me again."

Bobby Sue suddenly thought of Peter Smith and began to cry. *Peter was right about Mark! How could she have been so foolish?*

"I have an idea," advised Maria. "We will confront Mark together."

"I've seen his temper," objected Bobby Sue.

"He would never do anything to harm an innocent child," persisted Maria. "Let's go see him and find out what he has to say for himself."

"I'm not so sure that's such a good idea," differed Bobby Sue.

"Nonsense," determined Maria as she rolled down the car window. "Boys, get in!"

After waiting for her boys to comply, Maria started up the engine and headed directly for the barn.

"There he is!" Bobby Sue felt genuine fear at the very sight of Mark Killingham. "We can't do this."

"The only thing to fear is fear itself," assured Maria as she put the DeSoto into park and shut off the engine.

"No!" maintained Bobby Sue.

"I'll carry Kevin," informed Maria as she took Eric from Michael and instructed, "take Kevin from her."

Michael complied.

Maria then handed Eric to Bobby Sue and took Kevin from Michael. "Let's see if Mark even *knows* which one is which!"

"Wait!" pleaded Bobby Sue as Maria opened the car door.

"Boys, you will wait inside the car until I tell you otherwise," ordered Maria. "No matter what happens!"

"Yes, ma'am," answered the boys.

"Bobby Sue, you and Eric are with us."

"It's show time," mumbled Michael, who had a better understanding of the events at hand than his mother realized.

Mark was busy unloading a flatbed full of hay with a pitchfork. As he paused to wipe sweat from his brow with the back of his hand, he froze. *Maria and Bobby Sue were approaching with their babies! What was he going to do?*

April 24, 2023

It was almost 11:00 in the morning by the time Jim Otterman drove his Jeep Cherokee through the entrance gates of the Ocean Bluff Mental Institution.

"What are we doing here?" frowned Kevin.

"The cemetery is right out back, behind it," explained Jim.

A clean black hearse was already parked in the long, circular drive. Gold letters on its side read, "Ocean Bluff Coroner's Office."

"It is beautiful here," remarked Linda. "This was one place I never got to see when I went to school at Oceanview."

"I'm sure my wife wishes she could say the same," replied Jim. "She and Jon were committed here together, back in 1973."

"After the Joyce and Veronica incident?" guessed Linda.

"Yes, but both were released in March of 1983 after a ten-year commitment," confirmed Jim. "That was when they were married."

"It's just like a huge park with all the trees, flowers and pathways everywhere," admired Linda. She hoped to change the subject. "And, just look at all those white benches along the walkways where you can sit and enjoy the view as you listen to the sounds of the ocean below!" Situated on a high elevation of land overlooking the city below on one side and a vast expanse of ocean on the other, Ocean Bluff Mental Institution truly was a magnificent sight.

"How old is this place again?" asked Kevin as he studied the medieval looking brick building with its white spiraled steeples and clock tower.

"It was first established in 1887," reminded Jim. "Fifteen years after the lighthouse."

"It's hard to believe the lighthouse is older than this," marveled Linda as Jim pulled to a stop and shut off the engine.

"Oh, yes," assured Jim. "As I mentioned earlier, the lighthouse was originally built in 1872 by the first Killinghams to come here from Ireland."

"That would be the people in that photo?" questioned Kevin.

"Their grandparents, I believe," answered Jim. "At least according to Ann. We'll have to get a better look at her records when we get back."

"And the cemetery is right behind this?" marveled Linda.

"Right down that path," nodded Jim. "Around the side of the building."

"I'd like to get a better look at the front door first," informed Linda. "I'll follow you in a moment."

"We can wait," responded Jim.

Kevin and Linda then paused at the front steps long enough to read a large metal plaque centered over its ornate entry doors that read: "When the waves reach to our heads we begin to listen to anything; no advice is too contemptible for us; no person too insignificant for us to be willing to listen." by Johann Peter Lange - 1872.

"Can I help you?" questioned an older woman in an antiquated white nurse's uniform who had suddenly opened the front doors.

"Ah, Nurse Redden," greeted Jim. "So good to see you."

"Jim Otterman," recognized the woman. "Please, come in."

"Actually, we're expected out back, at the cemetery."

"You're with those other fellas that want to dig up Mark Killingham?" frowned Nurse Redden.

"I'm afraid so," apologized Jim. "This is Mark Killingham's son Kevin and his wife Linda."

"You don't say," muttered Nurse Redden as she put her hands on her hips and tipped her head back to get a better look at them through her bifocals. Nurse Redden was a short thin woman with pale skin and gray hair that had once been dark brown. Her piercing blue eyes usually made people who didn't know her uncomfortable.

"Nice to meet you, ma'am," acknowledged Kevin as he extended his hand to her.

"Likewise," responded Nurse Redden as she finally shook it.

Linda and Nurse Redden merely exchanged a polite nod.

"That was some terrible business when Mark Killingham fell in love with his older stepsister Linda," commented Nurse Redden.

"Excuse me?" scowled Kevin.

"Of course, Linda Dixon was already six months pregnant with Jon Roth, Sr.'s child at the time," added Nurse Redden.

"Yes, that's what my daughter Ann was saying," revealed Jim.

"Humph," snorted Nurse Redden. "Then you also know that was when Mark Killingham decided to be gallant and marry her to save her honor, as if that were possible!"

"That's right!" recalled Kevin. "Ann was telling us that Mark was only 14 years old at the time, so he lied about his age in order to get the marriage certificate."

"And I made a remark about that probably being the beginning of his life as a con artist," snickered Linda.

"How very perceptive of you, my dear," approved Nurse Redden. "I like her! Of course, I only found out about some of this last month myself."

"From whom?" urged Jim.

"From that lady friend of yours," winked Nurse Redden.

"Lady friend?" Jim furrowed his eyebrows.

"Carolyn Bennett-Hunter."

"Now, wait a minute," objected Jim. "It's not what you think. Carolyn and I really are only friends."

Linda could not help but smile with amusement at Jim's predicament. *Had there actually been some truth to the high school rumor that Jim and Carolyn were once an item?*

"If you say so," smirked Nurse Redden.

"Exactly what else did Carolyn tell you?" pressed Jim.

"Well, apparently your daughter Ann had Ginny's journal, as well as my mother Helen's diary, and shared the information she had with Carolyn. They were computer friends for quite a while, you know, something about electronic mail or some such nonsense."

"Go on," prompted Jim, who now had his arms folded.

"As you probably also know, Ginny Eggersol was actually my sister, though I never knew it when she was alive," revealed Nurse Redden rather sadly. "And, of course, it also mentioned the torrid romance between Jon Roth, Sr. and Linda Dixon, and how she became pregnant with Ray."

"Making Ray and Jon half-brothers," acknowledged Jim. "I know. Ann already shared that with the rest of us, too."

"Ann found the diary in a secret compartment of an old trunk that once belonged to my mother," Nurse Redden explained for Kevin's and Linda's benefit.

"She mentioned that, yes," nodded Jim.

"It also said that Mark Killingham met and fell in love with Linda Dixon when she was six months pregnant," continued Nurse Redden. "And that, rather than tarnish the stellar reputation of Jon Roth, Sr. - the man who had fathered her child – Linda Dixon went to her grave without revealing the secret to anyone but Jon Sr.'s wife Edith, who was her midwife."

"Hold it!" interrupted Linda. "I thought Mark and Linda *were* married. Isn't that what you told us earlier?"

"That's what Ann told us, too," confirmed Kevin.

"Of course, they were," grinned Nurse Redden. "That doesn't discount Linda's deathbed confession to Edith Roth of the affair she'd had with her husband. That was something Edith later shared only with her sister Helen. What no one else knew was that she purposely failed to mention the true identity of her baby's father to Mark."

"Why would she do that?" frowned Linda.

"How would I know?" shrugged Nurse Redden.

"Edith and Helen were sisters?" asked Kevin, as he suddenly made the connection.

"Yes," answered Nurse Redden.

"Making Ray your cousin," realized Kevin.

"By George, I think he's got it!" laughed Nurse Redden.

"So, what does that have to do with any of this?" questioned Linda, who still was perplexed.

"I'll tell you what it has to do with it," replied Nurse Redden. "Being a blood relative to Ray gave me the legal right to obtain any and all records and court documents pertaining to his mother – my aunt Linda."

"Oh, my God!" exclaimed Linda. "The actual marriage certificate of Mark Killingham's marriage to Linda Dixon?"

"I've got a copy of it inside," beamed Nurse Redden. "Would you like to see it?"

"Yes!" exclaimed both Kevin and Linda together.

"We'd love to get a copy of it, too," added Kevin.

"Sorry, but I gave my only extra copy to Ann last month," mentioned Nurse Redden.

"Oh, that's okay," grinned Linda. "I can just snap a photo of it with my smartwatch."

"Whatever," shrugged Nurse Redden. She had little use for modern electronic devices but was occasionally impressed by their capabilities.

"How come you never said anything about this to me?" demanded Jim.

"Most likely because you never asked," shrugged Nurse Redden. "No one ever takes me too seriously, anyway. Except Ann, of course."

"How long were Mark and Linda married?" questioned Kevin as they followed Nurse Redden inside the facility.

"I'd say about three months," guessed Nurse Redden. "Give or take a day or two."

"You seem pretty certain about it," commented Kevin.

"Well, his stepsister was six months pregnant when he married her," reminded Nurse Redden. "It was three months later when Linda died during childbirth. I've got her death certificate here, too, if you'd like to snap a picture of it."

"Yes, we would," assured Linda.

131

"What year was Ray born?" grilled Kevin.

"1944," answered Nurse Redden, "but you'll have to get his birth certificate from Ann. She was coming by here nearly every day for a while there."

"We will," agreed Jim. He was beginning to become concerned about keeping the coroner and medical examiner waiting, but knew this was important. *What else had Ann failed to share with them?*

"For whatever reason – and your guess is as good as mine – Mark took Ray and raised him as his own," described Nurse Redden.

"Who took care of Ray when Mark was away?" asked Linda.

"Mostly, I think he just left him alone, right there at the lighthouse," assumed Nurse Redden. "The man sure was gone a lot, though. Anytime we needed an order of ice cream filled, we'd nearly always have to put in our request a month ahead of time."

"So did the school," recalled Jim. That fact had never seemed significant until now.

"Here it is," nodded Nurse Redden as she opened a desk drawer in the reception area and took out a small stack of official looking papers that she spread out on top.

Kevin, Linda and Jim all three began snapping photos of the documents, including the marriage certificate of Mark Killingham to Linda Dixon in 1944.

"Thank you so much," smiled Kevin.

"No problem," beamed Nurse Redden. "Glad I could help. Anything else?"

"Uh, yes," replied Kevin. "Do you happen to recall whether Mark Killingham ever drove a 1948 DeSoto?"

"Oh, yes, he certainly did," confirmed Nurse redden. "Rickety old thing, too."

"What ever happened to it?" asked Jim.

"Probably just drove it into the ground," sighed Nurse Redden. "You'd think folks would take better care of their vehicles, especially driving out of state and such like he did. If it weren't for Ray being a mechanic, it probably wouldn't have lasted Mark as long as it did."

"You know for a fact that Mark drove out of state?" grilled Jim.

"He mentioned something like that, a time or two," nodded Nurse Redden. "Why?"

132

"Did he ever mention going to Alabama?" queried Kevin.

"Not specifically, but he must have," laughed Nurse Redden as she motioned toward the marriage certificate sitting on the desk beside her. "That's where he and Linda got married, most likely because of the lower age requirement there. Even at that, he no doubt had to lie about it and tell 'em he was 16."

"When he was actually only 14," nodded Linda.

"That's about the size of it," confirmed Nurse Redden. "Now it's my turn. You folks still haven't answered my question. Besides the fact that Kevin here is his son, why all the sudden interest in digging up Mark Killingham?"

"We have reason to believe that the man buried in your cemetery back there might be someone else," blurted out Linda.

"Really?" grinned Nurse Redden.

"We probably should get back there," urged Jim. "The coroner and medical examiner are back there now, waiting for us."

"As curator, you'll no doubt need my permission, too," reminded Nurse Redden. "Mind if I tag along?"

"Please do," invited Jim as he started for the large double doors at the front entrance.

"There hasn't been this much excitement around here since Jon Roth, Jr. was committed in '73," commented Nurse Redden as she followed them outside and down the cobblestone walkway leading around the building toward the cemetery behind it. Purple and yellow ice plants grew in the flowerbed alongside them.

"Sheree was committed then, as well," reminded Jim.

"Being comatose isn't nearly as exciting as being a raving lunatic," chuckled Nurse Redden.

"Jon Roth was a schizophrenic," clarified Jim for the others. "It was actually his Birdboy personality that murdered Joyce and Veronica. Then, after being released, Jon became the theology professor at Oceanview Academy. That was when he married Sheree. And, just for the record, Sheree suffered from Kahlbaum syndrome, which is a motionless type of affliction. In her case, it was from seeing something so traumatic that she suffered from post-traumatic stress disorder."

"At least she got over it," added Nurse Redden. "Too bad that husband of hers went wacko again and quit taking his meds in 2016."

"I guess that depends upon your point of view," replied Jim, rather uncomfortably.

"Wasn't that when Jon shot himself?" asked Linda

"Indeed, it was, honey," verified Nurse Redden. "Good thing old Jim here decided to take in Sheree and that daughter of hers after that. Heaven only knows what they would have done if he hadn't."

"Her daughter's name is Ann," reminded Jim, who was becoming increasingly irritated with Nurse Redden.

"I know that!" snapped Nurse Redden. "I thought I already told you that Ann comes here to see me!"

"Why don't we take this down a notch?" suggested Kevin.

"Ah, Jim Otterman," acknowledged the medical examiner as he approached and shook his hand. "Did the judge sign your order?"

"Of course," smiled Jim as he pulled up a signed copy of it on his smartwatch to show him. "I can get a hard copy of it from my Legal Secretary if you need one."

Bill Huong grinned at Jim as he held his smartwatch up to Jim's to upload an electronic copy of it. "This will be fine."

"I've never seen Judge Law sign anything that quickly in his life," remarked Tony Ledbetter.

Jim merely shrugged and returned Tony's puzzled look with a confident grin.

"Tony Ledbetter is our coroner," mentioned Jim for Kevin's and Linda's benefit. "And Bill Huong is our medical examiner."

"Very nice to meet you," greeted Bill, whose smile was sincere.

"You're Tony?" asked Kevin.

"No, I'm Bill, that's Tony."

"Oh, okay, sorry. Nice to meet you," nodded Kevin as he shook each of their hands. "This is my wife Linda."

Linda merely nodded at first, to be polite, but then Bill suddenly reached for her hand and flirted with her as he shook it.

"My pleasure," beamed Bill as he checked Linda out.

The exchange did not go unnoticed by Kevin.

"Nice to meet you both." Tony's smile was insincere. Unlike Bill, he had a million other things he could be doing.

"Kevin, as son of the decedent, we will need your signature on some paperwork we brought with us," informed Tony as he pulled an envelope from the pocket of his suit jacket and handed it to Kevin.

"Absolutely," agreed Kevin as he took it from him.

"I've got a pen," offered Linda as she hurried to retrieve one from her purse.

"Sorry it was necessary for Jim to get a court order," apologized Bill, "but since Kevin wasn't the one who originally signed for the interment, there was no way around it."

"Good thing old Jim here knows the judge," interjected Tony, just a little more snidely than necessary. He had always been somewhat jealous of Jim Otterman and all his many accomplishments, though Tony would never admit it to anyone.

"Good thing," agreed Jim with a crooked smile as he took the signed paper from Kevin and handed it to Nurse Redden. "We'll need the curator's signature, as well."

"Oh, that would be me, wouldn't it?" smiled Nurse Redden as she winked at Jim. "Just show me where to sign. I'm as anxious as you are to find out if the person buried in that grave is an imposter. We like to *know* who's buried in our cemetery!"

"Right there," pointed Jim as he handed her the pen.

Nurse Redden carefully signed the paper and handed it back to Jim with one hand as she handed Linda's pen back to her with the other.

Jim quickly snapped a photo of the fully executed document with his smartwatch before handing it back to Tony. "That should do it."

"Nurse Redden, will you be charging them any fees for the exhumation?" queried Tony as he folded the fully executed document and returned it to his suit pocket.

"Of course not," assured Nurse Redden as she waved him off.

"Can anyone who signs for the interment automatically sign for disinterment?" questioned Linda, who was interested.

"In most cases, yes," answered Bill, "provided the person is a close family member, but even heirs must get a court order in cases where they were not the ones to sign the original interment papers."

"So, where's the skip loader?" questioned Tony.

"Actually, I just texted the skip loader guy," advised Jim. "Apparently, he thought he was meeting us here after lunch."

"Perhaps we should all go get something to eat while we're waiting," suggested Bill as he flirted again with Linda.

135

"We serve a mean lunch in there," offered Nurse Redden with a wicked smile. "Chili beans and cornbread today."

"I've always wanted to eat at a mental institution," snickered Tony rather sarcastically.

Bill merely shrugged his shoulders and nodded. "Sure, why not? Let's have lunch at the looney bin. I'm hungry."

As the group followed Nurse Redden back toward the front entrance of the Ocean Bluff Mental Institution, Tony decided to razz Jim. "You know, you're pretty lucky Judge Law signed that order. Under modern law, courts usually do not allow exhumation unless there are substantial and compelling reasons to do so."

"I'm well aware of that," smirked Jim. "In the landmark U.S. Supreme Court decision of *Dougherty v. Mercantile Safe Deposit and Trust Company* in 1978, Justice Cardozo stated that, 'The dead are to rest where they have been lain unless reason of substance is brought forward for disturbing their repose.' I think this qualifies, don't you? In fact, there are three general principles that govern the law of disinterment in the United States. First, it is presumed that...."

"I get the idea!" snapped Tony. He was well aware of Jim's tendency to display his plethora of knowledge to unsuspecting listeners and was sorry already that he had opened the door to that conversation.

"Perhaps while we eat lunch, Kevin would like to pick up where he left off on the way over here," suggested Jim.

"I'm not sure I feel comfortable about it in front of so many people," mentioned Kevin.

"Why don't just the three of us go over there," motioned Jim. "I'm sure Nurse Redden can keep these other guys entertained."

"No food in the visiting room," cautioned Nurse Redden with finality. "But, there's no reason why you can't take your lunch outside and eat at one of the benches out there."

"That works," approved Kevin.

August 16, 1956

Bobby Sue could not help but notice as she held little Eric how closely he resembled Kevin. *What if Mark really couldn't tell them apart?*

Mark suddenly stabbed the pile of hay he had been unloading with the pitchfork and left it sticking there while he turned to face his approaching wives. There really wasn't much else he could do.

"How dare you!" screamed Maria as she unexpectedly charged at Mark and kicked him as hard as she could in the shin.

"How dare I?" laughed Mark as he grabbed little Kevin from her and roughly tossed him onto the bale of hay beside the pitch fork.

Kevin began screaming immediately, which caused Bobby Sue to dash over to where he was. She was still holding Maria's baby in her arms, who also began to cry.

By then, Mark had grabbed Maria by the arm and shoved her down onto the ground. *Should he kick her back?* Mark stood there glaring at Maria as he considered what he should do next.

"Go ahead!" screamed Maria. "It would be better than having to spend the rest of my life with *you!*"

"Take that screaming brat of yours and get!" commanded Mark as he let her go. "I'll deal with you later."

"Make me!" snapped Maria.

Enraged at being contradicted, Mark suddenly grabbed Maria by the hair and yanked her down again. "That can be arranged."

"Mark, no!" yelled Bobby Sue. "They would send you to prison for the rest of your life."

"Did I ask for your advice?" growled Mark as he finally let go of Maria again and shoved her away before starting toward Bobby Sue. "Why did you even bother to come?"

"So that you could meet your son," stuttered Bobby Sue. *Why was Mark acting this way?*

"Babies," laughed Mark. "How can you tell the difference?"

"Probably because they're both *yours,*" interjected Maria rather defiantly. "Bobby Sue is holding Eric. The one you just tossed over there is her child – little Kevin."

"I've heard enough," advised Mr. Johnson, who was now standing directly behind Mark holding the pitchfork and had it aimed toward him. "Maria, I suggest you take your child and go."

Mark started to leave with her, until feeling the points of the pitchfork against his back.

"Not you," specified Mr. Johnson. "You will be making a trip downtown with the Sheriff."

137

For a moment, Mark looked again as if he were going to try and make a run for it, but then decided against it.

"Good choice," fumed Bobby Sue's father. "My wife is calling the Sheriff right now."

Maria hurriedly came and took little Eric from Bobby Sue and then ran towards the rickety DeSoto.

"Wait! My suitcase is in the trunk," hollered Bobby Sue.

"Nothing that can't be replaced," assured Mr. Johnson. "I suggest you get that other child and go inside the house. Now!"

Bobby Sue thought of the barrel racing trophy inside her suitcase, and of the navy blue wool coat that Jill had given her and hesitated.

"Move!" commanded her father.

"Yes, sir," complied Bobby Sue as she scooped Kevin up and ran for the house. *She had planned on giving the belt buckle to Mark, anyway, hadn't she? Perhaps this was all a bad dream and she would wake up and find herself still at the bus station.*

It seemed like an eternity before her father came inside. Bobby Sue peered through the living room curtains, just in time to see the Sheriff's car pulling away with Mark Killingham in the back seat. Just at that moment, he turned to glare at Bobby Sue, causing her to shiver.

"I take it you fired him?" assumed his wife Evelyn.

"He's lucky that's all I did to him," advised Mr. Johnson as he shook his head with trepidation.

"This is Kevin," introduced Bobby Sue, rather nervously. "Your grandson."

"That illegitimate child is *not* my grandson and he can't stay here!" snapped Mr. Johnson. "First thing tomorrow morning, we'll be taking him downtown to Children's Services. I'm sure they can find an appropriate home for him."

"Father, please!" pleaded Bobby Sue. Tears were streaming down her face.

"I'm afraid his mind is made up," cautioned her mother as she poured herself another drink. "Better enjoy the time you have left with him, while you can."

Evelyn Johnson was a stay-at-home housewife who rarely spoke unless spoken to first. Although attractive when she was younger, the years had not been kind to her, particularly after burying

138

her troubles in a bottle for so many years. She had miscarried her other four children, leaving Bobby Sue as her only living child. Evelyn was lucid at the moment, but usually quite sauced by noon. Rum was her favorite poison, though she would consume whatever she could get her hands on when necessary. The stress of the current situation was too much for her and her hands had begun to tremble.

"Mother, please!" cried Bobby Sue. "Do something!"

"Like your father said, you'd best go to your room now," suggested Evelyn. "I'll be along shortly. I would like to see my grandson while I can, too."

"That child is NOT your grandson!" shouted Mr. Johnston as he stormed from the house. "And if Mark Killingham *ever* comes near our daughter again, I'll kill him!"

Both Evelyn and Bobby Sue jumped when Mr. Johnson slammed the kitchen door so hard that it broke off the top hinge and remained hanging at an odd angle.

"Best let him stew for a while," recommended her mother as she drank down an entire glass of rum in one swig before pouring herself another.

"Mother, please, don't do this to yourself," begged Bobby Sue. "Come with me. I know a place we can both go to be safe. We can take Kevin with us."

"Please don't tell me where it is," stammered Evelyn. "I wouldn't want your father finding out if he manages to beat it out of me."

"You'll help us leave, then?" Bobby Sue was hopeful.

"You'd best wait 'til your father's sound asleep tonight," described Evelyn as she staggered toward a picture on the wall and moved it aside. Behind it was the family safe where money and other valuables were kept. Evelyn hesitated before remembering the combination and then fumbled with it several times before finally managing to open it.

"Father will kill *you* when he finds out," feared Bobby Sue.

"Good," stuttered Evelyn. "I've had about all I can take of this, anyway." Evelyn then reached for and removed two small stacks of bills that were neatly wrapped with paper money bands. "There should be a hundred bucks in each stack."

"Oh, mother, we just can't," objected Bobby Sue.

139

"It's from selling Moose," informed Evelyn as she shoved the money at her. "Take it. It should be yours."

Bobby Sue's lower lip quivered as she thought of poor Moose. "Mother, what did happen to him, anyway?"

"Some man from out of town wanted a breeder," revealed Evelyn. "It's doubtful he's hamburger yet."

"Thank you!" wept Bobby Sue as she took the money and gave her mother a brief hug with Kevin still in her arms.

"You'd better get to your room before he comes back," urged Evelyn as she hurried to close the safe and put the picture back on the wall over it. "I love you, sweetheart!"

"I love you, too," replied Bobby Sue as she gave her mother another hug before hurrying up to her room with Kevin.

She would need to work fast to get everything ready. There would be little that she could take with her when she left. She would need to tear up some old rags and make diapers, too. Most importantly, she could not let her father find her in the middle of packing when he returned. She would need to hide her suitcase beneath the bed. *Did she still have the other suitcase?*

Bobby Sue had finally managed to get Kevin cleaned up and put down for a nap in the center of her bed. The peanut butter and jelly sandwich she had made herself for dinner that night sat half eaten on her dresser beside a half-consumed glass of milk. It was already well past 10:00. A rapid succession of knocks on her bedroom door caused her heart to race. *It was her father!*

"May I come in?" asked Mr. Johnson. "Are you decent?"

Bobby Sue swallowed hard before responding. "Come in."

Mr. Johnson walked over to the bed and sat down beside little Kevin, careful not to wake him up. After staring at him for several minutes, he sadly shook his head and turned to look at his daughter. "Why?"

"Because you sold Moose like you did," answered Bobby Sue.

He could tell by the way her lower lip quivered that she was ready to begin crying again.

"Where did your mother and I go wrong?" questioned her father.

Bobby Sue merely hung her head. She had no response.

"May I hold him?" asked her father.

"Why?" shrugged Bobby Sue. "All you plan to do is just give him away!"

Mr. Johnson tenderly picked up little Kevin and held him for several minutes, sadly shaking his head. "I'm sorry it has to be this way, Bobby Sue, but someday you'll thank me."

Was he going to take Kevin away right now? worried Bobby Sue. *How would she get him back in time before leaving?*

"Like your mother said," advised her father, "enjoy the time you have with him. Tomorrow will come soon enough." Mr. Johnson then carefully put Kevin back onto the bed.

Bobby Sue sighed with deep relief as she watched her father get up to leave, without Kevin.

"We'll talk more in the morning," promised her father. He was not looking forward to it.

"Yes, sir," agreed Bobby Sue as she watched him turn to leave.

Pausing at the door, her father added, "I hope you realize that this is for the best."

Bobby Sue merely nodded as he left and closed the door behind him. *She didn't dare try to sleep now, or she might not wake up in time. Did she have everything she needed? She sure hoped so!*

April 24, 2023

It was almost 2:00 in the afternoon before the skip loader could be seen slowly making its way up the circular drive in front of the Ocean Bluff Mental Institution. The 1989 John Deere Skip Loader had seen better days.

"It's about time they got here," muttered Jim. "You can tell me all about how Bobby Sue made her escape later, on our way back to the lighthouse."

"How come you never mentioned any of this to me?" Linda whispered to Kevin.

"I don't know," replied Kevin. "Until today, I didn't even want to think about it."

"And now?"

"Now, all I want to do is find that son of a gun and make sure he gets what's coming to him," answered Kevin through gritted teeth.

"Within the bounds of the law," reminded Jim with a knowing look. "And, provided he's still alive." Jim was always doing that, overhearing things other people said with his excellent hearing.

"We'd better let your friends know the guy's here," pointed out Linda. She was as anxious as they were to get on with the exhumation.

"Do you mind getting them?" asked Jim. "Kevin and I can meet the rest of you out back."

"I'd be happy to," agreed Linda as she got up and headed for the elaborately carved front doors of the institution. After pausing to admire it, she lifted the huge brass lion-head door knocker and let it fall against the huge brass plate beneath it.

Nurse Redden's rubber soles were virtually inaudible in their approach, so Linda was startled when the large front doors suddenly opened. Bill and Tony could be seen sitting in the visiting room behind her by the front desk.

"The skip loader's here," called Linda, to get their attention.

"Shh!" advised Nurse Redden as she put her finger to her lips. "Just because you're here to dig up a dead person, doesn't mean you need to try and wake the dead, too!"

"Sorry, ma'am," apologized Linda.

"Thank God!" exclaimed Tony as he and Bill got up and made a beeline for the front entrance.

"Jim and Kevin are out back," informed Linda as she turned to head out there.

Nurse Redden had been giving Tony and Bill a complete history of the Ocean Bluff Mental Institution, along with its policies and procedures, and was about to resume her narrative.

"I think we've heard enough," remarked Tony as he put a hand on her upper back to indicate that she should go first.

"Very informative, though," interjected Bill. *Even though he had been bored to tears, there was no reason to be rude.*

"You're very welcome," Nurse Redden smiled at Bill as she turned to follow after Linda.

"How long have you worked here?" Linda decided to ask her.

"Well, my mother had me when she worked here as head nurse, so I guess you could say I was born and raised right here," answered Nurse Redden.

"Where is your mother now?"

"Died earlier this year," explained Nurse Redden. "Right here, in her room. She was 97 years old."

"Really?" Linda was surprised. "You don't look a day over 50."

"I'm 47," advised Nurse Redden with some indignance. "My mother was 50 years old when she had me."

"What about your father?" pressed Linda.

"Name was Redden, but I never knew him."

"Was he a patient here?"

"I believe so, yes," replied Nurse Redden.

Tony and Bill exchanged a look of concern.

"Don't tell me you've spent your *entire* life here?" grilled Linda, hardly able to comprehend such a thing.

"I'm afraid so," shrugged Nurse Redden as she deeply inhaled the fresh ocean breeze and gazed at the ocean view below. "I could think of worse places to live."

"It is beautiful here," admitted Linda, "but, don't you ever worry about being around so many patients all the time?"

"Not particularly," grinned Nurse Redden. "Besides, who's to say who's sane or who's not – some of the sanest people I've ever known reside right here within these walls."

"And you *are* head nurse now?" questioned Tony, to make sure.

"That, I am," confirmed Nurse Redden as she narrowed her eyes at him. She did not particularly care for Tony.

Tony merely shook his head.

The aging skip loader was finally beside them, making its way across the lawn parallel to the walkway, on the other side of the flowerbed. The noise from its engine was becoming increasingly difficult to hear above, so Linda and the others continued their trek in silence until reaching the cemetery.

"Jim," yelled Tony, to be heard above the noise as he approached him and put one hand on his shoulder, "Do we know how much longer this will take?"

"It takes as long as it takes," advised Jim. "Besides, due to the fact that this person may be the victim of a homicide, I'll need both of you here as witnesses to preserve the chain of custody."

"Custody of what?" frowned Tony.

143

"Why, the casket of course," replied Jim with an imperceptible smile. "And the body inside. You two are the ones who originally signed the death certificate for Mark Killingham, are you not?"

Bill Huong nodded with understanding. *No wonder Jim had insisted on both of them being there.*

"Right over there, sir," pointed Jim as he hurried over to the grave and indicated to the skip loader driver which one.

The man merely nodded as he set up for the dig.

"Just how long were you the Sheriff of this town, anyway?" Bill suddenly asked Jim while the skip loader began its task.

"Longer than I've been the Mayor," grinned Jim, "but I'm still your boss, either way."

"Indeed," acknowledged Tony with a slight sneer.

"Tell me again why you think this isn't Mark?" asked Bill.

"Because Kevin and Linda actually saw and spoke with Mark subsequent to this person's burial," reminded Jim.

"That's right. It was in 2016 when we last saw him at the fish market in Seattle," corroborated Linda.

"Not only that," continued Jim, "there is the fact that Mark Killingham had an identical twin brother."

"Really?" Bill and Tony both seemed surprised.

"Who just happened to drop off the grid in 2009, right around the time that Mark Killingham allegedly died," described Jim.

"Did the guy have a name?" questioned Bill with a concerned look on his face. *How could something like this happen?*

"Jack Killingham, Jr.," revealed Jim. "My law firm will be looking into this, as well. You can count on it."

"Didn't you say something about Mark Killingham having had a broken arm at one point?" reminded Kevin.

"He sure did," Bill answered for Jim. "I was the one who set his arm when he broke it back in 2007, only two years before he died."

"Why would Mark have a medical examiner set his arm?" questioned Kevin.

"I also have a family practice in town," explained Bill. "And I do happen to have patients waiting for me right now – live ones."

"I think you'll find that your receptionist has rescheduled all your appointments for today," grinned Jim with a crooked smile.

Bill just shook his head, laughed, and then commented for the others, "I should hate it when he does that, but Jim always makes it

144

worth my while. Besides, if anything urgent comes up, I suppose there's always the 24-hour clinic."

Kevin raised an eyebrow at that and then turned to watch while more and more dirt was removed from the top of Mark Killingham's gravesite. *Who really was in that grave?*

"I'd better go get the hand shovels," realized Jim. "I'll be right back. They're in the Jeep."

"Hand shovels?" frowned Linda as she watched Jim leave. "What for? Don't they have to dig for at least six feet with the skip loader and then just yank it out with chains or something?"

"It's not that simple," chuckled Tony. Even when he smiled, it did not include his eyes. "That was only back when they needed to bury bodies deeply enough to keep wild animals from digging them up."

Everyone else but Linda laughed at that.

"He's right," confirmed Bill with a wide grin. "These days they put caskets in cement liners to protect them, so they don't need to go as deep. In fact, the very bottom of the cement liner would be about five feet down."

"How big is the cement thing?" frowned Linda.

"The cement liner is usually 30 inches wide, 30 inches high, and 86 inches long," elaborated Bill, who was becoming friendlier with Linda than Kevin felt comfortable with.

"Once they get to a certain point, they'll need to dig the rest out by hand," interjected Kevin.

"That makes sense," realized Linda.

"So, there would only be about 18 to 20 inches of dirt on top of the cement liner," added Bill with a wink at Linda.

"I have my best suit on," advised Tony as he watched Jim returning from his Jeep with the shovels.

"Me, too," shrugged Bill. "Not that it matters now."

"I'm sure Jim and I can handle it," volunteered Kevin, who had on his blue jeans, cowboy boots and a 10-gallon hat.

"I can still probably help," suggested Bill.

Just then, Jim returned with the shovels in time to hear Bill's offer. "Nonsense! We wouldn't want you ruining your good suit."

Kevin took a deep breath, shook his head, and reached for the other shovel. Bill merely shrugged in acquiescence.

"I can help, too," advised Juan, who had just shut off the engine and climbed down from the skip loader. He then reached for and pulled a hand shovel from beneath its seat but glanced with disapproval at the two suits. "Always come prepared, gentlemen."

"Exactly!" grinned Jim as he, Kevin and Juan began to dig. Jim's blue jeans were newer than Kevin's, but he had no compunction about getting them dirty.

A gust of ocean breeze unexpectedly swept over them, momentarily causing the heavy wet dirt on their shovels to seem even heavier than it was. The loud screech of a seagull flying past overhead was immediately followed by a sticky white deposit onto the headstone beside them. Kevin could not help but chuckle about it.

The diggers all paused to glace upward – as did everyone else – just to make sure no other seagulls were above them.

"They did the same thing to our car on the way up here," laughed Linda. "Messy things!"

The seagull could suddenly be seen circling nearby and then diving toward the shoreline below.

"Even he seems to know there's something fishy about that grave," commented Nurse Redden with her hands on her hips.

"We shall see," replied Bill, who had stepped closer to get a better look. "Hold on a minute." The others stopped digging while Bill knelt down in the mud and brushed what remained from the top of the cement lid on the casket liner. "We should at least double check the numbers before we go pulling off the lid."

The heavy lid of the cement grave liner had a series of numbers on it that had previously been stamped right onto the lid when the cement was still green.

"3-23-09-79-66? Is that right?" questioned Kevin. "Isn't March 23, 1930 supposed to be his birth date? Is that what the 3-23 part of it designates?"

"Apparently, March 23 was also his death date," advised Nurse Redden as she motioned toward the headstone beside them. "Looks like he died in 2009. The poor old guy must have died on his birthday, if it's him."

"The 79 indicates his age at the time of death," added Tony, who was familiar with the numbering system.

"What's the 66 for?" grilled Kevin.

146

"Why, the plot number, of course," revealed Nurse Redden. "This is space number 66."

"Of course, it is!" Linda rolled her eyes.

"What's the point of putting a cement grave liner around the casket, anyway?" questioned Linda. "Especially if they're just going to bury it in the ground."

"To preserve it as well as possible," advised Bill, "perhaps in case someone should ever come along later and decide to do what we're doing now."

"What we need at this point is a couple of crowbars," realized Jim. "One for each end. That lid looks pretty heavy."

"It weighs 300 pounds," advised Tony. *It felt good for once to know something that Jim didn't. Surely, he didn't plan to use a crowbar on it?* Tony began to smile.

"Crowbars?" laughed Bill. "Juan, where are the hooks?"

"Hang on," replied Juan as he retrieved a large sling from a compartment under the seat of the skip loader.

"We need to put the hooks on first," directed Tony.

"Well, I had to get the sling out first in order to get to them!" snapped Juan. Like the others, Juan was becoming increasingly irritated with Tony.

"If you'll look more closely at the concrete lid," elaborated Tony for Jim's benefit, "there are wire loops on each corner. They were cast right into the lid when the concrete was still wet."

Jim merely nodded and laughed. "Oh, okay. I see."

"Here we are," indicated Juan as he climbed down from the skip loader with four large hooks and attached one to each corner. Fastened to each hook was a four-foot section of sturdy chain.

"Nice," approved Jim as he grabbed the opposite ends of each chain and bundled them together in the center above the concrete lid with a large carabiner that still hung from one of the chains.

Juan then climbed back onto the skip loader, whose engine was still running, and steered the bucket over to where Jim stood holding the large carabiner that all four chains were clipped to.

"Just hook the carabiner right over the arm of the bucket," directed Juan. Jim quickly attached the carabiner to the hydraulic arm of the bucket and then jumped out of the way.

"The bottom part of that cement liner alone – even without the lid – weighs 700 pounds," added Tony with an irrepressible smile.

Linda merely nodded as she folded her arms and walked around to the other side of the huge pile of dirt, partly to distance herself from Tony and also to be where the shade of an overhanging cypress tree offered respite from the sun.

Nurse Redden immediately joined her. "Good thing it isn't hot today." It was already almost four o'clock.

"Good thing," replied Linda as she watched the cement lid being raised and moved over to one side.

Then, even though Juan tried to lower the lid as carefully as possible, the impact tremor of it coming into contact with the ground beside the open grave could easily be felt by everyone.

"Beautiful casket," admired Linda.

"That's the Royal Sunset model," recognized Tony. "It's made of 18-gauge steel with an ebony finish. They sell for about $10,000, depending on the internal amenities."

"Internal amenities?" scoffed Kevin. "It's just a coffin."

"It also has a lock on it," noticed Linda as she moved closer for a better look.

"We won't be opening it here, anyway," advised Jim. "They'll need to do that at the coroner's office."

"I have no problem with them opening it here," assured Kevin.

"No can do," advised Jim. "They still need to follow protocol and open it there. The contents of this casket must be treated as a crime scene – just in case it is."

"Absolutely," agreed Bill. "Thankfully, the Royal Sunset model is made of 18-gauge steel, so it should endure being lifted out of that liner with just a sling. A wooden casket, on the other hand, would be completely disintegrated by now and would crumble to pieces if we tried to lift it out."

"It's only been 14 years," mentioned Linda.

"That's long enough to do it," interjected Tony, "especially with the moisture and temperature changes over time. But, if this man had been buried in the mausoleum, then that would be a different story."

"What he means," clarified Jim, "is that there is no moisture inside the mausoleum, only temperature changes."

"So?" scowled Linda.

148

"The lack of moisture would basically cause the body to become mummified over time," added Tony with a triumphant glance at Jim.

"Excuse me, gentlemen," interrupted Juan as he proceeded to slide the sling beneath the coffin. "Good thing it's still got feet."

Kevin and Linda watched with interest as Juan slid the huge sling beneath the coffin, into the space created by its short sturdy feet. Juan then shoved the sling as far under the coffin as he could with the handle of his shovel.

"I got it," advised Jim from the other side as he reached down to grab it and pull it up.

"Hold it!" commanded Kevin. "Why don't you guys just use one of those casket-lowering devices? Wouldn't that be a lot easier?"

"A casket-lowering device is a highly specialized piece of equipment," chimed in Tony. "Any attempt to *raise* a casket with it would completely strip the gears."

"Not only that," interjected Bill, "a device like that runs the City about $5,000. Not something the taxpayers would be anxious to replace if they didn't have to."

"Is this sling made of the same type of material as the nylon webbing straps they usually have on those devices?" asked Jim, who was curious about how strong the sling actually was.

"Yes!" assured Tony. "Now, can we please get on with this?"

"What's your hurry?" questioned Jim as he and Juan hooked the sling to the carabiner that had previously been used to raise the cement liner lid. "You do enjoy your job, don't you?"

"Yes, I'm sorry, sir," apologized Tony.

"Restroom's inside," mentioned Nurse Redden with a smirk. It was obvious to her what Tony's problem was.

"Thanks," nodded Tony. "I'll be back."

"We can't wait," snickered Linda as she rolled her eyes.

"Just like before," directed Juan as he steered the hydraulic arm and bucket toward Jim.

Once Jim had managed to attach the carabiner to the arm of the skip loader again, he sprightly stepped to one side to watch with the others while the casket was raised and successfully transferred onto a waiting casket dolly. It could then be pushed to the waiting hearse.

"Bill, the first thing I'd like you to do is take an x-ray of his arm and compare it to the old x-ray you have in your file from 2007," directed Jim. "That should tell us what we need to know."

"And if we don't find what we're looking for?" prompted Bill.

"Then you look until you find it," instructed Jim. "DNA testing could prove whether or not this man was closely related to Mark."

"I'm sorry, Jim," apologized Bill, "but a DNA sample from Mark Killingham is one thing I don't have. However, the next best thing would be a sample from a close relative, like Kevin here."

"We'll follow you into town then," advised Jim.

"Wait just a minute," objected Kevin. "What kind of DNA sample are we talking about?"

"Probably a blood draw would be the simplest and most accurate," described Bill.

"And that's it, nothing else?"

"We could always drill into your leg and get a bone marrow sample," teased Bill.

"What!?" questioned Kevin.

"I'm kidding," laughed Bill. "The blood draw will be virtually painless. Well, almost."

August 17, 1956

Bobby Sue cautiously picked up the green Army duffel bag containing her things. Unfortunately, she had not been able to find the other suitcase. Fortunately, she had failed to return the duffel bag to her father after borrowing it the previous summer for girls' camp. That seemed like a lifetime ago.

It was 3:00 in the morning and she dare not wait any longer. Often, her father was up by 4:00 to begin his morning regime of chores.

After making sure her belongings were not too heavy for her to carry, Bobby Sue slipped the huge bag onto her back, picked up Kevin, and crept toward her bedroom door. *There was a light on downstairs! It was her father! What was he doing up this time of night? What was she going to do?*

Bobby Sue realized at once that she would have to climb out the bedroom window, though being upstairs presented some risks.

After tying her bedsheets together, end-to-end, Bobby Sue carefully tied one end to the duffel bag and began lowering it from the open bedroom window. Thankfully, she had left the window open earlier, especially since it had a squeaky hinge! Once the duffel bag made it safely to the flowerbed below, she carefully let go of the sheets so they would drop on top of it. *She could take them, too, and use them later for diaper material. What if her father should go outside before she could manage to get down there?*

"We can do this," she whispered to Kevin as she wrapped him lengthwise in an old green Army blanket. It had also belonged to her dad and gone to girls' camp with her the previous summer. Like the duffel bag, it was identifiable by a serial number stamped onto it.

Bobby Sue carefully tied two opposite corners of the blanket containing Kevin into a secure square knot before slipping it over her head and one shoulder. She had seen a documentary once at school showing mothers from third world countries carrying around their infants like that. *If they can do it, so can I,* reasoned Bobby Sue as she cautiously began to climb from the window with Kevin hanging in the large sling.

She would need to negotiate the narrow ledge for at least 15 feet before reaching her mother's rose trellis. From there, she should be able to climb down with relative ease. She had on the well-worn riding boots given to her by Jill, and there was no telling how far she might have to walk in them. She had cut off the end of a pillow case and made a secret money pouch that was sewed to the bottom of her bra in the front where it would be easy to get to but hidden beneath her long-sleeved flannel shirt. She even had on an old pair of blue jeans, even though it was not considered ladylike for a woman to wear them in 1956.

Hopefully, her father would not go to the kitchen, where he might look out the window and see her. Kevin suddenly began to whimper. "Shhh!" whispered Bobby Sue as she nearly lost her balance.

After pausing to stabilize herself – and so Kevin would go back to sleep – Bobby Sue continued. *We can do this!* Progress was slower than she would have liked. *Would they make it there before her father went to the kitchen for his morning cup of coffee?*

A loose brick on the ledge started to give way, but Bobby Sue managed to step around it. The cool night air did little to relieve the sweat now dripping down her face and back. *One wrong step and it would be all over.* The full moon offered some light, but not much. *The stars are sure beautiful tonight,* noticed Bobby Sue as she glanced up.

Finally reaching the trellis, Bobby Sue began her descent. That was when she heard her father's voice from inside.

"Bobby Sue, come down here," commanded her father. "We need to talk."

Had he been sitting there all night, just waiting for this moment?

The sound of her father's footsteps on the stairway leading upstairs toward her room echoed through the quiet house.

Bobby Sue jumped the last two feet to the ground and raced for the duffel bag. There was not time to fold up the sheets, so she hurriedly stuffed them into the top of it, slung the bag over her other shoulder, and ran for it. Kevin had woken back up and was beginning to cry.

"Kevin, it's okay," whispered Bobby Sue in what she hoped was a soothing voice. Carrying both Kevin and the duffel bag at the same time was more difficult than she had anticipated.

She had wanted to make it to the barn and hide in the loft until morning. But, now that Kevin was crying, she needed to be on her way as quickly as possible. The sound of a coyote in the distance caused her to hesitate. *Was this a mistake? No, it was not! She must not let them take Kevin away from her. Otherwise, she might never see him again!*

By morning, her father would no doubt be out looking for her, if not before! *Would she manage to elude him? She needed to get to a phone as soon as possible so she could call Peter.*

It was 37 miles from the Johnson Ranch to Sprague, so walking the entire distance in one day was out of the question. Hitchhiking was also out of the question, since people would be searching for her. There was a small country market about a mile away with a phonebooth outside. Sadly, all she had were the two stacks of bills her mother had given her from the family safe, but no coins. Sometimes, however, change could be found on the ground near phonebooths, and for long distance calls, it was usually necessary only to click the receiver until an operator came onto the line.

152

August 18, 1956

"Peter! Peter!" hollered Jill as she raced up to his cabin on Walter, hopped down and quickly tied him to the doorpost. Thankfully, there was a full moon and no alligators or snakes could be seen in the vicinity.

The front porchlight suddenly came on and a half-awake Peter opened the door. "What time is it?"

"It's 3:00 in the morning," advised Jill.

"What's wrong?" frowned Peter. "Isn't today Saturday?" *Was something wrong with one of the animals?*

"I just got a call from Bobby Sue!" exclaimed Jill. "She's in trouble and needs our help. Right away!"

"What kind of trouble?" frowned Peter.

"Just get dressed and come to the house as fast as possible," instructed Jill. "We're driving out to get her."

"Where is she?" asked Peter, who was suddenly wide awake.

"In Washington, of course," reminded Jill.

"What did she say when she called?" demanded Peter.

"She's hiding out in a shed behind some country market with Kevin, just a mile north of the Johnson Ranch," described Jill. "Pretty much in the middle of nowhere. Things did not go as expected with Mark, and now her father wants to turn Kevin over to Children's Services – unless we get there in time to stop it."

"Give me five minutes, I'll be right there."

"I figured you would be, but don't keep me waiting or I'm leaving without you," cautioned Jill as she quickly untied Walter, hopped on his back and took off at a full gallop.

Neither of Jill's other ranch hands was overly enthusiastic about being called at 3:15 in the morning, but both were easily persuaded to take on the responsibility of caring for the entire Circle K Ranch for a few days after being promised an adequate bonus.

Jill rapidly threw a change of clothes into an overnight bag and tossed it into the trunk of her late husband's baby blue Plymouth convertible, whose top was currently up. She was still wearing her riding clothes, but that didn't matter. Time was of the essence. Jill then grabbed several cans of beans, a can opener, and a loaf of bread,

153

and put them into a cardboard box, along with some extra silverware and plates. *Would that be enough for the trip?*

"What about water?" questioned Peter from behind her as he handed her two canteens.

Jill had been so involved in her preparations that she hadn't heard him ride up.

"Walter and Fred are unsaddled and wiped down," informed Peter. "They're in the barn together."

"Excellent," approved Jill. "Can you please fill the canteens while I go get that sack of oranges?"

Peter nodded as he raced for the garden hose and turned it on. "I hope you plan to elaborate on what's happened."

"On the way," promised Jill as she tossed the sack of oranges into the trunk, closed the lid, and climbed into the vehicle to wait for Peter.

"Did you reach the other hands?" questioned Peter as he climbed into the driver's seat. He was concerned about the animals, especially one of the longhorns that was getting ready to give birth any day.

"All taken care of," replied Jill. "Let's go!"

Just as Peter started to pull away, Jill remembered that her purse was still sitting on the hall table inside. "Wait! My purse."

Peter slammed on the brake, backed up, and put the car into park as he waited for Jill to hurry inside and retrieve it.

Once inside, Jill glanced inside her purse and noticed that all she had was $15 in cash. *We're going to need more than that!*

Jill raced upstairs to her room and retrieved a shoebox from the top shelf of her closet. It contained her entire life savings. Jill never had trusted banks. *How much should she take?*

After only a moment's hesitation, Jill grabbed a handful of bills and stuffed them into her purse. She then put the lid back onto the shoebox and returned it to its secret hiding place.

"Oh, heck!" cursed Jill as she paused again to open her purse back up on the bed. *She had better count it. The last thing they needed was to run out of money during a long-distance trip.*

Jill took a deep breath and began counting.

154

"$700 should be plenty!" acknowledged Jill with satisfaction as she returned the money to her purse, grabbed a sweater, and hurried back downstairs.

"I thought you were in a hurry," teased Peter as Jill climbed back into the car with her purse and sweater.

"I just needed to check everything one last time before leaving," explained Jill. "Everything's good. Let's go!"

Peter put the car back into drive and started out again. "So, what's the deal with Mark and Bobby Sue?"

Jill hesitated before answering.

"Well?" pressed Peter.

"The crumb already had another wife and family!" fumed Jill.

"Really?"

"Five boys," added Jill with disgust. "The youngest was born just 11 days before Kevin!"

"No kidding?" Peter shook his head with disbelief.

"There was some big confrontation between Mark and the wives," continued Jill.

"And?"

"That was when Mr. Johnson showed up and threatened Mark with a pitchfork," described Jill. "Bobby Sue said he held it to him until the Sheriff showed up and hauled Mark away."

"Mark was arrested?" Peter began to smile. They had reached the main road and were headed toward Mobile.

"And now Mr. Johnson wants to turn Kevin over to Children's Services," added Jill. "That's why we need to get there just as soon as we can. We can take turns driving if we need to."

"How could someone just turn their own grandchild over to Social Services like that?" scowled Peter.

"Bobby Sue is underage, unmarried, and there's really nothing she can do to stop them from taking Kevin away from her if that's what her parents choose to do," summarized Jill.

"What if I were to ask her father for permission to marry her?" proposed Peter.

"He could easily say no," pointed out Jill. "And then, it would be too late. Kevin would go to some foster home or maybe even an orphanage somewhere, and Bobby Sue would never see him again."

155

"What about me?" frowned Peter. "Kevin already thinks I'm his daddy."

"Do you care about him?"

"Of course I do," replied Peter. "I've already asked Bobby Sue to marry me and let me adopt him."

"Then we better not let her or Kevin down," advised Jill. "I care about Kevin, too! I've come to think of him as a grandchild."

Peter and Jill rode in silence for nearly an hour after that, each lost in his or her own thoughts.

"I know!" Jill suddenly exclaimed.

"What?" Peter had been so startled by Jill's outburst that he nearly drove off the road.

"I have a cousin who lives in Montana," revealed Jill. "He's got a ranch out there and is always looking for hands."

"What's the age requirement for marriage in Montana?"

"It doesn't matter," assured Jill. "All you need to do is marry Bobby Sue in Alabama first and then you'll already be married when you get there."

"What if her parents find us?" worried Peter. "Or Mark?"

"Once I explain to my cousin that an abusive ex-husband is on the hunt to do Bobby Sue and Kevin harm if he finds them, I'm sure he'll agree to hire you on and keep his mouth shut," elaborated Jill. "He owes me one, anyway."

April 24, 2023

It was 7:30 in the evening. Kevin and Linda had just finished eating a delicious meal of meatloaf, baked potato and green salad in the tower room of the lighthouse with Jim and Sheree.

"Wow!" Sheree shook her head. "Someday you really should write a book about all your mother's adventures."

"I doubt that," snorted Kevin. "I think most of her experiences with Mark Killingham are things she'd just as soon forget."

"So, did Jill and Peter ever get there in time?" asked Sheree. She had become quite engrossed in the tale.

"Uh, we're going to have to resume that later," interrupted Jim. "We're scheduled for a three-way conference call at 8:00 with Bill and Chip, so we need to get everything set up."

"Bill and Chip?" questioned Kevin.

"Bill Huong, the medical examiner that you met today, and Chip Priest, who is one of the partners in my firm," clarified Jim. "He's only up in Ocean Bay, so we're all in the same time zone."

"Do you think Bill has the results of the DNA test back yet?" wondered Linda.

"That's one of the things we hope to find out," described Jim.

"Hey guys," acknowledged Ted Jensen as he entered the tower room of the lighthouse carrying an older computer.

"This is our son-in-law, Ted," introduced Sheree as she proceeded to clear the dinner dishes from the table.

"Hello again," smiled Ted as he reached with one hand for a small slice of meatloaf from the platter Sheree was carrying.

"Better not get that on Ann's computer," warned Sheree.

"I wouldn't dream of it," grinned Ted as he devoured the piece of meatloaf while setting down the computer.

Ted was an extremely handsome Polynesian man, well-tanned from his many hours spent surfing, and in excellent physical condition. His shoulder-length hair was neatly pulled back into a ponytail. Kevin gritted his teeth when he noticed the continued attraction between Ted and Linda, despite the fact that she was clearly old enough to be his mother. Ted had flirted with Linda at the ice cream shop earlier, too.

"Fire it up," indicated Jim, who was already busy pulling up information on his own laptop.

"Sure thing," complied Ted.

"And this is Kevin and Linda," added Sheree, when it became obvious that Jim was not going to make the introductions.

"We've met. I'm Ann's husband," advised Ted as he pulled up a chair and sat down beside Linda to turn on Ann's computer.

"And I'm hers," indicated Kevin with a nod of his head at Linda.

"Nice to officially meet you both." Ted was oblivious to the innuendo, though it was not lost on the others.

"Let me just remote into it from here," muttered Jim as he keyed in the IP address of Ann's computer. "I can't stand Ann's ergonomic keyboard. Okay, where does she keep her genealogy notes? I'll need to refer to them during the conference call."

"Go to the desktop and click on the icon that says *Killingham*," suggested Ted with a crooked grin as he watched the cursor in front of him begin to move on its own at Jim's behest.

157

Just then Jim's smartwatch began to play the theme from *Man From U.N.C.L.E.*, a television series that had been popular in the 1960s.

"Sorry," grinned Jim. "I thought it was on mute. "Hello?"

"Jim this is Bill. Am I on speaker?"

"Yes, but can't this wait until our conference call at 8:00?"

"It could, but I thought you might like to know as soon as possible that we took two x-rays of each arm," described Bill.

"Don't keep us in suspense," replied Jim as he clicked on the *Killingham* icon.

"There was a broken arm, alright," advised Bill

Kevin and Linda began shaking their heads in the negative. *That just wasn't possible!*

"But," added Bill, "it was the left arm, not the right."

There was dead silence for several moments.

"Jim? Are you still there?"

"Yes. I'm certain it was Mark's right arm that was broken," remembered Jim.

"That's right," corroborated Bill. "I still have the x-ray from 2007 to prove it."

"So, it isn't Mark?"

"I'm afraid not," confirmed Bill. "We even located and compared the old dental records. It's definitely not him."

Jim sighed deeply and pursed his lips.

"Jim, I've put a rush on the DNA test and should have something by late tomorrow morning," added Bill.

"Good," approved Jim.

"Oh yes, the autopsy photos clearly show the decedent's face," informed Bill, "and it compares *exactly* to a photo taken of Mark that time we were at the golf tournament together in 2008. This guy just had to be his twin brother. There's no other explanation."

"Thanks for letting us know," mentioned Jim. "We'll continue this discussion at 8:00 on the conference call. I want Chip to be in the loop and up to speed on everything we've got so far."

"'Til then," bid Bill before hanging up.

"So, Mark's really still out there?" questioned Sheree.

"We already knew that," reminded Kevin.

"That we did," sighed Linda.

"Sheree, can you please fire up another laptop for the conference call?" asked Jim.

"I'll be right back with it," promised Sheree.

"Hurry, we've only got 20 minutes," reminded Jim. Then, turning to Kevin, Jim continued, "Okay, Kevin, in the time we have left before the conference call, I need you to *briefly* summarize all known contacts made between Mark Killingham and you or your mother. Besides what you've already told me. Can you do that for me?"

Kevin put his hands together in steeple shape, with the tips of his fingers touching. "Well, after my mother and Peter got married and moved to Montana in 1956, there was no contact until about 1961."

"How did he find you?" grilled Jim.

"There was a traveling rodeo that came to town, near where we lived, so my mother decided to try her hand at barrel racing again," revealed Kevin.

"Did she win?" asked Linda.

"Later," insisted Jim. "Right now, we're only interested in the contacts with Mark."

"Mark had signed up to work as a rodeo clown for the outfit," described Kevin, "and was there when she showed up for the event."

"He probably found the belt buckle trophy in her things from before and figured she would eventually compete in another rodeo," guessed Jim. "Go on."

"There was a horrible encounter between Mark and Peter at the barn while she was racing," continued Kevin. "It was not until she finished the event and found her husband left for dead that she realized Mark had been there. She knew for sure it was him because she saw Mark walking toward the DeSoto. Peter had a broken collar bone."

"Oh, my God!" exclaimed Linda. "And you never bothered to think I would want to know something like that?"

"Well, I had no intention of ever seeing the man again, anyway!" snapped Kevin. "Plus, I didn't want you to worry about it. I figured we'd both been through enough already."

"Enough, you two," interjected Jim. "Where was the younger *you* at that point?"

"Apparently, I was taken to his vehicle," continued Kevin.

"Attempted kidnapping," nodded Jim as he wrote that down. "And how did your mother get you back?"

"She ran over there right then, grabbed me, and screamed for the security guards to arrest him," elaborated Kevin.

"Which they did?" presumed Jim.

"No," replied Kevin. "He was somehow able to talk them out of it. They finally agreed to just let him go, provided he would go away and leave us alone after that."

"Did he?"

"Not really," recalled Kevin. "While my stepdad was in the hospital, my mother packed up everything we had and moved our stuff the very next day. I was five years old by then, so I do remember trying to help her. Mostly, I just got in the way."

"Did Mark try to come see you guys before you managed to get moved?" pressed Jim.

"No, I don't think so."

"What about after that?"

"About a year later, while I was in school one day, he showed up there and tried to have me pulled from class, but I never actually saw him," related Kevin.

"Then how did you know it was him?"

"Because my mother told me that the same man who had tried to take me at the rodeo was who it was. She just omitted the part about him being my real father. Unknown to me, the school had called my mother to verify that my father was actually picking me up, since they had never seen the man before."

"And then?"

"My mother had them keep me at the nurse's office until she could get there," recalled Kevin.

"What did Mark do then?"

"I have no idea," admitted Kevin. "They must have asked him to leave. All I know is that I was permanently pulled out of school, right then and there, and was home schooled after that until junior high."

"But you were never aware that the man who had tried to kidnap you at the rodeo or from school was your real father?" grilled Jim.

"No!" snapped Kevin. "It was during my first year of high school while milking the cows one morning that my stepdad and I got into it about something stupid. Then, in an unguarded moment of anger, he said something like, 'if you were my son.'"

Linda put a comforting hand on Kevin's shoulder.

"Were you under the impression that Peter Smith was your real father up until that point?"

"That's right," scowled Kevin. "That was also when I changed my name to Killingham, though I've certainly considered changing it back to Smith!"

"Understandable. So, you never saw Mark Killingham again until Detective Floyd Shoeman found him for you?" questioned Jim, more softly.

"That's correct," replied Kevin.

"And when you first met him, did Mark look familiar to you in any way whatsoever?" pressed Jim.

"No, not really," sighed Kevin. "It had been so many years, plus people change over time."

"So, you didn't recognize Mark Killingham as the man who had tried to take you from your mother at the rodeo when you were just a boy?" quizzed Jim.

"No! I've already told you that!" growled Kevin. "If only I had, perhaps Linda and I could have been spared the unfortunate experience of knowing him!"

"Amen to that!" exclaimed Linda.

"It's five minutes until 8:00," interjected Sheree, who had come in and set up the other laptop while Jim was busy interrogating Kevin. "Everything is ready."

"Sorry I had to do that," apologized Jim.

"No problem," muttered Kevin.

"Jim, can you see me?" It was Bill Huong.

"Yes," confirmed Jim. "Nice tie."

Bill merely shrugged as he loosened the knot in it just a bit. "It's been a long day."

"Where's Chip?" questioned Jim.

"It's ringing now," pointed out Sheree.

Just then, the face of Chip Priest appeared in its own box on the laptop screen by Sheree. "Jim and Bill, good to see you."

"Likewise," nodded Bill.

161

"Okay," began Jim as he quickly scrolled through the items on Ann's computer to refresh his memory. "Chip, this is Linda and Kevin Killingham, sitting here next to Ted."

"Hello! Jim's not only our silent partner and CEO, but also the financial muscle behind the Priest and Krain Detective Agency," grinned Chip.

"Just so we're clear on that," smiled Jim. "Okay, Chip. I've got a priority assignment for you, and will be describing it for you next."

"What?" Chip seemed surprised. "What about that other matter that the Seattle PD has us working on right now? Remember that guy they found under the bridge?"

"Believe it or not, it's related," advised Jim. "So, I'll need whatever Michael has on it." For Kevin's and Linda's benefit, Jim explained, "Michael Krain is our other partner."

"I'm all ears," encouraged Chip.

"Kevin's real father is or was a man named Mark Killingham," began Jim. "Earlier today we exhumed what we thought were his remains but Bill has just confirmed for us that the body inside the casket was not his. Bill can fill you in on the details later, as I want the two of you to work on this together."

"Go on," urged Chip.

"As most of us know, this lighthouse was originally built in 1872 by the first Killinghams to come here from Ireland."

Seriously? Chip mouthed the words.

"The builder's name was Jeremy Killingham, born in 1848 in Dingle, Ireland. Their daughter Daisy was born in 1869. She ended up committing suicide but left two young sons behind. One of them was named Jed."

"Who could barely keep his family fed?" teased Chip.

"I'm giving you the family history behind Mark Killingham in case you need this information while trying to find him," advised Jim rather tersely. "Anyway, Jed Killingham was born in 1890, right here at the lighthouse. His son Jack was Mark Killingham's father. Mark is the guy we're trying to find."

"What do we know about Jack?" questioned Chip, now more serious.

"Jack, Sr. married his half-sister Ellie Mae in 1929, right before the stock market crashed, but she was only 17 at the time so

162

they got married in Alabama where the legal age for marriage was lower."

"That makes sense," nodded Chip.

"The twin boys in this photo with them were their sons, Mark and Jack, Jr.," indicated Jim as he held up the photo. "I'll send a copy of this to each of you."

"Jack's the tall guy?" asked Bill.

"Yes," confirmed Jim. "And the other man was his younger brother James. There was some business about Ellie Mae leaving Jack, Sr. while he and his brother James were on safari in Peru. That was in 1932. Apparently, James was killed during a cave-in there." *Jim purposely omitted any reference to the gold disc.*

"What happened to the twin boys after that?" asked Chip.

"That's where you come in," advised Jim. "Jack, Jr. is a complete blank. We know absolutely nothing about him other than the fact that he's probably the man whose remains were in Mark Killingham's coffin."

"We'll know for sure when the DNA results come back tomorrow," clarified Bill.

"Where did you manage to get DNA evidence to compare it to?" wondered Chip.

"From me," informed Kevin. "I'm Mark Killingham's son."

"I drew a blood sample from him earlier today," explained Bill, "but won't have the results back until late tomorrow morning."

"Mark was a bigamist and a con artist," interjected Linda, "and all we want is to see him captured and brought to justice for the many crimes he's committed."

"Especially the crime of murder," added Jim, "if that happens to be the case."

"That's a pretty tall order," replied Chip, suddenly feeling overwhelmed by the task.

"I have a theory," advised Kevin.

"Let's hear it," replied Jim.

"What if Mark and his brother Jack, Jr. were actually working together, both of them running con games on people?"

"That could explain how the man was able to be in so many places at once," speculated Linda.

163

"But, don't forget," reminded Jim, "he did disappear quite a bit, too, for days at a time. We all thought that was peculiar, even though he'd always come up with a plausible explanation for it."

"Huh," nodded Chip.

"What if they did work together, though," persisted Linda. "Then, when they got together to celebrate their birthday on March 23, 2009, they could have gotten into an argument over the proceeds from their last job – whatever that might have been – and Mark either accidentally or on purpose ended up killing his brother. Then, to keep from going to prison for the rest of his life, he switched identities with him and went on his merry way."

"We actually saw and spoke with Mark in 2016, at the Seattle fish market," added Kevin. "There's no way he died in 2009."

"I concur. Gentlemen, I'll send both of you a complete synopsis of everything we know so far by tomorrow morning," promised Jim.

"This might cost you extra," teased Bill.

"No kidding," agreed Chip.

"Not a problem," smiled Jim.

164

5. Jack

Even at age two, Jack Killingham stood head and shoulders above the other toddlers his age. He could already carry on an intelligent conversation with most adults and was often assumed to be at least four or five years old.

In comparison, his younger brother James was a typical one-year old, not yet able to communicate very well at all but making quite an effort at it. Of the two, only Jack had learned to both walk and talk and was into everything – when he wasn't busy asking questions about it.

It was Sunday evening, July 7, 1912. Earlier that afternoon, their father Jed had taken Jack and James by trolley across town to see a magic show where they would meet his "Cousin Chris" when she got off work later. Chris was a telephone operator for Ma Bell. Horse drawn street cars were still in use and were less expensive, though not fast enough to get them there in time.

They were currently spending the summer with "Cousin Chris" in New York City, but would be returning by train to their lighthouse home at Ocean Bluff next month.

Jack watched with fascination as world famous Harry Houdini was placed in handcuffs and leg irons before being placed into a wooden box that was weighted down, nailed shut, and quickly thrown from a nearby tugboat into the East River. No more than a minute after the coffin sank, Houdini surfaced before hundreds of cheering spectators, reporters and photographers that were congregated onshore to watch.

James, of course, was too young to comprehend what was going on, but seemed to enjoy watching all the people around them, especially the street vendor selling hot dogs, popcorn and cotton candy.

"How did that man do that?" questioned Jack with awe.

"Who knows?" laughed Jed. "But, he sure is good."

"It had to be staged," opined Chris.

"Could *you* do that?" challenged Jack.

"You sure ask a lot of questions for such a little boy," responded Chris as she slipped her arm through Jed's.

"I wanna go home!" exclaimed Jack. He didn't like Chris being so friendly with his father, even if she was his cousin.

"Of course, you do," acknowledged Jed as he untangled himself from Chris long enough to hoist James up onto his shoulders.

"When do we go home?" pressed Jack as he glared with disapproval at Chris.

"Next month," assured Jed.

"We should probably get back to my place so you can put the boys down for the night," smiled Chris as she winked at Jed.

"It is getting late," agreed Jed. *How would he ever manage to tell the boys that their mother was never coming back? Or, that Chris wasn't really his cousin? Perhaps he wouldn't bother with that part.*

Besides, Jed had no desire to spoil their holiday in New York by dwelling on something so unpleasant. In fact, it was his earnest desire to persuade Chris to come with them when they left New York and returned to the Killingham Lighthouse. Then, if Chris were agreeable to it, Jed would ask her to marry him so she could become a mother to Jack and James. *We all could use a woman's touch at the lighthouse*, thought Jed as he gazed with longing at Chris.

Not only that, Jed felt a twinge of guilt as he thought of his grandfather Jeremy – who had been left alone by his two grandsons – to struggle with maintaining and operating the lighthouse on his own.

By 1922, most other lighthouses along the neighboring coastline had already made the switch to electricity, but not the Killingham Lighthouse. Its Dalén light was produced by burning carbide gas, also known as acetylene. One of the many duties of the lighthouse keeper was to place calcium carbide pellets into the lower generator chamber. The upper reservoir was then filled with water. A threaded valve or other mechanism was used to control the rate at which the water would drip into the chamber containing the calcium carbide. Only by controlling the rate of waterflow was it possible to control the production and flow rate of acetylene gas, the size of the flame at its burner, and the amount of light produced. Being able to predict how long the light would burn enabled the lighthouse keeper to determine how often the calcium carbide would need to be replenished.

Lighthouse beacons were routinely turned off during the daytime to conserve fuel costs, but often left on during emergencies –

such as a shipwreck – at the discretion of the keeper to project its guiding beacon. Such an exception would of course need to be promptly reported in writing to the United States Lighthouse Service (USLHS) District Superintendent.

For convenience, the vital supply of pellets used at the Killingham Lighthouse was kept in two small out buildings, situated relatively close to the lighthouse. Lighthouse keepers were also required by the USLHS to plant and tend a personal vegetable garden. Once each month, a new shipment of pellets and other necessary supplies provided by the USLHS would arrive either by horse-drawn delivery wagon or seaside by ship. In subsequent years, however, the pellet system would be replaced by a diesel-powered generator, and finally by a solar-powered turbine generator.

The turning of the huge lamp itself was controlled by a separate system of gears powered by a large weight that hung down the center of the tower, not unlike the counterweight system used by a grandfather clock. The huge 50-pound weight used in the Killingham Lighthouse would slowly drop for 8 hours before it needed to be manually cranked back up to the top of the tower and the gears reset on its giant spool for the next descent. It could be disastrous if the chain were to become tangled or hung up on something, such as the railing of the spiral staircase built around it, so frequent inspections of the chain and other lighthouse equipment was essential.

Angela was the last remaining member of the original contingent of servants and household staff that had once lived in the old servants' quarters nearby. Jeremy Killingham and his wife Bonnie had employed a butler, a maid, a nanny, a gardener, a cook, and even a tutor for their children. It had been Bonnie's idea to name each of their daughters after various flowers, and to name their rooms after them. But, Bonnie had never been well. Her health had been seriously compromised by the weather and constant dampness at the lighthouse. Weakened by one illness after another, Bonnie suddenly died – just after giving birth to their youngest child Petunia.

Her oldest daughter Daisy had been a wayward child who never actually married the father of her two young sons – Jed and Bill – and had kept the Killingham name for each of them. Their father had been a sailor who never stayed in one place for very long. Daisy had become so depressed after being abandoned by her sailor love that she flung herself from the blufftops onto the rocks below. The

167

isolation of the lighthouse and constant howling of the wind had become more than she could endure. Her other six sisters – Rose, Violet, Lilly, Rosemary, Heather and Petunia – had already married but then left the lighthouse for good, never to be seen or heard from again.

Jeremy had then been left to raise his daughter Daisy's two sons, not to mention the many responsibilities associated with caring for the lighthouse. Thankfully, many members of his original staff were still in employ at the time and were able to help. Jed and Bill did their utmost to pitch in, once they were old enough to be of any real help, but soon realized how confining and rigid a lighthouse keeper's life could be.

It was little wonder that both Bill and Jed had sought out opportunities to travel abroad when reaching manhood, though Jed had ultimately returned to the lighthouse from New York to help his aging grandfather with the lighthouse.

When subsequent budgetary cuts by the USLHS had made it necessary for Jeremy to dismiss his entire staff, only Angela and her mother had remained – without pay – to continue helping in exchange for a meager share of the supplies allotted by the USLHS to the lighthouse each month. It was Angela who singlehandedly maintained the grounds and tended the vegetable garden, so she and her mother were also allowed to keep and use part of the harvest it produced.

It was June 7, 1922. His mood was somber as Jed thought of what life would be like at the lighthouse without Grandfather Jeremy. *Would he be up to the challenge?* His brother Bill had no interest in helping whatsoever, and his children were far too young to be of much help yet. The family had lost all touch with his aunts, so there was no way to even let them know that Jeremy had passed.

Like his mother, Jed never married, though he did have three offspring to show for his years of philandering. Jack, James and Ellie Mae were ages 12, 11 and 10 in 1922, at the time of their great grandfather Jeremy's death. Though wanting for little and home schooled by Angela, the children understandably felt trapped at the lighthouse. Jack and Ellie Mae were particularly close.

Unfortunately, Angela's mother had suffered a severe stroke the previous year and was now living in an assisted care facility in Ocean Bay. With Jeremy gone, Angela would be leaving the

168

lighthouse permanently, to be closer to her mother. Tragically, her hope of kindling a romance with Jeremy had died with him. *Had Jeremy even known how she felt?*

Jed was numb with grief as he stood by his little family and watched the horse-drawn hearse pull away from the lighthouse doors. To save on burial costs, the Ocean Bluff Coroner had come out and performed the embalming right there at the lighthouse. The solid oak coffin in which Grandpa Jeremy had been placed would be buried at the Ocean Bluff Cemetery that afternoon.

"I am truly sorry about your grandfather," consoled Angela as she put a comforting hand on Jed's shoulder.

"Me, too," sniffed Jed. Men just did not cry, but the water escaping from the corners of his eyes threatened to betray him.

"It is okay to cry," Angela assured him.

"How come your suitcase is packed?" blurted out Ellie Mae, who had watched her pack earlier.

Angela swallowed uncomfortably. "I wasn't going to say anything until after the service."

"You're leaving?" Jed was flabbergasted.

"I'm afraid so."

"What will we do without you?" Jed could not comprehend life without Angela there. "What about the children and their studies?"

"They'll be okay," assured Angela. "I'm sorry, but my mother is failing fast, and I need to be there for her."

Jed merely nodded. That was understandable, but he felt as if someone had punched him in the gut.

His 12-year old son Jack put a comforting arm around Ellie Mae and pulled her close. The romantic feelings they had begun to have for one another was a carefully guarded secret, but even their brother James was beginning to suspect what was going on. James nervously fidgeted as he watched his siblings standing there, clinging to one another. *What would their father do if he found out?*

Both Jack and James were aware by now that Ellie Mae had been born practically nine months to the day following their visit with "Cousin Chris" in New York City. Neither would forget the weekend Chris had mysteriously showed up at the lighthouse with baby Ellie Mae and abandoned her there following a heated argument with Jed. *What if Ellie Mae wasn't actually their half-sister? What if someone*

169

else besides their father had been her dad? And, what had happened to their real mother? Why would she have left them?

Since the boys had been quite young at the time of their mother's departure, neither of them knew anything about her. Not even her name.

"Let's go," prompted Jed as a fancy horse-drawn carriage pulled up and stopped at the lighthouse doors. The driver patiently waited while everyone climbed in.

Jed, Jack, James and Ellie Mae were dressed entirely in black. Angela was dressed in a plain gray skirt and white blouse. Jed and Angela seated themselves beside the driver in the front seat. The Killingham children climbed into the back seat. Noticed only by James, Jack and Ellie Mae were holding hands.

"Giddyup," prompted the driver before quickly flicking the reins to the matched set of black quarter horses while they stepped up to an easy canter.

"How can we leave him now?" whispered Ellie Mae into Jack's ear, so no one else could hear.

Jack pursed his lips and shook his head. *How indeed?* Then, whispering back in her ear, "We can't. At least not yet."

Jack and Ellie Mae had talked for some time about running away together, just as soon as they were old enough. They had also heard that the legal age to get married was lower in some places than in others. *But, where was that?* They would need to find out. Meanwhile, they would have to bide their time at the lighthouse.

It was Tuesday, September 24, 1929, just one month before the infamous Wall Street Crash of 1929. Ellie Mae Killingham and her half-brother Jack had been in love for years, afraid to tell anyone but James of their true feelings for one another.

After taking on a job in town to help support the family, James had met a young waitress named Bell that he desperately wanted to marry. James was 18 years old, but Bell – who was the same age as Ellie Mae – was only 17. James had decided to bring Bell home with him to the lighthouse that evening for dinner, to meet the family.

"What a beautiful place to live!" marveled Bell as James pulled the one-horse carriage to a stop by the front entrance of the lighthouse. "You can practically see the entire ocean from here!"

"A good share of it," acknowledged James as he climbed from the carriage, tied the horse to a hitching post, and came around to the passenger side to help Bell down. "It's not a bad place to live, as long as leaving is an option – even if it's just to go on a holiday."

"I guess it would kind of tie you down, doing something like this," realized Bell as she slipped her arm through his and walked up the front steps with him.

"My sister's your age," James informed her as he opened the front door to the lighthouse and held it open. "And my brother's one year older than me."

"Well, hello!" exclaimed Jed as he took her hand and kissed it. He just happened to be in the front foyer at the time of their arrival.

"Father, this is Bell," introduced James. He was not overly pleased with the way his father was flirting with her.

"Jack, Ellie Mae, we have company," announced Jed. His loud booming voice echoed throughout the lighthouse.

Embarrassed by his father's behavior, James shook his head but remained silent about it.

"We're over here in the kitchen," called Ellie Mae. The large commercial kitchen was on the first floor.

"Set another place for dinner," directed their father.

Ellie Mae emerged from the kitchen wearing a bright yellow apron and was drying her hands on it.

"This is my sister, Ellie Mae."

"Nice to meet you," greeted Ellie Mae as she shook Bell's hand.

"Likewise," replied Bell.

"I'm Jack," announced a melodic bass voice from behind her. "And before you ask – yes, I'm 7 feet tall."

Bell turned to gaze up at Jack with awe. "I see you lift weights, too!"

"Three times a day," chuckled Jack as he flexed his arm muscles.

"He's talking about the 50-pound counterweight you see slowing making its way down here," pointed out Jed. "It's what keeps the lamp turning up there."

"He's 19 years old," grinned Ellie Mae as she openly flirted with her brother. If their father did notice, he did not let on.

171

"I see," nodded Bell. She was no slouch and suspected immediately that there was more to the relationship between Jack and Ellie Mae than mere sibling comradery.

After a simple meal of potatoes, green beans and canned tuna, Jed advised, "I can take care of the counterweight this evening, if you kids want to go down to the beach and hang out. Take some pop with you. I think there's plenty in the pantry."

"*Can* you stay any later?" James asked Bell.

"Oh, absolutely," answered Bell. "I wouldn't miss it for the world. Besides, my parents know I'm with you."

"Thank God the lighthouse has an electric lamp now," mentioned Jack. "No more making trips upstairs with buckets of pellets three times a day."

"Or buckets of water to go with it," nodded James.

"How true! And the new lens we have now is a Fresnel," added Jed rather proudly. "The light from our new lens can be seen all the way to the horizon, up to 20 miles away."

"We used to have a Dalén light," explained Jack.

"Before the USLHS decided to replace it with this one," continued Jed.

"The USLHS?" questioned Bell.

"The United States Lighthouse Service," clarified Ellie Mae. "Now, they don't have to worry about making a trip out here each month to deliver shipments of pellets for us to use."

"They still send us a small stipend to use for supplies, though," reminded Jed. "At least one of us has to go into town to get them."

"I guess you can't get away much," assumed Bell.

"Not since my grandpa passed," confirmed Jed. "I'm pretty much the main lighthouse keeper now."

"Huh," snorted Jack as he motioned with his head for Ellie Mae, Jack and Bell to follow him outside. *Good luck with that.*

"What time does the sun go down?" asked Bell.

"Not until a little after 7:00," volunteered Ellie Mae.

Ellie Mae and Bell genuinely liked one another almost instantly, and began chatting as if they had known each other for years. They had each removed their shoes to walk on the sand and were carrying them.

"Let's build a fire over there," suggested James. "By that log."

Jack flirted with Ellie Mae openly as he reached for some nearby flotsam to stack by the fire pit James was building.

"I take it your father doesn't know about you and Jack?" assumed Bell with a crooked smile as she winked at Ellie Mae.

Though flushing with embarrassment at first, Ellie Mae quickly managed to regain her composure. "How could you tell?"

"It's only obvious."

"We do have different mothers," informed Ellie Mae.

"And possibly different fathers," added Jack from behind them. He had a surprising talent for sneaking up on people like that, especially for such a large man.

"We hope to be married when I'm old enough," explained Ellie Mae as Jack put his arms around her, pulled her close, and gave her a passionate kiss in front of James and Bell.

"Indeed, we do!" agreed Jack, after he finished kissing her.

"When are you expecting?" blurted out Bell. She had instantly noticed the slight bulge in Ellie Mae's abdomen.

"What?" questioned Jack as he stood back to examine Ellie Mae more closely. He'd had no idea.

"Oh, boy," muttered James as he shook his head.

"I was waiting for the right time to tell you," explained Ellie Mae. "I don't think we can wait much longer to get married."

"I agree," nodded Jack as the reality began to sink in. "A baby?" Jack beamed with delight as he suddenly picked Ellie Mae up and spun around in a circle while holding her close. Then after carefully setting her back down, Jack knelt on one knee and proposed, "Ellie Mae, will you marry me?"

"Yes!" exclaimed Ellie Mae.

James sighed deeply as he struck a match to get the fire going. A pleasant breeze made it challenging, but perseverance paid off.

"When is high tide?" asked Bell, who had just noticed that the water was slowly moving closer.

"Not until after 10:00 tonight," assured James. "We should be good where we are for at least another hour."

"Wow," marveled Bell as she studied the colorful sunset. "Hey, I'm sorry about that."

"Sorry?" laughed Jack. "Young lady, you've made my day!"

"How will you get married if she's only 17?" queried Bell.

"That's what we need to figure out," remarked Jack as he added a small stick to the fire.

"I've heard that people can get married without their parents' consent in Alabama as long as they're over 16," recalled Bell as she used the bottle opener James handed her to remove the lid on her pop.

"That's a great idea!" exclaimed Ellie Mae.

"Perhaps the four of us should go there," suggested James.

"The four of us?" Bell tried to seem surprised that James would mention such an idea.

James suddenly knelt on the sand in front of Bell and took her hand. "Bell, will you marry me? We can to go Alabama with them."

Bell slowly began to smile and then broke into a huge grin as she embraced James and nodded her head yes.

"Is that a yes?"

"YES!" exclaimed Bell as she hugged him tighter. "Absolutely! Let's go to Alabama, just the four of us. It will be an adventure."

"It certainly will," agreed Ellie Mae.

"What will we tell our father?" James suddenly asked.

"He is 'pretty much the main lighthouse keeper now' – his words, not mine," reminded Jack.

"Do you think he can handle it?"

"Yes, I do," determined Jack. "Do *you* want to be stuck here for the rest of your life like that?"

James silently shook his head in the negative.

"Besides," added Jack, "after we're all of age, we can always come back for a visit. Then, there'll be nothing he can do about it."

"It probably will break his heart, though," contemplated Ellie Mae as she thought of what it would be like for their father to be completely on his own at the lighthouse.

"He's got that new lens now," pointed out Jack. "All he has to do is wind up the counterweight every eight hours. That's it. That's all he has to do. No more hauling pellets, or any of that. He'll be fine. Trust me."

Bell had decided to return home that night and pretend as if everything was status quo. After silently packing her suitcase and waiting until she was sure her parents were asleep, Bell left.

The stars were unusually bright that night. *Was she doing the right thing? Should she have left a note?* wondered Bell as she headed for the main road where James was waiting. *Oh well, it was too late now. They would just have to wonder about it. She could always write to them later and explain.*

Though the suitcase was unbelievably heavy, Bell somehow managed to half carry and occasionally drag it to the rendezvous point.

"What in the world do you have in this thing?" questioned James as he grabbed her suitcase and hoisted it onto the back of the wagon he was driving. It was actually more of a small trunk.

"Everything I didn't want to leave behind," grinned Bell as she allowed James to help her up into the wagon.

"We may not be traveling the way you think we are," informed James. "Jack thinks hitchhiking would be too risky."

"Why?" frowned Bell.

"For several reasons," answered James as the wagon began to move. "First and foremost, we want to stay together."

"Of course."

"Would *you* pick up four complete strangers with four huge suitcases? Even if you had the room?"

Bell slowly nodded. "I see your point."

"Not only that," continued James, "what if whoever picked us up were only going so far, and ended up having to drop us all off in the middle of nowhere? Then what?"

"What about a bus or even the train?"

"Out of the question. Not only would it cost more than we have," reminded James, "but with so many people at the bus or train stations, someone might see us and tell your parents or our father where we went."

"Then what are we going to do?" frowned Bell. "Ride horses all that way? That's over 2,300 miles!"

"Jack has another idea."

"Well?" Bell folded her arms.

"We'll definitely be going by train," revealed James, "but just not the way you think."

"You're not thinking what I think you're thinking?"

James smiled a crooked smile and nodded.

"Oh, James, we just can't! There are hobos and drunks on those trains. And, how in the world are we going to hop onto a moving freight train with our suitcases?"

"We'll all get on when it's stopped and then hide until it's moving again," laughed James. "Everything will work out. You'll see."

"What about Ellie Mae, and her condition?"

"You worry too much."

"I guess I'm just being silly," smiled Bell as she slid closer to James and put her hand on his leg. James rewarded her with one of his enticing smiles. Clearly, he was as anxious to be married as she was.

Once they had reached the freight yard, James spotted Jack and Ellie Mae where he had left them before going to pick up Bell.

"It's about time you got here," chastised Jack as he grabbed and tied the horses to a hitching post.

"What about the horses and the wagon?" questioned James.

"The guy at the store in there will drive 'em back to the lighthouse after we're gone," assured Jack.

"We paid him $5 to keep quiet about anything else he might suspect," added Ellie Mae.

"Do you trust him?" scowled James. "What if he just makes off with the horses and wagon?"

"He looks trustworthy," assured Jack. "Hey, we're committed now. No turning back." Jack then held his right hand out in front of him, palm down and looked at the others.

"No turning back," agreed Ellie Mae as she put her right hand on top of Jack's.

"No turning back," repeated James and Bell as they also put their right hands on top.

"Good," grinned Jack as they pulled back their hands. "Now that that's settled, we need to hurry and get on that far-left train."

"What about that man standing right next to it?" worried James. "The one with a conductor's uniform on?"

"We're going to need to circle around to the other side."

"But the doors are open on *this* side," objected James.

"Come on!" urged Jack. "Let's go. He just climbed inside and won't be able to see us. This side's fine."

176

The four runaways hurriedly grabbed their suitcases and began running toward the train. Bell, however, lagged behind as she struggled with her heavy load.

"Oh, for Pete's sake," muttered Jack as he came back to grab one end of her trunk-like suitcase and helped her carry it while also carrying his own.

By the time they arrived at the open door to the freight car on the train, James and Ellie Mae had already climbed inside with their suitcases and were waiting.

"It's starting to move!" yelled Bell. "We're not gonna make it!"

"Shh!" replied Jack as he hoisted his own duffel bag onto the train, and then grabbed and tossed her heavy suitcase in after it. James and Ellie Mae barely managed to avoid being hit by the flying luggage.

Jack then swooped Bell up into his arms and began running to catch up with the slowly moving train. "I'm gonna toss you in when we get there. Don't worry, James will catch you."

"Oh, my God!" screamed Bell as Jack caught up to the open car and tossed her onto the train.

The heel of her shoe caught on a metal grommet near the door and she started to lose her balance.

"I've got you!" hollered James as he grabbed and pulled his fiancé aboard.

"What about Jack?" shrieked Ellie Mae. *Where was he?*

Unseen by the others, Jack had managed to grab onto the rung of a ladder on the outside of the open car and was climbing his way toward its opening.

"What are we going to do?" wailed Ellie Mae.

"We're going to Alabama," replied Jack's booming bass voice as he suddenly leaped into the car. "That's what we're going to do."

"Oh, Jack!" wept Ellie Mae as she ran over to embrace him. "Don't ever scare me like that again!"

Both couples were aware of the close call they'd just had and sat there embracing one another for several minutes before taking in their surroundings. The open car faced the ocean side of the blufftop route their train was taking.

"Can we slide the door shut if we want to?" asked Ellie Mae, suddenly concerned about it when the train started around a bend and

177

caused the car to slightly lean in that direction. *What if they or their luggage should slide out, especially during the night?*

"Sure, if you like," replied Jack as he got up and reached for the heavy sliding door.

"No, leave it open!" Bell grimaced as she got a whiff of something foul. "What was in here?" The corner of her suitcase had landed in what appeared to be a pile of manure.

"Probably livestock," guessed James as he and the others suddenly started to laugh.

"It smells so bad, I don't think I could eat for a week," informed Bell as she folded her arms and glowered at the spot on her suitcase.

"Let's draw straws to see who gets her share of the food," teased Jack. He then reached for a piece of straw and broke it into pieces.

"Hey, wait a minute!" objected Bell. "I didn't say I *won't* eat, only that I can't right now."

"Nice try," grinned James.

"What kind of food did you bring?" questioned Bell as she gave Jack a questioning look.

"Several cans of beans," grinned Jack. "And a can opener."

"Beans?" Bell seemed indignant about it. "We're going to be on this stinky train for days, and all we have to eat is beans?"

"What did *you* bring?" challenged Jack. "Hopefully, that heavy trunk of yours is filled with cans of something."

"Shoes, clothes, and a photo album," revealed Bell, suddenly feeling rather foolish. "And a cast iron skillet."

Jack slapped his knee as he began laughing.

"A cast iron skillet could be useful," recognized Ellie Mae.

"But nothing to eat?" razzed Jack.

"Oh, give her a break," interjected James. "I've got a couple loaves of bread and some apples."

"What about water?" questioned Ellie Mae, suddenly worried about it. *She had not brought along any food or water, either!*

Jack just shook his head as he pulled a large canteen from his duffel bag. "For drinking only."

"Likewise," added James as he pulled his canteen out to show them. "If we're frugal, we should be okay."

178

"Ellie Mae is a priority," advised Jack, "so if need be, I'll forfeit any food or water necessary to be sure Ellie Mae and the baby are fed."

"He isn't even born yet, silly," flirted Ellie Mae as she playfully slapped him on the arm.

"All the more reason we need to take good care of you," replied Jack as he pulled her close and held her while they watched the passing view. Cypress and eucalyptus trees soon were replaced by redwood and other conifers as the train reached an old growth stand of trees.

"And you're positive this train goes all the way to Alabama?" grilled Bell as she scooted her suitcase away from the reeking end of the car and began wiping off the corner of it with her scarf.

"I hope you plan to throw that away," scowled Ellie Mae. The smell was making her nauseated.

The scarf had been a gift from her mother and Bell hated to do it, but she realized it was necessary. After using it to clean off the suitcase, she then scooped up as much of the remaining manure as she could with the scarf before tossing it out the open door. Bell did not look happy when she returned to sit beside James.

"I guess that's the corner we'll use if any of us needs to use the restroom?" asked Ellie Mae. *Thankfully, she still had her scarf!*

"That makes sense," nodded Jack.

"Good, the rest of you look the other way."

"I suppose none of that water is for washing our hands?" asked Bell with a pitiful look on her face.

"Not if we plan to stay alive," advised Jack.

"Here," indicated James. "Use this."

"Straw?"

"There's several large bales of straw stacked over on the other side of the car," pointed out Jack. "That's where we can all bed down for the night. It'll also be handy to use in the stinky corner whenever we need it."

"Amen to that!" exclaimed Ellie Mae as she dashed over to grab a handful of fresh straw and then quickly returned to the corner with it.

"Or to hide behind if the train stops for an unscheduled inspection," mentioned James.

"What do you mean?" Bell became alarmed.

"For bums hitching a ride on the train," interjected Jack as he tried not to laugh again. He was beginning to enjoy giving Bell a hard time, especially since she was so easy to fluster.

"I think they really do stop the train to do inspections once in a while," opined James. He was just as concerned about it as Bell.

"Then we'd better hide our luggage over there now," suggested Jack as he tossed his duffel bag toward the clean end of the car before grabbing Ellie Mae's suitcase and taking it over."

"What will we eat after we get there?" grilled Bell as she again looked to her fiancé's brother Jack for an answer. "The food we have isn't going to last forever."

"*Whose* food?" chortled Jack.

"Okay, the food you and James have isn't going to last forever," revised Bell.

"Especially if we eat it," pointed out Jack with a crooked grin as he grabbed Bell's huge suitcase and took it to the clean area and stowed it behind the large pile of straw. *Apparently, she had no intention of doing it herself.*

"I could have done that," objected James as he grabbed his suitcase and followed.

"Too late," shrugged Jack as he grabbed a handful of clean straw and headed for the dirty corner to sprinkle it over the area.

"Sorry," apologized Ellie Mae. "I should have put more down."

"We should be okay now," assured Jack as he wrinkled his nose. "We just need to make sure we're not overrun by flies." *The wind was definitely blowing in the wrong direction!*

"Especially once we get to the Alabama swamps," agreed James.

"You still didn't answer my question," Bell reminded Jack when he returned. "What will we eat when we get there?"

"Call it a guess, but probably *food,*" grinned Jack with a little more sarcasm than he intended. *But, Bell was such great fun to give a hard time to.*

"We won't have to change trains along the way, will we?" grilled Ellie Mae as she headed toward the clean end of the car. She was tired and wanted to lay down for a while.

"Hey, where you going?" flirted Jack as he grabbed her hand and pulled her down beside him.

"Call it a guess, but she's probably going to *Alabama,* just like the rest of us," interjected Bell with an even smirk at Jack.

"Not bad," nodded Jack. *Perhaps Bell had some redeeming qualities after all.*

"Seriously, what if they do find us?" questioned Ellie Mae.

"Or some bum or escaped convict just happens to climb inside this car while we're stopped somewhere?" worried Bell.

"Or while we're sleeping," imagined Ellie Mae.

"Ladies, just relax," directed Jack. "Remember, this is an adventure. Everything will work out. Trust me!"

After two uneventful days and nights on the train, the travelers were suddenly awakened by a harsh jolt, accompanied by the squeal of train brakes.

"What was that?" asked Bell.

All of them were wide awake and could feel the train struggling to stop. *Had the train hit something?*

"Stay here," instructed Jack as he stealthily made his way toward the car's large sliding door and began to open it back up. The train continued to slow until it came to a stop.

"What are you doing?" grilled Ellie Mae. "It's cold in here!"

"Not as cold as it's going to be if they find us in here and put us off," replied Jack. "They'll probably come back to inspect the cars, and we need to leave the door open the same way it was when we got on."

"And if they did hit something?" pressed James.

"Then we may not be going anywhere for quite a while," muttered Jack as he carefully glanced outside to see if he could see anyone coming.

"This was a mistake!" exclaimed Bell as she began to cry.

"Would you please do something about your fiancé," Jack instructed James. "We all need to get behind those bales of straw right now and remain absolutely silent until the train starts moving again."

"I'm sorry!" sobbed Bell as she and the others scrambled to secret themselves.

"Shh, it's okay," whispered James as he put his arms around Bell to try and comfort her.

Men's voices could be heard approaching. All at once, lantern light illuminated the car.

"Nothing in here," advised the conductor.

"I know I saw something," insisted the other man, as both of them glanced again into the car.

"Why would anyone be way out here, anyway?" grilled the conductor.

"I'm certain I saw someone hop onto the train when we were slowing down," persisted the other man.

"I suppose whoever it was also managed to chase that 8-point buck onto the tracks so we would hit him and then have to stop?" laughed the conductor.

"I know what I saw."

"Suit yourself," shrugged the conductor. "You finish looking in the other cars while I go skin out that buck. We'll be eatin' fine for a while now."

Jack, Ellie Mae, James and Bell continued to wait in silence for over an hour. Then, without warning, the train began to move again.

"Whew!" sighed Jack. "I was beginning to worry."

The others merely glared at him. Just at that moment, a tall, athletic looking black man suddenly leaped into the car with a tattered burlap sack tied to the end of a sturdy stick.

"Land sakes almighty!" exclaimed the man. "Anybody in here?" He then put one hand to his ear as he glanced about the car. "What in tarnation be that smell?"

"I'm Jack," advised a bass voice from behind the straw.

"Eweee!" exclaimed the stranger when he saw Jack emerge from the shadows behind the bales of straw and approach. "Jack be bigger den de beanstalk!"

"We really don't want any trouble," advised James as he also stepped out from their hiding place and made his presence known. Though not as tall as Jack, James was also in excellent shape and more than willing to take on the stranger if need be.

"Dat makes three of us," grinned the newcomer. His gleaming white teeth could easily be seen in the shadows. "Why, I's glad to make yer acquaintance. Name's Tom. Never did like travelin' alone much." He then reached out to shake their hands. "No trouble here."

"Where you headed, Tom?" grilled Jack, without shaking the man's hand at first. *There was no telling if the man could be trusted.*

"I just be headin' back to old Alabamy, where de kin folk are," Tom informed them.

"You're from Alabama?" questioned Ellie Mae as she and Bell came out and approached.

"Well, well," grinned Tom. "What have we here?"

"They're spoken for," answered Jack in an unfriendly tone as he put his hands on his hips and took a step closer to Tom.

"Okay, okay, Tom gets yer meanin'."

"I'm Ellie Mae." She then reached out to shake Tom's hand. *They would be traveling together, so the least they could do was be civil.*

Jack pursed his lips together and glared with disapproval at Tom while he unexpectedly bowed low and gallantly kissed her hand.

"And I'm Bell," mentioned the other woman as she shook his hand, but pulled it away in time to avoid having it kissed. "My great grandfather used to own a plantation, but that was before the family came out west."

James stepped closer and tried to jab Bell in the side as discretely as possible to try and shut her up.

"He had at least 300 negroes, I think," continued Bell.

"I see," nodded Tom, who was no longer smiling.

"Welcome aboard," grinned Jack as he suddenly slapped Tom on the shoulder with one hand and shook his hand with the other.

"Sorry about that," apologized James as he, too, shook Tom's hand. "I'm James. My fiancé pretty much speaks whatever's on her mind."

"Did I say something wrong?" Bell feigned ignorance.

"Hey, that's okay," Tom smiled again. "My wife's like dat, too. Kin hardly shut her up, once she gets a goin'. Just wait 'til yer hitched, permanent like."

"Well!" Bell stuck her chin in the air and folded her arms as she headed back to the bales of straw. "Just so you know, Mr. Tom, this area over here is *ours!*"

"Duly noted, ma'am," replied Tom with a courteous bow.

"Looks like Miss Bell knows how to dish it out, but just doesn't know how to take it," snickered Jack as he suddenly saw the humor in their situation. "I think that round goes to Tom."

Everyone but Bell began laughing as she went over to sulk, including James.

183

"Say, is ya'll hungry?" offered Tom as he sat down and opened his burlap sack. "Killed me a buck this trip, and so now I gots a whole mess o'jerky. Smoked it for two days."

"You made it yourself?" questioned Bell with a scowl of disapproval from where she sat. The very thought was sickening.

"Tom, you're okay," grinned Jack as he and Ellie Mae sat down beside him. "I'd be more than glad to help lighten your load, provided you'd agree to share a can of beans with us."

"Der be no twistin' my arm on dat," grinned Tom.

Had proposing to Bell been a mistake? wondered James as he closed the car door most of the way before joining them. Thankfully, the full moon helped light up the car just enough to see one another inside.

"Is it safe to eat?" questioned Ellie Mae as Tom handed a piece of it to Jack.

"Don't worry, dey be well dun," assured Tom.

"Not bad," approved Jack as he took another piece from Tom and handed it to Ellie Mae. "You need your protein. Both of you."

"Ya'll be expecting?" asked Tom with a raised eyebrow as he chewed on the piece of jerky he was eating.

"Yes, we are," advised Jack rather proudly as he pulled out a can of beans and a can opener and began opening it.

"Praise de Lord," beamed Tom. "Well, if ya'll needs a good mid-wife, den me Hattie's de one to see. She dun delivered all sorts of babies 'round de bayou."

"No kidding?" interjected James. "Hey, I think I will try some of that jerky."

"Enjoy," bid Tom as he handed him a piece.

"Could I try some, too?" came Bell's sheepish voice from behind them. None of them had noticed her approach in the shadows.

"Most certainly, perty lady," answered Tom as he handed her a piece. "Is ya'll expectin', too?"

"No!" replied James and Bell together as she sat down.

"We're actually hoping to get married, though," revealed Bell. "We heard that 17-year olds can get married without their parents' permission in Alabama."

"Den ya'll be just a bunch o' kids?" Tom was surprised.

"Only the ladies," assured Jack.

"But ya did bring 'em over de state line?" laughed Tom. "Ya'll is braver den ya look."

"Not to change the subject, but just how much farther is it to Alabama from here?" asked Ellie Mae.

"Ya'll got no idea where we is, do ya?" chuckled Tom.

"Do *you* know where we are?" questioned Bell, who was now quite subdued.

"Houston be comin' up real quick like," advised Tom as he accepted the can of beans from Jack and ate a single large spoonful before passing it along to James.

"So, we *are* still in Texas?" grilled Jack.

"Yep. And we'd best all hide real quick like when we feel de train a slowin' down," recommended Tom. "Gettin' off and back on again just be way too risky."

"Especially with all our luggage," recognized Jack as he glanced at Bell. *Why in the world had she brought that huge monstrosity of a suitcase?*

"Why is everybody looking at me?" demanded Bell.

James smiled and shook his head as he ate a spoonful of beans, and then handed the can to Bell.

"Thanks," accepted Bell as she, too, took a bite before handing the can to Ellie Mae.

"Where is ya'll from?" Tom suddenly asked, after taking another bite of jerky.

"They're from the Killingham Lighthouse," answered Bell. "I'm from Ocean Bluff."

"Huh," muttered Tom as he pulled out a bota bag, removed the lid, took a swig from the leather water carrier, and passed it to James.

"Are you sure you'll have enough?" questioned James.

"Gotta wash it down with sumthin'," grinned Tom as he saw the look on James's face after drinking some.

James coughed and cleared his throat. "What is this?"

"It's de good stuff," advised Tom. "Old family recipe."

"Please do keep it going," requested Jack as he and Bell glanced at one another in the shadows.

Bell cautiously sniffed the bota bag and then shook her head. "No way! Haven't you heard about Prohibition? All liquor was outlawed in 1920."

185

"Not for preachers or pharmacists," informed James with a crooked grin. "Or, for those who know how to make it themselves and don't get caught."

"I'll try some," decided Ellie Mae.

"Not in your condition," reminded Jack as he reached over and took the bota bag from Bell before Ellie Mae could manage to grab it.

Jack then took a long swig from Tom's bota bag, smiled and nodded with approval as he handed it back to Tom. "That's the good stuff, for sure!"

"So, Tom," asked Ellie Mae, "where are *you* from?"

"Bayou La Batre," answered Tom as he put away his bota bag and jerky.

"What brings you to Texas?" pressed Ellie Mae.

"De game," replied Tom.

"The game?" Ellie Mae did not understand.

"De animals," explained Tom. "De bayou may be good fer huntin' but ain't never seen a deer make it past all dem 'gators."

"'Gators?" repeated Bell with alarm.

"Alligators," clarified Tom.

"Huge reptiles with gaping jaws and lots of teeth," added Jack, with a wicked smile.

"I know what an alligator is!" snapped Bell. "I just didn't realize there were any where we're going."

"There be all sorts of critters in de bayou," chuckled Tom. "'Specially snakes."

"Snakes!" exclaimed Bell. *She hated snakes!*

"Then we'll just have to wait for the next stop," urged Ellie Mae. "We can't possibly get off in a place like that!"

"De next stop after dat wud be Florida," informed Tom.

"Then what are we going to do?" fretted Bell.

"Looks like we're goin' to – what was it called?" asked Jack.

"Bayou La Batre," repeated Tom.

"Bayou La Batre," nodded Jack. "That's where we're goin'."

A worried silence descended upon the travelers as they and their new friend Tom listened to the sound of the train wheels rhythmically clicking on the tracks for several minutes. The moonlit train car carried them ever closer to an uncertain future.

Would they be able to find work – or even a place to live – when they got there? worried James.

186

"I kin keep watch if ya'll wanna rest," offered Tom.

"I'll join you," advised Jack.

Even though Tom was a likeable sort and had done nothing to merit their distrust – at least not yet – Jack wasn't taking any chances. *The last thing he wanted to do was wake up in Florida and discover they'd missed their stop!*

James, Bell and Ellie Mae retired to the clean end of the train car and proceeded to spread out some of the straw. Jack remained seated by Tom, near the car opening.

"Hey, ya'll might wanna leave some 'o dat straw on de bale," called Tom. "Else wise der be nothin' to hide behind when we get to New Orleans. And dey will be lookin' in dez cars."

James and the others nodded that they understood and left the rest of the straw where it was.

"When might that be?" Jack asked Tom. "When will we get to New Orleans?"

"Shud be first light, but cause o' de deer stop, kud be later," replied Tom as he removed the bota bag again and took another swallow before passing it to Jack.

"Thanks." Jack took a smaller sip this time.

"Ya'll fixin' to get hitched in Mobile?" asked Tom as he reached for his bota bag. Half the moon shine was already gone.

"That's the plan. Say, just how far is it from La Batre to Mobile?" grilled Jack.

"A good half day's ride in de wagon," figured Tom.

"You have a wagon?"

"Yep." Tom nodded in the shadows.

"Can you take us there?" pressed Jack. "To Mobile?"

"Assumin' we makes it off de train widout gettin' caught," laughed Tom as he took yet another swig of moon shine and extended the bota bag to Jack again.

"Thanks, I've had enough," declined Jack. He could already feel the effects of it, much more strongly than anticipated.

"After we leaves New Orleans, de next stop is La Batre," informed Tom.

"When do we get there?"

"'Bout supper time," grinned Tom. "Ya'll shud join us."

"We wouldn't want to impose."

"Well, ya'll kin't stay out in de swamp, neither," insisted Tom. "Der be hungry critters all over de place who wudn't hesitate none to eat ya. Besides, ya'll needs to keep yer strength up, 'specially wid lady folk to look after."

"Then we'd be much obliged," agreed Jack. "Perhaps we can chop some firewood for you while we're there."

"Dat wud be good," accepted Tom.

"Say, what's the work situation like in La Batre?" Jack finally asked. "What do you do for a living?"

Tom chuckled before responding. "Folks like me, we mostly be livin' off de land. But, a big strong white guy like yerself shud have no trouble finding hire."

"Folks like you?" questioned Jack.

"Ya ain't never spent much time in de South, has ya?"

"No, not really," admitted Jack. "Living at a lighthouse keeps you pretty isolated from the rest of the world, always keeping it going and such." Jack thought of Jed for a moment but quickly dismissed it. *Their father would be just fine.*

"Ya ever do any fishin'?" asked Tom. "Der be all sorts of fishin' outfits hiring on in La Batre. Only thing is, ya'd be gone frum de ladies fer days at a time."

"That's no good."

"How 'bout fixin' stuff?" continued Tom. "Dey be hiring handy men over at de boat buildin' place all de time, too."

"James and I will have to look into that, once we find a place to stay and get settled in."

"I has a guest house ya'll kin stay in," offered Tom. "Fer as long as ya'll likes – 'til ya finds sumthin' better, dat is."

"How much will it be?"

"Ya shud see it first," cautioned Tom. "De place needs sum work. But, it wud be no charge fer me new handyman."

"Seriously?" grinned Jack. "You'll let us stay there in exchange for me being your handyman?"

"I figures ya kin keep de wife in firewood fer me, and dat oughta do it," described Tom. "And, maybe de roof kud use sum patchin' when ya gets around to it, no hurry."

"Anything else?" Jack raised an eyebrow. *The last thing he wanted to do was get wrangled into a full-time job fixing things again.*

"Just be a good pa to dat little one," grinned Tom.

Jack thought about it for several moments and then slowly smiled and nodded his head. "Tom, provided the ladies approve of the guest house, you've got yourself a new handyman."

Then they shook hands on it.

It was already light outside by the time the train began slowing down for its next destination. The unscheduled stop had indeed delayed its arrival time.

James hurried to quickly open the door again.

"Kin I hides back der wid ya'll?" asked Tom.

"Absolutely," called Jack. "You'd better hurry, too."

Ellie Mae could not help but notice in the daylight that Tom was actually quite handsome, and tried not to stare. She had never actually seen a black person before.

"It's not polite to stare," whispered James to his sister.

"Sorry," apologized Ellie Mae as she looked away. Fortunately for her, Jack had not noticed the way Ellie Mae had stared at Tom. Even though Ellie Mae was Jack's life-long friend and true love, she had yet to experience his jealous side.

"Dey may bring stuff in here," warned Tom.

"What are you saying?" questioned Bell. "More cows?"

"Kud be cows, kud be anything," smiled Tom.

"We need to remain hidden and silent, no matter what they bring in here," cautioned Jack. "Otherwise, there's no telling what might happen to us."

Once the train was stopped, it was less than a minute before the conductor and another man could be heard approaching.

"What about this one?" asked the man as he glanced inside the car. "Should I hose it out first?"

"Are you kidding?" chuckled the conductor. "We'll still have to hose it out again when we get there anyway. It's good enough."

"What are they talking about?" whispered Bell.

James immediately put a hand over her mouth and held it there until he was sure she would not try speaking again.

All at once, a crate of chickens was plopped into the car, followed by the worker, who shoved it back towards the "dirty corner." The birds inside began clucking and flapping their wings in protest.

Chickens? grinned Jack. *This ought to be good.*

After he left, it was a couple of minutes before the men returned with two more crates and loaded them into the car. The process was repeated until several dozen crates were stacked inside.

"Should we lock it?" asked the worker as he climbed back out.

The look of panic on Bell's face was shared by everyone. *What would they do if the men decided to lock the door?*

"What for?" laughed the conductor. "Just close it, that'll be good enough. We're only going as far as La Batre with 'em anyway."

"Should I at least tie the cages in place?" pressed the other man.

"Why bother?" replied the conductor. "They're just gonna slaughter 'em when we get there."

"Okay," relented the other man as he finally slid the car's door shut with a loud bang.

"That was close!" whispered Jack.

"Dat ain't nothin'," assured Tom. "De hard part will be gettin' off wid all dat baggage."

"How long do they stop at La Batre?" asked Bell.

"Just fer as long as it takes to unload de cargo," replied Tom.

"So, they'll probably come to this car first," realized Jack.

"More den likely," agreed Tom.

"What will we do?" worried Ellie Mae.

Just then, the train began moving again. The chickens squawked even louder and flapped their wings in protest as several of the cages slid haphazardly onto the car's floor at odd angles.

"This is no good," recognized James as he and Jack emerged from their hiding place and began restacking the chicken crates that were potentially blocking their avenue of escape.

"Oh, shut up!" barked Jack as one of the chickens tried pecking at him through the slats of its crate.

"Time to open de door, too," directed Tom as he went over to slide it open. "We needs to be ready to toss out de bags when I tells ya, just before La Batre. I knows a perfect place, by a big tree at de last bend. Lots 'o soft grass der fer it to land in."

"Let me get this straight," remarked Bell as she approached with her hands on her hips. "We're all just going to be jumping off of a moving train? Just like that? And what about Ellie Mae?"

"Not *us*," explained Jack with an irritated sigh as he shook his head. "Just the luggage. Then, we can come back and retrieve it after the train takes off again."

"That could work," approved James.

"When do *we* get off?" pressed Bell.

"When de train starts slowin' down," grinned Tom.

"So, we're still going to have to jump from a moving train?" persisted Bell.

"Pretty much," laughed Jack.

"What if anything inside our suitcases gets broken?" grilled Bell. She had not mentioned to them yet that she also had some of her mother's china with her, as well.

"And what if one of us breaks an arm or a leg?" added Ellie Mae. *Not to mention what might happen to her baby!*

"I'm sorry, ladies," apologized James, "but they're right. It's the only way. We can't afford to get caught."

"Dey kud even put yer guys in jail, fer bringing younger ladies like yerselves across state lines," interjected Tom.

"He's right," agreed Jack as he reached for Bell's huge suitcase and began scooting it toward the open door.

"You're not going to throw it out *now*, are you?"

"Perhaps I should," teased Jack.

"You wouldn't!" exclaimed Bell as she raced toward him.

"Relax," answered Jack. "I'm just getting things ready. Tom will tell us when it's time."

Jack began bringing over the other suitcases and stacking them beside Bell's. The train car's door was only open a couple of feet, but could quickly be opened further when needed.

"We're almost there, honey," flirted Jack as he pulled Ellie Mae close and gave her a hug. "Everything will be fine."

"How?" frowned Ellie Mae. "What if we can't find a place to stay once we get there?"

"Or jobs for you guys?" added Bell as she sat down on her suitcase, folded her arms in front of her, and began to pout.

"Ladies, I'd like you to meet our new landlord," grinned Jack as he motioned toward Tom.

Tom then grinned and bowed low in response.

James slowly began to smile and was clearly relieved. "Just when were you planning to tell us?"

191

"Right about now," laughed Jack. "We'll be staying in Tom's guest house, for as long as we like, in exchange for a few simple chores around the place."

"What kind of chores?" quizzed James.

"Chopping firewood," answered Jack.

"And fixin' de roof," added Tom. "No hurry, of course."

"Tom's invited us for supper tonight, too," added Jack.

"Den tomorrow, I kin drives ya'll over to Mobile in me wagon," grinned Tom. "Fer de hitchin'."

"Tom, you're okay," laughed James as he sat down beside Bell and put an arm around her. "I told you it would be fine."

"Shouldn't we even try to just go ahead and jump when we toss out the suitcases?" Bell suddenly asked. "What if we can't find 'em again? What if someone else grabs them first?"

"Wudn't be safe," replied Tom. "But, if we do dis right, den ders no way dey wud see us or de baggage. It'll be fine."

"We'll follow your lead," pledged Jack. The others finally nodded their consent, one by one. "Hey, we're going to make this work. Trust me!" Jack then put his right hand in front of him, palm down.

"This will work," remarked James as he put his right hand on top of Jack's, palm down.

"Let's hope so," muttered Ellie Mae as she and Bell each put their hands on top of his.

"All fer one, 'n one fer all," smiled Tom as he completed the stack by putting his hand on top of the others.

It was high noon on Sunday, September 29, 1929, as the overdue freight train finally approached the La Batre train station. The Alabama humidity was stifling. The five stowaways had successfully thrown their luggage from the train about a mile back and were positioned by the open door of the train car, ready to jump on Tom's signal.

"Hey look at this," noticed Bell as she snatched up one of the newspapers that had slid from a chicken coop. "It's yesterday's paper."

"We can read it later," advised James.

"It's dated Saturday, September 28," continued Bell as she ignored his direction. "It says the Bahamas hurricane passed over

192

Long Key, Florida yesterday – which would actually be two days ago, since this is yesterday's paper. Then, it goes on to say that although the southern peninsula was hit hardest by the strong winds, that damage was only moderate. Hey, didn't you say that Alabama's right next door to Florida? What if the hurricane hit *here,* too?"

"Here, give me that!" barked Jack as he snatched the newspaper from his brother's fiancé and tossed it out the open car door and caused it to fly away. "Now, pay attention!"

"Yes, sir!" responded Bell with a military style salute as she made a face at Jack.

"See dat big tree comin' up?" pointed out Tom. "We needs to jump, the moment it goes by. Den we lands in dat thicket jus' past it."

Jack unexpectedly swooped Ellie Mae into his arms.

"Hey, what are you doing?"

"Making sure you have something to land on," grinned Jack as he suddenly leaped from the train while holding her as the tree passed.

Bell then felt Tom grab her by one arm and James grab her by the other, as they jumped together, pulling her out with them. The three of them landed in a twisted pile, with Bell on top.

"Ya'll good over der?" called Tom as he untangled himself and stood up to brush off his ragged pants.

"We're great!" answered Jack, who lay on the ground with Ellie Mae on top of him and began to flirt with her.

"Den run!" commanded Tom. "As far as we kin before de train stops! Den we kin hide 'til it goes again."

"I think I've sprained my ankle," realized Bell when she tried to stand up.

"Oh, hell!" cursed James as he picked her up and began to run after the others.

After noticing that they were lagging behind, Tom paused and waited for them to catch up.

"Kin I spell ya?"

"Please!" agreed James as he handed Bell to Tom.

Like Ellie Mae, Bell had noticed Tom's rippling muscles and good looks, but could not believe how much faster Tom was able to run while carrying her than James had been able to manage.

"Keep a runnin'!" hollered Tom as he sprinted closer to where Jack and Ellie Mae were. "Watch yer step! Der be roots der."

Once he noticed that Tom was carrying Bell, Jack suddenly reached over and swooped up Ellie Mae.

"I can do this!" she objected.

"I know," answered Jack, "but we need to get as far as we can before that train stops, and besides, you shouldn't be running in your condition, anyway."

Ellie Mae merely nodded. She knew her brother was right.

The unbelievably thick brush beside them would provide perfect camouflage once they hid, but would anything else be lurking in the underbrush when they did? wondered Jack.

"Hide!" commanded Tom as the train finally came to a complete stop. "In der! Quick!"

No sooner had the five travelers managed to secret themselves in a dense thicket, then the conductor and his assistant began opening up the car doors. They were still easily able to see the train and the men now unloading it. Other men soon joined them, hosing out various cars after unloading the cargo.

"Won't the hose reach any farther?" frowned the conductor.

"We got another extender," replied one of the men. "I'll go hook it up."

"Good," approved the conductor. "We need to get as many of 'em hosed out as we can. Especially that one! It absolutely reeks!" He nodded his head toward the car where several chicken coops were haphazardly stacked but were being removed by the workers.

"They're going to remember the door was shut on that car!" fretted Bell. "What if they come looking for us?"

James merely clamped his hand over her mouth and gave her a stern look. *Didn't she realize how tenuous their situation was?*

The buzz of flies and other insect life around them was prolific as they waited in the muggy heat.

"Oh!" muttered Ellie Mae as she swatted at a mosquito on her arm.

"Shh!" cautioned Jack.

Bell grabbed James's hand and removed it from her mouth as she silently glared at him. *How could she have been foolish enough to have gotten herself into such a situation?*

It was over an hour before the freight train blew its whistle and began to move again. Workers at the La Batre Train Depot were still busy handling crates of chickens and other cargo as they placed it onto horse-drawn wagons that were waiting.

"What is taking them so long?" Bell finally whispered.

"It takes as long as it takes," answered Jack.

"Well, I have to use the restroom!" informed Bell. "I just can't wait any longer."

"Me, too," advised Ellie Mae with an apologetic look on her face. "Sorry!" The urge to urinate more frequently due to her pregnant condition was becoming more and more of an inconvenience.

Tom suddenly pulled out a wicked-looking knife from a sheath strapped to his leg, and began hacking away the undergrowth behind them. It was about 18 inches long and clearly home crafted. Then, after checking for snakes or other possible hazards, he nodded with his head.

"Don't worry," chuckled Jack. "We'll all look the other way."

Even after Ellie Mae and Bell had relieved themselves, it was nearly another hour before Tom indicated it was finally safe for them to resume their trek down the tracks, toward their luggage. *Would it still be there?*

At 3:30 in the heat of the afternoon, Tom, Jack, Ellie Mae, James and Bell, finally managed to locate their luggage. The humidity made it difficult to breathe and sweat was dripping down their dirt-streaked faces. Other wet places on their clothing was telling, as well. The hum of each attacking fly or mosquito would quickly be silenced after being swatted by its victim. For the most part, their suitcases were none the worse for wear, but something had savagely clawed open Tom's sack and stolen most of its contents.

"Der goes de whole stash," frowned Tom as he sadly shook his head.

"What was in there, anyway?" asked Jack as he set Ellie Mae down beside him. "And what could have done that to your sack?"

"Deer meat for sumthin'," shrugged Tom as he located the hide nearby, which was still in reasonable condition. "Kud be anythin' done did dis. At least de Missus will be happy fer dis hide." Tom carefully folded the deer hide and returned it to what was left of his burlap sack before spinning it shut and tying it to the sturdy stick on which he carried it.

195

"Do you go hunting like this often?" questioned James as he placed Bell beside her large suitcase.

"Now 'n den," revealed Tom. "We still gots plenty 'o food in de swamp, just nothin' like dat wud 'o been."

"Looks like I still have several cans of beans," notified Jack. "And my canteen's still half full." Jack then removed the lid, took a sip, and handed it to Ellie Mae.

"Mine's okay, too," apprised James. "Even what's left of the bread and apples is still here."

After each of them took a drink of water from Jack's canteen, he carefully replaced the lid and returned the nearly empty canteen to his large duffel bag. *How would he carry both his stuff and Ellie Mae's suitcase, and her, too?*

"I *can* walk," reminded Ellie Mae. Then turning to Tom, she questioned, "We won't be running again, will we?"

"Not if we get der by dark," replied Tom as he handed a piece of jerky to each of them. "Dat's all dats left. Was in de pocket."

"Thanks!" nodded Jack as he stuffed it into his mouth.

"Just how far is it?" grilled James as he quickly devoured the jerky. *Did he dare steal a drink from his canteen? No, he would wait. The others would need to drink again.*

"We kin do it," answered Tom, without directly answering the question. He was evasive like that when it suited him. "Wanna carry her or de suitcases?"

James then tested Bell's large suitcase and thought about it for a moment. Combined with the weight of his own suitcase, the total load would be just as heavy as Bell was, if not more. Not only that, it would be awkward.

"We kin trade off," grinned Tom.

After a deep sigh, James decided, "I'll start off with the suitcases."

"Shouldn't we check mine first to see if anything's damaged?" pressed Bell as Tom picked her up.

"Would it make a difference at this point if it was?" interjected James as he picked up the two suitcases, one with each arm.

Bell merely shook her head in the negative as Tom moved past Jack and into the lead. "Stay close."

196

The travelworn group trudged along in relative silence for quite some time. The continuous hum of insect life was soon joined by the noise of frogs, birds and other unidentifiable species.

Tom suddenly stopped and carefully set Bell down. By his posture, the others could tell that something was wrong. Tom put his finger to his lips to indicate silence as he reached for his knife and sliced it toward a low hanging limb by Bell's head.

When realizing that the limb had actually been a large snake, Bell screamed with fright.

"Looks like we got supper after all," grinned Tom as he put away the knife, handed Bell the headless reptile, and picked her back up.

Bell let out a series of shrieks as she tried to shove the snake away. *This was the last straw!*

Jack and the others could not help but laugh at the scene as Tom quickly hoisted the snake back onto Bell's lap with his knee before adjusting the weight in his arms again.

"Don't drop it," called Jack. "Otherwise, we may need to eat you instead!"

"Very funny!" retorted Bell, angry until she saw the amused smirk on Tom's face. She then nodded and began to smile, too. "Okay, I'll carry the snake."

"What kind was that?" grilled James.

"Cottonmouth," replied Tom.

"Isn't that the same thing as a water moccasin?" asked Bell.

"Yep."

"Those are poisonous! We can't eat this!"

"Just de sac," advised Tom. "Dat was on de head."

"Have you ever eaten one of these before?" grilled Bell.

"Many times, perty lady," flirted Tom. He was beginning to see why Jack enjoyed giving her such a hard time.

"It's actually quite heavy, isn't it?" realized Bell as she struggled to keep a grip on the large snake's body.

"Yep," agreed Tom.

"Huh," nodded Bell as she turned to study their surroundings.

Though heavily forested, the area they were in had few herbaceous plants, due to the lack of adequate sunlight. Mostly cattails, swamp lilies and other plants able to tolerate the high iron and low oxygen levels beneath the towering cypress and black gum trees that grew there. The winding trail they were on was slick and muddy, and in several places was barely discernable.

"Have you ever just tried bushwhacking it through here?" questioned Jack. He was becoming impatient by the many turns and twists in their circuitous route.

"Only once," answered Tom. "Lost me Uncle Joe to some quicksand a while back."

"You didn't even try to pull him out?" Bell was horrified.

"Not after dat 'gator got him by the leg," revealed Tom. "Joe wudn't 'o wanted to go thru life like dat."

"What *else* is in here?" asked Ellie Mae as she began to glance more nervously at either side of the trail.

"Bugs, bears, coons, snakes, thorns 'n quicksand, mostly," elaborated Tom. "Sum poison plants, too."

"Nice place," sniggered James.

"What do you do for fresh vegetables?" queried Ellie Mae.

"Ya sure asks lots 'o questions," chuckled Tom.

"Yes, what do you do for fresh greens and other salad stuff?" pressed Bell.

"We grows it," answered Tom.

"Where?" asked Bell. "Certainly not in here!"

"Der be places."

"Near where we're going?"

"Yes 'um."

"What kind of things do you grow there?" persisted Bell.

"Taters, maters, eggplant, peppers, squash and leafy stuff," described Tom.

Bell seemed surprised by his response. "So, you're telling me there's a place where these things can all be grown and get plenty of sunlight near your cabin?"

Tom merely smiled and nodded. "Near de guest house, too."

James was becoming tired of carrying the luggage, but decided not to mention it. *The longer Tom was willing to keep carrying Bell for him, the less likely he would be tempted to just toss her into some quicksand and leave her there!*

"Can we rest?" Ellie Mae suddenly asked.

"We's almost der," assured Tom.

"It's my ankle," apologized Ellie Mae. "Something bit me earlier, and it's starting to swell."

Tom's face took on a worried expression when he saw it. Then, turning to Jack, he instructed, "Leave de luggage. We kin come back. She shudn't walk on dat no more. We really is almost der."

Complying at once, Jack set down the two suitcases and picked Ellie Mae up. Tom then set Bell down long enough to put down his sack. He then tossed the snake onto the ground beside it and turned to James. "Kin ya watch de stuff?"

"Sure," agreed James as he watched Tom pick Bell back up and then race ahead with Jack close on his heels.

Seemingly alone in the primeval swamp forest with four suitcases, a worn-out burlap sack containing Tom's deer hide, and the large dead snake, James slowly sat down on Bell's huge suitcase to wait.

What if they didn't come back? What would he do? James knew of no way he could possibly find his way back out alone.

The deepening shadows seemed to come to life around him as the few remaining glimmers of sunlight disappeared for the night. *It was going to be dark in a matter of minutes.* All at once, a nearby log began to move towards him! The end of the log opened up, revealing a wicked-looking set of teeth inside its gaping mouth as it yawned. It was a huge alligator! *He had almost sat on that log!*

James hurriedly glanced toward a nearby tree. *Were there any snakes in it? Was it safe to climb?* The hanging moss on many of its limbs could potentially be hiding places for other dangers, too. What, he had no idea, but undoubtedly something deadly.

"James?" called an unfamiliar voice from the darkness.

Four tall, muscular black men were approaching, each carrying a torch. "James?" called another of them.

"Here!" answered James. "There's a huge alligator coming at me, right on the trail between us."

The sound of a machete being drawn could be heard. Then, by torchlight, James watched with disbelief as the four men converged upon the alligator, three of them holding it in place while the fourth hacked repeatedly at its huge head. Only after several tries, did the creature become still. Then, to make certain it was dead, he savagely hacked off its head.

199

"We'll need to come back for that guy in the morning, if it's still here," advised the man with the machete. "Hey James, you okay?"

"Yes, I'm fine," assured James, though he was badly shaken after what he'd just witnessed.

"I'm Tom's son Zeke," informed the man as he nodded cordially at James. "These are my brothers Nate, Shad and Bart." They each smiled and nodded as they were introduced. James noticed immediately that Zeke's grammar was much better than his father's.

"How's my sister?" questioned James as he reached for the nearest suitcase.

"She'll be fine," assured Zeke as he and his brothers grabbed up the luggage. "Can you just get pa's sack?"

"Sure," agreed James. "What about the snake he killed earlier? He seemed to want it."

"We can get that when we come back for the 'gator," replied Zeke. "Right now, we need to get you back. Not only that, ma's got supper on and they're waiting on us."

Tom's cabin was like nothing James had ever seen. The outline of its shape in the deepening shadows reflected in the eerie swamp beside it as lantern light shone from its front and side windows. The full moon could be seen overhead; its light was beginning to filter in through the thick canopy of cypress and black gum trees above. The entire cabin was built on huge wooden pylons, elevated several feet above the ground. A spacious deck surrounding the structure was enclosed by a sturdy wooden railing, designed to keep out as many swamp creatures as possible. It appeared to be roughly 60 feet square.

The wide steps and handrails leading up to its front door were partially covered in moss and other slime near the bottom, and separated from the deck by a small gate that swung open. Once inside the deck area, the gate would be securely latched to keep any creatures out that might decide to climb the steps behind them.

"Is this the guest house?" asked James as they climbed the steps.

"You'll see that tomorrow," advised Zeke. "It's too late tonight to try and go over there."

"And way too dangerous," added Nate.

After carefully stacking the four pieces of luggage on the deck beside the front door, Tom's sons opened it and motioned for James to come inside.

"You can leave pa's sack out here," indicated Zeke.

As James stepped inside the cabin with Tom's sons, the overwhelming smell of delicious food enveloped him. A sturdy wooden table with two long benches, one on each side, was neatly set with 10 place settings of elegant china and expensive-looking silverware. Candles in the middle between each facing place added to the atmosphere.

"Welcome!" greeted Tom as he motioned toward his wife. "Dat be Hattie."

"Hattie LaMont," smiled the woman as she came over to shake James's hand.

Hattie's light olive complexion and piercing green eyes were stunning. She would have to be at least 40 years old to have four sons as old as Zeke and his brothers, but her beauty was ageless. Her long, dark wavy hair clung seductively to her nicely shaped body. The red and black evening dress she wore was made of silk and looked quite expensive. Hattie also wore several diamond rings, golden bracelets, necklaces, and dangling earrings. One of the necklaces she wore had a tiny golden human skull attached to it.

James was speechless. This was not what he had expected, at all. *Why would someone like her have married someone like Tom?*

"I perceive that you have many questions," smiled Hattie. "Those can wait until we've eaten. I presume you have also met my four sons?"

"Uh, yes," stammered James. He had never seen anyone as voluptuous or compelling as Hattie before.

"They're quadruplets," grinned Ellie Mae.

"Really?" *No wonder they looked so much alike.*

"Hezekiah seems to think he should tell people his name is Zeke," began Hattie as she pulled out a chair and motioned for James to sit. "Nathaniel has chosen to tell people his name is Nate," added Hattie as she motioned for the others to join him.

"Would *you* tell people your name was Shadrak?" questioned Shad as he and his brothers sat down.

"It is an honorable name!" scolded their mother as she began pouring water in each of their crystal goblets from an elegant china

201

pitcher. "As is Bartholomew!" she added as she glanced at Bart with her piercing green eyes.

"But, my name's just Tom," grinned her husband. "Just plain Tom. Never nothin' else."

"Huh," replied Hattie as she gave her handsome husband an affectionate wink and a seductive smile. She clearly had not married him for his grammar skills. "Shall we join hands as our new friend Jack blesses the food for us?" Everyone quickly complied.

"Dear God," began Jack. "Thank you for sending Tom to save us, and for his help as we start our new lives. We thank you also for his lovely family, for their hospitality, and for this delicious meal. Amen."

"Amen!" chorused the others.

"Oh, veal!" exclaimed Bell as a large platter of meat was passed to her. "My favorite."

Without waiting for the next food item to arrive, Bell quickly sampled some of it. "Oh, this is amazing!"

"Thank you," smiled Hattie.

"She cooks de best 'gator in the bayou," grinned Tom.

Bell immediately stopped chewing the bite of food that was still in her mouth and questioned, "Alligator? This is alligator?"

"I'll take some of that," laughed James as he tried a bite. "That's actually quite good."

The others were amused as they watched Bell finish chewing and swallowing her bite. "Actually, it is."

"Yes, it's delicious," agreed Ellie Mae, who had also tried some.

Jack then took the platter from her and put a healthy portion of it onto his plate. Even as Zeke was still taking the platter from him, Jack stabbed a piece of it with his fork and devoured it. "Wow!"

"I'm glad you all like it," nodded Hattie.

"What's *that?*" frowned Bell as another unfamiliar dish was passed to her.

"Fried zucchini with bell pepper and onion," informed Hattie. "I trust you've had squash before?"

"Oh, okay," nodded Bell. "Yeah, sure. But this smells divine. I don't believe I've ever seen it prepared this way."

Hattie merely nodded before changing the subject. "You ladies are fortunate to be alive. Especially Ellie Mae."

202

"What was wrong with her?" asked James as he nodded toward his sister.

"Hattie said I was bitten by a spider," informed Ellie Mae.

"A brown recluse," clarified Hattie. "Very deadly without proper treatment."

"What did you do for it?" questioned James as he suddenly noticed the extensive pharmacopeia of herbs and dried plants hanging from the ceiling along one wall, along with several handwoven baskets with interesting patterns on them. A large stone mortar and pestle that had recently been used were still sitting on the wooden countertop beneath them.

"Luckily for us, Jewelweed grows in abundance in wet shady places like this," explained Hattie as she handed a platter of fresh tomato slices to James. "And, of course, it is always best when harvested during the summer months."

"How does it work?" asked James.

"The leaves and stems can be crushed and used as a poultice to help draw out the poison," elaborated Hattie. "It's also good for other things, too, including poison ivy."

"My ankle does feel much better," assured Ellie Mae.

"Mine, too," advised Bell. *How come James hadn't asked about her ankle?*

"That stuff helps with pain, too?" questioned James, almost as if reading her mind.

"Bell's treatment was different than Ellie Mae's," interjected Hattie with amusement. "Bunchberry, which is similar in appearance to Dogwood, is a ground covering of small greenish to brownish flowers, surrounded by four larger white petals. Its leaves and roots can be used to make a special tea that treats aches and pains."

"I read once that it can also be used for infant colic," remembered Ellie Mae.

"Wild mint tea is good for colic, too," interjected Hattie, "but most people use it for colds and fevers."

"That could be useful," nodded Jack. Even he was familiar with what wild mint was.

"How did you two meet?" questioned Ellie Mae.

"My father was a ship captain," replied Hattie.

"Frum de Caribbean," added Tom as he flirted with his wife.

"Tom was helping to unload it when I happened to come ashore," reminisced Hattie. "It was love at first sight."

"But der were problems," recalled Tom.

"Not from my father, though," Hattie quickly explained. "From the Government here."

"Because of your nationality?" frowned Ellie Mae.

"No, not because of that, either," answered Hattie.

"Cause 'o mine," informed Tom.

"I don't understand," admitted Ellie Mae. "Aren't you an American citizen?"

"Yes 'um, I is," replied Tom.

"You see," elaborated Hattie, "there are strict laws that prevent interracial marriage. They are called miscegenation laws."

"What?" scowled Jack.

"They ban the marriage between all whites and non-white groups, primarily blacks, but even Indians, or people such as myself from other countries," explained Hattie. "Someday that will change, I just know it. But, not in our lifetimes."

"So, you're not actually married?" pressed Ellie Mae.

"We were married by a licensed preacher, yes," confirmed Hattie. "We even have the license to prove it."

"Der be lots 'o those kind 'o preachers 'round dez parts," assured Tom, "'specially since dey outlawed all de liquor."

"What would that have to do with it?" wondered Jack.

"They allow preachers and pharmacists to buy liquor," perceived James as he nodded his head with understanding.

"So, everybody who wants to buy liquor has to become either a preacher or a pharmacist first?" asked Bell.

"Pretty much," laughed Zeke, who rarely interjected himself into his parents' conversations unless directly spoken to.

"Zeke here runs de family liquor business," grinned Tom. "He knows lots 'o preachers."

"But, we want to get married by a *real* preacher!" advised Bell.

"Dey's as real as it gets, miss," assured Tom. "Dey surely is."

"Your problems will be of a different nature," predicted Hattie. Her piercing green eyes seemed to look straight through each of them.

"Mother is a seer, too," informed Shad. "She knows things."

"Perhaps after dinner, you will allow me to do a reading?" offered Hattie.

"What kind of things?" questioned Ellie Mae with concern.

"Things to come, things that have been, or even things that might be," described Hattie as she gazed at each of her guests. "The future is never certain, but knowledge of its possibilities can be useful."

Once everyone had finished eating, Hattie announced, "The men will all sleep out on the deck tonight. Including you, Tom!"

"But ...," began Tom.

"That's what you get for gallivanting all over the countryside like that and leaving your poor family here to worry about whether you're dead or alive!" advised Hattie with finality. "Besides, it's the girls' wedding day tomorrow. They'll need a good bath first, and some private time."

"We'll get the tub," volunteered Zeke as he and his brothers got up to go retrieve it from the back deck.

Tom gave Hattie a pleading look but realized at once that it was in vain. He would need to wait until the following night to be with his wife again.

"I'm looking forward to tomorrow night," flirted Hattie in softer tones as she deliberately rubbed her hip against Tom while she passed.

Tom grinned and shook his head. "Come on, guys, we got us a 'gator to go fetch, anyway."

"And a snake," reminded James.

"Dat, too," nodded Tom as Zeke and Shad entered the cabin with a large washtub and carried it to the middle of the kitchen area before setting it down. Immediately behind them followed Bart and Nate, each carrying a large bucket of clean water.

"Go ahead and pour it in," directed Hattie as she relit the wood stove. "I'll heat up the rest on the stove."

Her boys quickly left but almost immediately returned again with two additional buckets of clean water, that they placed on the floor near the wood stove.

"Good night, mama," bid Zeke as he kissed her on the cheek.

"We'll be outside with the other men," grinned Shad.

"Last I checked, you boys are only 16," reminded Hattie with an amused smile.

"Does that mean we can stay inside tonight?" asked Nate as he flirted with Bell.

"Absolutely not!" exclaimed Hattie. "Now, run along! All of you. The ladies are going to need some privacy."

"Ladies," Bart bid them goodnight with a polite nod as he and his brothers left.

Hattie wasted no time pouring the water from one of the buckets into a large kettle on her stove to begin heating it.

"What about *our* suitcases?" asked Bell.

"Boys!" called Hattie through the open window. "Bring in the two biggest suitcases out there. I'm sure they must belong to the ladies here." And, of course, she was right.

Zeke quickly entered carrying Bell's large suitcase-like trunk, with Shad behind him carrying Ellie Mae's.

"That's the one!" beamed Bell. *Now she would finally have an opportunity to check on her things.*

"Thank you!" called Ellie Mae as they left.

Satisfied that the water was heating sufficiently, Hattie turned to a freestanding closet made of hand-finished wood. Inside were several shelves containing clean towels, linens and other things.

"You will need these," offered Hattie as she handed a bar of soap and a clean towel to Ellie Mae.

"Thank you!" exclaimed Ellie Mae. She looked as if she were going to cry. "How can we ever repay you?"

"You can't," smiled Hattie, "so don't even try."

"Thanks," beamed Bell as Hattie handed her a towel, also. She obviously was intended to use the bar of soap Ellie Mae had when she was finished with it.

"You don't have any curtains?" Ellie Mae suddenly noticed.

"They won't look," chuckled Hattie as she retrieved the kettle of water from the stove and poured it into the tub. "And even if they do, so what? Perhaps they might learn a thing or two."

After only a slight hesitation, Ellie Mae quickly disrobed and climbed inside the tub. The lukewarm water felt wonderful.

"There should be more in a few minutes," promised Hattie as she again filled the kettle on the stove.

"Do you know what you plan to wear tomorrow?" Hattie suddenly asked as she pulled up a chair.

206

"Just something clean," answered Ellie Mae as she lathered herself with the homemade lye soap.

"I might have something that will fit you," offered Hattie. "My only daughter was bitten by a snake and passed when she was quite young. She would be about your age by now. I was saving it for her."

"What was her name?" asked Ellie Mae.

"Elleanor. Elleanor LaMont." Hattie fought back a stray tear as she hurried over to the stove to check again on the water's temperature. "This should be perfect." Hattie then returned and poured it into the tub. "Good thing it was wash day today."

"I'd like to clean up, too," reminded Bell.

"Silence!" commanded Hattie with a look of censure that sent a chill to Bell's bones. "You will get your turn when Ellie Mae is finished soaking her ankle, and not a moment before! The warm water will help draw out any remaining poison, so she needs to soak a while longer."

"Will you be able to do that reading you were talking about after this?" Ellie Mae suddenly wanted to know.

"Do you feel comfortable and relaxed now?"

"Absolutely," smiled Ellie Mae as she piled her wet hair on top of her head and slid her naked body deeper into the warm tub.

"Excellent. Then we shall do it now," decided Hattie as she sat back down in the chair beside the tub, and took Ellie Mae's hands in hers. "And Bell, you must remain absolutely silent."

Bell merely nodded. Something about Hattie made her nervous enough to comply.

"Good," approved Hattie as she turned her piercing green eyes back towards Ellie Mae. "I want you to relax. Close your eyes and think of Jack, the love of your life, and how much he means to you."

Hattie then closed her eyes and almost seemed to be in a trance. "Is this true?" demanded Hattie as she unexpectedly opened her eyes and gazed at Ellie Mae with surprise. "Jack is your *brother*?"

"Half-brother," corrected Ellie Mae as she opened her eyes, too. "We have different mothers."

"And yet you bear his *children*?" grilled Hattie as she sadly shook her head.

"It *is* possible we have different fathers," added Ellie Mae.

"No, you do not," assured Hattie as she studied Ellie Mae more closely. "Do you love him?"

"Jack? Of course I love him."

"Your father, Jed," clarified Hattie. "Do you love him?"

"Yes," frowned Ellie Mae. *How did Hattie know his name?*

"He misses you greatly," continued Hattie. "The three of you have broken his heart, especially *you!*"

Ellie Mae's face took on a faraway expression.

"But, you will see him again," promised Hattie.

"What did you mean by *children?*" questioned Ellie Mae.

"There is more than one life within you," replied Hattie with a tender smile as she finally let go of her hands and then gently wiped the wet hair from Ellie Mae's eyes. "Twin boys."

"Really? Twins? Then it's a good thing we came here so we can get married," mentioned Ellie Mae as her mouth slowly widened into an irrepressible grin.

"I agree. It is very important that you and Jack get married soon, but the laws forbidding siblings to get married are very strict, even here in Alabama," Hattie informed her. "At *any* age."

"What are we going to do?" Ellie Mae's smile disappeared.

"I have an idea," advised Hattie as she opened the clean towel and held it for Ellie Mae to put around herself as she climbed from the tub. "Bell, it's your turn."

"Aren't we going to replace the water first?" frowned Bell as she hobbled toward the tub. She had already opened her suitcase and managed to sort through the fragments of broken china. *At least her clothing was undamaged, but bathing in someone else's dirty water seemed unimaginable.*

"Not unless you plan to go get it yourself," replied Hattie, without sympathy for Bell's sprained ankle. *Anyone foolish enough to wear high heels while trying to hop a freight train deserved to suffer the consequences. Perhaps it would teach Bell a valuable lesson.* "Besides, the trail would be covered with alligators and who knows what else this time of night."

"This will do," relented Bell with a deep sigh as she disrobed and climbed in. She was vaguely aware that another set of eyes was watching her through the open window but was too tired and dirty to even care.

Hattie rushed over to the closet and removed a small box from the top shelf. The box was shaped like a treasure chest and covered with tiny shells. Hattie carefully set it on the table by her

208

pharmacopeia and opened its lid. Inside were several important papers. "Here it is," informed Hattie after finding the item she was looking for. "The birth certificate for Elleanor LaMont, born in 1912."

"I was born in 1912," revealed Ellie Mae.

"I could sense it," nodded Hattie. "And fortunately for *you*, Elleanor's death was never officially reported, so as far as the authorities are concerned, she's still alive. Best of all, she was born right here, in Alabama. I'm telling you, it was destiny that brought you here!"

"Ellie Mae and Elleanor do kind of sound alike," recognized Bell. It was obvious to her what Hattie was suggesting.

"Why would you say that?" Ellie Mae did not understand.

"*You* can be Elleanor!" exclaimed Hattie. "It's perfect!"

The reality of what Hattie was proposing finally sunk in.

"That's not a bad idea," agreed Bell as she soaped herself up and began scrubbing her hair.

"Wouldn't that be illegal?" Ellie Mae was shocked by the idea.

"Not as illegal as marrying your own brother," Hattie assured her. "You try that around here, and they'll throw the book at both of you!"

Ellie Mae carefully opened her suitcase as she considered the idea, and removed a clean pair of underwear and pajamas that she put on before attempting to brush her hair. Her shoulder length medium brown hair was usually worn parted on the side, but just for fun she tried parting it in the middle. The small hand mirror she had brought with her was now cracked and caused her reflection to stare back at her in two halves. *Would she now have seven years of bad luck?*

"Hattie's right," opined Bell. "I'd listen to her."

Hattie then sat down beside the tub again, closed her eyes, and extended her hands towards Bell, palms up. Bell shrugged her shoulders and placed her hands on top of them, palms down. Bell's golden blonde hair was now hanging in loose wet strands around her face.

Hattie slowly opened her eyes and sadly shook her head.

"What?" demanded Bell.

"Danger follows you, my child," warned Hattie. "But, the future is not yet certain. You must exercise great caution while you are here in the bayou."

Hattie then glanced toward the window and noticed that Nate was peeking inside. He immediately ducked out of sight when realizing that his mother had seen him. *Would she know it was him, or think it was one of his brothers?*

"Here, put this on," indicated Hattie as she stood up, unfolded the towel, and held it for Bell, deliberately blocking any unsolicited viewing from the window as she did.

"What kind of danger?" scowled Bell.

"You must never go anywhere alone," elaborated Hattie. "Not even to the outhouse."

"Speaking of outhouse," interjected Ellie Mae, "I think I need to go there, most urgently."

"Not at night," responded Hattie. "There is a collection pot behind that curtain. Be *sure* you put the lid back on tight when you are finished. The boys will take it to the outhouse in the morning."

"Won't they be coming in here to use it during the night?" asked Bell, suddenly wondering about it.

"They have their own pot, on the deck," advised Hattie as she studied Bell more closely. She was well aware of the interest her son Nate had shown in Bell and that he had been the one peeking inside.

"What a shame they will have to wait until morning to bathe," added Bell, rather surreptitiously.

"They have a few buckets of their own water out there, too," smirked Hattie. *She would definitely need to keep Nate and Bell apart!*

Ellie Mae paused to admire the intricately woven pattern in the hanging curtain which covered the collection pot corner. It extended from ceiling to floor. The white lilies depicted had bright yellow centers, emerald green leaves, and gave the appearance of floating in a pond. Expensive-looking brass rings at the top were placed through small round grommets – like the ones normally found on a shower curtain – and hung from a hand-crafted wooden rod suspended from the ceiling. A series of alligator teeth had each been drilled at the root end and sewn to the curtain's bottom hem to keep it weighted.

Surprised after removing its lid to find a regular toilet seat on the collection pot, Ellie Mae carefully glanced inside for any possible snakes or spiders before sitting down. There was even a roll of toilet paper placed on a forked stick that had been fastened to the wall for that purpose. *There must be a store someplace nearby,* she reasoned. *Perhaps she could still get another mirror.*

"Are you okay?" called Hattie.

"Oh, yes, I'm fine," Ellie Mae assured her as she hurried to finish.

"You've got to see this," commented Bell.

When Ellie Mae pulled back the curtain, she could see Bell holding up a beautiful wedding dress while Hattie inspected it. An aging trunk lined with cedar and red satin sat open nearby.

"There you are," beamed Hattie. "I'd like you to try this on."

"It's beautiful!" gasped Ellie Mae as she studied the elegant ballroom style gown with its plunging neckline and delicate lace sleeves. Yards and yards of white satin ruffles hung from its diminutive waistline in stately fashion. Individual pearls had been sewn in a spiral design up the form fitting bodice sides and front, vaguely resembling the tentacles of an octopus reaching toward the wearer's bosom.

"Very beautiful!" approved Bell.

"It belonged to my mother," informed Hattie as she took the dress from Bell and held it up to Ellie Mae. "She would be pleased to know that the tradition of wearing it didn't die with me."

"What about the women your sons will marry someday?" asked Ellie Mae as she admired the dress.

"I would like *you* to have it," advised Hattie with finality as she handed the dress to Ellie Mae and went back over to the open trunk. "This veil was once worn by a Contessa whose father was unable to pay my father his gambling debt. It actually matches the dress rather well, don't you think?" Hattie then held it up for them to see. The hand-sewn pearls on its floor-length lace train were nearly an exact match to the pearls on the bodice of the wedding dress.

"Was your father some kind of a pirate or something?" teased Bell. She was only being facetious, of course.

"That's exactly what he was," revealed Hattie with a serious face. "He would make deliveries all over the world, including here."

"Were *you* raised on a pirate ship?" queried Ellie Mae.

"Indeed, I was," confirmed Hattie with a mysterious smile.

"Oh, try it on!" urged Bell.

Crouched in the darkness by the window outside, Nate studied the shimmering surface of the swamp for any sign of life. Moonlight streamed through the thick canopy of hanging moss on the cypress and black gum trees overhead. The symphony of frogs, crickets and other familiar night noises hinted of nothing unusual or concerning.

Tom had asked that one of his sons remain behind to keep watch over things while he and the other men went after the alligator and snake carcasses, a task for which Nate had eagerly volunteered. His firm muscular body was going through a number of changes that were typical and normal for any 16-year old boy, though Nate had no way of knowing why he was drawn to Bell like he was. Just watching her step into the tub to bathe herself had aroused desires within him that he had never experienced before. *Why was he so drawn to the blonde woman?* Nate knew it was wrong to have such thoughts about a woman getting ready to be married to someone else, but he could not help himself. His body responded to just the thought of her, though no one was there to see the embarrassing bulge beneath his clothing.

Unable to resist any longer, Nate stealthily crept toward the open window again. *He must have another look at her!* Much to his disappointment, Bell and the other young woman were now clothed in pajamas. *What were they doing with mother's wedding dress?*

Nate continued to watch while Ellie Mae removed her pajamas and stepped into the beautiful gown. Even the sight of Ellie Mae without clothes on created a deep stirring within him, but not nearly so much as Bell. Embarrassed and ashamed of himself for responding that way, Nate glanced around to be sure he was still alone on the deck.

Had he imagined the way Bell had looked at him earlier? wondered Nate. *After all, she technically wasn't married yet, so she was fair game, wasn't she? Could her head be turned before the ceremony tomorrow?* Nate tried to envision himself holding Bell in his arms, pulling her close and passionately kissing those delicate lips.

"It's beautiful!" he could hear Bell say as Ellie Mae swirled around in the stunning gown. *Bell would look even better in the dress than she does,* thought Nate as he noticed his mother glancing toward the window again and silently ducked in the nick of time.

Morning came way too early for everyone. It was Monday, September 30, 1929, so the courthouse in Mobile would be open.

Breakfast was over with and the entire wedding party was assembled on the deck of Tom's cabin. Ellie Mae was dressed in the elegant gown and veil given to her by Hattie, while Bell was dressed in a simple white wool skirt and suitcoat with a white silk blouse and was already sweating profusely. Jack and James were dressed in black rumpled suits that were in desperate need of an iron. Due to Jack's unusual size, the sleeves and pantlegs on his suit were insufficient in length and unusually snug. He and James were also sweating from the humidity. *What would they do as the day wore on and it really got hot?*

"Where's the wagon?" frowned Bell when she noticed Tom rowing a large rowboat up to the shoreline, just feet away from the bottom step to his cabin. Behind it was a second boat, tied to it by a sturdy rope with a square knot.

"At de barn," grinned Tom.

"It wouldn't be safe to take the horses through the swamp," explained Zeke, as he nodded towards the thickly overgrown trail behind them, that they had walked on the previous day.

"Not wid all dem 'gators," added Tom as he tied off the first rowboat by wrapping its mooring line around the closest pylon supporting his cabin.

"Huh," muttered Bell as she and Ellie Mae came down the steps and climbed into the first boat, closely followed by Hattie, Jack and James. Each of them glanced around first to be sure there were no alligators or other undesirable creatures blocking the way.

"Nate," nodded Tom. "Wud ya'll wanna help me row de weddin' party?"

Nate nodded exuberantly as he rushed forward to climb into the rowboat. He had mentioned to his pa earlier in private that he wanted to be the one to help him row the boat that Bell would be in.

Tom grinned a crooked smile at Nate. *What wud be de harm? Bell wud be hitched by noon anyhow.*

Nate, on the other hand, took seriously the opportunity to do everything in his power to turn Bell's head – even at the last possible moment – and intended to make the most of it.

Once Tom had climbed into the boat with Nate and the wedding party, Zeke untied their mooring line and gave them a little shove. The other rowboat had already been untied from the first and moored ashore by Shad and Bart.

213

"What are they doing?" questioned Bell as she noticed they had brought her large suitcase from the cabin and were coming down the stairs with it.

"Dey be takin' yer luggage to de guest house," advised Tom.

"They're not coming to the wedding with us?" asked Bell.

"No, child," interjected Hattie. "They need to get everything ready for you at your new home."

"Is it anything like yours?" pressed Bell. She was actually more worried about her possessions and not so sure she relished the idea of her suitcase being taken to some unknown destination like it was.

"You'll see," chuckled Hattie. "And don't worry, your things will be just fine."

Bell glanced at Hattie. *How did she do that? Hattie always seemed to know exactly what she was thinking.*

"This is Main Street," advised Nate as he picked up a long stick and began using it to guide the rowboat into the swamp by pushing off the bottom as needed. Meanwhile, Tom was busy at the opposite end of the boat doing the same. Naturally, Nate was at the rear end of the boat, closest to Bell and James.

"Main Street?" repeated James as he deliberately scooted himself closer to Bell and put an arm around her.

"That's our nearest neighbor," nodded Nate with a flirtatious grin at Bell. She and James turned in time to see a rickety floating shack come into view. It was about 20 feet square with a small front porch barely large enough to hold two chairs and an outdoor grill. One of the two trees it was tied to looked ready to collapse. The grill was actually an old 55-gallon drum with a metal grate laid across the top and served both as a way to dispose of trash and to cook meals. The lack of railing around the porch was concerning, especially in such an environment.

"Who lives there?" questioned Ellie Mae from the front end of the boat, where she and Jack were seated behind Tom.

"An old man whose wife died years ago," explained Hattie from behind them. She was seated in the very middle of the boat, wearing the same red and black silk evening gown she'd worn the previous evening. Like the others, she was beginning to suffer from the stifling humidity and increasing heat.

214

"Bob be his name," mentioned Tom as they floated past and continued deeper into the swamp. "De boat be gone, so Bob's probably in town."

"How can you possibly find your way around in here?" questioned Bell as she studied the never-ending view of huge moss-covered trees rising from the murky green depths they were traversing.

"It takes time," flirted Nate. "Just like falling in love."

James merely nodded, but Bell seemed to sense a hidden meaning in Nate's words and glanced up at him.

Nate stared at Bell with unconcealed desire, literally undressing her with his eyes. Bell blushed and suddenly turned away.

"How long have you two been in love?" grilled Nate, hoping to regain her attention.

"Not that long," admitted James. He was completely unaware that the question had been intended more for Bell.

"Better be careful," cautioned Nate, "or someone else might decide to steal such a pretty woman away from you."

The others in the boat had clearly heard Nate's remark and turned to observe the conversation more closely, including Tom and especially Hattie. She did not appear pleased.

"Perhaps you should do the same," advised James, "or some jealous husband might just have to put you in your place."

"Touché!" laughed Jack, who suddenly found the whole thing quite amusing. It was obvious to everyone that Nate was attempting to make a play for Bell and had a desperate crush on her.

"Can't blame a guy for trying," grinned Nate as he continued to flirt with Bell, despite everything.

"You'd best keep an eye on where you're going," recommended Hattie as she nodded at the water ahead.

Both Tom and Nate glanced ahead just in the nick of time to avoid pushing the boat into the path of a rather large alligator.

"That, of course, is one of the local residents," commented Hattie. "One that we normally try to avoid."

"We'll get him, eventually," promised Nate.

"That over there is the guest house," indicated Hattie as she nodded toward another floating house. It was newer, better kept, and moored to a stand of large gum trees on each side to prevent it from floating away, but entirely surrounded by water.

"It's a houseboat," realized Bell as they floated past it.

"Huh," grunted James. *Would it be big enough for both couples to share?*

"There's a curtain across the bedroom," described Hattie with a sly wink at James. It was as if she had read his mind.

"Same size as de other cabin," assured Tom. "Includin' de deck." Even the railing around it appeared to be identical, but without stairs leading up to it. It was only accessible by boat.

"How much farther to the barn?" questioned Jack, who was anxious to get there, drive into town, and be done with the wedding ceremony so he could change into something else.

"Not far," assured Tom as he continued to push against the bottom of the thick green water with his long stick.

Ellie Mae watched as the houseboat that would soon be their home started to disappear from view behind them. *Would they be happy there, and would their husbands be able to find jobs?*

"Oh, look!" exclaimed Bell. "Here comes our luggage!"

Zeke and his brothers smiled and waved at them from the other rowboat as they pulled up to the houseboat and tied off their mooring lines to its sturdy railing.

Tom and the others in his boat waved back before continuing on their way. Nothing else was said for several minutes.

"De barn be just 'round dat next tree," advised Tom as they finally approached a small dock that led to shore where several out buildings were located.

"It won't be long now," grinned Jack as he put an arm around Ellie Mae's waist and pulled her as close as he could in the ample wedding dress.

"Be careful with the dress," instructed Hattie from behind them.

"Sorry," apologized Jack as he loosened his grip.

"And don't forget, her name is Elleanor LaMont," cautioned Hattie as she gazed at the back of Jack's head.

"Oh, that's right," chuckled Jack as he turned around to grin at Hattie, but sobered at once by her intense expression. "Absolutely."

"So, don't slip up and call me by my real name," laughed Ellie Mae as Nate and Tom secured the mooring lines and stood ready to help everyone onto the dock.

216

When it was Bell's turn, Nate hurried over to assist, holding onto her hand longer than was necessary while he gave her a seductive smile. "If you change your mind ...."

"Not a chance," sniggered James as he grabbed her hand from Nate's grasp and pulled her onto the dock himself.

Bell turned to wink and flirt with Nate as they walked away. She just couldn't help herself.

"Enuf's enuf, son," warned Tom as he put a restraining hand on his son's shoulder. "Let's get de horses ready."

The five-mile ride to Mobile in Tom's horse-drawn wagon was dusty and hot, but not as hot as it would be coming back that afternoon.

"Let's stop at the courthouse first," instructed Hattie, who was seated in the front by Tom and Nate, with Nate driving.

Jack, Ellie Mae, James and Bell, were all piled onto the flatbed behind them, thankful more than once during the journey for the wooden side rails to hang onto.

"What about a place to freshen up first?" asked Bell.

"There is a ladies' room at the courthouse," advised Hattie.

"Do you think we have enough?" James whispered to Jack.

"Of course, we have enough," assured Jack. "We still have almost $75."

"Den ya'll better hang onto dat," interjected Tom, who had excellent hearing. "I gots ya covered."

"We've imposed on you so much already," reminded Ellie Mae, rather uncomfortably.

Tom then pulled a large jug of moonshine from beneath his seat and held it up for them to see. "De judge be one 'o my regulars."

"One of your regular customers?" perceived Jack with a crooked grin. "That's handy."

"Indeed," beamed Tom as he carefully put the jug away. "It be better dan money, trust me."

6. Lady Elleanor

It was nearly noon by the time the wedding party managed to reach the courthouse in Mobile, Alabama on September 30, 1929.

"Last chance to change your mind," Nate flirted with Bell as he helped her from the wagon.

"Not a chance," replied Bell as she turned to smile at James.

James merely shook his head and snickered with amusement as he climbed down behind her.

"Nate, really!" scolded Hattie as she gave him a look of censure.

Nate just shrugged his shoulders and gave his mother a sheepish grin. "You can't blame a guy for trying."

"This one's taken, too," advised Jack as he helped Ellie Mae from the wagon.

"We'd best wait outside," Tom suggested to Nate. "Only yer Ma shud go in wid 'em."

"What if I don't want to?" challenged Nate.

"Son, plez don't make me be takin' a whip to ya," implored Tom. "Yer 16 years old now." *The last time it had been necessary to beat Nate was when he was 12.*

"Your father's right," agreed Hattie. "Stay here. I'll make sure the Judge knows to meet us at the church for his *payment*." She was referring, of course, to the jug of moonshine that Tom had stashed beneath the seat in the wagon.

"All deys doin' here is gettin' de license, anyway," advised Tom. "De hitchin'll be at de church."

"Very well, then," agreed Nate as he leaned against the wagon bed and folded his arms with frustration.

"We needs to feed 'n water de horses," reminded Tom as he fetched an empty bucket from beneath the wagon's seat and headed toward the drinking fountains. A huge sign between them read, "DRINKING FOUNTAIN" – beneath it were two arrows, one pointing to the left and one to the right. Beneath the left arrow it said, "WHITE" and beneath the other arrow it indicated "COLORED."

"That's just so demeaning," muttered Nate as he shook his head.

218

"I knows ya'll kin read," replied Tom as he filled the bucket at the colored fountain. "Ya'll must surely get de meaning, too."

"Not *meaning*," corrected Nate as he pursed his lips together. "*Demeaning*, as in humiliating."

"Don't ya be disrespectin' me, boy," advised Tom as he held the bucket of water in front of the first horse and waited while it drank.

"I'm sorry, pa," apologized Nate rather insincerely as he took the bucket from Tom and headed back over to the drinking fountain area. In an act of defiance, he suddenly decided to use the white fountain.

"Nate!" barked Tom. "Don't be doin' dat!"

"If anyone asks," snickered Nate as he mimicked his father's poor grammar, "I'm just one 'o dem poor little swamp boys who can't read nor write a lick."

Tom hurried over to snatch the bucket from Nate and slapped his face quite hard. He then dumped out the water that had come from the white fountain before filling it with water from the colored fountain. "Don't *ever* let me see ya be doin' dat again! Yer lucky no one saw!" Tom then glared at Nate with disapproval as he went over to water the other horse. "Me 'n yer Ma don't need no trouble like dat here in town."

Just then, two well-dressed white men in suits emerged from the front doors of the courthouse, probably attorneys on their way to lunch.

One of them frowned with disapproval when he noticed Tom watering the horses out front and approached. "The colored entrance is over on the side, mister."

"Just waitin' fer sum white folk inside," replied Tom with a respectful nod.

"Very good," replied the man. "Carry on." The two men seemed satisfied with Tom's explanation for being there and went on their way.

Nate, on the other hand, was bristling with rage and appeared as if he were ready to shout something at them.

"No, son," commanded Tom in a low voice as he dumped out the rest of the water and stowed the bucket before putting a restraining hand on Nate's shoulder.

"How can you just let them talk to you like that?" demanded Nate in an angry whisper.

"It's de law," reminded Tom. "Dat don't mean we gotta like it. Dat's just de way it be."

"Is that why you and Ma live out there in the swamp?" Nate unexpectedly asked. "Because of all these stupid laws?"

"Yep," answered Tom as he grabbed a handful of hay for each horse and then handed one to Nate. "Most folks got no mind to bother us out der, neither."

Nate sighed deeply with frustration as he and his father stood feeding the two horses. "That includes any decent ladyfolk! At least none that's not already spoken for."

"Forget whatever ya's thinkin' about Bell," instructed his father. "Ain't no good gonna com from dat kind 'o thinkin'. She be taken."

Nate ground his teeth together and kicked at some loose rocks on the roadway. *Somehow, he would persuade Bell to change her mind about him, even if she did marry James first.*

"Dat oughta hold 'em," nodded Tom when the horse was finished nibbling.

Meanwhile, inside the courthouse, the wedding party had arrived only minutes before the lunch hour.

"Sorry," apologized the receptionist. "There isn't time to help you before lunch. You'll have to come back afterwards."

"Is Judge Brown in?" questioned Hattie.

"Maybe," answered the receptionist. She had naturally blonde hair and wore it up in a tight bun. Her long red fingernails drummed on her desk as she studied Hattie more closely.

"Please tell him that Mr. LaMont has a delivery for him," requested Hattie. "I'm certain he'd be disappointed not to receive it."

"What is it?" frowned the receptionist as she suspiciously glanced at the others. "Can't you just leave it here with me?"

"I'm afraid not," replied Hattie. "It's of a confidential nature."

It was still five minutes before noon, so the receptionist begrudgingly got up from her desk and headed down the hall.

"If I have to leave this suit on an hour longer than necessary because of her," began Jack, "I'm not going to be happy about it."

"Join the club," sniggered James.

220

"Gentlemen, please," admonished Hattie. "This is your wedding day! Just think how hot your lovely brides must be in what they're wearing."

"That's an understatement," agreed Bell.

"We'll be fine," assured Ellie Mae, even though her outfit was more cumbersome than any of theirs.

"Remember, it's Elleanor LaMont," whispered Hattie to Ellie Mae as they noticed the receptionist returning.

"Must be your lucky day," advised the woman. "Judge Brown said I could take the rest of the day off – with pay – provided I get you folks squared away first. He said he'll see you after that."

"Oh, thank you!" beamed Ellie Mae.

"I assume you're here for marriage licenses?"

"Yes, ma'am."

"I'll need to see your birth certificates," indicated the receptionist as she sat down, grabbed a blank marriage license form, and rolled it into her manual typewriter.

The shiny black Underwood Standard No. 3 typewriter had a 12" wide carriage, reel-to-reel ribbon cartridges, and individual striking arms attached to each key – the absolute latest in modern technology.

Realizing she had forgotten to insert a sheet of carbon paper in-between the pages of the form, the receptionist quickly removed it for another try.

"How many copies of that thing do you need, anyway?" asked Bell, worried that somehow one of them might fall into the wrong hands.

"One for us, one for you, and one for the County Recorder's office," described the woman as she lined up the form again by manually adjusting the roller so that the striking keys would hit in the correct box when she began typing. She then looked up at Ellie Mae expectantly. "Birth certificate?"

"Oh, yes," nodded Ellie Mae as she glanced at Hattie.

"I have it," indicated Hattie as she opened her purse and took out the carefully folded piece of paper.

The woman snatched it away and set it down on the desk beside her typewriter. "Elleanor LaMont?"

"Yes," answered Ellie Mae as she swallowed a lump in her throat. *What was the month and day again?*

"Nickname?" asked the woman when she got to that space.

"Ellie Mae."

"Elleanor Ellie Mae LaMont," the receptionist proofread aloud. "What year is this?" she squinted as she tried to read the birth certificate.

"1912," replied Ellie Mae rather nervously. *Please don't let her ask me the month or the day!*

"Pre-wedding jitters?" smiled the receptionist with a knowing look. She had seen that before.

Ellie Mae merely nodded.

"So, this is your mother, then?" questioned the woman as she glanced at Hattie.

"Yes," lied Ellie Mae and Hattie together. Even though Ellie Mae had dark brown hair and green eyes of her own, her skin was fair and nothing like Hattie's olive complexion.

"What about your father?" frowned the woman.

"Dead," blurted out Ellie Mae. "Killed by an alligator."

"My condolences," nodded the woman. "When was that?"

"Seven years ago," interjected Hattie. "On March 23, 1922." That actually was the date her own daughter Elleanor had passed, so it would be an easy day to remember.

The receptionist then adjusted the form in her typewriter to the other column so she could type in the information pertaining to the groom. "Birth certificate?"

Jack removed a crumpled paper from his front jacket pocket and unfolded it. It was tattered with age and barely legible.

"Oh, for crying out loud," muttered the receptionist. "Can you just tell me what it says, please?"

"Jack Killingham, no nickname."

"Date of birth?"

"August 16, 1910."

"Where?"

"Ocean Bluff," answered Jack as he watched her type it into the box. She apparently knew what state it was in without being told.

"Father's name?"

"Jed Killingham, also from Ocean Bluff."

"Mother?" frowned the receptionist. "How come this is blank?"

What could he say? He didn't even know who she was!

222

"Our mother abandoned us at an early age," interjected James. "I'm his younger brother. We think her name might have been Chris."

"So, you obviously have no idea what her last name was?"

"No, but she was from New York," lied Jack.

"That narrows it down," snickered the woman as she typed that into the form. "You wouldn't happen to know what city in New York, would you?"

"New York City," answered Jack. He had actually given the information that pertained to Ellie Mae's real mother, but could think of nothing else to say at the time.

"And who will be your witnesses?" pressed the woman.

"Can we just be witnesses for each other?" questioned Bell.

"Sure, that works," agreed the receptionist.

"I'm Bell Sanderson, by the way, and this is James Killingham."

"Hang on," instructed the woman. "One at a time."

She then pulled the completed form for the first marriage license from her typewriter and laid it on the counter, along with a fountain pen. "Oh yes," she muttered as she set a small bottle of liquid ink on the counter beside them. "You'll need to sign all three copies, starting with the top copy first. That way you won't smudge the other copies beneath it when you sign. Let each one dry for a moment or two before you go to the next. You can just leave the used carbon paper over there."

Jack and then Ellie Mae signed the form. She started to put Ellie and then hesitated. "I'm sorry, I started to sign with my nickname."

"That's okay," chuckled the receptionist. "Is Ellie LaMont how you normally sign your name?"

"Uh, yes," lied Ellie Mae as she proceeded to write LaMont after it and then exchanged a nervous glance with Hattie.

"Just think," grinned Hattie. "You'll be Ellie Killingham now."

"Indeed," laughed Ellie Mae with relief. *And she wouldn't have to lie about it, either.*

"That'll be $10," advised the receptionist as she looked at Jack.

"For both licenses?" questioned Jack.

"For each one," smirked the woman. "After all, I am working through my lunch."

Jack carefully pulled a $20-dollar bill from his wallet and laid it on the counter. He did not look happy about it.

After snatching away the money and putting it in her desk drawer, she carefully put the signed license into a folder. "The Judge will need to sign it, too, before we can tear off the copies, so I'll just keep that here for now."

"Okay, Bell Sanderson and James Killingham. Are you both from Ocean Bluff, too?"

"Yes," they replied together.

James and Bell's marriage license was completed more quickly, since the receptionist was able to copy much of the information from the other license. After they had both signed, the woman placed their license into the same folder as Jack and Ellie Mae's and got up. "Follow me." She then made her way down the long hallway with the folder to a closed wooden door and knocked.

"Come in," responded a man's voice.

The receptionist pushed open the door, approached the large oak desk where Judge Brown was seated, and placed the folder in front of him. "Anything else, sir?"

"Have a nice day off," bid the Judge. "See you in the morning."

"Shall I put out the closed sign?"

"Yes, please. There's nothing else on the docket, anyway."

"Good night, then," smiled the woman as she quickly left.

"Ah, Mrs. LaMont," acknowledged the Judge. "I understand Mr. LaMont has a delivery for me?" He smiled with amusement as he studied the marriage certificate where it indicated her husband had died in 1922.

"Outside in the wagon," clarified Hattie with a crooked smile.

"Have your husband come in through the colored entrance, please," requested the Judge. "We wouldn't want anyone seeing him come in through the front, especially being dead and all."

Hattie nervously laughed and shrugged her shoulders as she left to comply. "I'll be right back."

"We were hoping you could come to the church to marry us," interjected Bell. "It would be nice to have a church wedding."

"We can't just do it here?" sighed the Judge.

"I vote for that," urged Jack as he adjusted his collar. "These clothes are screaming to come off."

224

"Amen to that," agreed James.

The window to Judge Brown's office was open and the rotating electric fan on a small book stand in front of it offered some relief from the sweltering heat, but not enough.

"Where do you kids plan to live?" questioned the Judge as he signed each of the marriage licenses, tore off the top copies, and handed them to each of the brides.

"Aren't you going to have us say our vows?" asked Ellie Mae.

"Of course," grinned the Judge. "I thought you might like to wait for your parents to be present."

"Oh, yeah," nodded Ellie Mae. "I mean, yes, absolutely."

"So, you never answered my question," probed Judge Brown.

"What question, sir?" flushed Ellie Mae. She was so hot in the bridal gown that she felt faint – not to mention the fact that she was pregnant and had not yet eaten lunch.

"Where do you kids plan to live?"

Just then, Hattie and Tom entered the Judge's chambers. Tom was carrying a huge jug of moonshine and grinned at Judge Brown as he placed it on his desk.

"Dey plans to stay on de Lady Elleanor," advised Tom, who had heard the question as he came in. "Fer as long as dey need, 'til dey finds sumthin' else."

"How'd you all meet?" grilled the Judge with a wicked grin at Tom. He was aware of Tom's occasional hunting expeditions by railcar.

The two couples glanced nervously at one another and then at Tom and Hattie.

"Well, I suppose it's not important," laughed the Judge as he removed the lid from the bottle of moonshine and took a big drink. He nodded with approval as he made a sour face and smacked his lips. "Now, that's what I'm talking about!"

"We appreciate your services, sir," reminded Hattie as she motioned toward the two waiting couples.

"Very well," nodded the Judge. "We'll just do it as a double ceremony, if everyone is okay with that?"

There were no objections.

"Excellent. That way we won't have to do it twice," approved Judge Brown as he reached for a tattered book on his desk and quickly turned to the page he was seeking.

"Dearly beloved," read the Judge, "we have come together in the presence of God to witness and bless the joining together of these two couples in Holy Matrimony. The bond and covenant of marriage was established by God in creation, and our Lord Jesus Christ adorned this manner of life by his presence and first miracle at a wedding in Cana of Galilee. The union of husband and wife in heart, body, and mind is intended by God for ...."

Bell's mind had begun to wander as Judge Brown rambled on. Through the open window she could see Nate pulling the horses and wagon around to the side of the building, to get them out of the hot sun. The spreading oak tree near the colored entrance was also directly in line with the view from Judge Brown's chambers. Bell and Nate locked eyes from afar. Try as she might, she could not look away. Nate continued to gawk at her with unconcealed desire. *Why does he persist?* wondered Bell.

"Bell Sanderson, will you have Jack Killingham to be your husband ...."

"That's James," interrupted James. "I'm the one marrying Bell."

"Oh, sorry," chuckled the Judge. "Let's start that part again. Bell Sanderson, will you have James Killingham to be your husband, to live together in the covenant of marriage? Will you love him, comfort him, honor and keep him, in sickness and in health; and, forsaking all others, be faithful to him as long as you both shall live?"

After a slight hesitation at noticing the crestfallen look on Nate's face outside, Bell answered, "I do."

"Elleanor Ellie Mae LaMont – or whatever your real name might be – do you take Jack Killingham to be your husband, to live together in the covenant of marriage? Will you love him, comfort him, honor and keep him, in sickness and in health; and, forsaking all others, be faithful to him as long as you both shall live?"

"Absolutely, I do!" beamed Ellie Mae as she flirted with Jack.

"Gentlemen," continued the Judge. "Will each of you respectively have these women to be your wives; to live together in the covenant of marriage? Will you love them, comfort them, honor and keep them, in sickness and in health; and, forsaking all others, be faithful to them for as long as you each shall live?"

"We will," chorused Jack and James.

"Let's see, there is no congregation," muttered Judge Brown as he flipped past that page. "Okay, here we go. Do we have any rings to exchange here today?"

"Once we get jobs, sir," apologized Jack.

"Just not today," added James as he gave Bell an apologetic look. She merely nodded with understanding as she glanced out the window again, this time to see a slight smirk on Nate's face.

"The rings you will give one another – once you have jobs," clarified the Judge, "will be symbols of endless love. The rings are also unbroken circles, having no end, representative of the enduring and unending love you have for each other."

The two couples then stared lovingly into one another's eyes.

"May the challenges of your life together be met with courage and optimism," continued the Judge, "and may you learn from your failures and grow in your achievements. May life bless you with children, friends, and family in a wide network of mutual support and enjoyment. May you face pain, toil, and trouble with a stout but light heart. May you share with others the radiance of your seasons of joy and pleasure. And most of all, may you always remember that laughter is the medicine of God."

"Amen!" exclaimed Jack, who was about ready to tear off his suit on the spot.

"Now that each of you young people has given yourself to each other by solemn vows and with the joining of hands in the presence of God and these witnesses, I pronounce that you are each husband and wife, legally and lawfully wed, and those whom God has joined together let no one put asunder. Amen."

"Amen!!" exclaimed everyone as the two couples kissed.

The afternoon of Saturday, March 23, 1930, began like any other on the Lady Elleanor. Named after Tom and Hattie's late daughter Elleanor, the Lady Elleanor had been their home at the time of their daughter's death in 1922. Unable to live there any longer after the tragedy, Hattie had insisted that Tom build them another home nearby.

Jack, Ellie Mae, James and Bell had resided on the Lady Elleanor for only two weeks when the great stock market crash happened on October 24, 1929.

Not only were their lives still enveloped by the grip of the Great Depression, but also by the bayou in which they were now trapped.

Unable to find jobs at all, Jack and James had begun working for Tom in exchange for needed supplies. Making and distributing moonshine to remote areas within the bayou had also given the Killingham brothers an opportunity to become more familiar with their surroundings. Catching fish or killing whatever snakes happened across their path to take home for supper had become a routine practice. Even the occasional alligator would find its way to the Killingham dinner table, deliciously cooked in spices and herbs that enhanced its flavor.

Usually trapped on the Lady Elleanor when their husbands were away hunting or working for Tom, Bell and Ellie Mae were entirely dependent upon the charity of their friends and neighbors who happened by to look in on them. One such neighbor was Tom's son Nate.

"Thank you again for the firewood," nodded Bell as she indicated where he should stack it on the side deck. "I'm afraid if you bring us much more, the house might sink."

"Can you use any more potatoes?" offered Nate. He was determined to be of service to the Killingham wives – especially Bell – and had become obsessed with checking up on them daily to be sure they were okay.

"We're fine, really," assured Ellie Mae. She was ready to give birth any time but decided not to voice her concern about being stranded there when it happened. *The last thing Nate needed was another excuse to hang around or to make himself useful.*

"Let me just get you more water from the spring, then," responded Nate as he hurried to retrieve their water buckets from the rear deck. "Looks like your pot needs emptying, too."

"I know you mean well," began Ellie Mae, "but what we really need is another boat. That way we could take care of these things ourselves. Any idea where we could get one?"

"That would be nice," agreed Bell. "Maybe we could help out with the vegetable garden, too, if we only had a way to get there."

Nate could refuse Bell nothing, especially when she gave him that pleading look. "I'll see what I can do."

"You really shouldn't encourage him like that," whispered Ellie Mae as they watched him untie his mooring line and push off in the little row boat.

"Encourage him?" laughed Bell. "You're crazy!"

"He's never given up on you," differed Ellie Mae.

"Well, he's barking up the wrong tree," assured Bell as she sat down on the edge of the deck and allowed her bare legs to swing back and forth.

"You really shouldn't do that, either," cautioned Ellie Mae. "Next thing you know, some alligator will decide it's lunchtime!"

"Lunch was two hours ago," grinned Bell as she finally pulled her legs back onto the safety of the deck. "What we need is a safe swimming hole somewhere."

"Well, this isn't it," admonished Ellie Mae.

"Seriously, though," added Bell, "if it weren't for Nate bringing us firewood and fresh water each day, I'm not sure what we would do."

Ellie Mae sadly nodded in agreement. Bell was right. Their husbands were often gone for days at a time, only sporadically bringing them day-old fish and decapitated reptiles of questionable quality. *At least the fish Nate brought were cleaned first, as were the various other food items he would bring each day, including fresh vegetables.*

"Are you okay?" questioned Bell as she noticed Ellie Mae wince with pain.

"I'm fine," promised Ellie Mae. "It's just my back again. This is a lot of extra weight to be carrying around. I just need to sit down for a while."

Bell then smiled with amusement as she watched Ellie Mae struggle to lower herself onto the wooden bench beside her.

"Hey, look!" pointed Ellie Mae. Nate could be seen approaching with fresh buckets of water, and with a second small boat in tow.

"Oh, yes!" beamed Bell as she watched him tie off both boats and haul in the first two buckets of water.

Nate's tall dark body was well muscled, and watching him carry the buckets of water gave Bell a welcome opportunity to covertly watch him. Ellie Mae frowned with disapproval when she noticed the look of admiration on Bell's face.

The doeskin pants and sleeveless pullover top that Nate wore were always clean and well cared for. His face was always cleanshaven, and his close-cut afro neatly combed. When Nate did wear shoes, the simple homemade alligator skin sandals gave him a whimsical look, almost like that of a character straight from the *Adventures of Huckleberry Finn*.

Last of all, Nate hurried onboard the Lady Elleanor with the empty collection pot, that he carried inside to its designated location behind a curtain similar to the one at his parents' home.

"I think I'd like to go visit the vegetable garden," mentioned Bell. "I'm getting cabin fever, being trapped here like this all the time."

"You ladies really shouldn't go there alone," warned Nate. "Let me go with you."

"He's right, Bell. But, I'm in no condition to go anywhere right now," reminded Ellie Mae as she touched her large stomach when she felt a brisk kick from one of her unborn children. There was no doubt in her mind at this point that Hattie had been correct about twins.

"Perhaps I should go get my mother," suggested Nate.

"I'm not due for two more weeks," assured Ellie Mae. "Why don't you two go to the vegetable garden without me? I'll be fine. Maybe you could bring back some of those potatoes, though."

"Are you *sure* you're okay?" questioned Bell.

"Go," urged Ellie Mae. "At least I've got the extra boat now, should I need to get to Hattie's on my own."

"We shouldn't go," assessed Nate.

"I was just kidding," laughed Ellie Mae. "I'm fine, I promise."

Her performance was convincing enough that Nate and Bell finally left in his rowboat, leaving her alone on the Lady Elleanor.

"Thanks so much for all you do for us," mentioned Bell as she watched Nate row the small rowboat by himself.

Fingers of sunlight that managed to find their way through the dense moss-covered canopy above them gently reflected across the surface of the slimy green water. Bell slapped at a mosquito on her cheek and then rubbed the place with the back of her hand.

"I know something that might help with that," flirted Nate.

230

Bell studied him more closely. "Just how come none of the mosquitoes ever bother you, anyway?"

"I'll show you," smiled Nate as he undressed her with his eyes. "It's on the way to the vegetable garden. Well, kind of."

"This isn't just some trick to try and get me off alone with you, is it?" Bell became suspicious.

"I'm already off alone with you," reminded Nate as his gaze enveloped her.

The realization of that suddenly sunk in. "We are alone, aren't we?" Bell had tried for months to deny the attraction she felt for Nate. *After all, using her feminine charms to persuade him to bring them supplies each day couldn't be all that bad, could it?*

"I certainly wouldn't leave a beautiful woman like you alone in the swamp to fend for herself," remarked Nate as he began to row in a different direction.

"Seriously, what do you use to repel the mosquitos?" grilled Bell as she slapped at her arms and face. "They're eating me alive!"

"Rosemary and peppermint," replied Nate. "They work best when mixed with lard, then you can just rub it on."

"Lard?" frowned Bell.

"To keep the rosemary and peppermint from coming off too quickly," laughed Nate. "It also repels gnats and even lice."

"Is that why your skin always looks so shiny?" asked Bell.

"I'm afraid so," grinned Nate as he steered the rowboat into a secluded cove and moored it to a large gum tree.

"What are you doing?" demanded Bell.

"Getting you some mosquito repellant," answered Nate as he reached into the gum tree and removed a small burlap sack from a hollow in its trunk. "If the others knew I had this, they would all want some."

"Is it hard to come by?" asked Bell.

"Not really," replied Nate as he removed a mason jar from the sack and unscrewed its lid. "It just takes time to make."

"Thanks," nodded Bell as she cautiously reached into the jar with her fingertips and scooped out a small handful of the substance. After smelling it, she shrugged with approval. *It actually didn't smell that bad at all.*

Nate gazed at her with longing and desire while Bell rubbed the mosquito repellant onto her face, neck and arms. The lowcut pullover top she wore left little to the imagination.

"Would you like me to put some on your back for you?" offered Nate as he watched her rub the substance onto her long sensuous legs.

The lowcut top and shorts were all Bell had on besides a pair of leather thong sandals. Just then, a mosquito bit her on the back, but she was not able to reach the place to swat at it. She then turned around and gave Nate a pleading look. "If you don't mind?"

"It would be my pleasure," beamed Nate as he slowly pushed aside her blonde hair and deliberately began to rub the substance onto her shoulders and upper back. The embarrassing bulge in his groin area did not go unnoticed by Bell when she finally turned around to thank him.

"Uh, that does seem to help," she stuttered. *Why did she feel so drawn to him?*

"Does it?" asked Nate. He was not referring to the mosquito repellant and she knew it.

"So, what else do you have in there?" Bell suddenly wanted to know. "Any other good remedies?"

"You can't tell *anyone* about this if I show it to you," qualified Nate as he reached again into the sack and removed a small tin can.

"I won't tell, I promise."

Nate carefully removed the lid from the can and pulled out a small leather pouch.

"What's that?" teased Bell when she saw what she assumed was tobacco. "Something to keep away vampires?"

"Something like that," grinned Nate as he pulled out a pipe and stuffed some of the unusual tobacco inside. He then put the pipe in his mouth, pulled out a small box of matches, and lit it.

"Oh, I get it," assumed Bell as she watched Nate take a long drag from the pipe. "The smoke helps keep them away, too, doesn't it?"

"Try some," offered Nate as he reloaded the pipe and handed it to her. "See for yourself."

"I normally don't smoke, you know," advised Bell as she took the pipe from him and wiped off the mouthpiece before putting it in her mouth. Nate then lit another match and held it over the pipe's

232

contents while Bell inhaled. Suddenly, she began coughing repeatedly as she blew out the smoke.

"Try again," urged Nate as he lit another match.

Bell then nodded as she put the pipe back into her mouth and took another drag from it. This time she managed to hold in the smoke for a few moments before letting out the smoke more gradually.

Nate then took the pipe from her and relit what was left, inhaling it deeply. "You kind of have to stick with it."

"Okay, sure," agreed Bell, uncertain why she suddenly felt so strange. *Perhaps it was her imagination.*

After smoking two more pipe loads of the special tobacco, Bell felt a strange relaxed euphoria come over her. "What was that, anyway? Is it normal to feel like this?"

"It's a special herb," replied Nate as he flirted with her.

"I'm starving," Bell suddenly realized.

"Me, too," assured Nate as he moved closer and put a hand on Bell's cheek. "You are so beautiful!"

"I'm also married," reminded Bell.

"Then, where is he now?" questioned Nate. "Why is he never here for you?"

Bell had no answer for that.

"Who is it that makes sure you have fresh water, firewood, and whatever else you need each day?" grilled Nate.

"You do." Bell flushed with embarrassment at the feelings she had for Nate but yet she felt as drawn to him as he did to her.

"And where is your wedding ring?" added Nate.

"You know the guys haven't been able to find real jobs yet," answered Bell. "Since the Great Depression, gold has gone up from $20 an ounce to ...." she suddenly couldn't remember.

"To $286 an ounce," recalled Nate, who had also seen the newspaper article Bell was referring to. He was the one who had brought it to her, just the other day.

"That's right, gold has gone up to $286 an ounce," nodded Bell. "And movie tickets went up from 35¢ to almost $5."

"And yet, your husband and his brother have spent absolutely none of the money they've earned on you, have they?" questioned Nate.

"That's because they're saving up so we can return to the lighthouse someday," Bell assured him.

233

"Is it?" pressed Nate as his eyes enveloped her. "Do you really know how much money your husbands have made working for my pa?"

Bell shook her head in the negative. She suddenly realized that she had no idea.

"More than enough to buy you a dozen rings," assured Nate, "plus a first-class coach on the passenger train for all of you. And yet, here you are."

Tears began to escape the corners of Bell's eyes. *How could she have been so blind and foolish?*

"Don't cry, pretty lady," urged Nate as he gently wiped away her tears and pulled her close. "You should stay here with me when they go. I've been a good provider so far, haven't I?"

Bell slowly nodded as she looked up at Nate. *Was it so wrong to feel this way about him? At least Nate seemed to care what happened to her!* No longer able to resist the pull she felt towards him, Bell finally allowed Nate to kiss her.

The magnetic force between them was overpowering as the two of them lay down together in the bottom of the rowboat.

"I love you, Bell," declared Nate as he pulled her close and began to have his way with her. "I always have and I always will."

For a brief instant, Bell thought of Hattie and the admonition that she had once given Bell that she was in great danger in the bayou, and that she must never go anywhere alone, not even to the outhouse.

"You will never be alone again," promised Nate, as if he could read her mind. "Not with me by your side."

Unable to hold back any longer, Bell then gave herself to Nate completely and absolutely. She knew in her heart that there would be no going back to James after that, but she no longer cared.

Meanwhile, on the Lady Elleanor, Ellie Mae's water had broken and the labor pains were indescribable. *Should she dare to try and take the rowboat over to Hattie's? What if something went wrong?*

Realizing that she would need to deliver the baby by herself, Ellie Mae grabbed a stick and two clean towels from the unfolded laundry pile as she hobbled to the back deck. She carefully spread out one of the towels for herself beside the buckets of water. *She would use the other towel to wrap the baby in – unless there really were two!*

Perhaps Bell and Nate would be back in time to bring her another towel, hoped Ellie Mae as a scream of agony escaped her lips.

Ellie Mae put the small stick into her mouth to bite down on as the contractions became stronger. She carefully tried to lower herself onto the towel but lost her balance and fell backwards the rest of the way, landing butt-first on the towel. "Ouch!" came her muffled scream as more blood began pouring from her birth canal.

Unnoticed by her, another small rowboat had pulled up out front. It was Hattie. "Oh, child!" exclaimed Hattie as she hurriedly moored her boat to the deck's railing before rushing to the back deck where Ellie Mae was in labor. "I had a premonition that you were in trouble and came as soon as I could."

"Where are Bell and Nate?" Ellie Mae managed to say before the next contraction hit.

"Where indeed!" spat Hattie, who was clearly angry about the fact that they had left Ellie Mae alone at such a time.

"They're not with you?" mumbled Ellie Mae.

"Let's worry about them later," suggested Hattie as she hurried to put a kettle of water on to boil. "I'm going to make you something for the pain."

Ellie Mae then let out a blood curdling scream as another contraction hit. The stick had fallen from her mouth onto the deck beside her and the fingernails of her hands were digging into her palms.

Hattie quickly wrung out a wet rag and returned to dab the sweat from Ellie Mae's face. "Next time you feel a wave of pain like that, I want you to push, with all your might. Okay?"

Ellie Mae merely nodded.

"I'm right here," assured Hattie as she crouched in front of Ellie Mae with a waiting blanket. "You *can* do this!"

"I don't think I can!" wailed Ellie Mae. Tears were streaming down her cheeks.

"Oh, Ellie Mae," mumbled Hattie when she noticed the blood on her palms. Hattie immediately set down the towel long enough to rip a strip of fabric from her skirt and wrapped some of it around each of Ellie Mae's hands.

"Thanks," Ellie Mae nodded and tried to give Hattie a weak smile, but suddenly felt another painful contraction.

"PUSH!" screamed Hattie as she picked the extra towel back up and held it in place, ready to catch the first child.

"Ugggghhhh!" grunted Ellie Mae. *She was thankful that Hattie had wrapped her hands!*

"I see his head!" exclaimed Hattie. "Keep going!"

Even without waiting for the next contraction, Ellie Mae began bearing down and pushing with all her might. Her face was beginning to turn red from holding her breath.

"Breathe!" shouted Hattie.

Realizing that she had been holding her breath, Ellie Mae suddenly gasped for air as the next contraction hit.

"PUSH!!" screamed Hattie again. "I see his shoulders now! The worst is almost over."

Ellie Mae pushed again, with all her might, suddenly able to sense that the baby had come out. She started to relax and smile when another contraction suddenly hit. *The other child is coming, too!*

Hattie hurriedly held the first child up by his feet and gently swatted him on the butt as she wiped the afterbirth from his face and carefully wiped him off.

"Mark," mumbled Ellie Mae. "His name is Mark."

"Hello, Mark," beamed Hattie as she tenderly cradled him in her arms to admire him.

"The other baby's coming!" hollered Ellie Mae with a blood curdling scream.

Still holding little Mark, Hattie raced at once to the linen closet and grabbed two more clean towels. After carefully wrapping Mark in one of them, she brought him back out with her and placed him on the deck nearby. Hattie then grabbed the other clean towel and spread it out for the other baby. She would use the dirty towel for catching him, and then transfer him to the clean towel after wiping him off.

"Hurry!" wailed Ellie Mae. The baby's head was already showing.

"I'm right here, child," comforted Hattie as she crouched down in front of Ellie Mae again, ready to catch the next baby.

The next contraction hit, but Ellie Mae was already spent and barely able to push. *What if she couldn't do it again?*

"Listen to me," directed Hattie. "The head and shoulders are already out. One last big push should do it. You can't give up now! Now, PUSH!!!"

236

Ellie Mae nodded and then pushed for all she was worth. *She would either give birth to her second child or die trying.* Exhausted from exertion and loss of blood, Ellie Mae started to lose consciousness. Then, when the sound of her second child crying could be heard, she slowly opened her eyes and mumbled, "Jack, Jr."

"Jack, Jr.," nodded Hattie as she tenderly cleaned him up and wrapped him in the other towel.

"Hattie, a snake!" hollered Ellie Mae upon noticing that a water moccasin was slithering its way toward Mark. "Hattie, the baby!"

With surprising speed and alacrity, Hattie pulled out a rather large knife from a hidden sheath that she kept strapped to her leg and hurled it at the snake with such force that it pierced the snake's head and pinned it to the deck. She then hurried over to the snake, grabbed the knife handle, and with a swift slicing motion to each side, removed its head completely.

Ellie Mae stared with disbelief at what she had just witnessed while Hattie stabbed the severed head to pick it up and then hurled it over the deck's railing, into the swamp.

"We can have the rest for dinner," announced Hattie with a smile of relief. *Thankfully, she'd missed hitting baby Mark with the knife.*

Ellie Mae then fainted. It had all been too much for her.

Wakened at last by a steady sucking sound, Ellie Mae opened her eyes. Hattie was holding one of the babies to Ellie Mae's breast, and it was feeding. Ellie Mae stared at him with amazement and began to smile as she put her arms around the baby to support him.

"This is Mark," advised Hattie as she let go of Mark and let Ellie Mae take over. "He's the one with a small strip of leather tied around his right ankle."

"How long has it been?" questioned Ellie Mae as she admired him. While unconscious, she had been cleaned off, put in fresh clothing, brought inside, and was laying on her cot. There was even an absorbent leather pad spread out beneath her.

"Long enough," assured Hattie with a tired smile.

"You've even cleaned up the boys," noticed Ellie Mae. "Thank you so much!" She looked as if she were about to cry.

"You're welcome! Their cords are cut now, too," grinned Hattie as she took Mark from Ellie Mae and put him back in the makeshift crib.

Had Hattie used the same knife that she had used to kill that huge snake? wondered Ellie Mae.

"I hope you don't mind, but they needed a crib," added Hattie as she nodded at the nearby washtub. It had been cleaned out and lined with fresh blankets for the twins to sleep in. "There's still the other washtub out on the deck."

"That's fine," chuckled Ellie Mae. "What about Junior? May I hold him?"

"In a while. He ate while you were asleep and is resting now," Hattie assured her with a crooked grin as she headed for the kitchen and poured a cup of tea for Ellie Mae. "This is for you."

"What is it?" frowned Ellie Mae as Hattie brought her the cup.

"It's a special bark-root tea, made from the Aspen tree," described Hattie. "It will help slow the bleeding and also with the pain."

Just then, Nate and Bell pulled up in the other rowboat, each carrying a sack of potatoes as they came inside.

"That took long enough," teased Ellie Mae.

"Oh, my God!" exclaimed Bell as she set down the potatoes and rushed over to Ellie Mae.

"Meet Mark and Jack, Jr.," grinned Ellie Mae.

"Shhh!" Hattie held her finger to her lips. "They're resting. They've had a hard day."

"What's this?" frowned Nate upon seeing the headless snake on the kitchen counter. *Anything he had brought would have been butchered already.*

"Your ma's pretty good with that knife of hers," interjected Ellie Mae as she sipped on the tea. "It almost got little Mark."

"I'm sorry we weren't here," apologized Nate.

"Is there anything else we can still do to help?" asked Bell.

"There's a pile of bloody laundry on the back deck," advised Hattie. "If you don't mind."

"Oh, not at all," nodded Bell. It was the least she could do, especially after having been gone for so long.

"Ma, there's something else we need to tell you," began Nate.

238

Bell imperceptibly shook her head in the negative. This just wasn't the right time.

Ignoring her silent plea, Nate continued, "Bell and I have decided ...."

"We've decided to get married," interrupted Bell as she and Nate put their arms around one another and pulled each other close.

"Absolutely not!" forbade Hattie. "Bell is already married to James! That would be adultery!"

"I'm afraid it's too late," advised Nate as he pulled Bell even closer while he returned his mother's penetrating gaze.

"Is this *true*?" Hattie turned to glare at Bell.

"I'm afraid so," smirked Bell as she gave Nate a loving glance.

"The two of you have been together?" demanded Hattie.

Nate and Bell both smiled and nodded.

Ellie Mae was so stunned she was speechless.

"Get out!" ordered Hattie as she pointed toward the door. "Neither of you is welcome here or at the other house again. Now go!"

"I was thinking of staying right here," advised Nate.

"If James doesn't kill you first, your pa surely will," threatened Hattie. "You will both want to be as far from here as possible before either of them returns."

"And who only knows when that will be," sniggered Bell.

Hattie then slapped Bell across the face. "This is serious! You are in grave danger, both of you! I can sense their return, so you really should hurry."

"Hattie somehow knew I was giving birth to the twins," added Ellie Mae. "That's why she came over here."

Nate became serious. "Ma does know things, we should go. I know a place we can stay until this all blows over."

"It will not blow over until James is back at the lighthouse and your father is in his grave," predicted Hattie as she sadly shook her head. "Where did we fail you, Nathaniel?"

"Nate," corrected her son as he gave her an unexpected hug and a kiss on the cheek. "It wasn't you who went wrong, ma, so don't blame yourself."

"Please tell James how sorry I am," Bell mentioned to Ellie Mae as she grabbed her suitcase and began stuffing her possessions into it. "It would never have worked between James and me anyway. All we ever did was argue."

"He loves you!" advised Ellie Mae. "This will break his heart."

"Perhaps you should tell him that she was taken by an alligator," suggested Hattie, almost sarcastically. "Nathaniel, too."

Bell then rushed over to the makeshift crib and knelt beside it to admire the twins. A tear escaped onto her cheek as she tenderly touched each of their little hands. "I'm so glad I got to meet you both."

Without further comment, Nate picked up Bell's trunk and left, closely followed by Bell, who hurriedly grabbed one of the sacks of potatoes to take with them.

Jack and James were hot, tired and dirty after their most recent liquor run for Tom. They had been gone for five days, as the route had taken them to a remote area on the other side of Mobile.

"Think you're a daddy yet?" grinned James as they trudged through the dense brush. This had been their first solo delivery without Tom, so they were entirely on their own. *Too bad none of the horses had been available for this particular trip*, thought James.

"Who knows," replied Jack as he untied a filthy red bandana from a vaguely familiar cypress tree. "Good thing we marked the way."

"Should we stop in Mobile to pick up some supplies for the twins?" asked James with a crooked smile. "Just in case."

"We still have to get Tom's share of the money back to him," reminded Jack. "I'd sure hate to get robbed along the way."

"Nobody's gonna mess with a 7-foot tall guy like you," laughed James. "Nobody in his right mind, that is."

"I have an idea!" exclaimed Jack, suddenly enthused about it.

"Wanna fill me in?" requested James as he hurried to match his pace. Once Jack began walking faster, keeping up with him could be a challenge. "Hey, what's the rush?"

"You'll see," grinned Jack as they neared the outskirts of Mobile. "It's at least another hour before supper time."

"So?" frowned James. "The girls have no idea when we'll be back, anyway, so what difference does it make?"

"Look," indicated Jack as he nodded toward a nearby saloon. Only three horses were hitched out front. "All we need to do is double our share of the money, and then we're home free."

"You want to gamble away our hard-earned money?" James was appalled by the idea. "What would we tell the girls?"

"They have no idea how much money we have," reasoned Jack.

"And what about Tom?" pressed James. "We can't just gamble away someone else's money!"

"No, of course not," agreed Jack. "We'll only use our half. You can hang onto Tom's money for me while we're in there."

"I don't like it," objected James. "I don't like it at all."

Jack then stopped, turned to face his brother, and put a hand on his shoulder. "All we need is $50 more and we can afford a private compartment on the passenger train for all four of us, all the way back to the lighthouse! The babies can ride for free, if they're even born yet."

"And if you lose?" persisted James.

"We can't lose," assured Jack. "I have a good feeling about this. Just think what a nice surprise it would be for the girls to know we're finally able to leave this God-forsaken place."

"Nobody blames you for any of this," answered James. "There's no way we could have known about the stock market crash."

"Okay, if anyone's to blame, it's Bell," sniggered Jack as he removed his hand from James's shoulder and headed for the saloon. "It was her idea to come here in the first place."

"That's not fair," argued James as he hurried to keep up. "All of us agreed to come here."

"Oh, I know," chuckled Jack as he approached and pushed open the swinging saloon door.

"I really wish you'd reconsider," pleaded James as he followed his older brother inside.

"Here," muttered Jack as he stuffed a wad of bills into James's pocket. "You can keep a lookout for pickpockets."

James suddenly became more aware of his surroundings as he suspiciously studied the few people inside.

"Drinks all round," instructed Jack as he pulled his last remaining bottle of moonshine from his sack and plopped it onto the bar counter. "On me."

"Mister, we don't want no trouble," urged the bartender. He was a man of color. "We're a dry saloon, just like de law says, and all we serves here is water and pop."

"Gentlemen?" proposed Jack as he turned to a nearby table where three men were engaged in a hand of poker. Jack held up the bottle and raised an eyebrow at them.

"I'll take some in a soda glass," grinned one of the men as he began shuffling a deck of cards for another hand. "Name's Clay."

Clay was an aging fisherman who was currently gambling away what little was left of his hard-earned money. His frizzy white hair was long overdue for a visit to the barber, and his tattered clothing had seen better days. And, like so many other less fortunate individuals during the Great Depression, his loose clothing had once fit more snugly.

"Me, too," nodded another man, who was much younger, but basically fit the same description. "Clay, Jr."

"I'm Jack, and this is my brother James," nodded Jack as he pulled out the fourth chair and sat down. James remained standing behind him, with his back against the wall.

The bartender suddenly brought four soda glasses to the table and set them down by Jack's bottle of moonshine. "Mind you pour it quick like, and hide that bottle!" He then rushed back over to the bar.

"I didn't catch your name," added Jack as he glanced up at the other man while pouring moonshine into the glasses for each of them.

"Pierre," replied the man with a rather heavy French accent. "We all serve together on the M&J."

"The M&J?"

"It's a fishing boat," explained Clay as he quickly gulped down what was in his glass. "Whoa, Nelly!"

Pierre and Clay, Jr. then sampled theirs and each made sour faces as they swallowed. "Not bad," approved Pierre.

"So, what are we playing for?" questioned Jack as he glanced at each of them.

"I'll play you, for the rest of that bottle," offered Clay.

"And just what do you have to offer in exchange?" pressed Jack.

"I already lost all my cash to him," described Clay as he glanced at Pierre. "What about this? It was my father's."

"You can't gamble grandpa's watch away!" objected Clay, Jr.

242

"Don't tell me what I can't do," barked Clay as he glared at his son. "It's not like knowing what time it is will change anything, now will it?"

Jack merely shook his head. "Keep your watch. We play for cash or nothing at all."

Pierre and Jack studied one another carefully for a few moments.

"Ten dollars," proposed Pierre as he took out and plopped a small bag of coins onto the table. "It's all there if you'd like to count it." Pierre then grabbed the deck of cards from Clay and began shuffling them in an experienced fashion.

"Too rich for my blood," advised Clay, Jr.

"Ten dollars," agreed Jack as he pulled out a small wad of bills, peeled off a ten, and placed it on the table.

"What'd ya do, go rob a bank?" teased Clay.

"Don't be ridiculous!" interjected James from the sidelines.

"Five-card draw?" asked Pierre as he looked up at Jack.

"Go for it," smiled Jack.

Pierre then dealt the five cards, one at a time, all face down. The remainder of the deck was moved to one side and entrusted to Clay before Jack and Pierre picked up their hands, being careful to keep them concealed.

"Two," indicated Jack as he discarded them and waited for Clay to replace them, face down. Jack then swiftly picked up and added them to his hand so he would still have five cards.

"Pierre?" questioned Clay.

"I'm good."

"Showdown?" asked Clay.

Both Pierre and Jack nodded.

"Two pair," smirked Jack as he laid down his cards.

"Flush," grinned Pierre as he revealed his cards and then reached for the money.

"Now, hold on just a minute," instructed Jack as he pulled out another ten-dollar bill and laid it on the table. "Let's play again. Everything there, plus I'll raise you ten."

Pierre nervously reached into his jacket pocket and pulled out a tattered map. "This is all I got left, but it's worth at least $50."

"Let's see it," requested Jack as he reached for the map, opened it up, and began to study it.

"It supposedly leads to a lost city of gold," described Pierre, "down in South America."

"Exactly where in South America?" frowned Jack as he turned the map sideways.

"The man I won it from told me it was in Peru," replied Pierre. "Some place called Machu Picchu."

"Machu what?" laughed Jack as he shook his head and started to set the map aside.

"I've read about that," interjected James. "It was back in 1911, I believe. Some guy named Bingham discovered it."

"Let me see that," requested Clay. "Wasn't that one of the lost cities where the Incas lived?"

"I'm pretty sure it was," agreed James.

"What's that writing on the back?" questioned Clay, Jr.

"That sure ain't in English," assessed Clay upon noticing the unusual markings on it. "It looks like some kind of ancient language, or something."

"You're on!" advised Jack as he suddenly snatched the map away from Clay and moved it to the middle of the table.

"For $50, not $10," reminded Pierre.

Jack then pulled out $40 more and laid it on the table beside the $10 he had already put there.

Even the bartender had moved in closer to get a better look at the game. The stakes were getting high.

After several card exchanges and each man putting on his best poker face, Jack finally called it. "Showdown."

Pierre waffled for several moments before finally laying down his hand. "Straight flush," smirked Pierre as he laid down 9-10-J-Q-K.

Jack tried at first to look crestfallen but then broke into a huge grin as he laid down 10-J-Q-K-A. "Royal flush."

"Son of a sea serpent!" exclaimed Pierre as he pounded his fist on the table. "That's just not fair!"

"Sorry," apologized Jack as he scooped up all the money, and the map, and stood to leave. "Pierre, it's been a pleasure."

"I'll play you again, double or nothing on my next week's salary," proposed Pierre.

"He's good for it," assured Clay.

"Sorry, gentlemen," declined Jack as he and James hurriedly left with their winnings.

"Don't you *ever* pull something like that again!" scolded James as they headed for the swamp trail to resume their trek home.

"Told you we had nothing to worry about," insisted Jack.

"In a pig's eye!" differed James, who was still quite upset about the risk Jack had taken.

"Remind me of that tomorrow when we're all on the train for Ocean Bluff," laughed Jack. "We should be just in time for supper, and won't the girls be surprised."

James trudged along in silence the rest of the way. An uneasiness had descended upon him, and he wasn't sure why. *Had something bad happened while they were away? He needed to find out so he could put his mind at ease.*

"Hey!" exclaimed Jack as he stopped and put a hand on James's shoulder. "Do you hear *that*?"

Suddenly, the sounds of babies crying could be heard, echoing across the swamp. "Congratulations!" smiled James as he slapped Jack on the back.

"You, too, Uncle James," grinned Jack as he hurriedly climbed into a small rowboat docked at the vegetable garden and unmoored it while James clambered in after him.

"Won't Ellie Mae need to stay in bed for at least a week before she's up to traveling?" questioned James.

Jack sighed deeply and slowly nodded. "Probably so."

"Have you ever wondered how pa is making out, especially since the Great Depression hit?" questioned James.

"Yeah," admitted Jack.

"Do you think he'll let us come back?" pressed James.

"What's he going to do, turn all of us away? Besides, he's got grandkids now, too."

James merely nodded.

"He'll forgive us," assured Jack as he steered the rowboat up to the Lady Elleanor and moored it to the deck.

Jack and James swiftly scrambled from the rowboat and went inside, expecting to see their wives there waiting for them.

"Where's Bell?" questioned James.

"She's gone," advised Hattie. She was still there caring for Ellie Mae and the twins.

"Something sure smells good," noticed Jack as he glanced at the kettle on the stove.

"Jack!" exclaimed Ellie Mae as she motioned for him to come to the cot where she lay holding and nursing one of the twins. "I'd like you to meet your sons. This one is Mark."

Jack hurried over to kiss Ellie Mae and then started to reach for the infant, but Hattie put a restraining hand on his arm.

"*After* you've had a bath!" advised Hattie as she pointed to the rear deck where the only remaining washtub was located.

"Jack, Jr. is over there," indicated Ellie Mae as she nodded at the makeshift crib.

Jack stood there proudly admiring each of his sons, and then headed for the deck to clean up. "I'll be right back!"

James turned to Ellie Mae. "Where is Bell?"

Ellie Mae's face suddenly took on a frightened expression as she glanced at Hattie. "Like Hattie said, she's gone. Hey, wouldn't you like to meet your nephews?"

"Where are her things?" demanded James, ignoring the twins completely. The only thing he was concerned about at that moment was Bell. *Why wasn't she there?*

"She took all of her things with her," advised Hattie. "You really should join your brother on the deck. When was the last time you had a bath?"

"I'm not going anywhere until someone tells me where Bell is," persisted James. *Was this why he'd had such a bad feeling earlier?*

"Not until you've washed up," replied Hattie with an even gaze.

James was furious but realized Hattie was not about to tell him what he wanted to know until he complied. "Where's the other tub?"

"It's right there, being used as a crib," apologized Ellie Mae.

James then stormed to the back deck to wait for Jack to finish washing up so he could bathe, too.

"Aaahh!" beamed Jack as he climbed from the tub, dried off, and pulled on a clean pair of blue jeans and a t-shirt.

"I'll be right in," muttered James as he disrobed and climbed into the dirty water to wash himself off. *Where had Bell gone? Had she returned to Ocean Bluff without them?*

After bathing, drying off and putting on clean clothes, James hurried back inside just in time to see Jack pick up and admire little

246

Mark. "This is my first born," bragged Jack with a proud smile on his face as he showed him off. "The one with the leather ankle bracelet."

James merely nodded and then turned to Hattie. "Okay, I'm clean now, and someone had better tell me where Bell has run off to."

"What a shame she couldn't have waited only one more day," mentioned Jack as he handed Mark to James. "We finally have enough for a first-class train ride all the way back to Ocean Bluff, and she misses out on it."

"Even if Bell were here, Ellie Mae's not going anywhere, for at least a week," advised Hattie with finality.

"Guess Bell will just have to be surprised to see us when we get there, then," chuckled Jack as he picked up Jack, Jr.

Ellie Mae had begun to cry.

"You know where she is, don't you?" grilled James as he carefully put Mark back in the crib, pulled up a stool, and sat beside his sister's cot. "Tell me what you know."

Ellie Mae just shook her head and looked at Hattie. Her lower lip had begun to quiver, something she never did unless extremely upset.

"The twins look healthy," apprised James, "so I'm guessing that's not why you're crying."

"Leave your sister alone," commanded Hattie. "She's had a most difficult day."

"Not as difficult as it's going to get unless someone tells me right now where Bell has gone!" hollered James. Neither Jack nor Ellie Mae had ever seen him so angry.

Frightened and upset by the noise, both twins began to cry.

"Now look what you've done," frowned Jack as he gently rocked Jack, Jr. in his arms.

Hattie rushed over to comfort little Mark.

"We were going to tell you that an alligator got her," Hattie advised James, rather uncomfortably, "but then you'd still wonder what happened to that huge trunk of hers."

"Hey, where's Nate?" Jack suddenly asked. "Doesn't he usually stop by around this time of day with more water?"

"Nate will not be stopping by again," informed Hattie. "He and Bell have run off together."

James was thunderstruck. It took nearly a minute for what Hattie had said to sink in. "Say that again?"

247

"You heard me!" snapped Hattie. "I told them that if you didn't kill them first, that Tom most certainly would."

"That reminds me," fumed James, "I need to take Tom's share of the money to him."

"What are you going to tell him?" demanded Hattie.

"Back off!" hollered James as he took a menacing step toward her. "And don't wait up for me, any of you!"

"Shouldn't you eat something first?" blurted out Ellie Mae.

"She's right," agreed Jack. "Perhaps you should eat something first. Then we can go together."

"I'm not hungry," replied James as he snatched Tom's money from his dirty pants pocket before storming from the Lady Elleanor. The others watched in stunned silence as James got into the rowboat by himself, unmoored it, and headed for Tom's cabin.

Jack was torn. *Should he follow?*

"Leave him be," recommended Hattie as she gave Jack a warning glance. "He needs his space. Enjoy this special time with your family."

"How can I, when our brother is about to do something he will regret for the rest of his life?" Jack then handed Jack, Jr. to Ellie Mae as he sat down on the stool beside her and gently brushed a stray hair from her cheek. "I'm sorry sweetheart, but I've got to go after him."

"I know," nodded Ellie Mae, rather sadly. She knew that Jack would be impossible to live with unless he did what he could to try and stop James from doing the unthinkable.

"I love you," bid Jack as he kissed Ellie Mae and each of his new sons again. "And thank you for taking care of them," added Jack as he came over to give Hattie a kiss on the cheek, too. "I won't forget this."

It had been an entire week, but still there was no sign of Nate or Bell anywhere. Tom and James had spent each day and several nights in vain searching for them. Tom's other sons had helped, as well.

"Where could they be?" fumed James as he helped Tom row the small rowboat back toward the Lady Elleanor.

"Der be nowhere else to look," replied Tom. He had been as angry as James was at first but was starting to calm down. "Perhaps de swamp got 'em. Ya never know."

248

"Now I have to decide whether to keep looking, or just give up and return to Ocean Bluff with Jack and his family when they leave here tomorrow," mumbled James.

"I kin surely write 'n let ya know if dey do turn up," promised Tom. "Ya got my word on dat."

"Hey, thanks for everything you've done to try and help," mentioned James. "I can only imagine how you must feel about your son doing something like this."

Tom sadly nodded in agreement as they pulled up at the Lady Elleanor. *James had no idea!*

It was Monday morning, March 31, 1930. Tom, Hattie, Zeke, Shad and Bart had all come to see the Killingham family off at the train station in Mobile. Tom had driven them and their luggage into town on his horse-drawn wagon, while his sons followed on horseback.

"It almost seems strange not to have to worry about hopping on in time, before it takes off," chuckled Ellie Mae as she gave Hattie a one-armed hug. She was holding Jack, Jr. with her other arm. "Thanks so much for everything you've done for us!"

"Please keep in touch," requested Hattie as she hugged her back and handed Ellie Mae a folded slip of paper. "It's our address."

In all the time they had been there, Ellie Mae had not known what the mailing address was and suddenly smiled as she climbed onto the train. "I will."

Tom and his sons had already taken their luggage on board, and had come back out to say goodbye.

"Yes, thank you," nodded Jack as he hugged each of them with his free arm before climbing on board. He was holding little Mark against his chest with the other arm. "We appreciate everything you've done for us."

"And *you* be careful!" cautioned Hattie as she pulled James close and gave him a farewell kiss on the cheek. "Danger surrounds you."

"Ma, don't be scarin' him like that," objected Zeke.

"We'll let ya'll know when we find them," promised Shad.

"You got that right," agreed Bart.

249

"Thanks, guys, I know you will," bid James as he climbed onto the train. A deep sense of foreboding had descended upon James as he contemplated Hattie's warning.

Tom exchanged a farewell nod with James. He understood how James felt better than most of them, especially after having spent the last week together, and felt great empathy for him. *At least James might have a chance at starting over. For him, the search had only just begun.*

"Safe journey," bid Hattie as the train began to move.

The LaMont family stood there smiling and waving at them until the Killinghams were out of sight.

"Do you really think we'll find Nate and Bell?" asked Zeke as they watched the train disappear.

"Perhaps they don't want to be found," replied Hattie, rather mysteriously.

7. Expedition

Two years had passed since their return to the lighthouse. Ellie Mae had written to Hattie twice, but there still was no word from the LaMont family. *Had they forgotten their promise to keep in touch?*

It was Wednesday, March 23, 1932, and Jed had planned a big birthday surprise for his two young grandsons.

"We're all set for another eight hours," announced Jed as he motioned for little Mark to come to him. He had just finished hoisting the 50-pound counterweight to the top of the lighthouse tower for its next descent.

Mark had begun walking several weeks earlier – even before Jack, Jr. – and had been into absolutely everything ever since. Both twins were finally walking and talking and were quite a handful.

"Gramps!" hollered little Mark as he made his way toward him on his unsteady little legs.

"That's my boy," beamed Jed as he squatted and held out his hands, beckoning for his grandson to come to him.

"Are you sure we have enough food in here?' questioned Ellie Mae as she struggled to pick up the heavy picnic basket. She was being ironic, of course.

"I got that," advised Jack. He somehow sensed that it was too much for her to carry by herself.

Ellie Mae smiled with relief. The picnic basket was indeed quite heavy, and more than she felt was safe for her to carry. In fact, she was expecting again, but had told no one yet, not even Jack.

Ellie Mae then grabbed Jack, Jr.'s hand and patiently waited for him to make his way towards the front door.

"Wanna ride with Uncle James?" asked her brother as he motioned for Jack, Jr. to come to him. "We wanna eat lunch before supper time, don't we?"

Jack and Jed laughed as they watched James hoist Jack, Jr. onto his shoulders for the trek down to the beach.

Jed then put Mark onto his shoulders and followed. Ellie Mae was next, followed by Jack carrying the huge picnic basket.

"Hey, grab that blanket on your way out," nodded Jack as he motioned with his head toward a folded blanket on a small table by the front door.

"I can do that," agreed Ellie Mae as she grabbed the blanket and then followed the others outside and down the switchback trail that led to the beach.

"Someday we need to think about installing stairs here," mentioned James from the lead.

"That's not a bad idea," agreed Jed as he carefully stepped over a manzanita root on the trail.

Bright pink ice plant blossoms and other low-lying groundcover bordered both sides of the path, emitting a pleasant odor. The fresh ocean breeze also carried with it the odor of cypress and eucalyptus trees from the bluff above them. Stunning views of the ocean below could be seen from anywhere on the trail, with glimmering rays of sunlight reflecting off its surface.

"At least there are no mosquitos here," reminded Ellie Mae as she thought of the bayou where they had lived in Alabama two years earlier.

"Amen to that!" exclaimed James as he adjusted Jack, Jr.'s weight on his shoulders.

Just then a seagull flew by overhead, cawing as it dove toward the water below in search of some unsuspecting prey. A sticky white deposit suddenly landed on the trail beside Jack's feet, narrowly missing them. "One thing they don't have there is seagulls, though."

The others laughed in agreement. In spite of everything, they had all missed their ocean home at the lighthouse and were glad to be back. The one-piece swimsuits they had on were all basically nothing more than hip-length pullover tank tops.

Jack's was extra-large and had a two-inch white stripe near the bottom hem and another one around the chest. The remainder of his swim outfit was dark red. Jed's swim outfit was almost identical to Jack's, while James's and Ellie Mae's swim outfits were entirely dark red. The twins each wore nothing but a white cloth diaper pinned into place with giant safety pins. All of them were barefoot.

"Have I got a surprise for all of you!" exclaimed Jed as they finally reached the sand below.

"James and I have a surprise, too," advised Jack as he plopped the huge picnic basket down onto the sand.

"Really?" Ellie Mae raised an eyebrow as she began spreading out the blanket beside the picnic basket. *Did they already know she was pregnant again?*

"Should we draw straws to see who goes first?" grinned Jack.

"Grandpa goes first," insisted Jed as he handed Mark to Jack. "You know how Ellie Mae has been after us to get a family photo?"

"You didn't?" exclaimed Ellie Mae as her father came over, pulled aside the cloth on the picnic basket, and pulled out a new camera.

"I want all of you to stand right over there, with that big rock in the background behind you," instructed Jed as he unfolded and began fiddling with the contraption.

The *No. 1A Pocket Kodak Folding Camera* had come with an instruction booklet that he had inadvertently left up at the lighthouse, though he was fairly certain how to set it up for the shot.

Both Mark and Jack, Jr. were squirming and wanted to be put down onto the sand.

"Hold on," requested Jed as he finally got it ready.

"Did you remember to put film in that thing?" teased Jack.

"Yes, there's film," assured Jed. "I've taken several shots already. Can I get all of you to move a little closer to the water?"

"What about over here?" asked Ellie Mae as she moved nearer to the shoreline and sunk one foot into the sand.

Jack came over and stood beside her. He put one arm around her and pulled her close. Mark sat on his other arm, gazing over his shoulder at the ocean behind them.

James came over and stood on her other side. He had Jack, Jr. sitting on one arm and was holding one of the child's hands with his other hand. "Look at Gramps," urged James.

"Hold it right there," commanded Jed as he snapped the photo.

"Are we done yet?" sighed James, who was struggling to keep Jack, Jr. looking toward the camera.

"Let me take a couple more," urged Jed. "Just in case."

"What about *you*?" questioned Ellie Mae. "We should get one with you in it, too."

"Okay, okay, hold on," muttered Jed as he snapped another photo. "Oh, no, there's no more film."

"I guess that's it, then," laughed Jack as he set Mark down on the sand and shook out his arms.

"Amen to that," agreed James as he put Jack, Jr. down beside Mark and stretched his back.

"Someday we'll all be glad we took that photo," assured Ellie Mae. "The boys will only turn two once, you know."

"So, what's your surprise?" grilled Jed as he came and sat down on the blanket beside the picnic basket.

Jack and James exchanged a curious look and seemed to come to an agreement.

"Well?" pressed Ellie Mae as she sat down beside her father and began removing food items from the picnic basket.

"Potato salad," beamed Jack. "My favorite."

"What else do you have in there?" questioned James.

"Grapes and cheese," answered Ellie Mae.

"And a bottle of wine," grinned Jed as he reached in and pulled it out. "Soon-to-be legal, too."

"How do you figure?" frowned Ellie Mae.

"He's right," vouched James. "It was in the paper last week. If the legislation passes – and there's no reason it shouldn't – Prohibition will be lifted by next year."

"Well, it's not lifted yet," objected Ellie Mae. She was clearly not pleased. "And just what is your *surprise,* anyway?"

"Remember when we were in Alabama?" began Jack.

Ellie Mae just folded her arms and scowled at him. "As if I could forget! Why?"

"Did you ever wonder how we came across so much money all at once to get us home when we did?" continued Jack.

"I'm listening." Ellie Mae narrowed her eyes at Jack.

"We stopped by Mobile for a friendly game of poker that afternoon," recounted Jack.

"I was totally against it," reminded James.

"Thankfully, I didn't listen to him," smirked Jack as he reached into the picnic basket and pulled out a tattered looking piece of parchment paper. "I even managed to beat out the other guy with a royal flush."

"I suppose that's an IOU that he gave you?" asked Ellie Mae rather sarcastically. She was not happy about it.

"Better than that," assured Jack. "It's a treasure map!"

"A treasure map?" repeated Jed and Ellie Mae together.

"To a lost city of gold in South America," interjected James, who had a sly grin on his face.

"Hey boys, come away from the water," yelled Ellie Mae as she watched her sons wading in the water's edge. "Right now! There's an undertow out there."

"Get back here!" hollered Jack as he handed the treasure map to James and rushed over to grab up the twins, one with each arm. "Do as your mother says and stay away from that water, or a great big sea monster will get you."

"A sea monster?' questioned Jack, Jr., with frightened eyes. He was genuinely concerned about it.

"Nah ah," doubted Mark as he struggled to get down so he could head back to the water.

"You will not go near that water again, or I'll whip you but good," threatened Jack as he finally put the twins back down onto the sand. "I mean it."

Jack, Jr. waddled over to his mother and began to cry, but Mark merely folded his arms and glared up at his father in defiance.

"Do you understand?" grilled Jack as he put his hands on his hips and stared down at Mark.

"Yes," muttered Mark as he glanced up at his 7-foot tall father. *He understood perfectly, but would head back for the water the moment no one was looking.*

"So, about that treasure map?" prompted Jed. "What do you boys intend to do with it?"

"Go to South America," grinned Jack, "find the treasure, and get rich. What else would we do with it?"

"In case you haven't noticed," rebutted Jed, "the Great Depression is going on right now – not to mention the fact that you've got two small sons and a wife to take care of."

"Well, she's *your* daughter," reminded Jack with an even gaze. "And those are *your* grandsons."

"You're serious, aren't you?" Ellie Mae was furious. She had planned on sharing her special secret with all of them that day at the beach, but suddenly decided against it.

"Just how do you plan to get there?" questioned Jed.

"We can hitchhike, hop trains, and even walk if we have to," described Jack. "We'll be back before you know it, with riches beyond our wildest dreams."

255

"*Your* dreams, not mine!" spat Ellie Mae as she got up to leave. "Isn't finally being back here at the lighthouse good enough for you?"

"Not really," answered Jack.

"Come on, we're going back up to the lighthouse," advised Ellie Mae as she grabbed Jack, Jr.'s hand and headed for the switchback trail. "Father, can you keep an eye on Mark?"

"Absolutely," promised Jed.

"And see if you can talk some sense into *your* sons while you're at it," added Ellie Mae as she and Jack, Jr. began their ascent up the trail.

"Hey, wait!" called Jack.

"Oh, let her go," prompted James. "She'll come around."

"Don't be so sure about that," opined Jed. "And it does sound like a rather risky venture at that."

"*Adventure*," corrected Jack with a devious grin. "Everything will be fine. Trust me!"

Six months had passed since Jack and James had departed for South America. It was Monday, September 26, 1932. Ellie Mae and her father Jed were seated at the table in the kitchen, on the first floor of the lighthouse, ready to eat lunch. Mark and Jack, Jr. were seated in highchairs that Jed had made for them.

"You should have told Jack you were pregnant again," chastised Jed as he glanced at her swollen belly and shook his head with dismay.

"It wouldn't have mattered," replied Ellie Mae. "They still would have gone."

"I disagree," answered her father as he unfolded the morning paper that had just been delivered. Rarely did the morning paper get delivered before noon, way out at the lighthouse.

"Anything new?" asked Ellie Mae as she chopped up some fresh peaches for the twins, who were now self-feeding. After slicing a biscuit in half and putting one half on each of their plates with the peaches, she put them on their food trays.

"It says here that the Ierissos earthquake in Greece has killed almost 500 people, that they know of," answered Jed.

"How far is that from Machu Picchu?" grilled Ellie Mae.

"Over 6,000 miles," assured Jed.

256

"That's good," nodded Ellie Mae as she sat back down at the table to eat her lunch.

"Oh yes, this came, too," added Jed as he handed Ellie Mae a letter postmarked from Alabama. He had considered at first not giving it to her, but realized that wouldn't be right.

Ellie Mae glanced at the return address, but all it said was "LaMont" with no address listed.

"I'd hoped at first that it was from the boys," sighed Jed, who was quite worried about his sons.

Ellie Mae grabbed a knife and began slicing open the envelope. Inside was a handwritten letter. As she removed it, a black and white photo slid out and onto the table. It was of Bell and Nate! Bell was clearly quite pregnant in the photo, and Nate stood next to her holding a white baby in his arms. Bell had her arms wrapped around Nate's waist and her head on his shoulder.

"Oh, my!" exclaimed Jed upon seeing the photo. "May I?"

Ellie Mae merely nodded as her father picked up the photo to study it more closely. "There's something written on the back."

Jed turned it over. It said, "James, Jr., born December 21, 1930."

"Huh," nodded Jed as he handed the photo to Ellie Mae.

"Looks like you have more grandchildren than you thought," commented Ellie Mae as she stared at the picture. A flood of memories overwhelmed her as she thought of her experiences in the bayou.

"Read the letter," urged Jed. "Do you mind?"

Ellie Mae swallowed uncomfortably but finally opened the letter and began to read:

> *"Dear Ellie Mae,*
> *Miss you greatly, and thought you should have this photo of Bell, Nate, and James, Jr. It was taken last year, just before Gideon was born. Bell passed during the childbirth. Later that same day, Nate was bitten by a coral snake. Nothing we did could save either of them. The children are now in my care. I shall do my best to raise them as my own, but thought perhaps James might wish to claim his son. You are*

welcome to come visit, any time. With much love, Hattie"

Ellie Mae wiped a tear from her cheek as she carefully folded the letter and returned it and the photo to the envelope.

"Unbelievable!" exclaimed Jed with a heavy sigh.

"I'm going," advised Ellie Mae, with finality.

"Now, hold on a minute," entreated Jed. "What about the twins? You can't just go running off like that."

"Jack did," snapped Ellie Mae.

"That doesn't make it right, and you certainly don't expect me to watch two small children like this by myself!"

"No, of course not," relented Ellie Mae. "I'll take one of them with me."

"That's out of the question," protested her father.

"Mark, how would you like to stay with Gramps for a while?" asked Ellie Mae.

Mark smiled with delight. He loved his grandpa.

"That settles it then," advised Ellie Mae. "I'm taking Jack, Jr. with me and going to see Hattie in the morning. Mark can stay here."

"Is there nothing I can do to change your mind?" appealed Jed.

"I'm afraid not," replied Ellie Mae. "After all, James, Jr. is *your* grandchild, too! Don't you even care what happens to him?"

"Perhaps I should go and *you* could stay here?" proposed her father. "It sounds much too dangerous for you to go alone."

"Do you really expect me to hoist a 50-pound counterweight to the top of this lighthouse – three times a day – and in my condition?" questioned Ellie Mae.

Jed studied his pregnant daughter and dolefully shook his head. "Perhaps if you wait until after the child is born, then we could all go there together. I could get someone else to look after the lighthouse while we're away."

"I'll think about it," promised Ellie Mae.

April 25, 2023

It was 8:30 in the morning. Kevin and Linda had just finished having breakfast in the tower room of the lighthouse with Jim and Sheree, and were finishing off a final cup of coffee.

258

"As much as we appreciate everything you've done," began Kevin, "we don't want to wear out our welcome."

"He's probably right, we do need to get back," agreed Linda, although not as enthusiastically.

"Bill Huong should have those DNA test results for us sometime this morning," reminded Jim. "Perhaps you might want to wait for that."

"Sure," nodded Kevin as he shrugged his shoulders. *Still, it seemed improbable that any other avenues to pursue might present themselves anytime soon. Jim and his associates would need time to investigate the information they had already before moving forward again on the case.*

"I know cases like this can seem discouraging at times," advised Jim after reading Kevin's expression, "but sometimes when you least expect it, the smallest clue can break the case wide open."

"Just like that?" doubted Linda as she finished off her coffee.

"Just like that," assured Jim with a crooked smile. He then looked upwards and in a dramatic gesture with his hands commented, "We really could use some help here."

All at once, an unexplained coldness could be felt within the room that caused everyone to feel an involuntary chill. Sheree glanced around to see whether any of the windows was open, but none was.

"That was odd," frowned Jim. The last time he had experienced something like that had been when staying as a guest in a haunted room at the Powell Mountain Bed and Breakfast earlier that year. It had originally belonged to a woman named Angie, and each time her ghost appeared, the sickening odor of jasmine perfume could be detected in the room.

Jim sniffed the air in the tower room to see if he could smell anything unusual, but there was nothing.

"Look!" exclaimed Linda as she noticed one of the books in the bookshelf suddenly slide out from its place and fall off the shelf, onto the floor. It landed with an echoing thud.

Jim had turned just in time to see it happen and slowly got up. He wanted to see whether it was one of the two known faux books in the library, but it wasn't. "That's odd."

"I'll say," agreed Sheree. She had personally dusted the book shelves earlier that week, and none of them had been out of place.

"It's not one of the faux books," mentioned Jim as he reached down to pick it up.

"Most of these books have been here for a hundred years or better," reminded Sheree. "Perhaps it just got so old that the pages started to crumble, and caused it to fall from the shelf."

"This book's in fairly decent condition," assessed Jim as he brought the book over to the table and set it down.

"Alabama?" frowned Kevin, when he saw the title.

"It must be a book about Alabama," guessed Linda as she glanced at it with interest.

Jim slowly opened the front cover, but nothing was inside. He then began turning the pages. "It's exactly that. It's a book about Alabama."

"May I?" asked Linda.

"Be my guest," motioned Jim.

As Linda picked up the book to move it closer, an old photo and an envelope fell out from within its pages and slid onto the table in front of her. Again, a coldness could be felt within the room.

Linda and Kevin exchanged a look of concern with Jim and Sheree. "Did you feel that?" asked Kevin.

"Oh, yeah," responded Jim.

"He did ask for help," grinned Linda.

"Yes, indeed," nodded Jim as he came around the table to sit beside Linda. He wanted to see the old photo for himself.

"Oh, my!" exclaimed Linda as she turned it over. "It's a wedding photo, and it looks like the same people that were in that picture from the beach."

Jim quickly got up and retrieved the beach photo from the faux book where it was kept. He then laid it down on the table beside the other photo. Even Sheree had come over to see and was crowding close behind them to get a better view.

"It *is* the same people," agreed Kevin as he studied the two photos. "No doubt about it."

"I think there was something written on the back," stated Sheree.

Linda then turned the photo over. It said, "Jack and Ellie Mae with James and Bell, 9-30-29, Mobile, Alabama."

260

"That's right," remembered Jim. "Jack married his half-sister, Ellie Mae, at least according to what Ann told us. And James was their brother."

"Those two are your grandparents," marveled Linda as she pointed at Jack and Ellie Mae.

"Apparently so," replied Kevin as he studied them more closely.

"So, who's Bell?" asked Sheree.

"Obviously, she was James's wife," assumed Jim.

"Perhaps there's something in here that will tell us more about her," mentioned Linda as she picked up the envelope and pulled out a worn letter. Another photo slid out.

"James, Jr., born December 21, 1930," read Linda as she picked it up to turn it over.

"Hello!" exclaimed Jim as he saw the photo.

"Looks like James wasn't the only one Bell managed to marry," observed Linda.

"Read the letter," urged Sheree.

Linda carefully unfolded the letter and read out loud:

"Dear Ellie Mae,

Miss you greatly, and thought you should have this photo of Bell, Nate, and James, Jr. It was taken last year, just before Gideon was born. Bell passed during the childbirth. Later that same day, Nate was bitten by a coral snake. Nothing we did could save either of them. The children are now in my care. I shall do my best to raise them as my own, but thought perhaps James might wish to claim his son. You are welcome to come visit, any time. With much love, Hattie"

"How sad," muttered Linda as she carefully folded the letter and returned it to the envelope.

"If James, Jr. was born in 1930, this must have been around 1931," calculated Sheree. "James, Jr. looks like he's a year old already, and Bell must be about nine months pregnant in this photo."

"LaMont," read Jim as he took the envelope from Linda and went back over to his laptop to search for the name. *Why was there nothing on Hattie? Even dead, there should be some record of her.*

"Looks like Bell must have left James for Nate," deduced Kevin as he shook his head with disapproval. "Karma surely got 'em in the end, though."

"What a thing to say," objected Linda. "You have no idea what went on between those people. Bell might have had a very good reason for leaving him to marry Nate."

"I doubt they ever married," interjected Jim as he continued searching for information on his laptop. "At least not legally. Miscegenation laws were stronger in the south than anywhere else at that time."

"What?" scowled Linda. "What does that mean?"

"Laws that prohibited interracial marriage in the United States," explained Jim. "For example, it was illegal for blacks to marry non-blacks until 1948 in California, and they were one of the more liberal states at that time."

"You've got to be kidding me!" exclaimed Linda.

"Most other states waited until the mid-sixties to repeal their miscegenation laws," added Jim as he suddenly paused to read what was on his screen. He then continued searching for something else.

"What about Alabama?" questioned Kevin, suddenly curious about it.

"Well," replied Jim, "it was after the *Loving v. Virginia* case went to the U.S. Supreme Court in 1967, that miscegenation laws were condemned as unconstitutional across the board, and in violation of the Fourteenth Amendment."

"I didn't realize it was so recent," admitted Linda. "That's less than a hundred years ago."

"Actually, it was 56 years ago," corrected Jim.

"That really wasn't that long ago at all," agreed Sheree.

"In spite of that ruling, there were 17 Southern states that continued to enforce laws prohibiting marriage between whites and non-whites, even in 1967," continued Jim, "though South Carolina finally amended their state constitution in 1998 to remove the language."

"No way," doubted Linda.

"That was only 25 years ago," advised Jim.

262

"And what about Alabama?" pressed Linda. Jim had never answered Kevin's question and Linda was curious about it, too.

"I believe Alabama was the last," answered Jim as he finally seemed to find what he was looking for on his laptop. "It was not until the year 2000 – only 23 years ago – that Alabama officially removed the language from their constitution prohibiting miscegenation."

"That's unbelievable." Linda shook her head with disbelief.

"In fact," continued Jim, "there was a justice of the peace in Louisiana who refused to officiate a wedding for an interracial couple as late as 2009, only 14 years ago."

"That guy probably got sued," assumed Kevin.

"He certainly did," nodded Jim. "Okay, this might turn out to be worth checking out. There's an Alex Killingham living in Bayou La Batre, Alabama right now, which is only a few miles outside of Mobile. But, the guy's totally off the grid, no phone, no email, nothing."

"That's 2,300 miles away," sighed Kevin.

"Actually, it's 2,378 miles away," corrected Jim. "Anyway, according to this, he was born in 1956, right there in La Batre."

"He's our age," recognized Linda.

"I say let's go see him," suggested Jim as he powered down his laptop, stood up and tapped his smartwatch. "MIRA, prepare the Learjet for a trip to Mobile, Alabama. We will be leaving within the hour."

"Yes, Jim," answered a female voice.

"Who's Mira?" grilled Kevin.

"MIRA is an acronym for Modulated Interfacing Resonance Assistant and also the name my onboard computer system has been programmed to respond to," clarified Jim.

"You're serious?" questioned Kevin.

"It's only a 3-hour flight," assured Jim. "We can be back by tonight. I already did a preflight check this morning."

"He does one every morning," advised Sheree with a crooked smile. "Just in case he gets to go somewhere unexpected."

"I've never ridden in a Learjet," mentioned Linda as she gave Kevin a pleading look.

"And what if we're not back by tonight?" frowned Kevin. "It's not exactly like we have it in our budget to go stay somewhere else."

"Relax. There are comfortable couch seats right on the Learjet that have been slept on before," promised Jim. "Not only that, she's fully contained with satellite hookup for your devices and a well-stocked kitchenette."

"It does sound intriguing," remarked Linda. "And when else will we ever get to see Alabama, of all places?"

"You might want to grab a couple of things from your suitcases, just in case we are gone overnight, though," suggested Jim as he headed for the door. "I'll meet you on the runway in 20 minutes."

"Uh ..." Kevin started to protest, but Jim was gone.

Just then, Linda picked up the Alabama book by the ends of its spine and gently shook the pages as they hung over the table. Nothing else fell out. "Just checking," grinned Linda.

"You'll have a wonderful time," promised Sheree. "Don't worry, your room will be here waiting for you when you get back."

Linda had nearly twisted her ankle while trying to negotiate the spiral staircase at the lighthouse with her huge suitcase because of her stiletto heels. Fortunately for her, Sheree also wore a size 8 shoe and had lent her a pair of hiking boots for her expedition to the bayou.

"I still don't understand why you need the entire suitcase," complained Kevin as they walked along the blufftop trail toward the tiny airport at Oceanview Academy.

"You brought *your* entire duffel bag," pointed out Linda as she continued to struggle with pulling the suitcase along. The wheels kept getting caught on rocks and tree roots as she went.

"Give me that," instructed Kevin as he snatched it from her and hoisted it up onto his shoulders.

"Your back!" cautioned Linda.

"Here, carry this," barked Kevin as he shoved his duffel bag at her with one hand.

"You're as stubborn as they come," muttered Linda while she hurried to keep up with him.

Kevin merely smiled. There were times when he rather enjoyed giving Linda a difficult time, though he wouldn't change a thing about her, even if he could.

"You're enjoying this, aren't you?" grinned Linda, who was breathing heavily from the fast pace.

264

"You bet your stilettos, I am," laughed Kevin as they approached the Learjet, where Jim was already waiting. "Good thing Sheree had those boots she let you use."

Jim began to laugh, too, when he saw the suitcase, and abruptly snatched it away from Kevin to stow in the luggage compartment.

"I could need some of those things while we're still in flight," advised Linda from where she stood holding Kevin's duffel bag.

"Very well," sighed Jim as he took it back out and carried it into the passenger compartment. "I'll leave it beside the couch seat."

"Thanks," nodded Linda as she climbed on board with the duffel bag and gazed with wonder at the plush accommodations.

"Not to quote a line from an old movie," chuckled Jim, "but I always strive to 'spare no expense.'"

"How can you afford all of this?" questioned Kevin as he and Linda sat down. "Even having your own law firm plus being the Mayor – not to mention running the B&B – still wouldn't leave you with this much free spending money. You must have expenses."

"What Kevin's trying to say," interpreted Linda, "is that we both hope you're not putting yourself out onto a financial limb like this, just for us."

"Not at all," grinned Jim as he seated himself in the pilot's seat. "MIRA, secure aircraft."

"Securing aircraft now," replied MIRA. The sound of doors and windows locking could be heard from throughout the craft.

"And if I remember correctly, you said that you have done your preflight inspection already?" grilled Kevin. He was nervous about flying and rarely did.

"Everyone buckle up!" called Jim, ignoring Kevin's question. "MIRA, skip control tower sequence."

"Why would we skip the control tower sequence?" questioned Linda, suddenly concerned about it.

"Because there's no control tower here at this private airport," smiled Jim as he studied his passengers in the large rearview mirror installed above his complicated-looking instrument panel. "But, we do have a flight plan and will be cruising at 47,000 feet."

"I thought the cockpit voice and flight data recorders were supposed to start up automatically in one of these things," mentioned Kevin as he nervously glanced out the window beside him.

"MIRA is programmed to respond specifically to my own personal commands and will take care of all that for us," assured Jim.

Kevin merely nodded.

"MIRA, begin data recorder," commanded Jim.

"Data recorder engaged," verified MIRA.

"Today is April 25, 2023, at 9:05 a.m., Pacific Standard Time," mentioned Jim for the recorder. "Departing from Oceanview Academy Airport, destination Mobile Municipal Airport."

"Confirmed. Aircraft system and flight parameters have been uplinked to satellite relay," stated MIRA.

"Wait a minute!" objected Kevin as he glanced out the window and noticed that Jim had repositioned the Learjet so that it was headed toward the bluffs. "There's not enough runway for a plane like this!"

"That runway does seem to end pretty abruptly on the far edge of that bluff over there," agreed Linda, who was also concerned about it. "What if you can't get us up into the air before we reach it?"

"Don't worry, I haven't sailed over the edge or crashed onto the boulders yet," laughed Jim, half-jokingly. "MIRA, initiate takeoff sequence."

"Takeoff sequence initiated," responded MIRA.

Without further warning, the engines began to spool. "We are waiting for the engines to stabilize for a symmetrical thrust," described Jim. "Don't worry, we'll be fine."

Kevin reached over and put his hand over Linda's. "I hope this wasn't a mistake."

"There's nothing to worry about," assured Jim as he set his flaps, aligned his aircraft with the runway centerline, and advanced his throttles. "Just be sure your seatbelts are buckled."

"Symmetrical stabilization acquired," verified MIRA.

"MIRA, fire thrusters," ordered Jim. Then for his passengers, Jim advised, "Don't worry, we won't be doing a vertical takeoff or anything like that."

"Thrusters firing now," confirmed MIRA. The Learjet suddenly thrust off and began to accelerate at a rapid speed down the private runway at Oceanview Academy.

"146 knots indicated airspeed," advised MIRA.

"I love you," Linda whispered to Kevin as the precipice ahead raced toward them with finality.

"I love you, too." Kevin tried to force a smile.

"Positive rate of climb attained," announced MIRA. "Landing gear retracting."

The sound of landing gear being retracted could be heard and felt by Jim's passengers. The craggy ocean-top bluffs below quickly disappeared from beneath them as Jim's Learjet ascended into the airspace above the expansive ocean.

"It really is a beautiful campus," opined Kevin as Jim's aircraft circled back and flew over Oceanview Academy one last time before veering its course toward Mobile Municipal Airport.

"That it is," agreed Linda as she glanced at the scenic view beneath them.

"MIRA, continue to flight level four seven zero."

"Course plotted for Mobile Municipal Airport with an alternate destination at Gulfport-Biloxi International Airport," announced MIRA. "Winds aloft checked, weather en route and destination checked. Flight plan filed and release time within your timeframe, Jim. Squawk code entered. Fuel load is adequate with a generous reserve. Estimated arrival time in 3 hours and 23 minutes."

"Thank you, MIRA," added Jim.

"You are welcome, Jim," responded MIRA.

"Four seven zero is pilot talk for 47,000 feet," Jim informed Kevin and Linda. "The extra zeros are not spoken in altitudes of 18,000 or above, which are called flight levels."

"Just where did you learn to fly, anyway?" asked Kevin.

"Right there, at Oceanview Academy," answered Jim.

"He was in the aviation course they offered there," volunteered Linda. "Available only to those who were able to afford it."

"Okay," shrugged Jim. "What I'm about to tell you is something I'd rather not publicize, so I would ask that you keep it to yourselves."

"We're all ears," encouraged Linda.

"My parents were pretty well off, so I was not allowed to work when I went to school at Oceanview Academy. My mother always wanted me to focus my attention on photography, chemistry, biology, aviation, mathematics or anything else that might help me become successful later in life."

"Is that all?" laughed Kevin.

"Unfortunately, my parents were killed during an avalanche over in Switzerland while they were skiing in the Alps back in 2004.

267

Not only did I inherit their fortune, but also my dad's multi-million-dollar brokerage firm."

"Wow!" exclaimed Kevin, suddenly comprehending why Jim had so much extra spending money.

"The firm is run by an entire regiment of well-paid employees, though, so there's little else for me to do but show up via skype for board meetings and make a personal appearance at the home office once or twice each year. That's why I have the Learjet, to make the commute more enjoyable."

"Leveling off for cruising altitude now," announced MIRA.

"I'm jealous," mentioned Linda.

"Me, too," agreed Kevin.

"Cruising altitude attained," verified MIRA.

"You may now unbuckle your seatbelts and feel free to wander around the aircraft," Jim informed them as he unbuckled his seatbelt, came back to where they were, and headed for the couch seat. Jim then grabbed and pulled out a retractable table from the wall and pressed a button on the edge of it. The surface of the table suddenly became a computer display.

"Spare no expense, indeed," said Kevin as he stared at the entire setup with amazement.

"What time do you think we'll get there?" asked Linda as she sat down beside Jim.

"Well, it was 9:05 when we took off," calculated Jim, "and the flight should last about 3 hours and 23 minutes. So, that should put us there at the Mobile Municipal Airport at approximately 12:30, just in time for lunch."

Kevin merely nodded as he sat down across from them.

"This is the entire case file on *The Killingham Matter* so far," advised Jim as he pulled it up.

"We're not going to go over it again, are we?" asked Kevin.

"No, we're hoping to add to it, though," replied Jim. "MIRA, show us everything you have on Alex Killingham."

"Alex Killingham," repeated MIRA. "Born in 1956, month and day unknown."

"MIRA, what about his parents or any other known family members?" questioned Jim.

"Father was James Killingham, Jr., born 21 December 1930, in Bayou La Batre, Mobile County, Alabama. James, Jr.'s body was

268

found on 22 September 2005, presumed to be a victim of Hurricane Katrina."

"When did the hurricane take place?" asked Linda.

"Normally you would need to say her name when you ask a question," advised Jim, "but she's programmed to respond only to me, anyway. MIRA, when did Hurricane Katrina occur?"

"Hurricane Katrina formed on 23 August 2005, dissipated 31 August 2005. Highest windspeed 175 miles per hour. Fatalities between 1,245 and 1,836. Areas most affected included the Bahamas, South Florida, Central Florida, Cuba, Louisiana (especially Greater New Orleans), Mississippi, Alabama, Florida Panhandle, and most of eastern North America."

"MIRA, what is the weather forecast like for Mobile, Alabama, today?" grilled Jim.

"Clear and sunny all day, with a high of 81 and a low of 52. Humidity at 70% by noon."

"MIRA, is there any sign of inclement weather in the forecast for Bayou La Batre?" asked Jim.

"No, Jim."

"MIRA, what about in Ocean Bluff?"

"Scattered showers throughout the day today with a high of 66 by noon and a low of 48 by tonight. Increasing rain and cloud cover overnight."

"Thank you, MIRA."

"You are welcome, Jim."

"That thing is flying the plane *and* answering all these questions for you at the same time?" questioned Kevin.

"That she is," grinned Jim. "Programmed her myself."

"Ask her if there are any other known Killinghams in Alabama besides James, Jr. and his son Alex," requested Linda.

"MIRA, are there any other close relatives listed for Alex Killingham in the Alabama area?" asked Jim.

"Negative," reported MIRA.

"MIRA, please engage satellite imaging mode," commanded Jim with a sly smile.

"Satellite imaging mode engaged," replied MIRA. "Specify target."

"MIRA, please display a real-time image of Bayou La Batre, in the area where Alex Killingham currently resides," directed Jim.

Immediately, a real time moving image of the Bayou La Batre appeared on the tabletop. A dense canopy of huge cypress and black gum trees covered the entire tabletop display. Intermittent glimpses of green mossy swamp water beneath them almost seemed like something supernatural.

"Now, there's something you don't see every day," nodded Linda. She was grateful to be wearing Sheree's hiking boots, and not the stilettos as she had planned.

"MIRA, what about a Hattie LaMont?" Jim suddenly asked. "Is there anyone by that name, or any other LaMonts living in the Bayou La Batre area?"

"Negative."

"MIRA, what about any deceased persons by that name?" pressed Jim.

After a brief pause, MIRA responded, "LaMont, Hattie, date of birth 1895, place unknown. Body was found following Hurricane Frederic, which occurred on 12 September 1979."

"MIRA, describe severity of Hurricane Frederic."

"Hurricane Frederic was a category 3 storm with average winds near 130 miles per hour and occasional gusts up to 145 miles per hour."

"And we're sure there are no hurricanes in the weather forecast?" questioned Kevin.

"Not according to MIRA," assured Jim. "I think we're good."

"How are we going to get to Alex Killingham's house?" asked Linda as she frowned at the tabletop display.

"By swamp boat," replied Jim. "MIRA, please confirm reservations for Jed's Swamp Boat Tours at LaBatre."

"Reservation for private excursion is confirmed for 2:30 this afternoon, central standard time."

"MIRA, also please confirm the rental car reservation from Mobile Municipal Airport to Jed's Swamp Boat Tours," added Jim.

"Reservation confirmed and vehicle standing by."

"Good job, MIRA."

"Are we sure we really want to go someplace like that?" frowned Kevin. "Just look at it! The canopy is virtually impenetrable."

"I think I'd be more worried about snakes and alligators," chuckled Jim as he turned off the tabletop monitor.

270

"You are kidding, right?" worried Linda.

"We'll be fine," laughed Jim as he headed toward the kitchenette and pulled out three bottles of water from the refrigerator. "Trust me."

After safely landing at the Mobile Municipal Airport, Jim had taken Kevin and Linda to lunch at the La Batre Seafood Bar & Grill.

"Not bad, thanks," mentioned Kevin as he finished eating the last of his lobster.

"Yes, thank you, very much," added Linda as she devoured the rest of her baked salmon before gently dabbing the corners of her mouth with a cloth napkin.

"You're very welcome," grinned Jim as he grabbed the bill, headed for the cash register, and waved his smartwatch over its reader. Unknown to the others, he had left his usual $20 tip.

"Thank YOU!" beamed the cashier.

Jim merely smiled and nodded as he grabbed a toothpick and headed for the front door to hold it open for Kevin and Linda.

"Uh, do you mind if I use the restroom first before we go?" asked Linda.

Jim merely laughed and shook his head. "Women!"

"Amen to that," agreed Kevin as the two of them sat down on a bench in the lobby to wait for her.

"Have you considered what we'll do if Mark is here in the bayou?" Jim suddenly asked.

"We're both carrying," reminded Kevin with a pointed glance at Jim's boot.

"I hope you don't plan to do anything foolish," cautioned Jim as he raised one eyebrow. "You're not gonna go rogue on me, are you?"

"Absolutely not," promised Kevin as they watched a scruffy-looking man about 66 years of age approach the cash register.

"That'll be $12, Mr. Killingham," advised the clerk.

"It was only $11.50 last week," teased the man. "How can it go up 50¢ in just one week?"

"Alex, you ask me that every week," laughed the girl as she reached for his folding money.

"But, I'm the only one who pays you in cash," reminded the man rather proudly as he winked at the girl.

271

"Excuse me," said Jim as he got up and walked over to the cash register and swiftly waived his smartwatch over the reader. "I've got this."

Alex Killingham turned to see who had just paid his bill and frowned at Jim with disapproval. "Do I know you?"

"You do now," grinned Jim as he extended his hand to him. "I'm Jim Otterman."

"Jim Otterman?" repeated the man with astonishment. "You're not the same Jim Otterman who happens to have a reservation for 2:30 this afternoon over at Jed's Swamp Boat Tours, are you?"

"Well, as a matter of fact, I am," replied Jim as he studied the man more closely.

"Nice to meet you, sir," smiled the man. "You can call me Alex. And you really didn't need to go and buy my lunch, though I do appreciate it. I'm perfectly capable of paying my own debts."

"I'm sure you are," replied Jim as he motioned for Kevin to join them. "Alex, I'd like you to meet Kevin Killingham."

"Killingham?" questioned Alex as he folded his arms and studied Kevin with curiosity.

"Mark Killingham's son," informed Jim.

Kevin winced when hearing that fact spoken out loud, as it was something he had tried for years to forget.

"I take it you and your old man don't see eye to eye," assumed Alex upon noticing Kevin's reaction.

"Something like that," replied Kevin.

"That makes two of us, son," advised Alex as he extended his hand to Kevin. "Uncanny family resemblance between you, though."

Kevin swallowed uncomfortably as he shook Alex's hand. *The last thing he wanted to do was remind anyone of Mark Killingham.*

"Who's this lovely lady?" flirted Alex, upon seeing Linda approach. Two of his bottom front teeth were starting to decay and he was in desperate need of a visit to the dentist. His shoulder length, reddish-gray hair was pulled straight back and fastened with a leather thong, and a can of chewing tobacco could clearly be seen outlined inside his back right pocket.

"Honey, this is Alex Killingham," informed Kevin as he put an arm around her for reassurance. "Alex, this is my wife, Linda."

"*You* are Alex Killingham?" questioned Linda with disbelief as she forced herself to shake his leathery hand.

272

"Just call me Alex, please," requested the man.

"Okay, sure," agreed Linda as she quickly pulled her hand away and studied Alex's scruffy facial hair and tattered clothing with disapproval. The man obviously had not bathed yet that day.

"Our whole reason for flying out here from Ocean Bluff was actually to find *you*," informed Jim. "What a stroke of luck that we should run into you like this."

"If you don't mind my asking," responded Alex, "but why on earth would you be looking for the likes of me?"

"We are actually conducting a murder investigation," explained Jim. "The man buried in Mark Killingham's grave back in 2009 turned out to be someone else, so we're following up every possible lead, including distant family members."

"A murder investigation," smirked Alex. "You don't say. Ten bucks says Mark probably did it, too."

"You don't even know the facts of the case yet," pointed out Jim.

"I have no doubt you'll fill me in," chuckled Alex as he headed for the door. "Why don't we go out to my place, where we can talk more freely?"

"Exactly what we had in mind," approved Jim. "We were actually going to try and find you, and now you've saved us the trouble."

"Well, here I am," replied Alex as he shrugged his shoulders.

"What about the rental car?" Linda reminded Jim, upon seeing the filthy pickup truck Alex was heading for.

"Oh, save your money, you can ride with me," suggested Alex. "Especially after buying my lunch like that. Thanks again, by the way."

"No problem. MIRA, cancel rental car," directed Jim as he spoke into his smartwatch.

"Who's Mira?" grinned Alex as he opened the driver's side door. "You'll have to get in from this side. The other door hasn't worked in years. One of you will have to ride in the back, though."

"MIRA is an acronym for my Modulated Interfacing Resonance Assistant," clarified Jim as he motioned for Linda to climb inside.

"I can just ride in the back with Kevin," offered Linda.

"One of them fancy computer geeks, huh?" assumed Alex as he came around back and lowered the tailgate. "Sorry about the mess."

Linda gazed with horror at the fragments of some disgusting swamp creature – probably an alligator – that had recently been butchered in the bed of the pickup and then decided, "I think I'll just ride in the cab."

Kevin merely nodded with understanding and climbed into the back without her.

Since Jim was already inside the cab, Linda would be forced to sit next to Alex. She then leaned inside the cab and gave Jim a pleading look. "Trade you places?"

"Sure, why not?" Jim responded with a crooked grin as he climbed back out so Linda could get in first.

"I don't bite, you know," chuckled Alex as he undressed Linda with his eyes.

You obviously don't bathe much, either! thought Linda as she wrinkled her nose with disgust.

"Rental car cancelled," confirmed MIRA's voice on Jim's smartwatch.

"That's sure an irritating thing, isn't it?" asked Alex as he climbed inside the truck after Linda and Jim, and inserted its old-fashioned key into the ignition. The pickup was a dark green 1980 Chevy that had seen better days.

"Thank you, MIRA," Jim spoke into his smartwatch.

"Who would we see about cancelling our reservation for Jed's Swamp Boat Tours at LaBatre?" Linda whispered to Jim.

"No need, pretty lady," interjected Alex, who had easily overheard her. "That's exactly where we're headed."

"Will Jed Killingham be there?" Linda unexpectedly asked.

"Heavens, no," chuckled Alex. "He's long dead. Jed was my great granddaddy. The place is named after him."

"Really?" Jim and Linda exchanged a surprised look.

"I believe that's the name of my great grandfather, too," Kevin suddenly realized. He was easily able to be a part of their conversation through the open back window of the cab.

"Huh," grunted Alex as he studied Kevin in his rearview mirror more closely, as if he were sizing him up.

"You married?" Linda finally asked.

"Don't you already have a husband?" flirted Alex as he nodded toward the back where Kevin was riding.

"What I meant was ...."

"What she meant," interrupted Jim, "was to ask whether you have a family? We were hoping to meet them while we're here."

"And to find out more about Hattie LaMont," added Linda.

"So, you came here to uncover all the dark Killingham Family secrets, did you?" Alex gave them a wicked grin.

"That's exactly why we're here," advised Kevin from behind them. "And whatever else you can tell us."

"Very well, then, you're in luck," agreed Alex as he became more serious while he swerved to miss a pothole in the road. "I have some papers at the house that used to belong to my Grandma Bell. All sorts of juicy stuff."

"How juicy?" frowned Linda.

"You won't be disappointed," promised Alex. "Trust me."

Already feeling out of sorts from the bumpy ride to Jed's Swamp Boat Tours at LaBatre, Linda gazed with horror at the rickety boat moored to its pier. *Would they be eaten by alligators when it sank?*

"When was Jed last here?" asked Jim.

"Well, let me think," replied Alex as he climbed from the pickup and headed at once for the boat. "He's the one who started the place when he first came out here with my Aunt Elleanor back in 1932."

"Elleanor?" pressed Jim as they followed him to the boat.

"She also went by Ellie Mae when it suited her," added Alex.

"MIRA, please cross reference Ellie Mae Killingham with the name Elleanor," instructed Jim.

"How is that thing even working out here?" frowned Alex as he motioned for them to climb inside the boat.

"Satellite," replied Jim.

"Hold it," protested Linda. "I thought we were going to your house, now that we've found you."

"This is how we get there," revealed Alex.

"That's the only way, in that thing?" scowled Linda.

"I'm afraid so," chuckled Alex.

"What about life vests?" Linda suddenly asked.

275

"Oh, yeah, I'll be right back." Alex then hurried to an old shack to retrieve the life vests.

"Elleanor LaMont married Jack Killingham in Mobile, Alabama, on 30 September 1929," announced MIRA. It had taken her longer than usual to provide the information.

"Just like it said on that old photo," nodded Jim. "MIRA, please cross reference that to a James Killingham and a woman named Bell."

"Bell Sanderson married James Killingham in Mobile, Alabama, on 30 September 1929," confirmed MIRA.

"MIRA, confirm it was a double wedding ceremony," pressed Jim.

"Affirmative, Jim."

"I could have told you that," informed Alex as he approached and handed each of them an aging orange life vest. The one he handed Linda was still slightly covered with dried mud on one corner.

"I'll take that one," offered Kevin as he gave her his.

"Thanks, honey." Linda was grateful for the exchange.

"Lady in the middle," directed Alex, "and one man at each end. I can ride on the seat beside her."

"What if Kevin rides in the middle with me?" proposed Linda.

"Sure, he can do that," agreed Alex as he flirted with her. "Can't blame a guy for trying."

"You lay a hand on her, and you're mine," whispered Kevin as he walked past Alex to climb inside the boat.

"A good man like that's hard to come by," approved Alex as he winked at Linda. "Better hang onto him."

"I intend to," assured Linda as she put her arm through Kevin's when he sat down beside her.

"Looks like you and I are the pole guys," commented Alex as he picked up two long poles from inside the boat and handed one of them to Jim. "Wanna do front or back?"

"Which end does the most poling?" questioned Jim.

"They both do," grinned Alex.

"I'll take the back then," volunteered Jim.

"If you get tired, you and Kevin can always trade off," suggested Alex as he unmoored the boat and gave it a shove from the pier with his pole.

276

The afternoon sunlight could be seen intermittently streaming down through the canopy above them, and seemed to ripple across the thick green water. The knees of craggy cypress trees hugged the hidden shoreline on either side of them, intermingled with giant black gum trees, both of them covered with feathery strands of moss that dangled down from huge limbs. The humming buzz of insects and other swamp creatures surrounded them as they made their way into the swamp. Linda suddenly swatted at a mosquito on her arm, and then another one on her face.

"There's some insect repellent under the seat," revealed Alex.

Kevin quickly reached under the seat and retrieved an old mason jar filled with what appeared to be seasoned lard. "What is *this*?"

"Rosemary and wild mint in lard," replied Alex. "And it works, too."

Linda and Kevin exchanged a look of concern, but as more mosquitos began to bite, they each dug in and scooped out some of the vile looking substance to rub onto their arms and faces.

"When you're done, pass that back here," requested Jim. He, too, was being eaten alive by mosquitos.

"Yuck!" exclaimed Linda as she wrinkled up her nose.

"It does seem to work," admitted Kevin as he began to laugh at the expression on her face.

"We swamp boys know how it's done," advised Alex as he continued to flirt with Linda. His remark was intended to be taken any way she chose.

"So do us city boys," commented Kevin as he moved closer to Linda and glared at Alex with disapproval.

"Point taken," nodded Alex as he became serious and pointed to the water ahead of them. "Jim, we need to steer around that log."

"As slow as we're going, what difference does it make?"

"Because it's not a log!" exclaimed Linda.

Jim then nodded with understanding upon realizing it was an alligator. "Will he try to capsize us?"

"He'll leave us alone," assured Alex, "as long as we go around him. They just don't take kindly to being rammed by boats."

Linda was clearly afraid, and didn't even realize that her fingernails were digging into Kevin's arm.

"Hey!" yelled Kevin as he grabbed her hand and pulled it off.

277

"Sorry," apologized Linda. Just then, she looked up and noticed a giant snake hanging down from one of the low-hanging branches they were passing beneath and let out a blood-curdling scream.

"Water moccasin," Alex informed them. "Very poisonous."

"That's only one of the three poisonous types of snakes found here in the bayou," added Jim. "There are actually 57 varieties of snakes altogether, including the non-venomous ones."

"Oh, please don't get him started," begged Linda. She was in no mood for one of Jim's knowledgeable descriptions right then.

"A regular wise cracker," acknowledged Alex as he nodded with understanding. "Kevin's daddy was like that, too, by the way."

"Mark Killingham was like that?" questioned Linda.

"Yep," replied Alex. "Always seemed to know everything about nothing, and nothing about everything, anxious to impress the world with all his knowledge."

Jim's nostrils flared as he glared at Alex. "Sir, there's no need to insult me. I knew Mark Killingham, too, and the only thing he knew anything about was making good ice cream."

"That he did," agreed Alex as he thought of Mark Killingham.

"Huh!" scoffed Kevin as he thought of his estranged father and the turmoil he had caused in their lives.

"Just how much farther is it to your place?" questioned Linda. She was anxious to get indoors and away from the prolific insect life.

"Not far," replied Alex.

"Say, what's that over there?" nodded Kevin upon seeing the wreckage of an old houseboat.

"That, sir, is the Lady Elleanor," informed Alex as he paused from his poling to look at it. "Or – I should say – it was."

"What happened to it?" asked Kevin.

"First, Hurricane Frederic, and later, Hurricane Katrina," replied Alex. "What Frederic didn't tear apart, Katrina demolished. The only thing left is a small wooden sign that used to hang on its door. It's mounted on that cypress tree over there."

"Oh, so it is," noticed Kevin.

"Is that where Ellie Mae lived?" grilled Jim, suddenly very interested in it.

"For a while," answered Alex as he resumed poling. "It's also where Mark Killingham and his brother Jack, Jr. were born."

278

"No kidding," said Jim as he gave another push off the bottom with his pole.

Kevin merely scowled at the location.

"There's an old diary at the house that tells all about it," promised Alex. "It belonged to Grandma Bell."

"Why would you want to live in a place like this?" Linda suddenly asked. "Won't there be other hurricanes?"

"Most likely," answered Alex, "but most of us try not to think about it too much. This is the kind of place that grows on you. It's got a beauty all its own."

Linda then gazed up at the abundant moss clinging to the towering trees above them and noticed gossamer spider webbing silhouetted in between them in the afternoon sun. Just then the hoot of an owl could be heard as it unexpectedly flew past them.

"I thought owls were nocturnal," commented Linda.

"Usually, but it could have been startled by something," replied Alex as he glanced around. "All creatures need to be on guard around here at all times, especially humans."

"What's that place?" grilled Jim as they came upon a set of pylons and more wreckage along the shoreline.

"That's where Hattie and Tom used to live," informed Alex.

"Isn't Hattie the one who wrote Ellie Mae that letter?" Linda reminded Jim.

"That wouldn't happen to be a Hattie LaMont, would it?" Jim asked Alex.

"She was Nate's mother," revealed Alex. "You folks sure know a lot of names, but have no idea how they fit into the family puzzle, do you?"

"That's about the size of it," answered Jim.

"Well, Hattie LaMont was the daughter of a pirate who would come to Bayou La Batre to trade in exotic merchandise," began Alex as he took up a steady rhythm poling their boat. "When she came ashore one day and saw Tom unloading cargo at the dock, it was love at first sight. Her father's ship ended up leaving port without her."

"He just left her here?" Linda couldn't believe it.

"Well, yes," grinned Alex. "Tom was a black man, and in those days, it was illegal for folks to marry outside their race, especially here in Alabama."

279

"Is that why they came here to the swamp?" asked Linda, "so no one would find them?"

"Pretty much," nodded Alex. "They had four sons, quadruplets, all with Bible names. Nate was short for Nathaniel."

"What happened to the rest of them?" grilled Jim.

"It's all in the diary," assured Alex as he suddenly began steering their boat into a different direction. Straight ahead of them was an older houseboat that had obviously survived some catastrophic event and since been repaired. Mismatched boards on its sides were nailed in place at uneven angles, to cover holes or gouges.

"This is *your* house?" Linda stared at it with trepidation. "Do you have a restroom in there?"

"There's an outhouse," answered Alex. "Of course, you gotta check for snakes before you sit down. And, it never hurts to look for spiders, either."

Linda gave Kevin a pathetic look.

"You wanted to come," reminded Kevin as he started to smile.

"Are you cooking something in there?" questioned Jim as he detected a whiff of something delicious on the wind.

"Dinner," replied Alex as he began slowing his pace and allowed the boat to coast up to a small dock in front of the floating house. "This is where James, Jr. was born. It's the house that Nate built for Bell after they took off together. What they didn't know was that she was already pregnant with my daddy at the time."

"James, Jr.?" clarified Jim, just to make sure.

"Yes," replied Alex as he moored the boat to his dock.

"Who raised your father?" pressed Linda. She decided not to mention the contents of Hattie's letter just yet.

"Well, Grandma Bell died while giving birth to Nate's son Gideon," began Alex as he pulled his pole from the water, "and poor Nate was bitten later that same day by a coral snake. They are buried together in the old cemetery, right beside my great grandpa. But, it was Nate's mother who raised my dad. I knew her as Grandma Hattie."

"What about Gideon?" Linda suddenly asked.

"He and my dad were raised as brothers," answered Alex as he took Jim's pole from him and stowed both poles in the boat.

"Does Gideon live around here?" pressed Linda.

280

"No." Alex sadly shook his head. "He died during Hurricane Katrina, back in 2005."

"I'm so sorry," replied Linda.

"Is Jed Killingham buried around here?" grilled Jim.

Alex then shook his head and gave Kevin and Linda a crooked smile before glancing at Jim. "Is ya'll in some kind of a hell-fired hurry to get your questions answered all at once?"

Ignoring him, Jim spoke into his smartwatch. "MIRA, please confirm whether any Killinghams are buried in an old cemetery near Bayou La Batre."

"Maybe I should get me one of those," snickered Alex as he climbed from the boat and pulled it flush to the dock. "Ladies first."

Linda hesitated but then grabbed Alex's leathery hand and allowed him to help her from the boat. Despite his scruffy appearance and rotting teeth, Alex was actually rather handsome, and bore a remote resemblance to Kevin.

MIRA's voice could then be heard. "Jed Killingham is buried beside his daughter Ellie Mae Killingham aka Elleanor LaMont at the La Batre Pioneer Cemetery."

"Thank you, MIRA, are there any others?" pressed Jim.

"Negative," came the reply.

"We probably should go visit the cemetery while we're here, too," mentioned Jim as he and Kevin climbed from the boat on their own, without Alex's help.

"I can take you there later," promised Alex. "Hope ya'll like 'gator stew."

Linda's eyes widened and she swallowed an involuntary lump in her throat.

Jim and Kevin both grinned at her with amusement as they followed Alex into his floating home.

After glancing around for possible snakes or spiders on the porch, Linda reluctantly followed them inside. *At least there were screens on the windows!*

"Have a seat," invited Alex as he motioned toward a handmade burl table in the middle of the room.

"Nice work," admired Kevin as he touched the smoothly polished tabletop.

"A fellow carpenter?" asked Alex as he grabbed a potholder to remove the lid on his stewpot and began stirring its contents.

281

"My stepdad was a general contractor," revealed Kevin as he sat down on one of the tree stump benches surrounding it. "I've worked a bit with wood."

"He's being modest," added Linda as she sat down beside her husband, smiled and put her arm through his. Linda then noticed that the stewpot was actually a large crockpot and was plugged into an electrical outlet. "How do you have electricity out here?"

"There's a cable strung through the trees, clamped on where necessary to keep it in place," described Alex. "It also takes electricity to two other residents here in the swamp, just a little farther out."

"Pretty ingenious," appreciated Jim.

"Oh, and the outhouse is right through that back door and across a small footbridge, by the way," directed Alex as he put the lid back onto his stewpot. "Flashlight's by the door, in case it's dark before you work up the courage to venture out there. Just be sure to keep the door latched at all times. There's a hook on each side, just like the one over here. We don't want any snakes getting in."

"Is there any electricity in the outhouse?" asked Linda.

"Nope," replied Alex. "You'll need the flashlight. And the swinging footbridge actually leads to a small island where the outhouse is, but the 'gators rarely come out during the daytime."

"We won't be here after dark, will we?" Linda became alarmed.

"We very well might," interjected Jim. "We do have a lot we need to go over while we're here."

"That could mean spending the night here," warned Alex as he flirted again with Linda. "Don't worry, I've got enough extra cots."

"What about our suitcases?" Linda suddenly asked as she frowned at Jim. "It's not like we have an extra change of clothes with us! Everything's back on your Learjet, remember?"

"You could always borrow some of mine," teased Alex as he headed for a small hutch at one end of the room.

"I'm fine," assured Linda. *What a revolting thought! If the rest of his clothes smelled like the ones he had on ....*

"We'll be fine," promised Kevin, as he interrupted her thoughts by putting a comforting hand on her back.

Linda merely nodded.

"Here, read this," suggested Alex as he plopped a tattered old diary on the table in front of them. "I've got a box of other stuff

282

somewhere, too," mentioned Alex as he returned to the hutch to search for it.

"Is that Bell's diary?" questioned Jim as he scooted his stool close to Kevin and Linda so he could look on.

"That would be it," answered Alex from the other side of the room as he rummaged through the hutch. "Here's the other thing I was lookin' for." He then returned to the table with an aging metal box that looked like a treasure chest and placed it on the table. "There are some old photos and other things inside, and you're welcome to anything you want, since you're family, too. That stuff ain't doin' me no good, plus I ain't got kids."

"We don't, either," informed Kevin, rather sadly, "but definitely might take you up on that."

"Should we read the diary first, or look in the box?" asked Linda.

"Whatever you fancy," grinned Alex as he returned to the kitchen. "I make the best 'gator stew in the county, by the way. Won first place at the fair last year."

"That really is alligator stew?" questioned Jim with a raised eyebrow. He had assumed Alex was joking earlier.

"Tastes just like chicken," laughed Alex as he took off the lid and stirred it again. "It's got potatoes, onions, garlic, parsley and shredded cheese in it, too."

"How do you prepare the alligator?" questioned Kevin as Linda proceeded to open the diary and began reading.

"The tail," explained Alex, "is the tenderloin. It has four cylindrical tubes of muscle, four lobes, like tuna. It almost looks like a dunce cap, long and skinny. All you do is slice that and pound it like veal, and you can't tell the difference. Good for grilling, too."

"Huh," nodded Jim as he opened the metal box and began rummaging through a stack of photos and documents.

"Hey, you guys, listen to this," requested Linda. "When Bell first came here with Jack, James and Ellie Mae, she says they hopped a freight train."

"All the way from that lighthouse of theirs," interjected Alex as he pulled up a stool.

"Say, is there a place to wash up?" questioned Linda. "After using the outhouse, that is."

"There's a washtub out on the deck," mentioned Alex, suddenly perceiving why she was asking. "And if you folks are good for a few minutes, I might just go tidy up myself. Didn't get a chance to this morning."

"We'll be fine," assured Linda. She tried not to appear too overjoyed that Alex was about to clean himself up, but the relief on her face was obvious. Kevin then gave her a warning poke in the side with his elbow.

Jim began laying old photos out on the table. One was a wedding photo of Jack, Ellie Mae, James and Bell. On one side of them was a beautiful Latin woman and a black man. On the other side of them was a plump white man in a judge's robe holding what appeared to be a jug of moonshine.

"Wow!" exclaimed Kevin as he picked up the picture and took a closer look at it. "It must have been taken at the same time as that other photo from the lighthouse."

"Even though they were brother and sister, it's clear to see how much in love your grandparents were," assessed Linda.

Kevin then turned the photo over and read, "Hattie and Tom with Judge Brown and the Killinghams."

Then, turning back to the diary, Linda began to read out loud. Jim and Kevin listened with great interest.

"Sounds like Bell was smitten with Nate from the moment she first saw him," guessed Jim.

"Yet she married James anyway," added Kevin.

"Perhaps James shouldn't have taken her for granted and been gone all the time like that," countered Linda.

"That still doesn't make it right, her taking off with Nate like that," argued Kevin.

"Of course not," agreed Linda, "but James should have been observant enough to see that coming, before it was too late."

"It wouldn't have made any difference," opined Alex as he entered the room in a fresh pair of clothing. He had also shaved. "Bell and Nate were hopelessly in love, from day one."

Linda stared at Alex with amazement as he came over and sat beside them. Aside from his rotting teeth, he was actually quite handsome! The look on her face was not lost on the others.

"We swamp boys clean up real well, too," grinned Alex.

All except your teeth! thought Linda as she quickly turned her attention back to the diary. Kevin and Jim both smiled when they saw her reaction.

"How 'bout I just tell ya'll the tale of Bell's diary?" offered Alex. "You can always read it later."

"That would be nice," agreed Kevin.

"Before I get started, is anyone thirsty?" asked Alex.

"I could use a bottle of water," mentioned Linda.

Alex then took a drinking glass from the top shelf in his kitchen and poured some water into it from a pitcher on the counter nearby. "It's been boiled," promised Alex as he handed it to Linda.

"Thanks," nodded Linda as she stared at the lukewarm water with concern.

"Got any iced tea?" questioned Jim.

"Nope, but I got this," replied Alex as he quickly retrieved a large ceramic jug with a cork in the top and plopped it onto the table.

"Moonshine?" laughed Jim.

"Isn't that illegal?" challenged Kevin.

"Not since 2013," grinned Alex as he popped off the cork. "The High Ridge Spirits Distillery near Union Springs was the first legal distillery in Alabama since Prohibition."

"Sounds like MIRA's got some competition," razzed Kevin with a pointed look at Jim.

"I'll try some in a glass," requested Linda. Both Jim and Kevin turned to stare at her with surprise.

"A glass would be good," agreed Kevin. "Besides, who comes to the deep south without sampling a little moonshine?"

"I'm in," grinned Jim.

"Guess ya'll plan to help wash up the dishes?" teased Alex as he went to fetch more drinking glasses.

"What time is it?" questioned Linda.

"It's 3:45 in the afternoon," answered Jim.

"We're not really going to spend the night here, are we?"

"I can't guarantee we won't," replied Jim.

Alex then set several empty drinking glasses down in front of them, along with a bowl of pretzels.

"Now you're talking," approved Kevin as he poured himself a glass of moonshine and then grabbed a handful of pretzels.

Jim did likewise.

Alex then grabbed the bottle of moonshine and poured a glass for Linda, that he put beside her glass of water.

"Okay then," sighed Alex as he took a huge drink directly from the jug and then wiped his mouth on his sleeve. "It was in 1929 that Jack and James came out here with Ellie Mae and Bell. It was because both women were only 17 years old that they decided on Alabama, where it was legal to marry 'em."

"What about the train ride?" pressed Linda.

"I'm gettin' to it," assured Alex as he devoured a pretzel before continuing. "It was just before The Great Depression hit, too, but they were still quite broke at the time and figured hopping a freight train might defray their travelin' costs."

"That's one way of looking at it," remarked Jim as he took a sip of moonshine and then coughed and sputtered.

"Kind of gets ya right there, doesn't it?" laughed Alex.

Kevin then took a drink and had a similar reaction. "Whew! That stuff'll make your eyes water, too."

"Anyhow," resumed Alex, "they spent days in a smelly old freight car where cattle had been, and even some chickens, I believe, before arriving here. But, while the train was stopped after hitting an 8-point buck, they were joined by another traveler. That was Tom."

"Hattie's Tom?" Linda was surprised.

"One and the same," grinned Alex as he took another swig of moonshine from the jug. "That's how they all met."

"Wow!" exclaimed Kevin as he took another sip from his glass.

"Wow is right," agreed Linda as she picked up her glass and took a small sip. The others watched to see her reaction, but she merely reached for the glass of water with a perfect poker face and drank about half of it down.

Alex then flirted with her and undressed her again with his eyes before resuming his tale. Ignoring Kevin's look of disapproval, Alex explained, "When Tom took them back to his place that night, they stayed there."

"Was that when she first met Nate?" pressed Linda.

"Not just Nathaniel, but also Hezekiah who went by Zeke, Bartholomew who went by Bart, and Shadrak who went by Shad."

"They were religious, then?" assumed Jim.

286

"Hattie was," recalled Alex, "though Tom just went to church to make her happy when necessary."

"Was Tom French?" asked Linda.

"I doubt that," laughed Alex as he popped another pretzel into his mouth. "LaMont was Hattie's last name. He just acquired it upon marrying her."

"I thought they couldn't get married back then," reminded Jim.

"Just like there were black-market moonshine dealers during Prohibition," explained Alex, "there were also black-market preachers, willing to marry anyone for the right price – or a good bottle of moonshine."

The others chuckled at that.

"The Killingham brothers went to work for Tom, who just happened to be one of the major manufacturers and distributors of moonshine in these parts," revealed Alex.

"Is that why Ellie Mae and Bell were left alone so much?" asked Linda as she glanced again at the page in the diary she had been reading.

"That was one reason," confirmed Alex. "It was also because they were hit by The Great Depression only weeks after getting married, and legitimate jobs were not to be found."

"How did they get by?" grilled Jim.

"Hunting and foraging, mostly," answered Alex. "They also had a vegetable garden and a stable, up by where the boat dock is today."

"Where Jed's Swamp Boat Tours is located?" quizzed Jim.

"Yes, sir," confirmed Alex. "Anyway, Nate was only 16 years old, just a year younger than Bell, so no one took it seriously at first. He would go over to the Lady Elleanor, where the Killinghams were living, and cut firewood, bring in fresh water, whatever they needed, almost every day. He would bring them fresh meat and vegetables, too."

"He was also a very handsome young man," apprised Linda as she studied the photograph of Nate and Bell together with James, Jr. more closely.

"If you like that kind of thing," muttered Kevin as he gave Linda a pointed look. He could not help but think of Lenny Owens, the young black man he only recently learned had been Linda's main interest when she was in high school.

287

The exchange between them did not go unnoticed by Alex, who merely took it in and nodded.

"Go on," urged Linda.

"Well, on the very day that Ellie Mae gave birth to Mark and Jack, Jr. on board the Lady Elleanor – right while Hattie was midwifin' her – Nate and Bell showed up to announce that they had been together and were running away to live as man and wife."

"What did James do?" frowned Kevin.

"That's the strange thing," answered Alex. "James and Jack didn't make it back from their latest hunting trip until just after Nate and Bell had taken off, so they just missed 'em."

"Ouch!" exclaimed Kevin. "I'll bet that went over well."

"Anything but," assured Alex. "Tom and James went out day and night after that – for several days – searching everywhere for 'em. Their intentions were anything but good."

"Did they ever find them?" asked Linda. She had become quite engrossed in the story.

"No, they never did," responded Alex. "They were hiding on the island out back – the one where the outhouse is. It wasn't until they finally felt sure no one was still looking for 'em that Nate built this place. Bell wanted to help, but soon realized she was with child, so Nate built the entire thing by himself."

"They really do look happy in this picture," repeated Linda.

"That's what she says in the diary," confirmed Alex. "Theirs was the love of a lifetime. Her only regret was marrying James first."

"If she hadn't, then you wouldn't be here," reminded Linda.

"Touché!" exclaimed Alex as he took another swig of moonshine and devoured more pretzels.

"So, exactly when did Jed and Ellie Mae come out here?" questioned Jim. He felt a need to get back on track before it got any later, or they might not have time to visit the cemetery.

"It was on March 23, 1932, when they were all celebratin' Mark and Jack, Jr.'s birthdays there at the lighthouse, that Jack and Ellie Mae had a big blowout, right there on the beach. It was because Jack told her he'd won some treasure map in a poker game, two years earlier, and was determined to go to South America to find a lost city of gold," recounted Alex.

"I take it she wasn't too keen on the idea," assumed Jim.

"Especially with two young boys like that," opined Linda.

288

"That's an understatement!" exclaimed Alex as he rolled his eyes and shook his head. "That was when Ellie Mae decided to come back out here, to spend some time with Hattie and them."

"What about James?" asked Jim. "What did he think of the idea of going to South America?"

"James went with Jack, but was killed during a cave-in at the mine they discovered," recalled Alex. "That was the part Ellie Mae didn't learn until years later, when Mark came back out here for a visit. They sure had a nasty argument over it, too, and something about some treasure and who really had it."

"That's interesting," mused Jim as he thought of the gold disc.

"Mark came out here for a visit?" Kevin became concerned.

"The first visit was before my time," revealed Alex. "It was during World War II. According to Ellie Mae – who was actually my great aunt – Mark said the military had taken over the lighthouse and used it as a defensive seaside outpost. He needed somewhere else to stay for a while, so he came here."

"Where was Jack, Sr. all this time?" questioned Jim. "After he got back from South America?"

"He took over running the lighthouse," replied Alex, "until the military stepped in. That was when he started up some trailer park on the property next to it."

"I remember that trailer park," nodded Linda. "It was still there in 1972 when I went to school at Oceanview Academy."

"Isn't that where the golf course is now, where the trailer park used to be?" Kevin whispered to Linda. She merely nodded yes.

"So, Mark just left his dad there to run the lighthouse by himself?" frowned Jim. "That was quite a task back in those days."

"I'm sure it was," agreed Alex, "but Mark was like that. Never thought of nobody but himself. When he came out here, he was alone."

"When was that again?" pressed Jim.

"Sometime between 1942 and 1945, but I wasn't even born until 1956. Mark also told Ellie Mae how the lighthouse was used by the military to send light signals by Morse code to ally vessels at sea," described Alex. "It's all there in the diary."

"I thought that was Bell's diary," reminded Linda.

"'Til she died," explained Alex. "The last half is all written by Ellie Mae."

Linda thumbed through the diary until a page where the different handwriting began. "Huh."

"Ray told us about the military taking over the lighthouse once," remembered Jim. "He also mentioned that when Mark came back from a trip to visit relatives, that he set up the first ice cream shop and helped Jack, Sr. run that trailer park. At first it was just supposed to be temporary, until the military people left. Then, it became a lucrative business venture, especially with the ice cream shop. People love ice cream. So, they decided to branch out and set up the second ice cream shop in Ocean Bluff."

"I don't doubt it," responded Alex. "Mark made the best ice cream, hands down."

"Wasn't it after the military people left that Mark moved back into the lighthouse with his stepson Ray?" asked Linda.

"That's what Ray always told us," confirmed Jim. "Apparently Jack, Sr. passed away just before that."

"Interesting," nodded Alex as he put a hand on his chin and rested the elbow of that arm in his other hand.

"So, when did they get rid of the lighthouse light and put in that round wooden table up in the tower room?" grilled Linda.

"Ray said it was his stepdad Mark's idea to have the table put there to fill up the space after the lighthouse was decommissioned by the military at the end of World War II," explained Jim. "I thought I mentioned that to you earlier."

"I believe you did," corroborated Kevin.

"Why would they decommission it?" Alex was curious.

"Because you can't have a lighthouse without proper approval," replied Jim. "A valid permit is required to be in compliance with federal regulations, and since they're the ones who voided the permit and decommissioned the lighthouse in the first place, it hardly seemed likely they might change their minds."

"Interesting," nodded Alex, who was definitely beginning to feel the effects of the moonshine.

"Can we get back to the subject of Jed and his daughter Ellie Mae," urged Linda as she finally took another sip but still needed to chase it down with a gulp of water. "You were telling us about how they came out here in 1932."

"Oh yes," recalled Alex as he got up to go stir the alligator stew again before resuming his narrative.

"Why did they end up staying here?" questioned Jim.

"I thought you'd never ask," grinned Alex as he sat back down at the table. "Apparently, Bell wasn't the only Killingham woman to take a walk on the dark side."

"Just what's that supposed to mean?" frowned Linda.

"She and Zeke became an item," clarified Alex, pausing long enough to let the realization of it soak in for his listeners.

"Is this Ellie Mae with Zeke?" asked Linda as she suddenly reached for another photo and held it up.

"She looks like she's expecting there," noticed Kevin.

"She was actually pregnant with Jack Killingham's daughter Vivian, the child he never knew about."

"Jack, Sr. never even knew he had a daughter?" Linda could not believe it. "Why wouldn't she have told him?"

"She must have had her reasons," assumed Alex.

"Who's the child with them?" grilled Jim.

"That's Jack, Jr.," replied Alex.

"Why isn't Mark with them?" probed Jim.

"He was left at the lighthouse with some woman to look after him until Jack, Sr. got back from south America," described Alex.

"Mark was raised by Jack, Sr.?" asked Linda.

"Pretty much," verified Alex. "It was a splitting of property, so to speak, except all they really had were the twins."

"Incredible." Jim shook his head as he took another sip of moonshine, quickly followed by a pretzel to stave off the flavor.

"Where did Zeke and Ellie Mae live?" asked Linda.

"Out here, on the Lady Elleanor, of course," replied Alex. "Until they were both killed during Hurricane Frederic in 1979."

"What about Jack, Jr. and Vivian?" grilled Linda.

"They were both long gone and on their own by that time," described Alex. "If I'm not mistaken, Jack, Jr. was 49 years old in 1979, and Vivian was 47."

"Where did they each finally go?" delved Jim.

"Well, the last I heard, Jack, Jr. had headed back out to Ocean Bluff to try and straighten things out with his estranged brother Mark."

"When was that?" grilled Jim.

"In 2009, I believe," recalled Alex. "It was only a handful of years after Katrina killed my mom."

"Where were you during Katrina?" probed Jim.

"With her," answered Alex as his face took on a rather sad expression. "My wife and kids were killed that day, as well."

"Oh, I'm so sorry!" apologized Linda. She leaned over and put a comforting hand on Alex's shoulder.

"So, it's just me now," sniffed Alex as he took another swig of moonshine and then wiped his mouth on his sleeve.

"So, Jack, Jr. went to visit his brother Mark in 2009," repeated Jim as he considered the implications of it. "That's the very year that Mark allegedly died and was found on the floor of his ice cream shop by his stepson Ray."

"Except that the body we exhumed turned out to be someone else!" exclaimed Linda, suddenly seeing where Jim was going with that.

"We believe that Mark may have murdered his brother, left him there, and then took on his identity," elaborated Jim.

"That wouldn't surprise me one bit," commented Alex. "That Mark was a good-for-nothing two-bit con artist."

"What makes you say that?" asked Linda.

"Well, for one thing, he lied about his age to come out here and marry his older stepsister Linda when he was only 14 years old," related Alex. "Linda and her sister Cathy were the daughters of an older woman named Kate Dixon that Jack, Sr. married later on, several years after his divorce from Ellie Mae was final."

"We knew her sister Cathy," volunteered Linda. "Cathy Dixon was the Dean of Girls at Oceanview Academy when I went to school there."

"Small world," remarked Alex.

"That's right," confirmed Jim. "I remember her well. And it was later when I knew Ray that he told me how Cathy's sister Linda – who was Ray's mother – died during childbirth."

"That's right," recalled Linda.

"Ray's mother, who was Linda Dixon, had an affair with a married man –Jon Roth, Sr. – and was already pregnant with Ray when Mark married her," elaborated Jim. "They were married only a short time when she died during childbirth. Mark was Ray's stepfather."

"I take it Ray never found out who his real father was?" questioned Alex as he ate another pretzel.

292

"Not until later in life," interjected Jim. "My stepdaughter Ann was doing the family genealogy and finally came across it. It was quite a surprise for all of us."

"But you never knew about Mark marrying Linda Dixon before that?" probed Alex.

"Well, actually, Ray did mention that once," admitted Jim. "Ray also told us how Mark literally raised him on his own, which is astounding when you consider what a good and decent person Ray turned out to be."

"Perhaps Mark really loved Linda Dixon and thought of Ray as his own," assumed Alex.

"He sure thought of me as his own, for all the good it did!" fumed Kevin.

"Whatever happened between you two, if you don't mind my asking?" questioned Alex.

"The man is nothing but a bigamist and a con artist!" exclaimed Linda, suddenly becoming upset by the memory of everything Mark had done to her and Kevin.

"We just want him found and brought to justice for the things he has done," mentioned Kevin, more calmly.

"Well, get in line behind a whole lot of people," suggested Alex. "Each time he came out here, he tried to get Ellie Mae to tell him where that treasure was, that she had allegedly come and stolen from the lighthouse one weekend, while he was out of town."

"Did she?" grilled Jim.

"Of course not!" exclaimed Alex. "But, he was convinced of it and kept coming back. Each time he was in town, our homes got burglarized, and someone rummaged through our things. We all knew it was him."

"What a horrible man!" fumed Linda.

"Whatever happened to Vivian?" Jim suddenly asked.

"Vivian LaMont was what she went by," clarified Alex, "and last we knew she went to go live in Seattle. None of us heard from her again after that. Ellie Mae once said that Vivian was hellbent on finding Mark and getting him to tell her where the treasure was, but never got the opportunity. At least not that we knew of."

Jim suddenly thought again of the gold disc that they had found in the faux book at the tower room of the lighthouse earlier that year. *Had Jack, Sr. had it all along and hid it there when he was still alive?*

293

Kevin gave Jim an inquisitive look. He was thinking the same thing, and remembered Jim showing them the photo of the gold disc.

Jim mouthed the word "later" so only Kevin and Linda could see and imperceptibly shook his head in the negative. They immediately understood and remained silent about it.

"Who knows if she ever found him," shrugged Alex as he got up to stir the stew again. "Hey, looks like it's ready."

"Perhaps we can try some before we head out to the cemetery," suggested Jim.

"That might be too dangerous at night, with 'gators and all," cautioned Alex. "It really would be best if we go in the morning."

"Fine with me," agreed Linda, who was too drunk to care anymore. "I would like to visit that outhouse, though."

"Perhaps you should go with her, Kevin," advised Alex. "Just in case she runs into any trouble."

Moonlight streamed in through the shaggy moss on a nearby cypress tree as Linda made her way across the swinging bridge toward the outhouse. Kevin was close behind, holding the flashlight.

"What was that?" Linda suddenly asked when a loud whooping sound beneath them startled her.

"Sounds like a frog," assured Kevin. *He sure hoped it was!*

The sound could suddenly be heard again, but this time it was louder, and somehow closer.

"That wasn't a frog," persisted Linda as she nervously continued across the bridge.

The sudden screech of an owl as it flew past her face caused Linda to scream, lose her balance, and topple from the bridge, into the murky swamp water below.

"Help!! Get me out of here!!" hollered Linda as she frantically splashed her way toward the island.

"Stop!" commanded Alex from behind them. "There's a 'gator on the shoreline. I can see him."

Without any thought for himself, Alex suddenly leaped into the water, made his way toward Linda, and grabbed her from behind. Alex then swam for the floating house and swiftly grabbed the small ladder hanging from its side. By the time he managed to climb on board with Linda, Kevin had already made his way back to the rear deck.

Linda collapsed onto the deck and sat there crying. Jim had come out back to see what the commotion was.

"Help me get her up," ordered Alex.

Linda was trembling and nearly paralyzed from fright as Jim and Alex helped her back inside. Her breathing was shallow and she could not recall ever being so frightened in her life.

"Guess you'll just have to use the pee-pot," laughed Alex.

"You do have extra clothes she can borrow?" questioned Kevin, who was quite worried about her.

"Of course," grinned Alex. "Welcome to the bayou, by the way. Very few have the courage to actually jump in like that."

"I didn't jump," clarified Linda through chattering teeth. "I lost my balance."

"Well, I'll let you borrow some of my clothes on one condition," teased Alex.

"What's that?" scowled Linda.

"That you take a bath first," laughed Alex. "You smell as bad as I do now!"

Everyone but Linda began laughing, until she finally saw the humor in it and joined them.

After bathing in the tub on the back deck while Kevin kept watch, Linda hurriedly dried off with the towel provided by Alex before putting on an old pair of jeans and a tight-fitting top. They had previously belonged to Alex's wife. The hiking boots she had borrowed from Sheree were drying by the wood stove inside.

"Not bad," approved Kevin as he watched Linda turn around.

Just then a whistle could be heard from behind them. "Looks as good on you as it did on her," approved Alex as he studied Linda more closely.

"Thanks again," mentioned Linda as she reached for the cord on the tub's drain stopper.

"Hold it!" instructed Alex. "That water's still gotta wash me and then all these clothes."

"Don't you have any other fresh water on board?" frowned Linda.

"Not until I go get some more tomorrow at the spring and haul it over here in the boat," explained Alex. "And I'm sure not using up the rest of our drinking water inside for just laundry or bathing!"

295

"You haul all your water in that boat?" questioned Linda.

"Actually, I put it in buckets first," flirted Alex, "and then I haul it in the boat."

"That sounds like way too much work," opined Kevin as he frowned with disapproval at Alex's continued interest in Linda.

"Only when there's company," grinned Alex before turning his attention back to Linda. "So, pretty lady, would you like me to wash your clothes first before I take a dip in the tub? It might be your best option."

Linda thought about it for a minute but quickly realized it was the more desirable choice. "Uh, sure. Yes, absolutely."

"Then I'll see ya'll back inside when I'm done out here," advised Alex as he began pulling off his shirt.

Linda stared with disbelief at how muscular and well-built Alex actually was as she and Kevin headed inside.

"Come on," directed Kevin as he grabbed her by the arm to hurry her along.

"You're welcome to stay," offered Alex as he began to unbuckle his belt.

"We're good," assured Kevin with a warning glance as he ushered Linda back inside.

"Why is he taking his clothes off before doing my wash?" whispered Linda.

"He probably plans to wash his stuff with yours," guessed Kevin.

"I see," frowned Linda. She was clearly displeased by the idea.

"At least you have these to wear now," reminded Kevin.

"And there's the pee-pot he was talking about," indicated Jim as he got up from the table to stretch and approached. "Right over there, behind that curtain in the corner."

Jim had been busy reading the diary and studying the various photos and documents.

"Excuse me then," said Linda as she headed for the curtain.

"Be sure you get the lid back on when you're done, nice and tight," came Alex's voice from outside.

Was he able to hear everything they said and did? wondered Linda as she used the pee-pot.

As soon as Kevin and Jim were seated at the table again, Jim leaned over to whisper. "There's a Vivian LaMont living in Seattle. According to MIRA, she was born in 1932. It's got to be her."

"That would make her 91 years old," calculated Kevin.

"Huh. Well, there are two things certain in this life," began Jim. "First is, that hell hath no fury like a woman wronged, regardless of the reason and even if it's a sister."

"And the other?" prompted Kevin with a raised eyebrow.

"That revenge is a dish best served cold," answered Jim.

The two of them considered that as they each took another sip of moonshine, and made sour faces from the taste afterwards.

"I think we need to go talk to her," continued Jim.

"Right now?"

"When we get back," clarified Jim with a crooked grin.

Both he and Kevin were definitely feeling the effects of the moonshine.

"Anyone up for some 'gator stew?" came Alex's booming voice when he entered the room. He was wearing a black tank top that allowed his muscular chest to show, and a tight-fitting pair of jeans. Except for the rotting teeth, he was actually very handsome.

"Where are *my* clothes?" asked Linda as she emerged from the curtained off area where the pee-pot was located. For a moment, she was caught off guard by Alex's appearance but tried not to show it.

"Got 'em hanging on the clothesline out back," winked Alex as he grabbed a potholder, removed the lid, and began stirring the stew.

"Thanks again," mentioned Linda as she glanced at the various pots and pans Alex had hanging from the ceiling of the kitchen. "Is there anything I can do to help?"

"*You* can go sit down," advised Kevin as he got up and came over to where Linda was. "I can help him."

"Just in case you're worried about it," Alex assured Kevin as he pulled four large bowls from the shelf above him, "going after another man's wife is not my style. I just like to be friendly, that's all."

Kevin imperceptibly nodded as he and Alex made eye contact.

"Just so we're clear," added Alex, more seriously.

"So, after we go visit the cemetery tomorrow," interjected Jim to change the subject, "what else is there to do here in Bayou La Batre?"

"Here in the swamp?" scoffed Linda.

"You'd be surprised," replied Alex as he filled one of the bowls before handing it to Kevin. "Bayou La Batre was featured in a movie called *Forrest Gump,* back in 1994."

"I remember that movie," commented Linda. "Wasn't that when Forrest got a job working on a shrimp boat and the guy who hired him talked about all the different ways to cook shrimp?"

"That's the one," laughed Alex as he filled up another bowl and set it on the counter. "Bayou La Batre is also known as the seafood capital of Alabama, and packages seafood from hundreds of fishing boats from all over the world."

"Isn't it also a major center for ship building?" asked Jim.

"You've been talking to MIRA again," razzed Alex as he filled the last of the bowls and brought it to the table.

"What kind of ships?" questioned Linda.

"Shall I tell her, or would you like to be the one?" grinned Alex as he glanced at Jim.

"It's your home town," deferred Jim with a polite nod.

"Okay then," beamed Alex. "It was in 2005 that one of the major shipyards here was commissioned by Walt Disney Studios to build a pirate ship. It was called *The Black Pearl.*"

"The one used in *Pirates of the Caribbean?*" grilled Kevin. He and Linda both were surprised.

"One and the same," assured Alex. "It was actually built on top of a modern steel utility boat, with the pirate prop built right over it. It was then sailed from here to the Caribbean for filming."

"Small world," nodded Kevin as he sampled the 'gator stew.

"This is amazing!" complimented Linda as she, too, took a sip after blowing on her spoon to cool it off.

"Wait 'til you try the meat," smiled Alex as he picked up his bowl with both hands and blew on its contents before slurping some down.

Jim went straight for the meat, stabbing a piece with his fork. "Nice and tender," remarked Jim as he blew on it before tasting.

The others paused to watch as he chewed the piece in his mouth. From the expression of satisfaction on his face, it was obvious that he enjoyed it.

Linda then stabbed a piece of meat and carefully took a bite, being careful not to burn herself. "It does taste like chicken."

298

"Glad you like it," responded Alex, pleased that she enjoyed it. "Whatever's left is what we'll have for breakfast."

The morning of April 26, 2023, began as it frequently did in the swamp with an eerie fog that would quickly burn itself off as the day progressed. Craggy knees of cypress trees nearby almost seemed to take on human form. The prolific insect life surrounding them would soon reach its zenith, as well. Alex Killingham and his band of unexpected house guests rode quietly in his flat bottom boat, gliding over the thick green swamp water toward the La Batre Pioneer Cemetery.

"Are you sure this is the right way?" questioned Linda as they made their way deeper into the swamp.

"It's not too much farther," assured Alex as he pushed off from the muddy swamp bottom with the long pole he was holding.

"Are you sure?" pressed Linda. There was no solid mass of land anywhere in sight. *What if they were lost?*

"It's on an island," revealed Alex as he and Jim continued to push the boat along.

"Are there alligators there?" worried Linda.

"Most likely," laughed Alex. "Probably snakes, wild hogs, and other things, too."

"I'm prepared if there are," promised Jim.

"Me, too," added Kevin.

"Me three," laughed Alex.

"You're *all* carrying?" Linda was surprised.

"Good thing I wasn't carryin' last night, though," reminded Alex. "Swamp water is murderous on guns."

"Why weren't you?" questioned Kevin.

"I always take off my side arm and stow it in the pantry when I get home," explained Alex.

"I think most guys do something like that," agreed Jim. "Especially if it's handy and they know right where it is."

MIRA's voice could then be heard. "La Batre Pioneer Cemetery is straight ahead, Jim."

"Well, hello MIRA," chuckled Alex. He had almost forgotten about Jim's Modulated Interfacing Resonance Assistant. "Is she always like that?"

"Thank you, MIRA," said Jim before responding to Alex. "I asked her earlier to let us know when we got here."

"I definitely gotta get me one of those," nodded Alex as he and Jim steered his boat up to an aging dock.

Alex then grabbed the mooring lines, hopped out onto the dock, and began securing his boat to its aging railings.

"What if it floats away with your boat still tied to it while we're here?" questioned Linda as she stared at the rickety dock and the dense undergrowth beyond it with concern.

"Let's hope not," answered Alex as he held the boat steady. "Welcome to the La Batre Pioneer Cemetery."

After climbing from the boat, the others followed Alex toward an overgrown trail. Linda was behind Alex, with Jim and Kevin taking up the rear. Both Jim and Kevin had their weapons drawn, just in case they should run into trouble. Alex's gun remained holstered, but he had pulled a rather large Bowie knife from the scabbard on his belt and was using it to whack away some of the brush as he went.

"How long since you've been here?" asked Linda from behind him as they trudged along.

"Not long enough," answered Alex as he unexpectedly whirled around and sliced at a coral snake above Linda's head, swiftly managing to cut it in half.

Linda then screamed with fright and jumped back immediately when she saw the portion with the head land within inches of her feet.

Kevin hurried over to stomp on its writhing head with his boot before kicking it aside. Then looking up at Alex, Kevin nodded and said, "Thanks!"

"You're welcome," acknowledged Alex as he resumed his trek toward the old cemetery.

"There's not any quicksand or anything like that on this island, is there?" Linda suddenly asked.

"Let's hope not," chuckled Alex.

"You don't *know*?" pressed Linda.

"I've never seen any," clarified Alex, "but who knows?"

"That's reassuring," muttered Kevin from behind them.

"How far is it to the cemetery?" questioned Linda.

"MIRA, how far from our current location to the entrance of La Batre Pioneer Cemetery?" queried Jim. He wanted to know, too.

"Five hundred meters," answered MIRA.

"This island is bigger than it looks," apprised Jim. "Thank you, MIRA."

A rustle in the bushes beside them caused everyone to glance in that direction.

"What was *that*?" demanded Linda.

Jim and Kevin each took the safety off on their weapons and Alex suddenly drew his. "Time to make lots of noise, folks."

"La, la, la, la, la," shouted Linda.

"Have you actually seen any animals on this island before?" asked Jim in a rather loud voice.

"Saw a bear once," replied Alex, "but that's not what this is."

"What do you think it is?" demanded Linda in a loud voice.

"Skunk!" hollered Alex as he began hurrying forward. "I wouldn't dally, folks."

It was then that Linda noticed the black and white striped skunk beside her and broke out into a run. "Wait for me!"

Jim and Kevin both laughed as they dashed after her.

"That was close!" exclaimed Linda as they reached the rusty wrought iron cemetery gates.

"Especially since I'm plumb out of tomato juice right now," agreed Alex as he put the safety back on his handgun and sheathed it.

Jim and Kevin finally did likewise.

After Alex chopped away a dried blackberry cane from the previous year that had attached itself to the entrance, he then kicked the gate open with his boot and motioned for the others to follow.

"This place is like something out of a creepy horror movie," opined Linda as she glanced around.

Aging headstones that had been left unattended for years were overgrown with weeds and moss.

"You can't even read the names on them," noticed Kevin.

"The tall one on the end is where Jed Killingham is buried beside his daughter Ellie Mae," indicated Alex as he walked over to it and whacked away the weeds before carefully scraping the moss covering its lettering with his knife.

"That's amazing," marveled Linda. "Who would have ever thought your great grandpa and even your grandmother would be buried here, of all places."

"Better get all the pictures you want," recommended Jim. "It's doubtful we'll be back."

301

"Amen to that!" agreed Linda as she glanced around. It felt as if they were being watched by something, and it was not a good feeling.

Both Linda and Jim proceeded to take several photos of the obelisk shaped headstone belonging to Jed and Ellie Mae.

"This next one is Gideon," pointed out Alex as he cut away the vegetation and scraped away the moss. "Hattie and Tom are over there."

"What about your wife and children?" asked Linda.

Alex became sullen and his eyes took on a faraway look. "Over on the end."

"Ann will be most interested in getting these photos," assured Jim as he proceeded to help clean off and photograph every headstone in the cemetery, along with several establishing shots of the area and the entrance gate.

"Who owns this place?" asked Kevin. "How come it's been allowed to deteriorate like this?"

"No one owns it," replied Alex. "And since I'm about the only family left, I guess it's my bad that the place has come to this."

"I think between this and the information we've gotten from you, this trip has been quite a success," acknowledged Jim.

"And we appreciate your hospitality, too," added Linda, just a little too enthusiastically for Kevin's liking, though he remained silent about it. *After all, he would probably never see his cousin again.*

"Does that mean you'll be heading back for home after this?" inquired Alex.

"I'm afraid so," smiled Jim, "but you're welcome to come visit the lighthouse, anytime. You might find it interesting."

"I might just do that," agreed Alex as he flirted again with Linda. "It's always nice to keep in touch with family."

That's what you think, reflected Kevin as he thought of Mark.

8. Chance Encounter

Mark Killingham had just finished cleaning up and closing his ice cream shop in Ocean Bluff for the night, but hadn't yet locked the front door. He still needed to get over to his other shop at the trailer park to close it up, as well. His stepson Ray was looking after it at the moment. Ice cream was especially popular with tourists – when there were any – and with most of the students over at Oceanview Academy.

He had not bothered to remind anyone that it was his birthday. It was Monday, March 23, 2009, and he had just turned 79. Most likely his stepson would remember, though. Ray usually managed to surprise him with a cake or something unexpected. Thankfully, Ray had never known about the many horrible things Mark had done during his life, especially the women whose lives he had left in ruins. Mark's greatest regret of all was the children he'd had with two of them, none of whom wanted anything more to do with him.

His second wife Maria had been mother to most of them – or was she his third? It was hard to keep track anymore. He had been married so many times, with only a divorce or two to show for the entire lot. *What were his children's names again? Oh yes, there was Michael, and then Justin, and Philip, and baby Evan. Wait a minute! There was Baby Eric, too. Eric had served several tours of duty in the military, and Mark had followed his career from afar over the years.* Mark hoped that all his boys were happy and had good lives now, wherever they were.

Mark's thoughts then turned to Bobby Sue Johnson, the mother of his son Kevin. *He'd almost managed to have a relationship with that one. If only he'd been more careful, perhaps Kevin would still be a part of his life. Unfortunately, times had been hard and Mark had done what he needed to in order to survive financially. Besides, Kevin had been young at the time and would recover. Was he still married to Linda? Perhaps he would look them up on FacePal and find out. Maybe there was still some way to patch things up.*

Just then, the bell on his shop's front door suddenly rang. Someone had come inside.

"I'm sorry, but we are closed for the day," apologized Mark as he headed for the front portion of his shop.

"I hear it's your birthday today," came an unfamiliar voice.

"What the heck?" Mark stared with disbelief. It was like looking into a reflection of himself in the mirror. "Jack, Jr.?"

"Happy birthday, brother," grinned the man as he approached. "Long time no see."

"Uh, that's an understatement," muttered Mark as he gaped at his long-lost twin with astonishment.

"What's it been, 77 years?" grinned Jack, Jr.

Mark then sat down on a stool at the counter. Hugging his estranged brother just didn't feel right, so he refrained. "That sounds about right."

"You probably wonder what I'm doing here," guessed Jack, Jr. as he glanced at a newspaper laying on the counter. The caption read, "Monday, March 23, 2009. Wreckage of Federal Express cargo plane lies on tarmac at Narita International Airport in Chiba, Japan. Two crew members killed when plane crashes and bursts into flames as it lands."

"Horrible things always seem to happen on our birthday, don't they?" chuckled Mark.

"Indeed," agreed Jack, Jr. as he sat down on the stool beside him. "That's why I'm here."

Mark narrowed his eyes at Jack, Jr. and studied him closely.

"I'll be honest with you," continued Jack, Jr. "I was hoping that we could arrive at a family truce of some sort. I know about the threats you made last time you came out to Alabama. Ma told me all about it."

"I'm listening," prompted Mark.

"There were also several break-ins coinciding with the time of your last visit to the Bayou," accused Jack, Jr. "Ma said you were looking for some sort of treasure, that you thought she had."

"Is that what she said?" sniggered Mark as he drummed his fingers on the countertop. "It wasn't until after her last visit to the lighthouse to see Dad that the treasure disappeared from where Dad always kept it!"

"What sort of treasure?" demanded Jack, Jr.

"You tell me," urged Mark, "You knew what it was."

"Why don't you enlighten me," suggested Jack, Jr.

"The treasure that Dad brought back from south America," reminded Mark. "Ring a bell?"

"No, it doesn't," answered Jack, Jr. "I've never even seen it."

304

"Well, Ma's seen it!" hollered Mark. "She obviously has it stashed someplace where nobody can find it."

"Let's just say for argument's sake that she did have it," conceded Jack, Jr. "Why in the world would she continue to live on a floating house in the swamp? Especially if she could afford to live anywhere she wanted?"

"Where's she residing now?" delved Mark.

"At the La Batre Pioneer Cemetery," revealed Jack, Jr.

Mark was silent for several moments as he considered the information. "How did she die?"

"On the Lady Elleanor, during Hurricane Fredric, back in 1979," answered Jack, Jr. "She and Zeke were together when they died."

"Now that's another thing," fumed Mark. "Why would Ma go and marry one of them colored fellas, anyway?"

"Zeke and Ellie Mae were very much in love," answered Jack, Jr. "What difference does the color of a person's skin matter, anyway?"

"Of course, we both know what happened to Bell after she left Uncle James for one of Tom's boys," reminded Mark. He'd heard the story over and over again from his dad.

"From what I heard, Uncle James didn't fare too well himself," commented Jack, Jr.

"True enough," acknowledged Mark. "Uncle James was killed during a cave-in when he and Dad found that treasure down in South America, and of course Ma knew about it. She obviously told you."

"James had a son, you know," mentioned Jack, Jr. He hoped to guide the conversation into a different direction. "Bell was already pregnant with him before she took off with Nate."

"I know. I met him during my last visit," informed Mark. "He claimed to know nothing about the treasure, either."

"Well, he didn't!" exclaimed Jack, Jr.

"He's probably off living it up in the Caribbean by now," assumed Mark.

"Actually, James, Jr. was killed during Hurricane Katrina. His body was found on September 22, 2005."

"Huh," muttered Mark. "Perhaps the treasure is buried somewhere in that precious swamp of yours?"

"Would I be here if it was?" laughed Jack, Jr.

305

"What about Nate's son Gideon?" grilled Mark.

"Died during Hurricane Katrina."

"So, just who's left back there, anyway?" demanded Mark.

"Just Alex," replied Jack, Jr.

"Alex?" scowled Mark. "Who in the world is that?"

"James, Jr.'s son Alex," clarified Jack, Jr.

"Okay, I remember him now. What about his family?" pressed Mark.

"His wife and family were all killed during Katrina."

"Sounds like I'd better look up the weather forecast before my next visit," snickered Mark.

"There's nothing left to go back to," assured Jack, Jr.

"If that treasure is still there, then Alex knows where it is and he's going to tell me," threatened Mark.

"Well, if he did have it, he wouldn't still be there!"

"I don't believe you! One of you took Dad's treasure, and I plan to get it back!" hollered Mark as he suddenly pounded his fist on the counter.

"Are you threatening me?" challenged Jack, Jr.

"You bet I am!" barked Mark. "You're the one who has the treasure, aren't you? That's how you were able to afford to come out here in the first place!"

"No, I don't have it," yelled Jack, Jr., "but I intend to get what's rightfully mine! I'm tired of living hand-to-mouth while you live out here in luxury in that lighthouse! It belongs to me just as much as it does to you, right along with this ice cream shop!"

"I don't think so," informed Mark as he suddenly grabbed his handgun from its holster and coldcocked his brother across the top of the head with it.

Surprised by the attack, Jack, Jr. had not been prepared to fend off the blow and fell to the floor unconscious.

Without hesitation, Mark grabbed a large plastic bag from behind the counter, knelt down, and pulled it over Jack, Jr.'s head. Mark held it tightly in place while Jack, Jr. regained consciousness and struggled, but finally asphyxiated from the lack of air and died.

Mark then hurried over to lock the front door of his shop and furtively glanced outside to make sure no one was there before pulling down the window shade on the top half of the door. The bottom half

306

of the door was made of solid metal and was opaque. *Thankfully, no one had happened along during the murder, but what now?*

Unseen by Mark, a woman unknown to him had seen the entire thing but had stealthily managed to hide herself beside the door outside in time to avoid being seen. Vivian LaMont hurriedly took off her shoes and tiptoed back to the vehicle she had parked nearby. It was her plan to duck down and wait until Mark left, as he no doubt would. *Something would definitely need to be done to avenge the death of her brother Jack, Jr.! At least Mark has no idea I exist,* Vivian reminded herself. *There was only one of two ways this could be played. Either she made her presence known and confront Mark right then – and risk ending up like Jack, Jr. – or she could bide her time and go from there. Definitely the latter,* decided Vivian with an evil smile.

Several of Mark's prior wives had finally managed to find him and had each filed a lawsuit against him for spousal support and other damages. The consolidated matter was scheduled to be heard in two weeks. Mark slowly smiled and nodded his head as he grabbed his dead brother by the armpits and dragged him to the back room. *Even if he didn't have the treasure just yet, this would give him a clean break from everything else that had happened. It would be a chance to start over. Ray would find the body in the morning and assume it was him, since Ray had no idea that Mark even had a twin brother. Then, Ray would inherit the lighthouse, the trailer park, the ice cream shops, and what little was left of his ill-gotten gain, and his ex-wives would not be able to do a blessed thing about it.*

"Sorry about that, Ray" muttered Mark as he began to undress Jack, Jr. "but that's the only way I can ensure your inheritance at this point." Then, to his dead brother, Mark sniggered, "I presume we wear the same size?"

Mark's evil laugh could be heard outside from where Vivian waited in the dark green 2005 Plymouth sedan.

Once Mark had managed to swap clothes with his dead brother, he carefully checked the crime scene to be sure no telltale traces remained that would arouse anyone's suspicions. Mark then leafed through Jack, Jr.'s wallet. Besides the driver's license and a couple of credit cards and photos, the only thing of value totaled less than a hundred dollars in cash. *What a shame to leave his own cash-filled wallet behind,* regretted Mark.

Mark was tempted to clean out the cash register and make it look like a robbery, but knew he'd better not. *That might lead to additional investigation into the matter. He would need to leave absolutely everything behind, and not look back.*

Vivian LaMont waited for what seemed an eternity for her estranged brother to exit the ice cream shop. She was not surprised to see that he had swapped clothes with Jack, Jr.

I will get you for this, Mark Killingham, if it's the last thing I ever do, thought Vivian as she watched Mark remove a set of keys from the pocket of the pants he was now wearing.

Realizing at once that he was looking for Jack, Jr.'s car, Vivian grabbed a blanket from the back seat under which to hide. Thankfully, Mark suddenly returned to the ice cream shop for one last look around, giving Vivian the opportunity she needed to vacate the vehicle and tiptoe into a nearby alley. She left the car door ajar to avoid making any noise from shutting it. *That was close!* thought Vivian as she hugged the wall of the alley where she remained in the shadows.

Vivian LaMont was two years younger than her brothers, Mark and Jack, Jr., though her existence had never been revealed to Mark. Fortunately for her, she had either not been home or had managed to hide on the occasions he had come to Alabama to try and find some treasure he claimed they had.

Who did have it, if Mark didn't? wondered Vivian to herself. *Could the treasure be hidden somewhere inside the lighthouse? Mark would obviously have to go elsewhere to hide for now, but would eventually return either to Alabama or to the lighthouse to look for it again. It was inevitable.*

It was Saturday, April 11, 2009. Mark Killingham had managed to establish himself as Jack, Jr. in Seattle. His tiny upstairs one-bedroom apartment overlooked the fish market where local farmers and other vendors brought in their wares to sell each Saturday at the farmers' market. The first Social Security check for Jack, Jr. had just arrived at his new address. He would still need to do more research to find out what other pension benefits were out there for his late brother, but there would be time for that. What he really needed was to find another wealthy widow, ripe for the pickin'.

308

Mark had a copy of his own obituary carefully clipped and placed inside his desk drawer. He was finally free from his past. Perhaps in time, he might return to the lighthouse to search again for the treasure. *What if it was still up in the library somewhere?* He had looked inside each of the books, even the faux one he knew about, but had not looked *behind* them. He would definitely need to do that at some point.

The migraine headaches he'd suffered from before had returned with a vengeance, but Mark did not place much confidence in the medical profession. Perhaps there was a phytotherapist in the area who specialized in the use of herbal medicines. There had been one in Ocean Bay that he had visited for a while the previous year, but would be recognized if he tried to show up now. *Imagine that, a dead guy showing up to see his doctor again*, smiled Mark to himself.

Mark then turned his attention to the laptop he had just purchased and finished setting up. *Perhaps he should send himself a friend request*, snickered Mark. *No, but he could certainly check out his old account, and just leave no trace he was there.*

The whistle on his tea kettle sounded. Mark paused to go pour himself a cup of ginger tea. Hopefully, it would help his headache. As he returned to his laptop and started to sit down, Mark noticed a new message notification. *Who would be sending a message to a dead guy?* grinned Mark as he set down his cup of tea on a coaster nearby.

After clicking on the message to see who it was from, Mark began to smile. *Marilyn Monroe? Seriously? Obviously, an alias name.* Mark impatiently waited as the message opened.

It read, "No, Marilyn Monroe is not my real name. All you need to know for now is this – I know who *you* are and I saw what you did at the ice cream shop that night. I'll be in touch."

Mark's nostrils flared with anger as he read the message again. *Was this someone's idea of a bad joke? Had someone really seen him at the ice cream shop that night? What would he do? He certainly couldn't answer it! Did he dare? If someone had seen him murder Jack, Jr., then it wouldn't matter now anyway.*

Mark blew on his tea and took a sip as he considered his options. Then, without hesitation, he clicked on reply and wrote, "Who is this?"

Mark took another sip of tea as he waited to see if anyone would answer, but nothing. He then glanced over the other messages and posts, being careful not to click on anything that would reveal his presence on the website. *The useless junk some people post,* thought Mark as he started to turn off his computer.

Just then, a new message notification popped up. It was from Marilyn Monroe! Mark froze for a moment before opening up the message. It said, "Someone you should be afraid of."

Furious, Mark replied, "Prove it! Tell me something only you and I would know."

Within less than a minute, the response came, "I saw you murder your twin brother. You are *not* Jack, Jr."

"What do you want?" wrote Mark.

"I haven't decided yet," came the response.

"Don't play games with me!" answered Mark.

Several minutes passed before the reply arrived. "Play games with you? I'm just getting started."

"You have no idea what I'm capable of," wrote Mark.

"The same could be said of me," answered the other party.

Mark got up and paced the room for a moment, pausing to glance out his window at the courtyard below. Crowds of people, tourists and locals were busy buying and selling things at the farmers' market.

Mark then sat back down and typed, "Tell me your demands."

After another long pause, the next message said, "I told you, I haven't decided yet. Perhaps that treasure you have stashed up in the lighthouse might be a good place to start."

Enraged, Mark picked up his cup of tea and hurled it across the room, causing it to shatter when it hit the wall. Ginger tea covered the wall, and broken china fragments littered the floor. "How dare you!" shouted Mark to no one in particular.

After regaining control of himself, Mark answered the message. "Alex Killingham, is that you?"

"No," came the quick answer. "We've never met."

"When and where can I meet you, then?" asked Mark.

"I'll let you know tomorrow," came the final response.

Mark waited for several more minutes, but there were no additional messages. "Son of a gun!" hollered Mark as he walked over to clean up the broken tea cup and ginger tea.

310

Vivian LaMont smiled to herself as she powered down her computer. *This was going to be more satisfying than she'd imagined.*

Just then, her long haired white Persian cat jumped up onto her lap for attention.

"I know, you're hungry," recognized Vivian as she petted the animal before setting it back down. She then got up and walked over to the kitchen where she pulled out a can of cat food and began to open it.

"Meow!" sounded the cat as it impatiently waited for its meal.

"Here you are, sweetheart," said Vivian in a soothing voice as she set the animal's bowl down on the floor nearby. "Bon appétit."

The cat rubbed against Vivian's legs and purred before returning its attention to the cat food.

Vivian had studied herbal remedies for years with Grandma Hattie when living in the Bayou, and had just opened up her own shop in Seattle. She also knew that Mark Killingham frequented such establishments, and that it was only a matter of time before he dropped in. Naturally, she would be there to help him out in any way that she could. Vivian smiled an evil smile to herself.

Vivian had opened her new shop under an alias name: Bell Sanderson. It was doubtful that Mark would make the connection, even if the name sounded familiar to him, especially since he had never personally known his Aunt Bell. Neither had she, for that matter, but Vivian had grown up hearing about Bell from her mother, and how Bell had left poor James to be with Nate. *What a tragic story,* thought Vivian as she shook her head.

Her dark red hair and hazel eyes were similar in coloring to those of her brothers. Vivian kept her hair dyed to match her original color, but then so did Mark. Jack, Jr. had done likewise. *Would Mark see the family resemblance?* She hoped not. The type of revenge she had in mind would take time, an experience to be savored, just like a fine wine.

Like her mother Ellie Mae, Vivian had clear alabaster skin and a vivacious smile. Men just could not resist her, so Vivian had learned to use that to her advantage over the years. Unfortunately for him, her first husband had cheated on her with some floozy he'd met at a church function, of all things. In the end, he'd paid for his indiscretion, more dearly than anyone would ever know. The actual process of poisoning him with small doses of arsenic had taken several months, but Vivian was a patient person and had nothing but time on her side.

After moving to Seattle to get a new start in the late 1950s, Vivian had taken her time before getting married again. Her second husband was a true gentleman at first, and things had looked promising. She had met him at a symposium on the latest in herbal remedies. But, over time, their relationship had waned. After learning that he was gambling away what little was left of the life insurance money from her first husband, Vivian knew what had to be done. It was clearly a situation that needed to be remedied as quickly as possible, and had taken far less time to execute than the demise of her first husband. It had been in 1969, when the Hong Kong flu was going around, so his other symptoms had gone unnoticed by the coroner. She had begun by giving him massive doses of vitamin C laced with zinc to cause nausea, diarrhea, and stomach cramps. Toward the end, she had substituted his vitamin tablets with sleeping pills, until finally giving him a sufficient quantity to put him out of her misery once and for all.

Her third and fourth husbands had not fared much better, though she had managed to take out and collect sizeable life insurance policies on each of them. It was when the attention of a Detective Phillips had been drawn to the matter that Vivian finally moved to another part of Seattle and changed her name to Patty Dupont. That was in 2004, only five years ago.

It was in 2007 that her brother Jack, Jr. had moved to Seattle from Alabama to stay with her while he looked for a job. They had secretly kept in touch and he was well aware of her need to keep a low profile because of insurance fraud, but had no idea of her part in the demise of her late husbands. As far as he knew, they were unfortunate but explainable circumstances.

Together, she and Jack, Jr. had planned a way to confront Mark Killingham and recover the treasure he had wrongly accused the family of having. Besides, they had just as much right to it as he did, if it were to be found! It hadn't taken long to discover the ice cream shop down in Ocean Bluff and the other one near the lighthouse, but they had waited until 2009 to finally go and pay Mark the long overdue visit. Vivian had wanted to follow his movements for a while and learn what she could about what was going on in his life before just inserting herself into it.

It was Saturday, April 11, 2009, just over two weeks since the useless murder of Jack, Jr. at the ice cream shop. *Vivian sadly shook her head. How dare Mark do that!*

Now that Mark had answered her FacePal message, it would only be a matter of time before she pinpointed his exact location. She was fairly certain that he was in Seattle but just didn't know where.

Vivian decided to go visit the farmers' market for a while. She occasionally bought wholesale herbs from a local vendor there and needed to replenish the stock in her new shop, anyway.

Frustrated that he had so foolishly wasted the last of his ginger tea by hurling it at the wall like that, Mark Killingham suddenly grabbed his wallet and hurried down to the farmers' market. Perhaps he would be able to buy more of it before the vendors closed up shop for the day.

There was a local vendor nearby who sold wholesale herbs and had excellent ginger tea.

Mark stopped to buy a small bag of apples at a fruit stand on his way. He squinted against the late afternoon sun as he approached the stand where the herb dealer was located. Just then, he noticed a stunningly beautiful woman close to his own age looking at herbs. Not many women his age were still that attractive. Her clothing and jewelry looked expensive and were a clear indicator to him that she might be well off.

"Well hello there," flirted Mark as he approached the woman. "Have we met before?" Something about the woman seemed familiar, but he could not put his finger on it.

"Hello yourself," responded the stranger with an enticing smile. "I'm sure I would remember it if we had."

"I'm Jack Killingham," lied Mark as he grabbed her hand and bent down to kiss it.

"I'm Bell Sanderson," lied Vivian as she allowed him to believe he was luring her in.

"I know we've never met," continued Mark, "but I've never seen anyone like you in my life. It's as if we were led here for this very moment, to meet one another for the first time."

Vivian fought back a crooked grin. *The hook was set. All she needed to do now was reel him in. She couldn't have planned*

313

anything as perfect as this if she'd tried! What an amazing chance encounter.

"Are you sure we haven't met?" asked Mark as he studied her more closely. Her beauty was overwhelming.

"I have a small shop nearby," revealed Vivian as Mark continued to hold her hand. "Herbal remedies, that sort of thing."

"Really?" marveled Mark as he finally let go of her hand. "That's amazing. I just came down here hoping to find some ginger tea for my headache."

"I might have something even better than that at my shop," Vivian informed him as she continued to flirt with Mark.

"Excuse my manners," apologized Mark. "Have you had dinner yet? Perhaps we could dine together?"

"Well, I normally don't go out with perfect strangers," chuckled Vivian, trying to appear as if she were about to decline.

"What about over there, across the street?" indicated Mark. "At that little sidewalk café?"

Vivian paused for effect before finally accepting. "Well, I do need to eat. Okay, sure, why not?"

"After you," motioned Mark with his most charming smile.

"What about your headache?" reminded Vivian.

"Perhaps we can visit your shop after we eat?" suggested Mark.

"We'll see," replied Vivian as she put her arm through Mark's and began to walk with him toward the sidewalk café.

"Have you lived in Seattle long?" grilled Mark as they made their way across the pedestrian-filled street. The entire block was closed to auto traffic during the Saturday market.

"For a while now." Vivian was in no hurry to give him any definitive information. "How about you?"

"I just moved out here," answered Mark as they arrived at the café where he gallantly pulled out a chair for her to sit on.

"Thanks, Jack," smiled Vivian as she sat down and allowed Mark to help scoot her chair forward for her.

Mark then hurried around to sit across from her and motioned for a waiter to come help them.

"So, Jack, where are you from?" poked Vivian as the waiter arrived with two glasses of water and handed each of them a menu.

314

"Hi, I'm Mike and I'll be your waiter," interrupted the man as he set down the waters. "Would you like to hear our specials?"

"We're good," advised Mark.

"I'd like to hear them," differed Vivian.

"Of course," beamed Mike. "Our most popular selection for today is grilled salmon with a hint of rosemary on a bed of jasmine rice, served with freshly grilled asparagus."

"That sounds amazing," commented Vivian. "What else?"

"Our other special for today is an 8-ounce Porterhouse steak grilled to order with baby red potatoes sautéed in butter, and a side of salad with your choice of dressing."

"What kind of dressing do you have?" pressed Vivian. It was obvious that Mark had no patience for taking the time to listen to the specials, so she was enjoying the opportunity to make him do so.

"We have blue cheese, raspberry vinaigrette, creamy garlic with sage, or a special house blend of ranch," elaborated Mike.

"The Porterhouse sounds good," remarked Mark.

"Are you ready to order, then?" asked Mike.

"Well, I think I'd like to look over the menu first," decided Vivian. "Can you give us a few minutes?"

"Absolutely," agreed Mike. "Can I start you off with anything else to drink while you're deciding?"

"Do you have any ginger tea?" Mark suddenly asked.

"Sorry, we don't," apologized Mike. "But, we have a whole selection of herbal teas. I can bring you an assortment to choose from."

"Sure," shrugged Mark. He was becoming more agitated by the moment but trying not to show it to his new lady friend.

"I'll be right back," remarked the waiter as he hurried off.

"So, Bell, where were we?" flirted Mark.

"You were about to tell me where you're from, Jack," reminded Vivian with an innocent smile.

"Oh, yes," laughed Mark. "I'm from Bayou La Batre."

"Really?" Vivian tried to seem ignorant. "Where's that?"

"In Alabama," replied Mark, obviously relieved that she was unfamiliar with the place.

"Huh," nodded Vivian. *That's right, you scoundrel!* thought Vivian to herself. *That is where you're from.* She was actually surprised by his candor.

315

"Here you are, sir," interrupted Mike as he showed up with a basket of herbal teas and set them on the table. "May I bring you a pot of hot water and a tea cup?"

Mark merely nodded.

"Make that two," added Vivian. "I see you have Egyptian licorice. That's one of my favorites."

"Is it good for headaches?" questioned Mark as the waiter hurried off.

"Actually," stipulated Vivian, "if taken for longer or in greater doses than recommended, it can actually cause headaches, fatigue, high blood pressure, water retention or even heart attacks."

"Then why on earth would you take it?" frowned Mark as the waiter returned with a pot of hot water and two empty teacups.

"Are you ready to order yet, or do you need more time?"

"I think I'll have the grilled salmon special," advised Vivian.

"I'll take the Porterhouse, with blue cheese on the salad," added Mark. "On second thought, make that raspberry vinaigrette."

"Very good. Can I interest you in anything for dessert after that?" questioned Mike as he started to hand them another menu.

"This'll do it," informed Mark with finality.

"Thank you, sir," nodded Mike as he hurried away with their order.

"Licorice root can act as a soothing agent or even as an expectorant," resumed Vivian. "So, it can be useful for reducing phlegm and other upper-respiratory symptoms, such as sore throat and coughing. Licorice root is even used to treat ulcer symptoms, canker sores and digestive problems, such as acid reflux and indigestion. And, as a weight loss aid, licorice tea may help reduce body fat."

"Just how do you know all this?" grilled Mark.

"I'm a phytotherapist," revealed Vivian with a slight smile.

"You don't say?" Mark was suddenly quite interested.

"Licensed," added Vivian rather pointedly.

"So, Bell," continued Mark, "if licorice tea can do everything you say it can, then why would it cause headaches and such?"

"Because higher doses of licorice tend to pose the most glycyrrhizin-related risks," explained Vivian.

"Gly what?" scowled Mark.

316

"Glycyrrhizin," repeated Vivian. "It is the sweet-tasting component. But, when over-used, even in lesser quantities, licorice can sometimes cause arm and leg numbness and muscle pain."

"Then why on earth would you use it?" persisted Mark.

"Only occasionally, and for its soothing properties," revealed Vivian. "Besides, I like the taste of licorice."

"What would you recommend for a headache, then?" asked Mark as he began rifling through the selection of herbal teas in the basket on their table.

"Green tea would be a good choice," advised Vivian as she reached for the Egyptian licorice, tore open the bag's wrapper, and put the tea bag into her cup.

"Allow me," insisted Mark as he poured some water into it for her. "Green tea it is," added Mark as he tore open the wrapper on some green tea, put it into his cup, and poured in the hot water.

"Some fresh bread?" offered Mike as he showed up again with a wooden paddle on which some fresh baked bread and a small dish of freshly whipped butter sat.

"Please," nodded Mark as he indicated for Mike to set it down.

"Your order should be ready soon," assured Mike as he left.

"Good waiter," approved Vivian as she blew on her tea and took a small sip. "Delicious tea, too."

"You'll never believe this," mentioned Mark, "but I've actually been looking for a good phytotherapist to go to."

"And here I am," flirted Vivian.

"Yes," grinned Mark. "Here you are."

"Perhaps it was destiny that brought us together, then," said Vivian as she reached for a piece of bread.

"Bell, tell me something," requested Mark. "Are you married or attached to someone at this time?"

"No, Jack, I'm not," answered Vivian. *This was going to be even easier than she had anticipated.*

"If I'm not being too forward," continued Mark, "perhaps we could see each other personally, as well?"

"You mean, besides being your new phytotherapist?" Vivian grinned a crooked smile.

"Yes, exactly," flirted Mark as he took her hands in his. "You are the most beautiful woman I've ever seen in my life."

"I'll bet you say that to all the girls," replied Vivian.

317

"No, not really," assured Mark as he continued to hold her hands and studied the expensive looking diamond rings she wore. Her long red fingernails were perfectly manicured.

"Perhaps tomorrow you can stop by my shop," suggested Vivian as she unexpectedly pulled her hands away, and pulled a business card from the purse on her lap.

"What about tonight?" pressed Mark.

"What's the rush?"

"I do need to get some more ginger tea," reminded Mark.

"Let's see how the green tea works first, shall we?"

"Sure, we can do that," relented Mark as he took the card from her and studied it. "That's in the next block."

"It is," confirmed Vivian.

"Then we're neighbors," informed Mark. "My apartment is right over there, above the fish market."

"Does your apartment smell like fish, then?" teased Vivian.

"Sometimes," admitted Mark, "but it's not that bad."

"It sounds like my place might be the better option," suggested Vivian. *It was important to get his hopes up, especially now.*

"Is that an invitation?" flirted Mark as he undressed her with his eyes, actually causing her to blush.

"Only a possibility at this point," replied Vivian. "Like I said, what's the rush?"

"Neither of us is a spring chicken," reminded Mark.

"Speak for yourself," snickered Vivian as Mike arrived with their dinner and put the plates down in front of them.

"Fresh pepper?" asked Mike as he stood ready with a pepper grinder.

"Yes, please," smiled Vivian. "I always love lots and lots of pepper."

"Salt?" added Mike.

"Just the pepper," replied Vivian.

"Sir?" questioned Mike as he turned to Mark.

"None for me," answered Mark.

"Very good," grinned Mike. "Just let me know if you need anything else."

"We will," promised Mark.

Despite Mark's best efforts to convince her otherwise, the woman he knew as Bell had managed to evade an after-dinner tryst with him after getting him to admit that his headache was better.

Discouraged as he climbed the steps to his apartment alone, Mark reminded himself that he would be dropping by Bell's shop to see her the following day. He looked again at her business card. The shop opened at 9:00 a.m. *He would be there.*

Mark noticed at once upon entering his apartment that he had failed to sweep up the remaining fragments of broken china. *Good thing I didn't bring her here,* realized Mark as he began straightening up.

After vacuuming and dusting the living room furniture, Mark nodded with satisfaction. *He did want to make a good impression upon Bell when he brought her to his apartment for the first time.*

His thoughts suddenly turned to the mysterious person who had sent him the message as Marilyn Monroe. *Was there another message yet?* Mark hurriedly turned on his laptop computer and waited for it to boot up. *He would check it before retiring for the night.*

Mark drummed his fingers on the small computer desk as he waited. *Why was this taking so long?* Mark stripped off his outer clothes and took off his socks, leaving them on the floor beside him. *He would pick them up in the morning.*

Mark then opened up his old FacePal account and checked to see if there were any new messages. *That figures,* frowned Mark as he started to close the program.

Just then, a new message popped up on his screen. *It was from Marilyn Monroe!*

"There you are," muttered Mark with pursed lips as he clicked on the message to open it.

"Plans have changed," read the message. "We will need to wait until next week."

"Why?" questioned Mark out loud as he glared at the message. He then responded to the message, "Why until then?"

Almost immediately, the answer came. "Because I'm in Alabama at the moment and need to make travel arrangements."

Mark grinned an evil smile and nodded his head. *So, it was someone from Bayou La Batre that was sending him these messages.*

"How do you know where I am?" wrote Mark. "Perhaps I'm in Alabama, too."

"You're in Seattle," came the response. "That's what the GPS indicator on your messages shows."

GPS indicator? scowled Mark as he studied the computer more closely. *Where would he look to find something like that? Was there such a thing?*

Mark then right clicked on the message. A dropdown menu appeared. He certainly didn't want to "save" it or "select" it. "View Page Source," read Mark. *Perhaps that would show something.*

Mark then clicked on it and an entire screen of computer code appeared. *Gibberish!* Mark scowled as he studied it. *What in the world did "crossorigin = anonymous" mean? And what did all the rest of it mean?*

Mark sighed with frustration as he clicked on each of the other options in the dropdown menu, with equally unhelpful results.

"Whoever you are, you're good," admitted Mark aloud. He then typed, "Are you so sure that's where I really am? Perhaps your GPS indicator is connected to a faulty subspace relay station that has malfunctioned." *It sounded good, anyway.*

"You don't even know what a GPS indicator is, do you?" came the snide response. "Good night, Mark. I'll be in touch."

"Ooooh!" hollered Mark as he refrained himself from grabbing his laptop and smashing it against the wall.

Two weeks had gone by since meeting Bell Sanderson, and the ginger tea she gave him each day at her shop was amazing.

It had been years since Mark had allowed himself to care for anyone else, and that was going to make the inevitable all that more difficult. *I'm in it for the money,* Mark reminded himself. *What possible future could there be with Bell, anyway? She was 77 years old already, and he was 79.*

His date with Bell for mid-morning tea at the sidewalk café was not until 10:00, so Mark decided to check his computer to see if there were any more messages from Marilyn Monroe. *He had heard nothing since last week, and it was only 8:30.*

Thankfully, Bell had pointed out to him that he was consuming well over the recommended daily dosage of supplemental nutrients on top of everything else he was doing already. As it was, he ate fortified cereal for breakfast, grabbed an energy bar between meals, and frequently had enriched processed food for dinner.

320

The truth be told, he did feel much better now that he was no longer overloading on vitamins and minerals, some of which could become toxic in his system. Bell had even pointed out to him that one of his daily vitamins contained a high level of selenium and could lead to hair loss, gastrointestinal upset, fatigue, and mild nerve damage.

Mark was already fighting the expanding forehead scenario that comes in time with age-related hair loss in some men, and was in no rush to hurry that process along.

His laptop had finished updating itself and was ready for him to use. Mark checked to see, but there was nothing from Marilyn Monroe. *Was she traveling by car? Is that what was taking so long?*

On another whim, Mark decided to look up Bell Sanderson. Several names popped up from his search, but none that was a phytotherapist or that lived in the Seattle area. "Hum," muttered Mark as he began looking at the other listings. All at once, his attention was drawn to the census records for a Bell Sanderson, wife of James Killingham, who had lived in Bayou La Batre. It had Mark's undivided attention. *That's where he'd heard the name before! Bell Sanderson was the one who had abandoned his uncle to run off with that colored boy. What was his name again? Nate! That was it.*

Mark had heard the stories of how Bell and her illicit lover had perished before their time. *If he remembered correctly, she had died during childbirth and Nate had died that same day after being bitten by something. A snake? A spider? Something like that. Served them right!* fumed Mark as he did another search. He decided to look up the address of Bell's shop and see who the owner actually was.

"Patty Dupont," read Mark as he rubbed the stubble on his chin. *He would need to shave before heading for his date at the sidewalk café.*

After an unsuccessful search for the name Patty Dupont, Mark powered down his laptop and went to go shave. *He would definitely ask Bell – if that's who she was – if she knew anything about a Patty Dupont. Just who was she, anyway?*

"There you are," smiled the woman who called herself Bell. "I was beginning to think you stood me up."

"I wouldn't dream of standing up a beautiful woman such as yourself," flirted Mark as he grabbed her hand to kiss it before sitting down across from her at the tiny table.

"The usual?" grinned Mike as he arrived at their table to wait on them with the basket of herbal teas already in hand.

"Yes, thank you," approved Mark with a friendly nod.

"I'll be right back with your water," advised Mike as he hurried off to get some.

"Here," said Vivian as she covertly slid a ginger root tea bag to Mark under the table.

"Thanks," chuckled Mark as he took it from her and waited for the hot water to arrive.

"Better tear open one of theirs, so he doesn't get suspicious," snickered Vivian with a crooked grin.

"I got it covered," assured Mark as he reached for an Earl Grey from the basket. "They actually aren't bad together, anyway."

"Here you are," smiled Mike as he arrived with a teapot of hot water and two cups. "May I interest you in anything else?"

"Nothing you'd have on the menu," informed Mark as he began undressing Vivian with his eyes.

Mike understood at once and flushed with embarrassment as he hastily retreated from the table. *Clearly, the older couple wanted to be left alone. Why didn't they just get a room somewhere?*

"Okay, then," laughed Vivian as she flirted back.

"Hey, thanks for the ginger root tea," acknowledged Mark as he placed it into the cup with the Earl Grey he had selected. Before pouring his own water, Mark carefully poured some hot water for his lady friend.

"Thank you," smiled Vivian as she grabbed the string on her tea bag and began swishing it around in the water.

"What kind is that?" probed Mark.

"Apple cinnamon," pointed out Vivian.

"Okay, yeah," realized Mark. "That does smell good."

"I trust your headaches are still at bay?" questioned Vivian.

"Oh, absolutely," promised Mark. He was well aware of the fact that the woman who claimed to be Bell Sanderson would need to open her shop when they were done having tea. "I hope our morning tea hasn't cut into your business too much."

"No one usually shows up until the noon hour anyway," admitted Vivian. "We're good."

"Who is Patty Dupont?" grilled Mark, his face taking on a serious expression.

Though caught off guard, Vivian hid it well. She studied her estranged brother for a moment before responding. She then leaned in close and spoke in almost a whisper. "You got me. My name's not really Bell Sanderson."

"Really?" Mark's penetrating gaze began to make her feel uncomfortable, especially when he began drumming his fingers on the tabletop beside his cup of tea.

"Just something I made up," answered Vivian as she looked him in the eyes with as much sincerity as she could muster.

"There was nothing on Patty Dupont, either," revealed Mark with a wry grin. "Care to tell me who you really are?"

"We should go back to the shop for this conversation," decided Vivian as she suddenly stood up.

"Very well," agreed Mark as he got up, too, and laid a $5-dollar bill on the table. He then extended his arm for her to slide her arm through as they left their tea behind.

"I'm wanted by the authorities," whispered Vivian to Mark as they walked toward her shop.

"What for?" pressed Mark.

"For insurance fraud," confessed Vivian as she gave Mark a sheepish look. "My real name's Marsha Waynecroft."

"Marsha," repeated Mark as he nodded his head.

"Please don't turn me in," pleaded Vivian as she did her best to look pathetic. "I can explain."

"I wouldn't dream of turning you in without hearing your explanation first," assured Mark.

"No," persisted Vivian. "You must promise, or I can't tell you."

"Very well," Mark finally agreed as they arrived at her shop. The hand-carved wooden shingle above the door merely said, "Herbal Remedies."

Vivian left the "closed" sign showing as they went inside, and relocked the door behind her to make certain they were not disturbed.

Shelf upon shelf of glass jars carefully labeled with handmade labels lined one wall, around 300 of them. Bulk herbs, blends, supplements, essential oils, homeopathics, tinctures, and even empty capsules were among the inventory. Healthy snacks and beauty products lined yet another wall. Near the small counter where the cash register sat was a circular rack filled with greeting cards made from

323

recycled products, most of them nature scenes and tasteful artwork. Beside the cards was a display of prepackaged herbal teas, for those not adventurous enough to create their own tea from the bulk supply of herbs on the opposite wall. Out of necessity, to protect her inventory, her long haired white Persian cat was now in a new home.

"You've got quite a place here, Marsha," complimented Mark as he stood there with his arms folded.

"Thanks," replied Vivian.

"Insurance fraud, huh?" Mark began to snicker as he looked around at her little shop. "Is that how you were able to afford all of this?"

"Something like that," admitted Vivian with a shrug of her shoulders.

"And Bell Sanderson is just 'something you made up'?" doubted Mark as his face suddenly took on an ominous expression.

"Yes, it is!" Vivian became defensive.

"You'd better tell me who you really are," threated Mark as he suddenly grabbed Vivian by the arm and held it securely while he waited for her explanation. "And something tells me it's not Marsha, either."

"I've told you the truth!" shouted Vivian as she struggled to free herself from his grasp. "Let go of me! Just who do you think you are?"

"Who do *you* think I am?" grilled Mark as he waited for her to respond. "You'd better tell me."

Vivian glared at Mark for only a moment with undisguised hatred before regaining control of the expression on her face.

"So, you *know who I am and you saw what I did*, did you?" pressed Mark as he continued to study her.

"What?" Vivian put on a convincing performance. "Jack, you're scaring me. What are you trying to say?"

"Tell me it wasn't you who emailed me and told me that on my FacePal account two weeks ago," demanded Mark.

"Why would I do something like that?" asked Vivian. "And, while we're on the subject, just what did you do?"

"It's not important," replied Mark as he suddenly let go of her. "Hey, I'm sorry. It's just that I thought you might be someone else."

324

Vivian rubbed her arm in an exaggerated fashion where Mark had been holding it. "Does this mean the authorities are after you, too?"

"I don't know," admitted Mark as he shook his head.

"Perhaps we should team up," suggested Vivian as she tried again to flirt with him, but guardedly.

"Hey, I'm really sorry, sweetheart," apologized Mark as he put his arms around Vivian and pulled her close. "Forgive me?"

Vivian deliberately took her time before finally nodding her head. *Mark was smarter than she had anticipated, so she would have to be very careful from here on out.*

"Is that a yes?" asked Mark as he gently put one hand under her chin and forced her to look up at him.

"Yes, I forgive you," answered Vivian as she visibly relaxed.

Without further comment, Mark unexpectedly kissed her on the mouth. The electricity between them was undeniable.

Well aware of the need to play the part, Vivian kissed him back with unbridled passion. *Is this how our parents felt when they were together?* she wondered. *After all, they were siblings, too.*

"Let's go upstairs," pressed Mark as he grabbed her hand and began leading Vivian toward the narrow staircase at the back of the store. "Is that where you live? Up there?"

"I kind of would like an opportunity to straighten up first before letting you see my flat," stalled Vivian. "I wasn't exactly expecting company today."

"How 'bout I help you?" flirted Mark as he pulled her close and began kissing her again.

Vivian then remembered her open laptop sitting on the desk upstairs, and of the logon and password for "Marilyn Monroe" taped to the wall beside it. *Mark could not be allowed to see it!*

"Why don't we go to your place instead?" suggested Vivian.

"We can do that," agreed Mark without argument. He clearly had one thing on his mind at the moment and wasn't hard to persuade.

"Let me just go get something," responded Vivian. "I'll be right back, I promise."

"Take your time," grinned Mark as he glanced about the shop. "I'll just have a look around while I'm waiting."

Vivian hurriedly climbed the stairs to her flat, raced over to her computer desk, and snatched the large post-it note from the wall beside

325

it. *It could no longer be kept hanging in plain view. Where should she hide it?*

"Hey," greeted Mark as he entered her flat, without being invited. "I just had to see where you live."

Vivian quickly stuffed the incriminating post-it note into the pocket of her skirt. *She could find a better place for it later. It just could not be left in plain view!*

"Looks pretty tidy to me," opined Mark as he approached.

"I guess it's not so bad," shrugged Vivian. "I was thinking I hadn't put away my undies yet."

"Just what were you looking for then?" questioned Mark as he began to study the room.

"Oh, here they are," indicated Vivian. "My reading glasses. I was going to make up some special tea for your headache. Something better than ginger root."

"What did you have in mind?" quizzed Mark.

"Either Feverfew or Skullcap," replied Vivian as she quickly put on her glasses and headed for the staircase leading back downstairs.

"What's your rush?" flirted Mark as he grabbed her hand and pulled her back. "The tea can wait."

"Skullcap is not only used for stress headaches, but it has a relaxing effect, as well," explained Vivian.

"Sounds like you could use some," suggested Mark.

"You know, that's not a bad idea," agreed Vivian. "Not only will it help both of us feel more relaxed, but it also has antioxidant and anti-inflammatory properties and is great for migraines. It almost acts as a mild sedative."

"By all means, then," agreed Mark as he motioned toward the staircase. "After you."

"Just two grams of the leaf in tea, three times a day, can work wonders," promised Vivian as she hurried down the narrow staircase to her shop below. "It can also be taken in capsule form."

"Do you have any of those handy?" asked Mark as he followed.

"Not made up, but I do have a supply of empty capsules," replied Vivian. "Your choice."

"Is it addictive?" grilled Mark.

"Not really," assured Vivian, "though anything with a sedative effect can be over-used by consumers."

"I'll have some if you do," grinned Mark.

Vivian walked over to a large glass jar on the bulk wall, removed the lid, and used a pair of prongs to put a small amount into a tiny plastic bag. "This should do it."

"Why don't we take it back to my place?" offered Mark.

"Jack, that's exactly what I had in mind," promised Vivian. *If only she could get him to become dependent upon the Skullcap tea, then she could begin lacing it with something else over time.*

"So, Marsha," began Mark as he followed Vivian from her shop, "is that really your real name?"

"Actually, no," confessed Vivian as she locked the door to her shop behind them. "My real name is Melody McCauley."

"You're sure about that?" snickered Mark as he extended his arm to her.

"It's a gentleman's duty to believe what a lady tells him," smirked Vivian as she put her arm through his.

"You are convincing," laughed Mark as they walked toward his apartment. "But don't worry, I'll learn your secrets."

"You seem mighty sure of yourself," challenged Vivian.

"Your name wouldn't happen to be Marilyn Monroe, would it?" pried Mark with a mischievous grin.

"And I suppose you're Elvis?" laughed Vivian.

"Just checking," replied Mark as they made their way down the sidewalk, past various shops.

It was nearly supper time on Saturday, April 25, 2009, and the Saturday market below was filled with people.

Vivian lay beside Mark in his bed, unable to believe that she had actually allowed herself to be with him. Surprisingly, he had been a most satisfying lover, and she had no complaints in that department.

"So, Melody," teased Mark as he brushed a stray hair from her face. "Is that your real name?"

"For now." Vivian rewarded him with a crooked grin. "I really should get down there and open shop, especially with Saturday market going on."

"Care to join me later for some more Skullcap tea?" tempted Mark as he watched her get up and dress.

327

"I wouldn't miss it for all the tea in China," flirted Vivian as she quickly grabbed her purse and left. "Until then."

"I'll be counting the moments," flirted Mark from where he lay.

Unseen by Vivian, the post-it note in her pocket with the logon and password for "Marilyn Monroe" had fallen out and onto the floor. Fortunately for her, a gust of wind created by opening the door to Mark's apartment had sent it flying under his bed.

Vivian decided on a whim to leave her shop closed for a while. It was time for Marilyn Monroe to send Mark Killingham another message. Vivian smiled to herself as she reached into her pocket for the post-it note she had put there earlier. *It was gone! Had it fallen out while she was at Mark's apartment?*

After thoroughly searching every square inch of her shop and the flat upstairs, it was obvious that the post-it note must have fallen out when she was with Mark. Vivian rushed over to the window and glanced outside. Nothing resembling a post-it note of any kind could be seen laying on the pavement outside, or anywhere else.

This was not the first time she had been forced to relocate her shop unexpectedly. She would have about five hours in which to move her inventory before Mark would come looking for her. Vivian always kept preassembled cardboard crates ready to go, for just such an emergency, but usually had an entire night within which to accomplish the task.

There was no choice now. She would need to take what she could and leave the rest. She would start with the 300 glass jars of bulk herbs, blends, supplements, essential oils, homeopathics, tinctures, and other things. *Where would she take them all? To the UPS station on the next block! They would hold everything for 24 hours until she came up with a delivery address, and they were open until 5:00. They had done it for her before.*

"You can do this," Vivian assured herself as she glanced in the mirror before grabbing the keys to her van and putting them in her pocket. *Hopefully, she wouldn't lose them, too!*

Vivian speedily began grabbing the most valuable or difficult to obtain items first, carefully but quickly sliding them into the cardboard boxes. Slotted dividers to keep the glass jars from bumping against one another were already in place inside of each crate.

Once her van was full, Vivian quickly drove to the UPS station and explained to the worker on duty that she would be bringing more boxes and needed for them all to be held until the following day.

"Sure, for a deposit," agreed the worker.

"How much?" grilled Vivian. *There had been no deposit the previous time, but she didn't have time to quibble.*

"A hundred bucks ought to do it," agreed the worker with a raised eyebrow.

Vivian hurriedly opened up her purse, took out her wallet, and removed a hundred-dollar bill.

"You did say until tomorrow, right?" questioned the worker as he took the money from her and began filling out a form.

"Can't we just finish filling that out when I return?" asked Vivian. "I do have a few more loads."

"You in some kind of a hurry, lady?" asked the worker.

"Yes, I am," admitted Vivian. "I need to clean out my entire inventory before a very bad man shows up to try and destroy my shop and who knows what else."

"Has someone threatened you, ma'am? Perhaps we should just call the police."

"That won't be necessary," Vivian assured him as she pulled out another hundred-dollar bill and handed it to the worker.

"How many more boxes are we talking about?" questioned the worker as he took the money from her.

"Just a few more loads, I promise," answered Vivian with a pleading look.

"Very well, but only what will easily fit on the loading dock," indicated the worker. "There still needs to be room for customers who come in to walk around them."

"There will be," pledged Vivian as she hurried to her van and drove back to the alley behind her store.

It took her almost two hours and five more trips, just to get the glass jars safely to the loading dock at the UPS station. *This was taking way too long!*

Vivian then packed up the healthy snacks, beauty products, prepackaged herbal teas and greeting cards. She would take the cash register in her final load, as that was not something she felt comfortable leaving at the UPS station. She then threw as many of her

329

clothes into the last crate as would fit before hurrying to the UPS station with her final delivery.

"I'll be back by noon tomorrow with an address for you to send everything to," promised Vivian as she signed the worker's form.

"It'll be here," agreed the worker.

"You're the best," replied Vivian as she kissed the man on the cheek before hurrying away.

"No problem," smiled the worker as he watched her dash off.

After returning to her shop for one final look around, Vivian grabbed the handcart she kept on hand with which to move her cash register and safe. *Thank goodness for the automatic lift on the back of her van!*

It was 4:30 already, and she needed to hurry. Vivian glanced outside in time to see Mark Killingham headed towards her shop. She ran upstairs as fast as she could to grab her suitcase and literally tossed her most treasured possessions inside. Her photo album, her laptop, her jewelry box, two changes of clothes, and her makeup bag.

A knock could be heard on the door downstairs. Vivian took a deep breath as she tiptoed down the stairs with her suitcase, carefully placed it on the handcart with her cash register and safe, and then headed for the back door. *If Mark were to see her now, especially with the shop emptied out, there was no telling what he might do.*

Mark scowled as he shaded his eyes with one hand and tried to peer inside the shop. *How odd that the blinds were drawn.*

"Melody?" called Mark as he rapped on the front door and waited for her to come answer. "Hey, where are you?"

Mark then walked over to the sidewalk café where they usually met for tea, but she was not there.

On a hunch, Mark returned to the shop and then circled the building. He wanted to see if her van was parked where she usually kept it. *It was gone. Perhaps she had an emergency of some kind, but why hadn't she called?*

Just as Mark turned to leave and head for his apartment, he noticed that the back door to her shop was ajar. After glancing both ways to make sure he was alone, Mark pushed the door open and went inside. *He certainly would not want someone to see him at the scene of a crime, if there was one.*

Stunned to see the shop shelves empty, Mark angrily raced upstairs. Everything but a few dresses and two pair of shoes was gone. There were also some miscellaneous toiletry items left behind in the bathroom, but nothing of any consequence. *Perhaps she'd run out of time and had to leave them behind,* fumed Mark. *But why?*

After searching everywhere for any possible clues, Mark headed back downstairs and angrily kicked an empty rack of shelves with his steel-tipped cowboy boots. The entire section collapsed onto the floor with a loud crash.

"Who in blazes are you, anyway?" shouted Mark before kicking yet another shelf. It, too, toppled onto the floor with a mighty bang. "How dare you!" hollered Mark as he viciously kicked the fallen shelves one more time before finally turning to leave.

Not only that, what would he do for his Skullcap tea now? It was not as if he could just go out and find it anywhere.

On his way back to his apartment, Mark stopped at the wholesale herb dealer at the Saturday market to see if he had any Skullcap tea, but he just happened to be out of it that day.

"Of course, you are," snorted Mark as he turned to leave.

"Would you like me to call you when we get some in?" asked the dealer. "I should have some by next week."

"I'll check back then," replied Mark. "Thanks, anyway."

"Have you tried Herbal Remedies?" questioned the dealer. "It's just right over there, in the next block."

"Yes, I did, thank you," answered Mark in a controlled tone, "but they're out of it, too."

"Can I interest you in some ginger root?" offered the man.

"Actually, yes," agreed Mark as he whipped out his wallet. "How much?"

"Fresh Adrakam ginger root runs between $5 and $7 a pound," described the dealer, "but there is also Shunthi ginger; Sunth ginger; black ginger; race ginger; African ginger; Sheng Jiang ginger . . ."

"Hold it," interrupted Mark. "I get the idea. Is there a major difference in price between them?"

"One of them runs $11 a pound," clarified the dealer. "The others are all in the $5 to $7 range."

"Does that one work better than the others for a headache?" probed Mark.

"Some say it does," shrugged the man. "Personally, I couldn't see any noticeable difference."

"Surprise me, then," requested Mark. "Give me the $11 one, if you think it's better."

"Yes, sir," beamed the merchant as he placed one of the fresh ginger roots onto a scale. "This one weighs 12.2 ounces, so that would be, let's see, there are 16 ounces in a pound, and 16 divided by 11 is $1.45. So, multiply that by 12.2 and that comes to $17.69."

"How do you figure?" scowled Mark. "If it's only $11 a pound and this thing weighs less than that, how could it come to $17.69?"

"I don't know," admitted the merchant as he shrugged his shoulders. "That does sound wrong. Let me figure it again."

"Never mind," snapped Mark as he handed the man a $20-dollar bill and started to grab the ginger root. "Keep the change."

"Do you have a grinder?" asked the merchant.

"A grinder?" questioned Mark. He was about to lose his patience with the man.

"Even a simple cheese grater will work," suggested the merchant. "Just shred off a small portion for an individual cup of tea."

"I can do that," nodded Mark.

"Oh, wait a minute!" called the dealer. "It's only $8.38. I knew that $17.69 sounded too high. When 11 is divided by 16, it comes to 68¢ and when you multiply that by 12.2, it comes to $8.38. That means I owe you $11.62."

"How 'bout you just give me your best ginger root and we'll call it good," recommended Mark. "Any one."

"You choose," motioned the man.

Mark could not help but chuckle to himself as he grabbed the largest and most expensively labeled root from the collection. It was marked at $23.

"Enjoy," bid the man as he watched Mark walk away with his prized ginger root.

I will, grinned Mark as he headed for his apartment. *Perhaps he should check on Marilyn Monroe to see if there was any word from her yet.*

After making himself a cup of fresh ginger root tea, Mark sat down at his small computer desk to power up his laptop. He blew on his tea to cool it down but it was still too hot to drink.

332

The coaster he normally put his tea on had fallen to the floor, so Mark bent down to pick it up. Just then, a small piece of paper laying under his bed caught his eye. *What's this?*

Mark carefully set down his tea before kneeling down beside his bed to reach underneath it. The large post-it note did not look familiar. Mark put on his glasses and sat back down at his desk.

One side of the post-it note read "Marilyn Monroe" – the other side of it said "logon Vivian, password LaMont."

Mark glared at the post-it note for at least a minute before reacting to it. His face became flushed with anger and he gritted his jaw as he considered the information. *He was not going to toss his tea against the wall, smash his laptop, or kick anything this time! She was not going to get to him again.*

"Vivian LaMont?" questioned Mark out loud.

He quickly logged onto FacePal and tried to access the Marilyn Monroe account using the Vivian LaMont logon and password. "Password incorrect, try again," came the immediate message.

Before he could do anything else, there was an incoming message for him from Marilyn Monroe. "There you are," recognized Mark with a sinister smirk as he opened the message.

"Looks like I changed my logon and password just in time," advised Marilyn Monroe.

"Who are you?" demanded Mark. "Really?"

"Vivian LaMont," came the immediate response.

"Any relation to a Hattie LaMont?" typed Mark.

"Just by marriage," replied Vivian.

"I'm listening," answered Mark.

"She was my stepdad's mother."

"Who was your stepdad?" grilled Mark.

"Zeke," came the reply.

"Zeke LaMont?" wrote Mark as he narrowed his eyes at the computer screen. "The *same* Zeke who was married to Ellie Mae Killingham?"

"Yes."

"Jack, Jr. mentioned to me that she and Zeke were together when they died during Hurricane Fredric, in 1979."

"That's right. Ma was pregnant with me when she first left pa and took Jack, Jr. to go live with Hattie on The Lady Elleanor."

Mark's nostrils flared as he read the message. "Would that have been on March 23, 1932?"

"Yes."

"And just when were *you* born, sis?"

"December 21, 1932."

"You *knew* I was your brother and yet you let me make love to you anyway?"

"You didn't seem to mind it at the time," reminded Vivian. "Besides, our parents were siblings, and it didn't stop them."

"So, if you really did see what I did to Jack, Jr., then why would you have come to me?" grilled Mark.

There was a delay before the next message came.

"Revenge at first."

"What made you change your mind?"

"You did."

"That doesn't answer my question," pressed Mark.

"I don't know," admitted Vivian. "I guess you were not what I expected."

"What now?

"I need time to think," replied Vivian. "Don't worry, your secret is safe with me, so long as my secrets are safe with you."

"You never really did tell me your secrets," reminded Mark.

"In time," promised Vivian.

"When?" asked Mark, but no further messages came. *He would have to wait until she was good and ready.*

It was Saturday afternoon, April 9, 2016, and the farmers' market was in full swing downstairs. There seemed to be more people congregating in the area than usual.

Seven long years had passed since Mark had seen his sister Vivian in person, and his only contacts with her had been through FacePal. For all other purposes, he continued to use Jack, Jr.'s identity and remained where he was in Seattle, just in case she should change her mind and come back. *He was 86 years old now, and she was 84. They certainly weren't getting any younger. Perhaps it was time he finally settled down with the right woman.*

Strange that the most intriguing woman he'd ever met would turn out to be his own sister, thought Mark, but he could not get her off his mind. That afternoon he had spent with her continued to haunt

334

him. *Why had she done it? Why had she allowed him to get so close to her, only to disappear? She certainly knew what he had done to their brother before that, so what difference would it make now? He'd told her repeatedly in his email messages ever since how sorry he was for it, and how much Vivian had come to mean to him. All he wanted was another chance with her.*

Mark felt certain that Vivian would have turned him in to the authorities by now if she were going to, especially with him remaining where he was for so long, so she posed no viable threat. *Not only that, she was certainly his match in every way, cut from the same cloth. Perhaps together they could try and find that treasure and enjoy what was left of their lives together. He was finally convinced that she had no idea where it was, no more than he did. What they needed to do was find a way back into that lighthouse for one last search.*

Mark glanced out his apartment window at the crowd below and suddenly noticed a familiar woman. *It was Vivian LaMont!* He wasted no time hurrying outside to try and find her. *Had she come for the new herb dealer that had just set up shop two doors down?*

Unexpectedly, Mark came face-to-face with his estranged son Kevin and his wife Linda. All thoughts of Vivian vanished for the moment. "Kevin!" greeted Mark. "And Linda."

Kevin and Linda both stood there silently glaring at him with disapproval. *They were clearly not glad to see him!*

"I've been hoping our paths would cross again," mentioned Mark. "Hey, I'm so sorry about what happened before."

"As you should be!" snapped Linda.

"Chinook?" asked Mark as he turned to Kevin and nodded at the wrapped fish his son was carrying under one arm. He decided to ignore Linda's outburst for now.

"40-pounder," advised Kevin, rather coldly.

"Where you headed?" pressed Mark. "I haven't had any salmon for ages."

"There's the fish store, right over there," informed Linda.

"Can't we just put what happened behind us and start over?" asked Mark. He tried to appear charming and just a touch sad. "What brings you two to Seattle? Are you living here now?"

"Wouldn't you like to know," growled Linda.

"There are some bridges that just cannot be rebuilt," Kevin advised Mark rather coldly. "You made your bed."

"I'm sorry you feel that way, son," lamented Mark.

Kevin looked for a moment as if he wanted to club Mark over the head with the wrapped fish he held, but restrained himself.

"Hopefully, our paths will *never* cross again!" exclaimed Linda as she put her arm through Kevin's and glared at Mark with open defiance. *Her ill feelings toward Mark had obviously not diminished over the years.*

"You don't know how sorry I am for what happened," repeated Mark. "If there's anything at all I can do to make things right ...."

"Stay away from us," interrupted Kevin in a commanding tone as he and Linda began walking away.

Mark stood there watching them as they left. *They never even looked back.* Then, all at once, Mark remembered why he had come downstairs in the first place. *Vivian! Where was she?* He began searching the crowd, making his way from one end of the farmers' market to the other, but in vain. Vivian was nowhere to be found.

9. Happy Acres

Michael Krain paused to glance from the upstairs window of his Ocean Bay office at the Priest and Krain Detective Agency. A stunning view of Ocean Bay's scenic harbor could be seen below. Morning rays of sunlight glistened across the water and across the many boats docked there. The surrounding piers were coming to life with merchants and customers as local fisherman, yachts and sailboats headed out for the day. The endless sea beyond reached toward infinity, the view of it lost only as it met the horizon.

His partner, Chip Priest, could be seen pulling up out front and parking his sleek black Maserati in its assigned parking space. Chip's new car was one of the perks Jim had offered Chip to induce him to relocate to Ocean Bay, though it didn't take much convincing, especially after everything they had been through in solving *The Powell Mountain Matter* earlier that year.

It was Friday morning, April 28, 2023, and the new matter that the Seattle PD had turned over to the Priest and Krain Detective Agency to work on was still troubling. *Who on earth would murder a 93-year old man and just leave him under a bridge like that?* wondered Michael. *At least now they knew who the poor guy was, thanks to some astonishingly fast turnaround time from the Medical Examiner. How had Jim managed to get results from them so quickly, anyway?*

It seemed like a lifetime ago that Michael had resigned his position as presiding judge at the St. Diablo County Courthouse up north to join Jim and Chip, though that had only been a few short weeks ago. Michael's late father had also been a presiding judge at the St. Diablo County Courthouse at one time and had presided over the infamous Woodcutter's trial when he was alive. Both Michael and his father had also each been members of the Crusading Knights of Powell Mountain, something which Michael now regretted deeply.

Michael then thought of the late Jerry Krain, a fellow Knight who in the end had been the real killer in that case, a horrific crime for which the Woodcutter had been falsely accused and convicted by an all-white jury. The Woodcutter had been a man of color and hadn't stood a chance of defending himself against the false charges that had been pitted against him. Saddest of all was how the poor man had

337

languished and died in prison only a handful of years later under suspicious circumstances for a crime of which he'd been innocent.

The burden of knowing that his own father had been responsible for sending the Woodcutter to his death would haunt Michael Krain for the rest of his life. His goal now was to seek justice where it could be found, which was part of why he had joined forces with Jim Otterman and Chip Priest, the very men who had gone out on a limb to exonerate the Woodcutter posthumously of the horrific crimes attributed to him. Michael had been the judge to affirm that ruling, a decision which had prompted him to resign from his judicial career thereafter, but he would do it again.

"Good morning," greeted Chip as he entered the office, took off his black leather overcoat, and carefully hung it on a padded hanger first before placing that on the office coat tree.

"Hear anything from Jim yet?" asked Michael as he picked up his over-sized coffee cup and stared with concern at the syrupy-looking brew left inside from yesterday. *Was it safe to drink?*

"Actually, yes," replied Chip as he put his tattered briefcase down on his desk and opened it. "How can you drink that stuff?"

Michael simply smiled and shrugged his shoulders as he set the cup back down without drinking any of it.

"Is Avis coming in today?" grilled Chip.

"I don't know why not," answered Michael as he studied his partner. Charles Priest was much shorter and slimmer than he was and Chip's distinct Jewish features were unmistakable.

"Good," nodded Chip. "I have something else for her to scan into the system." Unlike Michael, Chip was a very neat and fastidious man, always obsessing over little details.

Michael, on the other hand, was slightly overweight with balding white hair that he kept in a crewcut so he didn't have to comb it. However, he had put a good deal more time into his appearance as of late. "I can't believe you still use paper files," razzed Michael.

"Somebody has to," grinned Chip as he removed the shadow file he had been keeping on their new case and set it down beside his briefcase.

"What'd you find out?"

"That there was another death about the same time," replied Chip as he sat down at his desk. "Also from Happy Acres."

"Really?" Michael raised his eyebrows with interest.

"Good morning, gentlemen," greeted Avis as she entered the office with a cardboard cupholder containing three cups of fresh coffee.

"It's about time you got here," razzed Michael. "Old Chip here's already got some work for you."

"Well, that can wait," informed Avis as she hung up her coat and put her purse inside a drawer at her desk. "First, we have to save you from food poisoning."

Michael merely chuckled as Avis came and snatched away his old cup of coffee and handed him a fresh cup from the cardboard cupholder. "Black, just the way you like it."

Since Avis was a beautiful woman of color, and quite aware of Michael's undeclared attraction toward her, she took advantage of the opportunity to wink and smile at him.

"That's enough, you two," teased Chip as he shook his head and grinned like a Cheshire cat. *Who would have ever thought that the former head of the Crusading Knights of Powell Mountain and a woman of color would have a budding romance in the offing?*

"Something else you want to share?" prompted Michael.

"Nope. That's it for now," answered Chip as he handed a piece of paper to Avis. "This needs to be scanned into our computer file for the new Seattle case."

"An obituary for Vivian LaMont?" questioned Avis as she studied the newspaper clipping.

"A resident from Happy Acres who is believed to have died on the same day as Mr. Killingham, also under suspicious circumstances," clarified Chip.

"It doesn't say anything about the cause of death in the obituary," frowned Avis as she finished reading it.

"No, it doesn't" agreed Chip. "The guy from Happy Acres that I called last night was pretty vague, too."

"I take it you two are headed for Happy Acres?" teased Avis as she walked over to the scanner and placed the newspaper clipping on the glass.

"Seattle?" questioned Michael. "It rains there all the time!"

"Then we'd better take umbrellas with us," smirked Chip.

"Does Jim know about this?"

"I was just getting ready to call him," replied Chip.

"Jim's still on his way back from Alabama," reminded Avis as she handed the newspaper clipping back to Chip. "He should be here within the hour, though."

"Good," sighed Michael. "Maybe he'd rather go with you himself."

"We'll let Jim decide," answered Chip as he took one of the cups of coffee from the cardboard cupholder on Avis's desk and blew on it before taking a sip. "Thanks, Avis, what do I owe you?"

"Lunch," smiled Avis. "And it doesn't have to be today."

"Guess that means I owe you lunch, too," interjected Michael.

"We can make it a threesome," flirted Avis.

"Hey, we also got back the DNA and other results from the man they found under the bridge," Michael mentioned to Chip. "I think we've finally got a match."

"Then it really is Mr. Killingham?" guessed Chip.

"It appears that way," confirmed Michael. "Of course, the Medical Examiner has asked that we stop by his office later today for his off-the-record opinion on something else related to the matter."

"Bill Huong? Off-the-record?" snorted Avis. "I doubt that!"

"He said there was something else he wanted to discuss with Jim," clarified Michael.

"At least Bill's just down the street," sighed Chip as he took another sip from the fresh cup of coffee provided by Avis.

"I'll let you gentlemen know the moment Jim arrives," Avis assured them as she sat down at her desk and turned on her desktop computer.

The sound of Kevin and Linda loudly snoring from behind him caused Jim to smile with amusement as he prepared to land his Learjet on the tiny runway at Oceanview Academy.

"Better put your seatbelts on," called Jim from where he was seated in the cockpit.

"Are we there yet?" questioned Linda as she yawned and sat up. "Oh my gosh!" exclaimed Linda as she suddenly realized they were about to land.

Both Kevin and Linda quickly fastened their seatbelts.

"Landing sequence initiated," advised MIRA.

Without further warning, the aircraft aligned itself with the runway centerline and began its descent from the airspace above the

340

expansive ocean, racing ever closer toward the craggy ocean-top bluffs below with the tiny runway on its crest. The sound of landing gear being lowered could be heard.

"Don't you need to call somebody or something?" grilled Linda with concern.

"There's no control tower here," reminded Jim with a chuckle as he winked at Linda in his rearview mirror. "You know that. We're completely on our own, except for MIRA, of course."

"Oh, that's right," realized Linda as she grasped Kevin's hand and gave him a look of concern.

"You wanted to do this," reminded Kevin with an amused smile.

"MIRA, release autopilot," commanded Jim. "I'll take it from here." Jim liked to land his own planes.

"Yes, Jim," responded MIRA as she released the controls.

The small out buildings at the Oceanview Academy landing field sped toward them at an alarming rate as Jim touched down and engaged the brakes on his Learjet.

"Today is Friday, April 28, 2023, at 14:45, Pacific Standard Time," volunteered MIRA as they continued down the runway. "Currently landing at Oceanview Academy Airport. Weather conditions optimal."

Linda let out a stifled scream when the wheels on Jim's aircraft momentarily bounced on the runway.

"We're good," promised Jim as he steadied their approach.

"Oh, my God!" exclaimed Linda when they finally came to a stop, just feet from the out buildings. She had been holding her breath without realizing it.

"Jim!" beamed Sheree as her husband entered the Killingham Lighthouse Bed and Breakfast with Kevin and Linda. She raced over to give him a hug. Then when seeing their mud-stained clothing, she became serious and asked, "What happened to you?"

"It's a long story," interjected Linda as she struggled to pull her huge suitcase toward the spiral staircase.

"Give me that," commanded Kevin as he snatched it from her and began carrying it up to their room.

"I think all of us could use a good shower and a nap," opined Jim as he pulled up and checked the messages on his phone.

341

"Ann skyped us today," revealed Sheree, "at the usual time."

"How is everyone?" questioned Jim as he scrolled through his list of messages to see if any were urgent.

"Susan and Rupert are just fine," mentioned Sheree as she took Jim's coat from him and hung it up. "So are Sherry and Ann."

Jim paused from what he was doing and gave Sheree an inquisitive look.

"Oh, yes, Carolyn's fine, too," added Sheree. She had pointedly waited until last to mention Carolyn. She was well aware of her husband's continued feelings for Carolyn, despite his repeated denials of it, feelings he'd had since high school.

"I suppose they're ready for me to fly down and bring them all home?" assumed Jim with a heavy sigh. He was already exhausted from the trip to Alabama.

"Actually, no," smirked Sheree. "They've found another way."

"What do you mean?" grilled Jim with narrowed eyes.

"Well, Carolyn did win the Powerball," reminded Sheree. "I'm sure she can afford to hire anyone she wants to fly them back."

"All the way from Machu Picchu?" frowned Jim.

"Relax," laughed Sheree. "I told them you were busy working a case and couldn't be disturbed."

"You did, did you?" Jim gave Sheree a crooked smile as he pulled her close and gave her a kiss.

"Chip called, too," revealed Sheree as she quickly returned his kiss and then pulled away. "I'll get dinner ready while you call him back. Apparently, it's urgent."

"Of course, it is," frowned Jim. Then, Jim commanded to his phone, "Call Chip."

Saturday morning, April 29, 2023, was overcast and drizzly. Increasing wind brought with it the sharp sting of salt air.

"Are you sure you're okay staying here?" asked Kevin as he and Jim headed for the front door of the lighthouse to leave.

"I just need a day to rest and relax," assured Linda. "Besides, you're only going as far as Ocean Bay, right?"

"That's where my office is," interjected Jim, "but there's no guarantees we won't be headed off on another lead after that."

"Chip wouldn't tell you anything else?" frowned Linda.

342

"Not over the phone," assured Jim. "He said he wanted to see the look on my face when he told me whatever it is."

"Perhaps I should go," waffled Linda.

"We're only a phone call away," reminded Kevin as he pulled Linda close and gave her a hug. "Jim and I will be fine."

"You'll let me know right away if you're flying someplace else?" grilled Linda.

"Of course," promised Kevin.

"Scout's honor," added Jim with a crooked smile. "Come on, we need to get going."

"Remember I love you," whispered Linda to Kevin as she gave him one last hug before he left with Jim.

It was well after 9:00 in the morning before Jim's bright red 2023 Jeep Cherokee began its journey along the narrow blufftop highway near the lighthouse and meandered its way toward Ocean Bay.

Morning sunlight rippled across the ocean surface to their left, framed by cypress and eucalyptus trees growing beside the winding road. A small bird could suddenly be seen darting past overhead as it zoomed toward the beach below where several established nesting sites were located.

"What kind of bird was that?" questioned Kevin.

"That was a Snowy Plover," advised Jim.

"So, you're a bird watcher, too?" grinned Kevin.

"The entire campus of Oceanview Academy, the lighthouse, and the golf course have a permanent easement as a wildlife management area," revealed Jim.

"Your doing?" guessed Kevin as he raised an eyebrow.

Jim merely nodded but couldn't hide his slight grin from Kevin.

"You really are responsible?" grilled Kevin. "I was just kidding."

"I'm sure anyone else with the means and opportunity would have done the same," shrugged Jim. "Besides, the beach along both the campus and the Killingham properties are now designated as an official site for bird enthusiasts to come and enjoy watching Snowy Plovers, Lesser Terns, and other endangered species in their chosen nesting grounds."

343

"Sounds like you're a good guy to know," nodded Kevin.

"Let's hope you still feel that way after we find out what Chip has to tell us," answered Jim. *Had something gone wrong on the case? Why was Chip waiting to share what he knew except in person?*

"What is it, about a two-hour drive to your office from here?" asked Kevin as he continued to stare at the scenery surrounding them.

"Or less," replied Jim with a crooked smile. "Depending on how one drives."

"Please take your time," chuckled Kevin as Jim slowed to negotiate another hairpin turn.

"I always do."

"So, if you don't mind my asking, were you and Linda ever an item back in high school?" pressed Kevin.

Jim suddenly started to laugh. "Me and Linda? No way!"

"I thought that's what you'd said earlier," smiled Kevin. "Just making sure."

After several awkward moments of silence, Kevin continued. "Tell me more about this Lenny Owens character."

Jim gave Kevin an odd look. "What would you like to know?"

"Everything."

"You really should be asking Linda this."

"I'm asking you."

Jim sighed deeply before responding. "Alright. I guess you noticed the photo they showed at the reunion of Lenny and Linda that was taken at our high school prom?"

"Yeah," confirmed Kevin. "The one where she was wearing the bright red prom dress, arm-in-arm with a tall, good-looking black guy."

"I take it she never bothered to mention it?" assumed Jim.

"Uh, no." Kevin folded his arms in front of him as he waited for Jim to continue.

"Linda was absolutely crazy about him," described Jim. "He was all she ever talked about."

"So, just where do you fit into the picture?"

"Me?" chuckled Jim. "I was crazy about Carolyn Bennett, the girl that Lenny was interested in."

"Lenny was interested in Carolyn, and not Linda?"

"Bingo," replied Jim. "You see, Linda and I were co-conspirators. It was our goal to keep Carolyn and Lenny apart so that

344

Linda would be free to move in on Lenny. And of course, I would then be free to move in on Carolyn."

"Troublemakers, huh?"

"Sometimes that can backfire," admitted Jim as he became serious. "It can also be hurtful, but high school kids often don't consider the consequences of things like that."

"What happened?" pumped Kevin.

"Well, Carolyn was quite shy, but so was Lenny. Neither of them had the courage to ask each other to the prom."

"That must have been handy for you and Linda."

"Let me finish," chided Jim. "Lenny had found out from some of Carolyn's friends that she would be wearing a baby blue dress to the prom that night, so he had a special baby blue corsage made up that he'd planned on giving to her when she showed up."

"But she didn't?" guessed Kevin.

"Not in time," replied Jim. "Linda managed to get there first and convinced Lenny that Carolyn wasn't coming. That's why the corsage on her bright red dress was baby blue in that picture."

"I see."

"Carolyn did show up, though, but not until Lenny had already pinned the corsage on Linda's dress. The look on Carolyn's face when she saw it spoke volumes," confessed Jim.

"What did Carolyn do?" questioned Kevin.

"She fled the place in tears, of course," answered Jim. "That was when Lenny left Linda alone at the prom to run after Carolyn to try and explain what happened."

"And?"

"She got away before he had a chance."

"And you know this how?"

"Because I followed and watched them from the shadows." Jim decided not to mention the other baby blue corsage Linda had ordered later to replace it, or how Carolyn had reacted to that.

"Youth is definitely wasted on the young," remarked Kevin as he shook his head.

"And you already know that Lenny was 59 years old when he died," reminded Jim as he slowed for another hairpin turn.

"So, Lenny was never interested in Linda at all, then?"

"No, he never was," assured Jim.

Kevin merely nodded.

345

"It was only Carolyn that turned Lenny's head," continued Jim. "But, that's another story."

"I take it that *you* still have some interest in her?"

Jim flushed deeply with embarrassment at Kevin's direct question and remained silent for several moments before responding. "I've been happily married to Sheree for seven years now."

Kevin tried to suppress a tight-lipped grin. "Good answer." It was clear that Jim had no intention of admitting the obvious.

"Not to change the subject," prefaced Jim, "but one of the things Chip mentioned to me was that we've gotten the rest of the results back from Bill Huong already."

"The Medical Examiner that you skyped with the other day?"

"One and the same," answered Jim. "He also reconfirmed for us that the guy in the grave was not Mark Killingham."

"I thought he was so busy working on some other case that he couldn't get to it until tomorrow," reminded Kevin.

"Things have changed," advised Jim. "Looks like both cases are one and the same. *The Killingham Matter* is what we're going to call it from here on out. Apparently, the ID found in the decedent's pocket in the Seattle case was for that of a Jack Killingham, Jr."

"Really?" Kevin was surprised.

"That's another reason why the Seattle PD wanted my help in the first place, because of my association with The *Killingham* Lighthouse Bed and Breakfast."

"That makes sense."

"The other thing Chip learned from Bill this morning is that Jack Killingham, Jr., was also a 93-year old resident from Happy Acres Nursing Home up in Seattle," described Jim.

"Mark would be 93-years old," muttered Kevin.

"Chances are pretty good its him."

"Then what is it that Chip won't tell you?" pressed Kevin.

"I guess we'll find out when we get there."

"Jim's here!" hollered Avis to Chip and Michael.

"Where?" demanded Chip as he emerged from his office. He had been pacing the floor again.

"Relax, honey," instructed Avis from where she stood by the front window gazing out. "He's just now pulling up. And he's got some guy with him, too."

Chip suddenly joined her by the window. "That's Kevin."

"Kevin Killingham?" grilled Avis.

"Yes, Mark Killingham's son," confirmed Chip.

"Good lookin' devil, too," commented Avis as she finally returned to her desk.

"I heard that," answered Michael from his office. Avis grinned with delight at his response.

The sound of footsteps outside the office entrance could be heard as Jim and Kevin walked up, opened the door and made their way inside.

"Greetings," smiled Jim. "This is Kevin Killingham."

"How do you do?" acknowledged Chip as he approached and shook Kevin's hand. Chip had a magnetic personality, usually well-liked by most people who met him.

"We met on skype," reminded Kevin.

"And so, we did," smiled Chip. "Glad to finally meet you in person."

"You must be Mark Killingham's son," commented another man who had just come into the room. "I'm Michael Krain."

Kevin nodded and cautiously shook hands with Michael, but there was something about the man he just didn't like. It was nothing tangible, just one of those things where you meet someone and either you like them or you don't. Perhaps it was Michael's abrupt manner.

"Come into my office," invited Chip. "I have something to show you two that I think you'll find of interest."

"I'll just be in here if you need me," advised Michael. It was clear from Chip's mannerism that Michael was not included in the invitation.

"Close the door," directed Chip.

Once Jim and Kevin were seated across from Chip at his desk, Chip grabbed a huge paper file and shoved it across the desk toward Jim. "Take a look at this."

Jim slowly began to smile. Jim loved paper files, even though most of his items were now stored electronically. "Has Avis scanned all of this in already?"

"Absolutely," promised Chip as he watched Jim open the file.

"Vivian LaMont," read Jim as he studied the obituary on top of the other papers.

347

Kevin moved closer to get a better look at it. Both he and Jim slowly nodded their heads as they read the article.

"You don't look surprised," admitted Chip.

"Take a look at this," suggested Jim as he pulled his laptop from his briefcase and put it on the table. "I guess I should forward my stuff to Avis, too."

"And you talk about me," teased Chip as he came around the table and stood behind Jim and Kevin so he could see the screen on Jim's laptop. "Are you kidding me?"

"Looks like Vivian was quite the busy little widow," assessed Chip as he watched Jim scroll through the electronic file.

"It would seem that a trip to Happy Acres might be in order," decided Jim.

"Way ahead of you," answered Chip. "I had Avis call them earlier to see if there's someone there we can talk to."

"Excellent," approved Jim.

"That's almost 900 miles from here," reminded Kevin.

"Then the sooner we get started, the sooner we'll be there," smirked Jim.

"Shouldn't we drive back and get your Learjet or something?" grilled Kevin.

"That'd take two more hours, just to do that by car," objected Jim. "I've actually got my Cessna here, so let's just fly the Cessna back for the Learjet. That should only take about 30 minutes, and then it'll take us another hour and a half to fly the jet up to Seattle. We can be back by tonight."

"Two hours if we get started now?" asked Chip, to make sure.

"Yep," answered Jim. "Give or take a little preflight check time. I think the three of us can handle this."

"I suppose I should stay here to keep an eye on Avis," came the voice of Michael over Chip's intercom system. He had been listening in on their conversation.

"Somebody's got to keep an eye on her," chuckled Jim. He did not seem the least bit surprised or upset that Michael had been eavesdropping.

"I should probably call Linda," reminded Kevin.

"Call her on the way," directed Jim as he pressed a button on his laptop before returning it to its case. "Avis, I just sent you another document for our new case," informed Jim as he opened the door to

348

Chip's office. "We'll be calling it *The Killingham Matter* from now on."

"Got it. Have fun in Seattle," bid Avis with a crooked smile. She had been listening in, too.

Five Weeks Earlier

Thursday morning, March 23, 2023, seemed to start out like so many others at the Happy Acres Nursing Home and Retirement Community in Seattle, Washington, except for the noticeable lack of rain or visitors.

It was one of those rare spring days in the Pacific Northwest that was blessed with sunshine and the hope of warmer weather to come. Yet, torrential precipitation and flooding in the area during the past two weeks had made it next to impossible for many of the usual family members to come see their loved ones, especially now that the southbound Seattle Bridge across the Duwamish River had collapsed. Thankfully, no one had been on it at the time, as it had happened around three o'clock in the morning.

Meanwhile, southbound traffic was being diverted toward the north. The 45-minute detour ultimately led to a congested cloverleaf interchange where it was finally possible to access the northbound Seattle Bridge over the Duwamish River. Two of its six lanes had been temporarily cordoned off to allow for a southbound direction of travel as part of the detour. The morning commute was often at a standstill during this process while angry drivers tried to reach their destinations.

High on a nearby hill sat Happy Acres. The narrow, winding road leading to its entrance gate had seen better days but at least it had not washed away and was surprisingly little-traveled. Eric Santori had been forced to commute to his new job alone since losing his carpooling companion, so was glad to finally be off the main freeway and on the road to Happy Acres. He would miss Ken Smithers, the coworker with whom he had carpooled, but at the same time was happy for Ken, who had found a better job closer to the end of town in which they both lived.

Eric slowed and pulled over to the side of the road for an ambulance to pass. *Who was it now?* Another Happy Acres resident was being taken to the local hospital. *Hopefully, it was not Vivian*

349

LaMont. Eric was not sure why, but he had come to think of Vivian as a dear friend. *How sad that no family or friends ever bothered to visit the poor lady,* thought Eric. He normally did not fraternize with the residents, let alone allow himself to develop personal attachments to any of them, but Vivian was different. There was just something about her, though he wasn't exactly sure what it was.

At 67 years of age, Eric wanted nothing more than to be retired, yet the recent loss of his mother had made that impossible. Instead of inheriting the anticipated fortune from her estate, Eric – who was executor of her Will – had learned too late of the dire financial circumstances she had been in. *Why hadn't she said something?*

It had been years since his mother Maria had inherited and taken over her parents' exclusive Italian Restaurant up near Bellevue, Washington. Santori's Italian Dining had been an icon in the community and the closing of its doors following Maria's death had been a blow to many long-time loyal customers.

Maria had once been a beautiful young Italian woman but had never married again after divorcing her no-good husband. It had been when Eric was a baby that she had learned of her husband Mark's other marriage to a young girl named Bobby Sue Johnson. That was enough for her. Maria had taken her five boys – Michael, Justin, Philip, Evan and baby Eric – and moved from their home in Sprague up to Bellevue, Washington, to help her parents run the restaurant.

Mark Killingham had attempted repeatedly to contact Maria and had even made threats, but the business end of Mrs. Santori's rifle had changed Mark's mind. Maria's mother was not about to allow Mark to see her daughter or grandchildren again, and that was that.

Michael, Justin, Philip, Evan and Eric's last names were legally changed from Killingham to Santori at that time, as well. The older children, especially Michael, were well aware of the fact that their father was a bigamist and a con artist, and had no desire to see the man again.

Eric, on the other hand, had been only a baby at the time and had no memories of his real father. He had been told, of course, that he had a younger half-brother named Kevin, who was only 11 days younger than he. Eric had been born on January 18, 1956, while Kevin had been born on January 29, 1956.

Eric had even tracked Kevin down once, and learned that he was married to a woman named Linda. *He'd married a woman named*

Linda once himself, before meeting Rose, but it had been annulled. Eric had watched Kevin from his car in the parking lot of Kevin's and Linda's apartment in Ashton. *What if Kevin did not know the truth about their father? What would inserting himself into Kevin's life do to him?* In the end, Eric had forced himself to abandon the idea, but had always wondered whether he had made the right decision. *It might have been nice to meet Kevin.*

After several more years of searching to try and locate Mark Killingham, Eric Santori had finally learned in 2009 of his real father's untimely death at an obscure ice cream shop. He still kept a carefully folded copy of the obituary in his wallet. He had later visited Mark Killingham's gravesite at the Ocean Bluff Cemetery, up on the hill by The Ocean Bluff Mental Institution. *If only he could have found Mark Killingham before that! Perhaps then he could have asked him WHY he had done what he did. It was something Eric had always wanted to find out for himself but had been denied the opportunity.*

Eric finally reached the top of the hill where Happy Acres was located and pulled into the long circular driveway at Happy Acres. It led to a covered drop-off area by the front door. Just beyond it was a small parking lot beside the building for its employees. Only guests were allowed to park alongside the circular drive.

Eric was deep in thought as he pulled into his assigned parking space and grabbed his sack lunch before exiting the older vehicle. It was hard to believe that his 1995 Camry still ran at all. *Not many people drove 28-year old cars*, mused Eric as he manually locked the doors. *At least he had a new smartwatch, so he wasn't entirely in the dark ages.* Eric smiled to himself at the irony of it.

"It's about time you got here," razzed Wilbur Hansen, a fellow worker who had also just arrived.

"At least we're here," pointed out Eric as the two of them walked toward the building's front entrance.

"Did you see the ambulance?" grilled Wilbur.

"Yeah, I did," answered Eric.

"Who do you think it was?" pressed Wilbur.

"I guess we'll find out when we get inside."

"Have you heard anything about a replacement for Ken yet?"

"Smithers?" chuckled Eric. "I doubt it."

"That's just not fair," complained Wilbur. "They can't expect us to keep doing all that extra work without hiring someone to replace him. If it keeps up, Ken might not be the only one to quit this place."

"Is that a threat?" challenged Eric as they reached the front door.

Wilbur merely shrugged his shoulders as he and Eric went inside. He certainly did not want the head shift nurse at the main desk to overhear them.

"See ya at break then," called Eric as he headed toward the south wing. Wilbur worked the north wing.

"You're late!" snapped a stern-looking Hispanic woman named Consuela as Eric reached the south wing nurse's station. She was in her late fifties and clearly fond of food.

"You're lucky I'm even here," retorted Eric as he flashed her one of his winning smiles.

Consuela backed down immediately, of course, and smiled back. Like most other women in Eric's life, she was unable to resist his charm, or his smile, and even had a bit of a secret crush on him.

Although Eric Santori did have the distinctly recognizable Killingham family facial features, his Italian side had left him with black hair, dark eyes, and a Roman nose. Eric managed to keep his hair and goatee free of gray hair through the miracle of hair dye, and was thought to be years younger than he actually was. Eric also worked out each day and was in excellent physical condition, for any age.

Women were drawn to him like moths to a flame, but Eric's second wife Rose had died years ago in a plane crash while flying out to be with him when he was stationed in Okinawa during the tail end of the Vietnam War. Rose had been pregnant with their only child at that time. Eric had never found anyone else adequate to replace that missing piece in his life, even after finally retiring from the service after repeated tours of duty in nearly every branch of its military. *Of course, there was his first wife Linda, with whom he was still very much in love, but she had managed to disappear from his life without a trace. Linda was most likely married to someone else, and probably had kids and grandkids, too.*

"Whatever made a highly qualified guy like you even want to work at a place like this?" grilled Consuela as she handed Eric one of the patient charts.

352

"I don't know," replied Eric as he flipped it open. "Just seemed like the thing to do at the time."

"You must enjoy it," chuckled Consuela. "You're still here. I can't believe we haven't gone paperless yet."

"Probably never will. Hey, who'd they take out in the ambulance earlier?" questioned Eric as he glanced at the various charts to try and find Vivian's.

"Mr. Henderson," advised Consuela. "Why?"

"Just curious."

"Vivian was asking for you earlier," remembered Consuela. "Something about not wanting her meals in the dining room anymore."

"Really?" frowned Eric. "Guess I should go find out why."

"Yeah, yeah, go ahead," sighed Consuela. "Nothing pressing here, anyway. Just the usual."

"Thanks," flirted Eric as he handed the chart back to Consuela and suddenly gave her a kiss on the cheek before heading down the hall.

Why would an outgoing and vivacious woman like Vivian suddenly decide to become a recluse? wondered Eric as he approached and knocked on her door.

"Come in, Eric," came Vivian's voice.

"How'd you know it was me?" flirted Eric as he entered the room. He enjoyed flirting with her, even if she was 91 years old.

"Sit down," motioned Vivian, without answering his question. She was seated at one of two Queen Anne style chairs at a small round wooden table at one end of her room. The window beside it overlooked the well-manicured grounds outside and the old growth forest beyond. Two specially-placed hummingbird feeders outside her window had been put there and maintained by Eric at her behest.

"I am on duty," reminded Eric as he sat in the overstuffed chair. The plush maroon and gold floral brocade pattern gave the chairs a distinctive look.

"When do you get off?" pressed Vivian.

"What's this about you becoming a recluse?" asked Eric. He was truly concerned.

"There's a new resident that I wish to avoid," explained Vivian. "Someone from my past. He just checked in today, so I was fortunate indeed to have avoided him at breakfast."

"An old flame?" teased Eric.

353

"Something like that," confirmed Vivian. "Someone who is not who he purports to be."

"What's that supposed to mean?" frowned Eric.

"He goes by the name of Jack Killingham, Jr."

Eric Santori looked as if someone had suddenly punched him in the gut and stared at Vivian with disbelief. *Who was she, anyway?*

"Please stop by when you get off duty," requested Vivian. "There is much I need to tell you."

Eric studied her more closely. "How would you know someone named Jack Killingham, Jr., anyway?"

"I'll tell you all about it later," assured Vivian. "For now, I need to know you will be careful. Under no circumstances are you to tell that man who you really are. The consequences could be dire."

"And just who am I?" tested Eric.

"Cut the crap, Eric," responded Vivian. "Your birth name is Eric Killingham. You are the youngest son of Maria and Mark Killingham."

"Just who are you?" demanded Eric.

"I'm your aunt," revealed Vivian.

"Prove it."

"Count on it," promised Vivian as she finally gave Eric a slight smile. "When you stop by later. There are things you need to know."

"Why haven't you said anything until now?"

"Because there wasn't a need."

"But there is now?"

"Eric, just promise me you'll be careful, please!" exclaimed Vivian. "Your father is a very dangerous man."

"My father is dead," informed Eric.

"That's what Mark would have the world believe."

"I'm not leaving here until you tell me right now what you know," persisted Eric.

"Very well," sighed Vivian, "but you're not going to like it."

"Try me."

"Mark had a twin brother named Jack, Jr.," began Vivian as she pulled an old tattered photograph from the drawer of her table and laid it down in front of Eric. "Here is a picture of my mother Ellie Mae with her two brothers, Jack and James. Her brother Jack was also her husband, and was my father."

Eric stared with amazement at the old, black and white photo. "What beach is this? Where was this taken?"

"At the Killingham family lighthouse," revealed Vivian. "The twin boys are Mark and Jack, Jr."

"How can you tell them apart?"

"Mark is the one being held by Jack," elaborated Vivian. "He's the tall man. Your grandfather."

"Where were you when this was taken?"

"My mother was pregnant with me when this photo was taken," replied Vivian. "Eric, listen to me. I saw Mark murder my brother Jack, Jr. with my own eyes and am the only person in this world who knows what he did or can identify him. The man buried in Mark's grave is Jack, Jr."

"You actually *saw* my father murder his own brother?" scowled Eric. "Why on earth didn't you go to the police when it happened?"

"Because I was in some pretty bad trouble with the law myself at the time," confessed Vivian. "For something completely unrelated."

"Does Mark know what you saw?"

"Yes, he does," admitted Vivian. "It's complicated. I promise I'll tell you all about it when you stop by later, but you *must* trust me on this. You cannot let that man know who you are. He would recognize the name Santori immediately."

"It's a good thing we only have first names on our name badges, then, isn't it?" nodded Eric. "Okay, but I will be back. Meanwhile, I'd like you to keep your door locked. I'll bring you your dinner myself."

"Thank you," Vivian smiled weakly.

"'Til then," bid Eric as he got up and locked the door to Vivian's room before leaving.

Consuela had grown impatient as she waited for Eric to return. When she saw him coming, she began, "Eric San ...."

"Consuela," Eric cut her off. "We do not use our last names in front of the residents, remember?"

Consuela narrowed her eyes at him but merely nodded. "You're right, I'm sorry."

"Just don't let it happen again," flirted Eric, in the hope that she would comply.

355

"Meds or meals?" questioned Consuela.

"I'll do the meals tonight," offered Eric. He usually prepared the meds, so Consuela gave him a puzzled look.

"To make up for making you wait," grinned Eric. "Okay?"

"Ah, yeah, sure," smiled Consuela. "You are full of surprises."

Delivering meals and picking up trays afterwards was far more involved than just getting the meds ready, especially since the regular server had quit, leaving the nurses on their own to do just about everything. Thankfully, most residents ate in the main dining room.

"That doesn't include bed pans, though," clarified Eric with a mischievous wink. "Perhaps you can get Wilbur to take care of that. Besides, most of the residents are potty trained, right?"

"Wilbur, huh," snickered Consuela. "He already does the north wing. Why in the world would he come do the south wing, too?"

"There could be a reason." Eric did not elaborate.

"You must have something pretty good on him," chuckled Consuela as she unlocked the medicine cabinet and began organizing the various pills that would be needed to accompany the dinner trays.

"I'll get the food trays from the kitchen," advised Eric as he headed down the long hallway, then toward the main dining room on the east wing. The kitchen was located just beyond it.

"Eric," called Ms. Billingsly as he passed her station. "There's someone I'd like you to meet. This is our newest resident, Jack Killingham."

"Jack Killingham, Jr.," corrected the man. He was seated in an overstuffed chair in the lobby nearby, busy reading a newspaper as he waited for the dinner hour.

"Sir," nodded Eric as he studied the man. He hoped it wasn't obvious that he was trying to appear uninterested. The sudden knot in his stomach upon seeing what he knew might be his dad was nearly overwhelming. *Could this **really** be his father?*

"This is Jack's first day here," pointed out Ms. Billingsly, rather loudly. She usually assumed that most of the residents were hard of hearing, whether they were or not.

"Welcome aboard," greeted Eric as he politely nodded at the new resident before continuing his trek toward the kitchen. His palms had begun to sweat as he clenched and unclenched his fists. *Hopefully, Mr. Killingham hadn't noticed.*

"Guess he must be in a hurry," apologized Ms. Billingsly to the new resident.

"The man's got a job to do," flirted Mr. Killingham. *Perhaps there was a way to work an angle on the nurse.*

"How's the room?" continued Ms. Billingsly.

"Actually, I'm in one of the cottages," reminded Mark. He was trying his best to be charming.

"Oh, that's right," flirted Marge Billingsly in return. "The courtyard is especially lovely this time of year, too, with all the tubers coming up."

"Ah, Marge, or should I call you Miss?" questioned Mark with a sly smile as he studied her name badge. "That's a lovely name," he added with a wink.

"Actually, it's Ms. Billingsly," whispered the woman, "but we don't normally give out our last names to the patients. You can just call me Marge."

"I would love to call you, anytime," advised Mark with a naughty smile. *The hook was set already, all he had to do now was reel her in.*

"Please let me know if you need anything at all," encouraged Marge, who was not immune to Mark Killingham's charm, even at his age. She secretly wondered how well off he was financially, particularly because of the nice clothes, expensive shoes and smartwatch he had on.

"Actually," mentioned Mark, "I was wondering if you have a patient here by the name of Vivian LaMont. I could have sworn I saw her in the dining room this morning, but then she disappeared."

"Someone you know?" questioned Marge with a raised eyebrow as she pushed down her glasses and looked at him over the top of them.

"An old flame," grinned Mark.

"Oh, I see," smirked Marge as she slowly nodded her head and pushed her glasses back into place. "Well, let's see." Marge began thumbing through a list on her clipboard.

"You haven't gone paperless yet?" razzed Mark.

"Not here, no," sighed Marge. "Perhaps someday."

"How do you keep track of everything?"

"We manage," assured Marge, unconvincingly.

357

"Do you have any sort of internet connection here, for the residents who might want to use it?" pressed Mark.

"Oh, of course, absolutely. We have Wi-Fi in each of the rooms and also in the cottages," assured Marge. "Here we are, Vivian LaMont, room 23, south wing."

"Thank you, Marge," flirted Mark as he unexpectedly took her hand in his and gallantly kissed the back of it.

"You're welcome," blushed Marge as she smiled back at him.

"I think I'm gonna like it here," responded Mark.

"And don't forget to let me know if there's anything else you need, Jack. Anything at all."

"Trust me, I will," promised Mark as he turned to saunter toward the dining room. *At least he knew where to find Vivian now. Had she seen him earlier and been hiding out in her room all day?*

It was 7:30 p.m. on Thursday evening, March 23, 2023. Eric Santori's shift had just ended.

"Wanna stop by Frank's on the way home for a cold one?" asked Wilbur as he approached him in the lobby.

"Not tonight," declined Eric. "I've got some personal things to take care of."

"What kind of personal things?" grinned Wilbur as he raised his eyebrows up and down a couple of times. "Anyone I know?"

"Perhaps," smirked Eric. He was not about to tell Wilbur anything else.

"Not Consuela?" pressed Wilbur with a crooked grin.

"Not Consuela," confirmed Eric with a mysterious smile.

"Oh, come on!" exclaimed Wilbur.

"Nothin' doin'," insisted Eric, who was clearly amused by Wilbur's persistence. "I might tell you about it later. Maybe."

"You'd better," said Wilbur as he grabbed his satchel and coat from the employee closet before heading for the front door. "See ya tomorrow."

"So, Eric, aren't you going home?" grilled Marge as she began straightening up her desk. As soon as the night nurse arrived, she would be on her way.

"Not just yet," replied Eric. "I need to talk with Ted."

"Is there anything in particular that I can help you with?" questioned Marge. She was suddenly curious.

358

Eric was actually waiting for Ted, the night nurse to arrive, so he could let him know he would be with Vivian. *Besides, Marge had a big mouth, so there was no need for her to be aware of his friendship with Ms. LaMont. Perhaps he should tell her something else, just to satisfy her curiosity.*

"About today," began Eric.

"Yes?"

"Earlier, before you introduced me to Mr. Killingham, did you know he was wandering the south wing?"

"Really?"

"And while he was down there, Consuela started to call me by my first *and* last name," continued Eric.

"Like she does when you're late or in trouble for something?" grinned Marge.

"Yes," answered Eric. "Exactly like that. I just don't want my last name used in front of the patients, especially that man."

"Why him?"

"It's personal."

"If it concerns the safety of our residents, then you'd better start talking," cautioned Marge as she took off her glasses, laid them down on her desk, and folded her arms.

Eric waited for several moments before responding. "I have reason to believe he is someone from my past that is using an alias name, and could potentially be untrustworthy."

"But he seems so nice," argued Marge. She was clearly distressed by what Eric had said.

"I would just like time to check him out," requested Eric, "and don't want him to know who I really am, just in case he's who I suspect. That's all I can tell you."

"That's a pretty tall order, mister," sighed Marge as she folded her glasses and put them in their case for the night before tossing it into her purse. "There must be something else you can tell me."

"I wish there was," assured Eric, "but, what if I'm wrong?"

"We do a thorough background check on all the residents," reminded Marge.

"Nevertheless," sighed Eric, "just give me a day or two to check him out. It couldn't hurt."

"Fair enough," agreed Marge as she finally grabbed her purse and stood to leave.

"Good evening," greeted Ted as he entered the lobby and approached the front desk nurse's station, where he would be working until morning.

Like Eric, Ted was in his mid-sixties, and finances were such that retirement was not possible. Ted thought often of the time he and Eric had served together in the '91 Gulf War, and were both present during a friendly fire incident where two soldiers of the U.S. Army had been killed and six wounded. They had been among the lucky ones, to come out unscathed, at least physically. Each had suffered from varying degrees of PTSD, and had also attended group therapy sessions together.

The incident had happened when an AH-64 Apache attack helicopter misidentified and fired upon a U.S. Army Bradley Fighting Vehicle and an M113 Armored Personnel Carrier during night operations. It was a tragic case of confusion between the Coalition Air Operations Center, which advised the Apache pilot that there were not blue (Americans) or green (allies/friendlies) in the area, and the inherent limitations of the Apache pilot's third generation night vision goggles. The NVGs had caused friendly ground fire to appear as hostile ground-to-air. The Bradley and APC were assumed to be Iraqi Republican Guard, and the Apache pilot was cleared by the CAOC to engage, with unforgivably lethal results.

Several of their comrades had been diagnosed with the Gulf War Syndrome, reporting symptoms such as memory loss, brain fog, night sweats, relentless fatigue, and intestinal and joint pain. There had also been reported birth defects among infants born to some of them, though neither Eric or Ted had ever remarried or had children since the war.

"Hey, Ted," acknowledged Eric.

Marge merely nodded.

"You takin' over my job?" Ted razzed Eric as he tossed his lunch sack under the desk.

"Not yet," grinned Eric.

"Anything new?" asked Ted.

"Same old, same old," replied Marge as Consuela emerged from the south wing hallway and stopped to grab her coat from the employee closet. "Oh yes, Mr. Henderson was taken to County General."

"Will he be alright?"

"I'm sure they'll let us know," answered Marge as she grabbed her coat and began putting it on.

"There's also a new resident," reminded Eric.

"Perhaps you can fill him in on that," suggested Marge as she and Consuela headed for the front door.

"Sure," agreed Eric. *That would give him the perfect opportunity to talk with Ted about Vivian, as well.*

"Good night, gentlemen," called Consuela.

"See you tomorrow," added Marge as the two women left.

"Let me just get my coffee first," requested Ted. "Do you mind?"

"Of course not, I'm in no hurry."

"I'll be right back."

Eric noticed the file for Jack Killingham, Jr., sitting on the head nurse's desk. Marge had not yet finished processing it.

Unable to resist, Eric sat down at the desk and quickly opened the file. Until assigned to a particular nurse or nurse's station, the files were usually considered to be privileged and confidential. Eric glanced toward the hallway leading to the kitchen, where Ted had gone to get some coffee. Ted was nowhere to be seen. *True, he and Ted were close friends, but there was no reason to involve him too deeply. Not just yet.*

Eric quickly opened the file and began reading. *No history prior to 2009? How odd.* After glancing again to be sure he had time, Eric rapidly began photographing the various pages in the file with his smartwatch. He would study them more closely later, at home.

Just as Eric finished and closed the file, he could see Ted approaching from the corner of his eye.

"It fits you," teased Ted as he arrived at the station and set down his cup of coffee on the desk.

Eric gave him a puzzled look.

"Being head nurse," clarified Ted with a twinkle in his eyes.

"Oh, not me," grinned Eric as he quickly got up. "Just keeping your seat warm."

"I should have asked if you wanted some coffee, too," apologized Ted as he sat down in the chair.

"I'm fine."

"So, what did you want to talk to me about that you didn't want big-mouth Marge getting ahold of?" Ted smiled a crooked smile. He and Eric occasionally shared gossip about the other workers.

"The new guy," answered Eric.

"What about him?" frowned Ted as he noticed and picked up the new file in front of him. "I trust you had sufficient time to look this over?"

Eric merely smiled and shrugged his shoulders as he watched Ted peruse the file.

"Everything looks in order."

"What about the history?"

Ted took another look and then furrowed his eyebrows. "That's odd. It only goes back to 2009."

"I did mention to Marge that I suspect the man of being someone from my past, who might be using an alias name."

"You told her that?"

"Yes," replied Eric. "I also mentioned that he might not be trustworthy, and that I would like a day or two to check him out."

"You actually told Marge all that?" smirked Ted as he shook his head. "What'd she say?"

"Well, she did remind me that a background investigation is done on all the new residents," elaborated Eric, "but that I was welcome to see what I could learn covertly, especially if the man is not who he claims to be."

"That explains why she left the file sitting out," realized Ted. "So, what didn't you tell her?"

"I don't want her to know that Vivian LaMont and I are personal friends," blurted out Eric. "If so, Marge could slip up and mention it to that man. And, from the looks of things, she seems more than casually interested in him, if you get my meaning."

"He's 93 years old!" laughed Ted.

"But, if he's who I suspect he is, then he's also an experienced con artist," rebutted Eric. "One who has left a long line of broken hearts and emptied bank accounts behind."

"Was Vivian one of his victims?" guessed Ted.

"No," answered Eric. "But, she was a witness to one of his crimes and is in fear for her life. She wouldn't even come to the dining room today. I personally took all her meals to her room for her."

362

"Perhaps she has mistaken him for someone else?"

"If only that were true, but I'm certain it's him. I believe his name is Mark Killingham, and if so, my own mother was one of his victims," revealed Eric.

"That's not good," frowned Ted.

Eric pulled up an empty stool and sat down beside Ted. "This place is full of wealthy widows."

"Lonely ones, too," added Ted.

"Did I ever tell you that I have a brother that is only 11 days younger than me?" asked Eric.

"No," replied Ted, "but if that man is your father, wouldn't he have recognized you by now?"

"I doubt it," replied Eric. "He hasn't seen me since I was a baby. Still, if one of those other nurses slips up and calls me by my last name, he'll know who I am. My mother changed our last names from Killingham to Santori when I was just a baby, so Mark would know the name if he heard it again. It was her maiden name."

"Just tell me if it's none of my business," mentioned Ted, "but why wouldn't you want him to know who you are?"

"Because he could become dangerous toward Vivian," answered Eric. "As I told you, she is an eyewitness to one of the crimes he committed."

"What kind of crime?" delved Ted.

"Murder," answered Eric as he folded his arms.

"What room is he in?" grilled Ted as he glanced again at the file.

"He's out in one of the cottages," replied Eric.

"We're gonna have to tell Marge about this," advised Ted. "We can't have someone like that in here."

"Marge did say I could have a day or two," reminded Eric.

"You still carry?"

"Never leave home without it," assured Eric.

"Me, neither."

"I promised Vivian I would come back to her room after I got off duty," said Eric. "There was more she wanted to tell me."

"You'd better fill me in," warned Ted.

"I will, later," promised Eric. "Just keep an eye out for our new resident, and warn us if you spot him. I don't want him to see me anywhere near Vivian or her room."

363

"Just how are you and Vivian related?"

"I never said we are."

Ted met Eric's gaze with his penetrating blue eyes. He was not about to let it go. Unlike Eric, Ted did not dye his hair but had allowed it to go completely white, which made him somewhat intimidating when he chose to be. Eric, on the other hand, had a full head of thick dark hair that was in excellent condition. Eric also worked out at the gym each day and had the body of a much younger man.

"Very well, apparently she's my aunt," admitted Eric.

"Mark's sister?"

"If it's him."

"Okay. I got your back."

"Thanks, man, I owe you," nodded Eric as he got up.

"Several times over," agreed Ted with a tight-lipped grin as he thought of their time in the Gulf War together. "Alright, get out of here. I'll call her room if he comes back up here tonight."

Unseen by Eric or Ted, Mark Killingham had managed to stealthily slip past them and make his way down the south wing's long hallway. Upon arriving at room 23, Mark looked each way first to be sure he was alone before silently testing the doorknob to find out whether it was locked. *Of course, it is,* frowned Mark as he tried to decide what he should do next.

After all, he and Vivian had continued emailing one another for several years, always with the promise on her part that one day she would see him again. Most of her emails started with "Hi Sweetheart" or something similar, and usually were signed "Love always, Vivian."

Mark took a deep breath as he thought of the afternoon they had spent together in 2009, and of the passion between them. *He had relived the experience over and over again in his mind. No other woman before or since had come close to satisfying the unquenchable desire he still had for Vivian. Even her emails had been suggestive and enticing. So, why had she avoided seeing him in person for so long, especially after all that had passed between them? It was finally time to find out!*

Quickly rapping on her door with three quick knocks as he had seen Eric do earlier, Mark waited for her response. *Hopefully, she would open it before Eric returned.*

From inside, her voice could be heard. "Eric, is that you?"

"I'm off duty now," replied Mark, hoping that his imitation of Eric's voice was adequate to fool her.

Footsteps approached from inside.

Though slightly slimmer than he had been 14 years earlier, Mark was still quite healthy for a man his age, including the ways that counted most. He had taken great care to look his best, with his silver hair neatly combed back on each side and parted down the middle. Mark's face was clean shaven, and the scent of an expensive men's tonic surrounded him. The small lead crystal vase he held contained a single daffodil. He had just picked it from the courtyard outside, near his cottage.

The sounds of a deadbolt being unlocked, and then the lock on the door handle, were carefully followed by an almost silent turning of the doorknob. Just as the door started to inch its way open, Mark adeptly inserted the right toe of his steel-tipped cowboy boot into the space and left it there.

"Mark?" muttered Vivian as she slowly backed away from the door. The look on her face revealed grave concern.

"Hi Sweetheart," flirted Mark as he pushed open the door, just enough to go inside. "This is for you."

Vivian made no effort whatsoever to take the vase from him as he closed the door behind himself, so Mark went ahead and placed it on the table by the window.

"How did you find me?" demanded Vivian as she studied her unwelcome visitor, almost as if he were an insect.

"Is that any way to treat the love of your life?" grinned Mark as he approached, put his arms around Vivian, pulled her close, and began ardently kissing her on the mouth. It was several moments before she began to relax and kiss him back. Finally, she put her arms around him, as well. The electricity that passed between them was extraordinary.

In his haste to see Vivian again, Mark had forgotten to relock the door to her room.

"Vivian, I thought we agreed you would keep this locked," came Eric's voice as he unexpectedly entered the room. Upon seeing Mark and Vivian locked in a romantic embrace, Eric froze. *Awkward,* thought Eric as he studied them. *Had Vivian lied to him?*

"Oh, Eric, thank God you're here!" exclaimed Vivian as she suddenly began struggling to free herself from Mark's grasp.

"Get away from her!" commanded Eric as he took a menacing step towards Mark.

Vivian cleared her throat uncomfortably. "Eric, this is your father, Mark Killingham."

Mark slowly began to smile as he let go of Vivian and turned his attention toward Eric. "Hello, son."

Eric folded his arms and silently glared at him.

"Perhaps we should all sit down," suggested Vivian as she motioned toward the table by the window. "Thank you for the flower, by the way."

Mark smiled and nodded as he waited for Vivian to sit down first. He then sat down across from her.

Eric grabbed another chair by the wall and pulled it up to the table. He studied Mark carefully for several moments before finally sitting down. Both he and Mark had folded their arms, and were waiting for Vivian to begin.

"Eric, there are some things you should know."

"There are some things I'd like to know myself," interjected Mark.

"Okay, we can start there," agreed Vivian. *Perhaps hearing their conversation might answer some of Eric's questions, as well.*

"I would like our conversation to be private," clarified Mark.

"I'm afraid this is as private as it's going to get. There's nothing you have to say that you can't say in front of Eric," persisted Vivian. "Besides, it's time he knew the truth, don't you think?"

"What truth?" challenged Mark.

Vivian glanced at Eric and then at Mark again. "Well, as both of you know, my real name is Vivian LaMont. My mother, Ellie Mae, was pregnant with me when this picture was taken." She then pulled out and placed an old black and white photo on her table that showed Jack, James and Ellie Mae Killingham standing on the beach, with Jack and James each holding one of the twin boys. It was the same picture she had already shown to Eric Santori earlier that day.

Mark frowned at the photo but remained silent. He was clearly troubled by it.

366

"I've already mentioned to Eric here that our parents were siblings, just as we are," continued Vivian, "and that the tall man holding you, Mark, was our father."

"Meaning, of course, that you and I are the only two left in this photo that are still alive," observed Mark.

"Actually, I wasn't born yet," pointed out Vivian.

"And yet, there you are," flirted Mark as he pointed at Ellie Mae's slightly enlarged abdomen in the photo.

"Only in the making," corrected Vivian with a sly smile. "Don't forget, I'm only 91."

"Is it true that you murdered your brother Jack?" demanded Eric as he turned to Mark.

Mark remained silent for several moments before responding. "I've already told Vivian how very sorry I am for what happened, and she and I have been in touch by email for years now. She is well aware of why I did it."

"Why don't you fill me in," pressed Eric, his arms still folded.

"I'm surprised Vivian hasn't told you about the treasure yet," commented Mark as he unfolded his arms and put his hands on his knees. "The same one she's been after herself for all these years."

"I was planning to tell him about it tonight," advised Vivian with a tight-lipped grin.

"Treasure?" sniggered Eric as he shook his head with disgust. "You killed your own brother for some treasure? Really?"

"It's not what you think."

"Then fill me in," fumed Eric. "You've got a lot of nerve faking your own death like that!"

"It was either that or prison," justified Mark.

"He does have a point," agreed Vivian.

"Do you know how it felt to finally FIND you, but only to learn that you were DEAD?" questioned Eric. "I had searched for you for years before that."

"Just how did you learn I was dead?" asked Mark with a mischievous grin. "From what I understand, you were busy serving one of your many tours of duty overseas."

"From your obituary," replied Eric, "right before I went to visit your grave. They do give us leave once in a while, especially when there is a death in the family."

367

"Sorry about that," shrugged Mark, "but you have to admit, it's not a bad place for poor Jack to be buried."

"What made you decide to steal his identity?" grilled Eric.

"Like I said, it was either that or prison."

"If no one knew what you did, then what for?" delved Eric. "Bigamy, perhaps?"

"Among other things."

"And you don't even try to deny it?" scoffed Eric as he shook his head. "Unbelievable."

"If I understand correctly," commented Mark, "you did eight tours of duty, and served in every branch of the military."

"Not the Marines." Eric narrowed his eyes at Mark.

"Okay, all the others, then."

"You never answered my question," reminded Eric.

"Which one?" asked Mark with a crooked smile.

"Don't you get smart with me!" snapped Eric as he unfolded his arms, pounded his right fist on the table, and leaned close to Mark in a menacing manner. "I'm in no mood to play games!"

"Definitely a chip off the old block," laughed Vivian as she watched the interaction between Eric and his father.

Both men paused to glare at her for a moment before resuming their conversation.

"Tell me," shouted Eric, "why would you murder your own brother for some stupid treasure?"

"Probably for the same reason I was married to two beautiful women at the same time," answered Mark. "I'm no good."

"That's what Mama always told us," fumed Eric. "I grew up all my life hearing about how I have a brother only 11 days younger than me. I even tracked him down once, between tours, but decided against contacting him."

"Why?" Mark seemed genuinely surprised.

"Because I didn't want to ruin his life, finding out something like that," replied Eric. "Just in case he didn't know about it already."

"Unfortunately, he did find me once," revealed Mark. "It had been Kevin's lifelong dream to finally meet me."

"And you ended up doing the same thing to him that you've done to everyone else in your life," interjected Vivian. "You stole the poor kid's identity and put him and his young wife through hell before they were able to finally elude you."

"What do you know about it?" demanded Mark as he turned his attention toward Vivian.

"I keep up on things," assured Vivian.

"At least Kevin *has* a wife," muttered Eric as he sat back down. "My wife Rose was killed in a plane crash while flying out to be with me during my first tour of duty in Okinawa, right at the tail end of the Vietnam War. She was pregnant with our first child at the time."

"I'm sorry," responded Mark. "I didn't know."

"Did you ever marry again after that?" asked Vivian as she put a comforting hand on Eric's arm.

"Not in my line of work," replied Eric. "Besides, there was no one left who could have replaced her, even if they'd tried."

"Exactly what was your specialty in the military, anyway?" grilled Vivian.

"I was a field medic during my first tour," revealed Eric.

"I see," nodded Mark. "So, that's what made you decide to work in a place like this. I was wondering why a highly trained soldier would settle for working here."

"Eric, what else did you do in the military?" pressed Vivian. "What about during your other tours? Were you still a medic?"

"Not after that, no," answered Eric. "I went to the dark side."

"The dark side," repeated Mark with a grin on his face.

"My Killingham side, no doubt," retorted Eric.

"How many people did you actually kill in the line of duty, anyway?" grilled Vivian. "Do you even know?"

"That's classified."

"Weren't you a shooter?" queried Mark.

"Even if I was," replied Eric, "that's not something I can talk about. Clearly, you were never in the military, or you'd know that."

"Then why should we tell you about the people we've killed?" asked Mark in a slightly mocking tone.

"What does he mean?" demanded Eric as he turned to Vivian.

"Perhaps you should ask her about some of her husbands, and what finally happened to them," suggested Mark.

"I was going to tell him about that tonight, too," snapped Vivian, "but we're still talking about *you two* at the moment."

"Husbands?" Eric gave Vivian a concerned look.

"Mark has accused me of being a black widow," indicated Vivian, "so I've made it a point to prove him wrong."

369

"By avoiding me?" grilled Mark.

"Yes, and to make sure that I didn't end up killing my only remaining brother," indicated Vivian. "I don't think I could live with that, even with it being you."

"It hasn't been easy living with what I did to Jack, Jr.," admitted Mark, "but I truly do regret it. I've told you that countless times in my emails, and begged your forgiveness."

"All you wanted was to get on my good side," sighed Vivian, "just so you could have another roll in the sack with me."

Eric was clearly upset by the revelation, and it was all he could do to contain the sudden anger he felt.

"That's not true," differed Mark.

Mark and Vivian were oblivious to the rapid change in Eric's demeanor.

"Nevertheless," countered Vivian, "nothing excuses what you did to all those women you allegedly married. What about Linda Dixon or Betty Jean White, or even the one after that?"

"Be very careful what you say next," cautioned Mark. He was clearly becoming agitated with Vivian.

"Just how many women did you marry, anyway?" demanded Eric as glared at Mark.

"Your father had several other women after that," interjected Vivian, "but not until after Maria or Bobby Sue, and then there were countless others after that, as well."

"I think you've said enough," Mark advised Vivian as he got up and started to make his way around Eric to get to her.

"Not so fast," cautioned Eric. He was about to lose control.

"I'll bet you don't even know how many kids you've got out there, either," added Vivian as she smirked at Mark.

"You hypocritical inbred!" hollered Mark as he reached for Vivian's arm.

Without thinking, Eric intervened. He instinctively grabbed Mark's hands and easily held them in place behind his back as he pulled him close to restrict his movements. "Were you legally married to my mother or not?"

"Who do you think helped her keep that restaurant going while you were off gallivanting around shooting at people in Afghanistan?"

"My older brothers were all here to help take care of her."

"Your mother was too proud to ask any of them for help," advised Mark as he struggled to escape Eric's firm grasp.

"And, of course she would come to you?" scoffed Eric. "After everything you did to her?"

"Yes!" hollered Mark. "Maria was still very much in love with me, even after all of that."

"I don't believe you." Eric's inner rage was about to take over.

"I was the one who gave her the $30,000 to keep her afloat," revealed Mark. "You can look it up if you don't believe me."

"She would *never* have taken money from you!"

"Believe what you want, but I'm telling you the truth," promised Mark as he attempted again to pull free from Eric's tight hold on him. "She was also very lonely during that time."

"You're the one that had better be careful what you say next," cautioned Eric. He was about to explode.

"Maria was a very beautiful woman, and hopelessly in love with me," answered Mark with a naughty grin. "I'll never forget the time ...."

Sudden banging on the door to Vivian's room was what triggered the flashback that Eric experienced next.

Eric had not had an outright episode of post-traumatic stress disorder since retiring from the military in 2012, following his 32 years of service. It was what happened to him just before that, that had finally convinced him to retire and return to civilian life. Eric had purposely sought out the Happy Acres Nursing Home and Retirement Community in Seattle, Washington, due to its remote location and simple environment.

* * *

"Ted, behind you!" hollered Eric as he unexpectedly grabbed Mark's head in his hands, expertly breaking his neck before shoving him to the ground.

"The others are all dead, soldier," assured Ted. He was well aware that Eric was having an episode of PTSD and that he needed to play along with it. "No worries."

Eric suddenly drew his concealed weapon and took off the safety. "We need to get the remaining civilians out of here, sir."

"You worry about her," indicated Ted as he nodded towards Vivian. "I'll look after the others."

"Where's your weapon?" demanded Eric. "What if more of the insurgents show up?"

"Good point," agreed Ted as he drew his weapon, but left the safety on. "I'll be ready for 'em."

"Ted, your safety's still on," cautioned Eric as he gently put his free arm around Vivian. He was prepared to lead her from the enemy compound in which they were trapped.

"We don't want to end up shooting any innocent civilians, do we?" chuckled Ted. "You should put your safety on, too."

"Very well, sir," agreed Eric as he let go of Vivian long enough to return his handgun to safe mode.

"Perhaps we should wait here for backup," suggested Vivian.

"We're it," assured Eric. "The rest of our platoon is gone."

"Enemy snipers," interjected Ted.

"Then there's no way I'm going out there," argued Vivian.

"You're safe with us," promised Eric. "Just stay behind me."

"We just need to make it to the river," informed Ted. "There should be a bird waiting for us in the LZ."

"Agreed," nodded Eric. "That means landing zone, ma'am."

Realizing there was nothing she could do to dissuade him, Vivian finally decided to play along.

"At least no one else in the village is still up," Ted whispered to Vivian. He was, of course, referring to the other residents at the nursing home, and hoped that was indeed the case.

"Let's hope you're right," responded Vivian as she let Eric lead her from the room and down the long hall.

Ted decided to lock the door to Vivian's room behind them as they left. They would have to worry later about what to do with Mark Killingham, if that's who he really was.

Eric stealthily made his way down the south wing and past the nurse's station there.

"Strange that no one is here," remarked Ted.

"Perhaps they've gone for reinforcements," suggested Eric.

"Then we'd better hurry," recommended Ted. The last thing he wanted was for one of the residents to wander out into the hallway and see the two nurses armed with weapons while escorting Vivian outside.

"What about in the supply room?" questioned Eric as they reached the main nurse's station. "Perhaps they're hiding in there?"

"Let's not wait around to find out," insisted Ted. "We need to get her to safety first before we check it out."

"Agreed," nodded Eric as he proceeded toward the front door. He had a tight grip on Vivian's hand, and it was all she could do to keep up with him. Eric looked both ways with his weapon drawn before darting across the courtyard outside.

"The daffodils are sure beautiful this time of year," pointed out Vivian. It was her hope that noticing them might help Eric snap back to reality.

Eric merely nodded as he continued past the park benches and onto a curving cement footpath that continued to a lookout point nearby. The park bench at the lookout point was quaintly situated beneath a towering redwood. Several hundred feet below was the Duwamish River. Its sandy banks could be seen in the moonlight.

"She should be safe here, but she shouldn't be left alone," insisted Ted. "Eric, you wait here with this woman while I go back to secure the compound."

"Perhaps I should go," differed Eric.

"I am your commanding officer," reminded Ted. "It's my call."

"Yes, sir."

"You two have a seat on that bench and I'll be back shortly," indicated Ted as he nodded toward it.

Eric then sat down. He was still holding Vivian's hand.

"A cup of tea would be nice," mentioned Vivian as she wriggled her hand free from Eric's grasp.

"Are you okay?" asked Ted.

"We'll be fine," promised Vivian.

Eric seemed dazed for a moment as he put both hands on either side of his face and began to shake his head.

"I'll just hang out a bit longer," decided Ted. He wanted to be sure Eric was safe to leave alone with Vivian.

"What just happened?" asked Eric as he gave Vivian and Ted a questioning look. "What are we doing out here?"

"You can holster your weapon," mentioned Ted.

373

"Oh my God!" exclaimed Eric as he checked his weapon to see if any of the rounds had been fired. "What happened? I didn't shoot him, did I?"

"No, you didn't," promised Ted, "but I think you should stay here with Vivian until I get back." He then left.

"I am so sorry!" apologized Eric as he made sure the safety was on before putting his weapon away. "I hope I didn't frighten you."

"Not that much," assured Vivian. *How in the world had Eric managed to beat her to the punch? It had been her intention to finally do Mark in, but not like this!*

"Where's Mark?" grilled Eric.

"He won't be bothering us again," replied Vivian with a slight smile on her face.

"Please tell me what happened."

"Not until you calm down first. Let's wait for Ted to return."

"What aren't you telling me? What did I do?" demanded Eric.

Vivian then reached for Eric's hands and wrapped her own hands around them. "Some things happen for a reason in this life."

"I killed him, didn't I?"

"You've killed people before," reminded Vivian.

"Not like this."

"You don't even remember it, do you?"

Eric shook his head in the negative.

"There you go, temporary insanity." Vivian smiled a crooked smile. "You were simply saving my life. Mark was about to do me in when you intervened."

"Is that how it really went?"

"That would be my testimony, if anyone were ever to ask," assured Vivian. "And yes, that's how it went down."

"I can't believe I had another episode." Eric shook his head with dismay. "I haven't had one for over 14 years."

"Been there myself," came the voice of Ted from behind them. He was pushing a wheelchair in front of him, in which Mark Killingham's lifeless body was poised with a blanket draped across his lap. "Mr. Killingham said he needed to go for a walk."

Vivian slowly began to smile and nod with approval when she saw Ted toss the blanket aside and begin pulling Mark's body up from the chair.

374

Eric quickly got up to help.

"I kept telling him not to go for walks at night," mentioned Ted. "They really should have a railing here, too, just in case folks get too close to the edge."

"I see what you mean," replied Eric as the two of them finally managed to get Mark's body into standing position.

"Whoops!" grinned Vivian as she suddenly kicked Mark's body in the butt from behind, as hard as she could.

"Oh my," muttered Ted as Mark's body slipped from his grasp and toppled from the edge of the lookout point, toward the sandy beach below. It was several moments before the lifeless body finally landed.

Eric, too, had lost his grip on Mark when Vivian unexpectedly kicked him. *Unbelievable that a woman her age could kick like that!*

"Mark was right, you know," informed Vivian. "I did poison my husbands, all of them. They were each two-timing creeps that deserved it, though. Any one of them could have chosen to be faithful to me, and would still be here today."

"Not all men are like that," replied Eric.

"I know," smiled Vivian. "You will find a complete account of my many crimes in a journal inside my table drawer, but may want to think twice about telling anyone."

"Why?" frowned Eric.

"Because you are my sole heir, nephew dear," advised Vivian. "Insurance companies don't take kindly to paying out survivor benefits to the beneficiary of a murderer."

"Perhaps no one needs to know," suggested Ted. He was more than willing to split the proceeds with Eric, if he were amenable to it.

"Did I mention that I was diagnosed with stage 4 cancer and have only a short time left to live?" questioned Vivian as she got up and sat down in the wheelchair.

"I'm so sorry," apologized Eric. "I had no right to bring you out here like this."

"I can push her back up," offered Ted.

"Nonsense, gentlemen," differed Vivian as she took the safety off on the wheelchair. "I'm sure I must have died trying to save him."

"What do you mean?" grilled Eric as he watched Vivian suddenly push the wheels of the wheelchair toward the precipice.

375

"Farewell, gentlemen," bid Vivian as she and the chair suddenly were propelled by momentum off the edge. "Remember me, Eric," came her voice as it trailed toward the bottom before landing near Mark's body.

Eric and Ted stood there for several moments staring with disbelief, unable to grasp at first what had happened.

"Do you think she's still alive?" asked Ted.

"Seriously?" asked Eric upon seeing the position of her body where it had landed.

"I think we'd better keep this between us, and let the chips fall where they may," suggested Ted.

Eric merely nodded. He was still numb from the experience.

"It will all work out," promised Ted. "The bridge is not too far from here, and bodies do occasionally turn up there."

April 29, 2023

Saturday afternoon was every bit as overcast and drizzly as the morning had been. Increasing wind and rain were in the forecast.

"Perhaps flying isn't such a good idea," mentioned Kevin as he followed Jim and Chip onto Jim's waiting Learjet.

"She is weatherproof," chuckled Jim as he carefully set down his laptop before heading back outside to unmoor his craft.

"He did the preflight check already," advised Linda from the couch seat.

"What are *you* doing here?" frowned Kevin. "I thought you were tired and needed a rest."

"I'm good," grinned Linda. "Sheree let me know what you guys were up to, so I thought I'd come along."

"She's not coming," Kevin advised Jim as he came back on board. He could feel Linda's scowl of disapproval without even bothering to look.

"That's entirely up to her," smirked Jim as he sat down in the pilot's chair. "MIRA, prepare flight plan for Seattle."

"My wife's the same way," grinned Chip. "Once a woman's mind is made up, there's usually no changing it."

Still troubled by what Jim had told him about Linda's obsession with Lenny Owens during high school, Kevin was in no mood to deal with it.

376

"You're not the boss of me, you know," whispered Linda to Kevin when he sat down beside her. *She was sick and tired of him trying to tell her what to do. She had just as much right as he did to decide whether or not she wanted to come along.*

"That's not it," replied Kevin in a soft tone. *He did not want Jim or Chip to know that he and Linda were arguing.*

"Buckle up, folks," reminded Jim in a loud voice.

"I don't try and tell you what to do," grumbled Linda as she buckled her seatbelt and gave Kevin a stern glance.

"Perhaps going to the reunion in the first place was a mistake," muttered Kevin as he snapped his seatbelt into place. He then folded his arms and turned to stare out the window.

"MIRA, begin data recorder," commanded Jim.

"Data recorder engaged," verified MIRA.

"Today is April 29, 2023, at 3:35 p.m., Pacific Standard Time," mentioned Jim for the recorder. "Departing from Oceanview Academy Airport, destination Seattle-Tacoma International Airport."

"Confirmed. Aircraft system and flight parameters have been uplinked to satellite relay," stated MIRA.

Linda was clearly frustrated with Kevin's behavior and had no idea what she had done to upset him so much.

"MIRA, initiate takeoff sequence."

"Takeoff sequence initiated," responded MIRA.

Without further warning, the engines began to spool. Jim quickly set his flaps, aligned his aircraft with the runway centerline, and advanced his throttles. "Everyone buckled up?"

"Yes, Jim," came the voices of Chip, Kevin and Linda.

"Symmetrical stabilization acquired," verified MIRA.

"MIRA, fire thrusters," ordered Jim.

"Thrusters firing now," confirmed MIRA. The Learjet suddenly thrust off and began to accelerate at a rapid speed down the private runway at Oceanview Academy.

"146 knots indicated airspeed," advised MIRA.

Kevin and Linda both silently watched through the window as the precipice ahead raced toward them again.

"We'll be there before you know it," remarked Chip in an effort to lighten the mood.

"Positive rate of climb attained," announced MIRA. "Landing gear retracting."

377

The craggy ocean-top bluffs below them quickly disappeared from view as Jim's Learjet ascended into the airspace above the expansive ocean.

"A lot of memories down there," mumbled Linda as Jim's aircraft circled back and flew over Oceanview Academy one last time before veering its course toward the Seattle-Tacoma International Airport.

Kevin merely nodded but did not respond. *Would Linda have really given herself to that colored boy if he'd been interested in her instead of that other girl?*

"MIRA, continue to flight level four seven zero."

"Course plotted for Seattle-Tacoma International Airport with an alternate destination at Snohomish County Airport nearby," announced MIRA. "Winds aloft checked, weather en route and destination checked. Flight plan filed and release time within your timeframe, Jim. Squawk code entered. Fuel load is adequate with a generous reserve. Estimated arrival time in 1 hour and 47 minutes."

"Thank you, MIRA," added Jim.

"You are welcome, Jim," responded MIRA.

"Didn't you tell us before that 'flight level four seven zero' means 47,000 feet?" questioned Linda, loud enough for Jim to hear.

"You *were* paying attention," grinned Jim.

"Don't encourage him," teased Chip. He had flown with Jim often enough to know better.

Kevin then nodded in agreement.

"I'll keep that in mind, gentlemen," smiled Linda. *Just because Kevin was in a foul mood, that was no reason she needed to be!*

"MIRA, engage autopilot," instructed Jim as he took off his headset and stood to stretch.

"Autopilot engaged," responded MIRA.

"So, Chip, tell me what you've got," directed Jim as he grabbed his laptop and headed for the couch seat where Linda and Kevin were seated. Jim quickly slid the work table out in front of them. He and Chip then sat down across from them.

"Well, as I mentioned earlier, we got back the DNA and other results from Mr. Killingham and it looks like a match."

"To Mark Killingham," recalled Kevin. "Yeah, we know."

"At least it appears that way," advised Chip. "Of course, the Medical Examiner did ask us to stop by his office later today for his off-the-record opinion on something else related to the matter."

"But he didn't say what it was?" grilled Jim.

Chip merely shook his head in the negative.

Jim pressed a button on his smartwatch. "MIRA, call Bill Huong." After only two rings, Bill answered.

"Jim? Where are you? I thought you guys were stopping by."

"We're in flight to Seattle."

"Who's with you?"

"Chip, Kevin and Linda."

Bill seemed to hesitate before continuing. "If my suspicions are correct, Mark may have murdered his twin brother Jack before assuming his identity thereafter."

"Are you certain?" questioned Jim.

"As certain as I can be with what little we know," answered Bill. "Too many things about Jack Killingham from March 23, 2009 forward just don't add up."

"Don't forget, that was his birthday," interjected Linda.

"Not a very good one, apparently," mentioned Chip.

"And, this is strictly off-the-record," added Bill. "What we have is pure speculation, based on circumstantial evidence."

"Of course," smirked Jim. "What do we have?"

"Well, for one thing," elaborated Bill, "Jack had a life insurance policy that named his sister Vivian as the sole beneficiary."

"Would the company have known Jack was dead if Mark assumed his identity after murdering him?" grilled Jim.

"Apparently, they received an anonymous tip about it, someone claiming Jack had been murdered," replied Bill.

"And?"

"The company searched for both Jack and Vivian for years, without success."

"Vivian LaMont?" questioned Jim as he nodded towards Chip's tattered briefcase where the obituary was stashed.

"I wonder ...," mused Bill as he broke off in midsentence.

"Bill, Chip's got something," indicated Jim as Chip opened up his briefcase and began thumbing through the paper file inside.

"Here it is," offered Chip as he handed a piece of paper to Jim.

379

"Bill, we've got an obituary here for a Vivian LaMont. She was a resident from Happy Acres," revealed Jim.

"Huh," muttered Bill. "I guess I'd better run a sibling DNA test on her. We should still have what we need to compare her against Mr. Killingham, from when we tested him against the guy buried in Mark Killingham's grave."

"Yes, please do that right away," agreed Jim.

"The guy we spoke with at Happy Acres mentioned that Vivian may have died on the same day as Mr. Killingham," revealed Chip. "He also said they suspected some sort of foul play, but just couldn't be sure. He wouldn't tell me anything else."

"Who is *they*?" Linda whispered to Kevin.

Kevin shrugged his shoulders but remained silent. His arms were still folded. *Why would someone from Happy Acres suspect foul play if the body of Mark Killingham had been found nearly a mile away?*

"It doesn't say anything about foul play in the obituary," frowned Jim as he finished reading it.

"No, it doesn't," agreed Chip, "but that's what the guy from Happy Acres told me on the phone when I called him last night."

"I wonder why he would think that?" asked Jim.

"That's a good question," agreed Chip.

"Well, the bodies I have down here at the morgue were each either thrown or voluntarily jumped from somewhere pretty high up, and at least one of them appears to have been moved," advised Bill. "They were both in pretty bad shape when they got to us, but of interest, Mr. Killingham appears to have other injuries inconsistent with the fall that allegedly killed him. The final results should be back by tomorrow."

"Perhaps they were both murdered before being thrown from a drop-off," speculated Jim.

"Or perhaps it was a murder suicide," guessed Chip.

"If that's true, then why would Mr. Killingham have gone somewhere else to kill himself?" Kevin finally asked.

"That's a good point," acknowledged Jim.

"Mr. Killingham's and Vivian LaMont's postmortem conditions are way too similar to overlook. They've got to be connected," deduced Bill.

"If the man was Mark Killingham, and the woman was his sister Vivian," questioned Jim, "then who else might have wanted them dead? And why?"

"That's what we'd all like to know," assured Kevin.

"Perhaps when we talk to the people at Happy Acres," reminded Chip, "they can help us get to the bottom of this."

"You guys be careful," cautioned Bill. "Odds are good that someone who either works there or goes to visit is responsible. That place is pretty far off the beaten path."

"Don't worry, Kevin and I are both prepared," grinned Jim.

"Hey, I carry, too," reminded Chip.

"Just be safe, and don't trust anyone from that place," bid Bill as he ended the call.

"Hey, I'm always safe," promised Jim. "We'll be in touch."

It was almost 7:00 p.m. on April 29, 2023, and none of them had eaten yet. Finding an empty hangar for Jim's Learjet and obtaining a rental car at the Seattle-Tacoma International Airport had taken much longer than expected. And now, they were stuck in endless traffic while Jim negotiated the 45-minute detour forced upon them. Even Chip was in a disagreeable mood, and that was rare.

"How does it make sense for the southbound traffic to be diverted this far north?" demanded Linda.

"It should eventually lead us to an interchange, and then across the river," advised Jim.

"Perhaps we should be looking for a restaurant in the meantime," suggested Chip. *He could not remember being so hungry, at least not anytime recently.*

"Even a gas station would be good," added Linda. "I'm not sure how much longer I can wait to use the restroom."

"I'll see what I can do," promised Jim.

"At least the rush hour seems to be tapering off," pointed out Kevin as they reached a congested cloverleaf interchange where it was finally possible to access the northbound Seattle Bridge over the Duwamish River.

"I'll bet the people going the other way aren't very happy, either," mentioned Chip as he shook his head.

"At least they still have four lanes of travel," reminded Kevin.

381

"That's true, we have only two," snickered Jim as he followed the other southbound vehicles onto the portion of bridge that had been temporarily cordoned off to allow for a southbound direction of travel as part of the detour.

"Look, there it is!" exclaimed Linda.

High on a nearby hill sat Happy Acres, prominently indicated by a huge roadside sign.

"Let's just eat there," suggested Kevin. "They would have to have a public restroom and a place to eat."

"Well, there sure aren't any gas stations or restaurants down here," pointed out Jim as he pulled onto the narrow, winding road leading to the Happy Acres Nursing Home and Retirement Community.

"They must've had quite a storm recently," recognized Chip as they made their way up the mountain, past some fallen trees and an excessive amount of other natural debris.

"You may need to stop before we get there," warned Linda. "I can't wait any longer."

"We're almost there," advised Jim as they finally reached the entrance gate. It had seen better days but was in good repair.

"You'd better hurry up!" exclaimed Linda. "Otherwise, I'm opening the door and hopping out right here."

"Alright, alright," responded Jim as he zoomed to a stop under a covered drive near the front entrance.

"I sure hope they're not closed for the night." Kevin suddenly grinned as he watched Linda fumble to unfasten her seatbelt before exiting the vehicle and urgently dash toward the front door of Happy Acres Nursing Home.

"You and me both," agreed Chip as he got out of the vehicle. "I'm next after Linda."

"I'm sure they have more than one restroom in a place this size," chuckled Jim as he got out and stood up to stretch.

Chip was close on Linda's heels as she pushed open the heavy glass door to go inside. *Strange that it wasn't automatic,* she thought as she glanced around for the nearest restroom.

"Down there," indicted Chip as he pointed toward an open area by the nurse's station.

"May I help you?" asked Ted as he watched her dash inside the ladies' room without answering.

382

"Where's the men's room?" demanded Chip.

"Right over there, on the other side," answered Ted.

"Hey, thanks man, I'll be right back."

Just then, Jim and Kevin came inside and approached the nurse's station. "Are you Eric?" questioned Jim.

"No, I'm not. But, you must be Jim Otterman."

"Sorry we're later than expected," apologized Jim as he gave Ted a puzzled look. "We weren't expecting that detour."

"Understandable," smiled Ted. "My name's Ted, by the way."

"Nice to meet you, Ted," acknowledged Jim as he shook his hand. "This is Kevin Killingham, and that woman who just raced past you is his wife Linda."

"And I'm Chip Priest," came the voice of Jim's partner from behind them, as he emerged from the men's room.

Kevin merely nodded in acknowledgment before heading for the restroom himself.

"Sorry about that," apologized Linda as she finally approached the nurse's station. "My name is Linda."

"Ma'am," smiled Ted. *She certainly was easy on the eyes!*

"Where can we get something to eat?" questioned Linda. "None of us has eaten yet."

Jim frowned at her but she ignored him.

Ted began to laugh. "Well, technically the kitchen is closed for the night, but we can certainly make you folks some sandwiches. I'll call Eric and let him know you're here. I'm sure he'll want to see you. In fact, you just missed him, so he probably hasn't gotten too far yet."

"How long will it take for him to come back?" grilled Jim.

"Probably as long as it will take us to make up those sandwiches," replied Ted. "Follow me."

"I'll join you in a minute," promised Jim. "I'm next in line after Kevin."

"Understandable," nodded Linda. *She had barely made it to the restroom in time herself.*

"Call Eric," said Ted to his smartwatch as he headed down the long hallway behind the nurse's station, and then toward the main dining room on the east wing.

"Yes?" came Eric's voice.

"They're here."

383

"I'm turning around now."

"We'll be in the kitchen, making up some sandwiches," advised Ted. "They haven't eaten yet."

"Make one for me," requested Eric.

"Sure thing," agreed Ted as he ended the call. Then, turning his attention to Linda and Chip, Ted nodded with his head toward an open doorway ahead. "That's the kitchen."

"Nice," approved Linda when she saw the large, commercial food prep area. "I wouldn't mind having a kitchen like this."

"Maybe someday," remarked Kevin from behind them.

"Well, I'm not exactly ready for Happy Acres just yet," reminded Linda with a mischievous grin as she turned around. *Perhaps flirting with Kevin might help him get over whatever was bothering him, and who knew what that might be.*

Linda's alabaster skin and piercing blue eyes were what had attracted Kevin to her in the first place, especially framed by her luxurious, dark brown hair. Besides, he never could stay mad at her for very long.

"Anything we can do to help?" offered Chip.

"Yeah, sure," replied Ted as he grabbed a loaf of bread from a nearby shelf and tossed it to Chip. "The island countertop is clean."

Chip wasted no time in opening the package to the loaf of bread and began laying out slices of it on the island's white marble countertop.

Ted then handed a huge container of mayonnaise to Kevin.

"I'll just have mustard on mine," indicated Linda.

Ted then handed a giant jar of mustard to Linda. "Knives are in the third drawer on the right."

Linda carefully set the jar down and went over to wash her hands at the large, stainless steel sink.

Chip then attempted to remove the lid from the mustard jar.

"Try this," suggested Ted as he tossed him a rubber lid remover.

Jim arrived on the scene just in time to watch the assembly line. "Is that turkey breast?"

"Chicken," answered Ted. "But, we do have some turkey breast in there somewhere." He then opened the huge double wide commercial refrigerator and began searching.

"Chicken's fine," relented Jim as he waved his smartwatch over Ted's to send him payment for the meal.

"That's not necessary," objected Ted.

"It's the least I can do," insisted Jim.

Ted then looked on his watch to see how much Jim had sent him and was flabbergasted. *Two hundred dollars?*

"For your trouble, too." Jim smiled a crooked smile. He loved seeing the look on people's faces when he was generous. *Perhaps now, Ted might be more forthcoming with information when it was time to question him.*

"Thank you very much!"

Eric Santori was irritated with himself for giving up so easily and leaving when he did. *Was he afraid of finally meeting his half-brother for the first time? What would he say to him? Would Kevin even know who he was?*

These and other thoughts troubled Eric as he made his way back toward the Happy Acres Nursing Home. Try as he might, he simply could not remember the PTSD episode where he had killed Mark Killingham. *How in the world would he ever explain that to Kevin? Could Kevin be persuaded to agree with the decision he and Ted had made to keep it to themselves? After all, Mark had been a very bad man and had truly deserved what happened to him.*

Upon finally reaching the parking lot at Happy Acres, Eric was still deep in thought when he parked his 1995 Camry. He had chosen not to insert himself into Kevin's life when locating him back in 1983. That had been between his first and second tours of duty.

Would Kevin's Linda turn out to be anything like the Linda he had married before Rose? Sadly, the marriage had ended in annulment when she had learned of his decision to join the military. True, he should have consulted with Linda first before taking such a step, but he had run out of options. No other employer would take him at the time and he needed to provide for his new bride. That had been in 1977. It was two years later in 1979 that he had met and married Rose, but only after finally realizing that Linda was never coming back.

In some ways, Eric had loved Linda even more than Rose, and had never gotten over losing her. *What had happened to her, anyway, and why in the world was he thinking of her now?*

Eric's thick black hair gently fluttered in the breeze as he made his way inside. After stopping inside the front door to straighten his hair with a comb that he kept in his pocket, Eric admired the reflection of his handsome Italian face in the door's glass. He quickly ran his comb through his neatly trimmed goatee, as well. Eric wanted to look his best when meeting Kevin. Eric was in excellent physical condition, and worked out each day. Was Kevin still in shape, too? He was about to find out. Eric then made his way toward the nurse's station.

Kevin immediately noticed Eric Santori's distinct Killingham family facial features the moment he saw him, but continued to stare with disbelief as Eric approached. *Why hadn't Jim warned him he would be meeting this man? Was he a sibling he had never met?*

What Kevin didn't see at first was the expression on Linda's face when she saw Eric Santori. Even Eric had not seen Linda yet, as he had been completely focused on Kevin at that moment.

Eric Santori? Linda silently gasped as she stared at him with disbelief. *Why was he here?* She suddenly thought of her marriage to Eric Santori in 1977 and how she'd had it annulled after only 11 months, something she had never mentioned to Kevin. Even her parents had kept silent about it. It had not been until Valentine's Day in 1979 that Linda married Kevin. Nevertheless, Linda had thought of Eric often over the years and had wondered what happened to him, but never imagined she would see him again.

"Kevin, I'm your brother Eric." Eric extended a hand to Kevin.

Kevin appeared for a moment to be in shock, and did not shake hands with him just yet.

"Santori was my mother's maiden name," added Eric. "My real name is Eric Killingham."

Linda suddenly fainted onto the floor beside them, gaining their attention at once.

10. Artifact

Eric and Kevin both knelt beside Linda at the same time.

"Linda?" muttered Eric as he gently reached for her and pulled her close. Eric suddenly felt tears welling up in his eyes, something that had not happened to him for years, not even after killing Mark.

"Excuse me," said Kevin as he reached for Linda and carefully extricated her from Eric's grasp. "That's my wife."

"This is *your* wife?" questioned Eric.

"For 44 years now," informed Kevin as he studied Eric more closely. *How did Eric know who she was? He had clearly said Linda's name, even though they had not yet been introduced.*

"I'm sorry," interjected Jim. "Perhaps I should have stopped at that sandwich shop we saw this afternoon, but how could I know there wouldn't be anyplace else to eat until now?" He was trying to change the subject before things got out of hand.

"Let's get your wife onto that couch over there," suggested Eric. "Mind if I help you move her?"

"I got her," advised Kevin as he stubbornly picked Linda up by himself and struggled to carry her.

"Are you sure you don't need some help?" pressed Eric. He could tell from a glance that lifting Linda was hard on Kevin's back.

"Just how do you know my wife, anyway?" demanded Kevin as he turned to face his half-brother after placing Linda on the couch.

Before Eric could answer, Ted quickly grilled him, "How come you never mentioned having another brother?" *The resemblance between Eric and Kevin was undeniable.*

"He's my half-brother," advised Eric.

"Did you know Kevin's half-brother would be here?" Chip whispered to Jim.

Jim smiled a crooked smile and imperceptibly nodded.

"Older or younger?" pressed Ted. *He had served with Eric in the military during four tours of duty, yet Eric had never mentioned having a half-brother.*

"Older," answered Eric. "I was born on January 18, 1956; Kevin was born on January 29, 1956."

"That's only 11 days," calculated Ted.

"That's right," confirmed Eric. "My father Mark was married to two women at the same time. Maria Santori was my mother and Bobby Sue Johnson was Kevin's mother."

"Your mother actually told you this?" questioned Kevin. *His mother had never told him anything about it while he was growing up.*

"It was no secret," replied Eric. "Mama told me often of the time our mothers decided to confront Mark together when we were just babies. My mother held you, Kevin, while your mother held me. They wanted to see if Mark would even know the difference between us when he saw us together."

"Did he?" scowled Kevin.

"No."

"What a sleazebag he was," responded Kevin.

"No argument here," agreed Eric.

"You two clearly have a lot to talk about," interjected Chip, "but I'm starved. Can we continue this over a sandwich? I'm Jim's partner Chip, by the way."

"Pleased to meet you," acknowledged Eric as he shook Chip's hand.

Kevin then unexpectedly shook Eric's hand, too, and gave him a brief hug and a slap on the back. "Hey, it is good to finally meet you, but I would still like to know how you know my wife."

"You will need to ask Linda how we know each other," advised Eric as they sat down at one of the tables to eat.

"I'm asking you."

"She might not appreciate my saying anything without her consent."

"Listen, Eric," began Kevin as he got into his half-brother's face and suddenly grabbed the front of his shirt. "You'd better start talking."

"Very well," agreed Eric, though he was clearly not the least bit intimidated. "Linda and I first met when her parents were on holiday up in Bellevue, Washington in 1977."

"Keep going," urged Kevin as he finally let go of Eric's shirt.

"It was a whirlwind romance," added Eric.

The others were silent, anxiously waiting for Eric to continue. All but Kevin were quietly eating their sandwiches.

"It was less than a year later when she had our marriage annulled," continued Eric.

Kevin looked as if he had been punched in the gut, and it was several moments before he was able to speak. "You were married to my wife?"

Eric nodded, raised his eyebrows and shrugged his shoulders. "It was before she ever met you."

"I can't believe she never mentioned it."

"She was pretty upset with me for joining the military without her consent," described Eric. "That was one of the reasons she decided to have the marriage annulled."

"What was the other?" pressed Kevin.

"There was another woman," admitted Eric, rather sheepishly. "I really blew it. Linda was probably one of the best things that ever happened to me, and I couldn't even get that right."

"What about Rose?" grilled Ted from behind them.

"That was the woman I ended up marrying in 1979," explained Eric. "On Valentine's Day."

"Seriously?" chuckled Kevin as he shook his head. "That's the exact same day Linda and I were married."

"You don't say. Well, Rose was killed in a plane crash," replied Eric. "If I hadn't joined the military and been in Okinawa in the first place, Rose and our unborn child might still be alive today. She was flying out to be with me when the plane went down."

"Perhaps if you hadn't joined the military, you'd still be married to Linda," pointed out Kevin as he folded his arms and narrowed his eyes at Eric.

"You never know," grinned Eric.

"Sounds like you two have a lot in common," opined Jim as he finished his sandwich. "But, I do need to ask Eric some questions about Mark and Vivian, specific to our case."

Ted and Eric exchanged a peculiar look before Eric finally nodded his consent. "Ask away."

"Eric?" mumbled Linda from the couch. She had just regained consciousness. *Had she imagined seeing Eric Santori again?*

"I'm right here," assured Eric as he got up and started to go to her. Kevin then put his hand on Eric's arm to stop him and shook his head in the negative.

"Perhaps there's a room somewhere else where I can interview you alone, Eric," suggested Jim. "Linda probably needs her rest right now anyway."

"Why can't you question him here?" demanded Linda as she tried to sit up. "Oh, I think I hit my head."

"You are somewhat of a distraction," advised Jim with an even smile. "Though I do agree, they both have great taste in women."

Kevin and Eric both gave Jim a surprised look.

Jim gave them both a crooked grin and shrugged his shoulders.

"I'll get her some ice," volunteered Ted as he jumped up and headed for the large commercial refrigerator.

Linda then saw the look on Kevin's face and glanced at Eric with a questioning look.

"I had to tell him," mentioned Eric.

"I see," nodded Linda as she turned to look at Kevin.

"Hey, it was before you even knew me," commented Kevin. "And Jim's right. My half-brother does have good taste in women." Kevin did not want Linda to know how much it bothered him to find out about her previous marriage and gave her a smile of reassurance.

"I'm sorry I never said anything," apologized Linda, "but that was a long time ago."

"Water under the bridge," assured Kevin.

Then, turning to Eric, Linda questioned, "Why on earth wouldn't you have told your own wife that your real last name was Killingham?"

"Sorry about that," apologized Eric as he gave Linda a longing glance. *With every fiber of his being, he still wanted her!*

"Didn't you think I would have wanted to know something like that?" pressed Linda.

"My father Mark was a very bad man," replied Eric. "My mother was so ashamed of the name Killingham that she had all of our last names legally changed to Santori when we were quite young."

"All of you?" frowned Kevin.

"You have four other half-brothers besides me," informed Eric with a slightly mischievous smile.

"Really?"

"Michael, Justin, Philip, Evan and me," elaborated Eric. "I'm the youngest."

"Guys, we really need to get down to business," interjected Jim, but it was of no use.

"It was right after Mama learned about you and Bobby Sue that she left our home in Sprague and moved up to Bellevue, Washington,

390

to help her parents run their restaurant. Apparently, we all fled from Mark in the middle of the night with only the clothes on our backs."

"I'm not surprised," muttered Kevin.

"Why?" asked Eric.

"That's pretty much what happened to my mother, too," revealed Kevin. "Mark tried for years to find us, but we just kept moving, though I was never told why."

"She never told you?"

"No," answered Kevin. "It was not until I was in high school that my stepdad accidentally spilled the beans."

"What did you do then?"

"Tried to find Mark Killingham."

"Me, too." Eric shook his head with disbelief. "I had always wanted to find out why he'd done what he did. Apparently, Mark had tried repeatedly to see us and even made threats, but the business end of Grandma's rifle changed his mind."

"My parents hired a PI to finally find the creep for us," blurted out Linda from the couch. "It was a wedding gift."

"How'd that work out?" Eric's penetrating glance caused Linda to blush. It did not go unnoticed by Kevin.

"The creep stole my identity," advised Kevin. "Among other things. Thankfully, we fared better than some of his wives."

"That's right," corroborated Linda. "The jerk left a whole string of wealthy widows behind."

"Not so wealthy after meeting Mark Killingham," interjected Jim. "From what we know, he did have at least a dozen confirmed marriages, only two of which were legal."

"Too bad someone beat me to the punch on putting that guy out of our misery," commented Linda. "If I ever find out who did it, I'd like to shake that person's hand. They certainly did the world a service."

"It sounds like Mark was bad news for just about everyone who ever knew the guy," opined Ted. "Assuming it was actually him."

Again, Eric and Ted exchanged a meaningful glance. Jim tried to appear as if he did not notice, but had a hunch the two men were hiding something. *After all, they had served together in the military, and soldiers were frequently known to be more loyal to their comrades than to their own families.*

"Tell me about Vivian LaMont," began Jim. "How long was she a resident here?"

"About six months," volunteered Ted.

"Thank you, Ted, but for right now I'd like to direct my questions to Eric, if that's okay."

"Fine with me."

"Okay, then, Eric," clarified Jim. "Did you know Vivian before she came here to live?"

"No."

"How long after she became a resident here did you strike up your friendship with her?" grilled Jim.

"Probably about four months ago," replied Eric.

"Had Vivian ever given you any reason to believe she was related to the Killingham family?"

"Absolutely not."

"Had you ever mentioned to Ms. LaMont that you are a Killingham?"

"Why would I do that?"

"Just answer the question," prompted Jim.

"No!"

"Is it common for the workers here to establish personal relationships with the residents?" questioned Jim.

"It's actually against policy," interjected Ted.

"That's right, it's against policy," agreed Eric.

"And yet you and Vivian became personal friends anyway?"

"Yes," admitted Eric.

"Why?"

"I don't know," responded Eric. "There was just something about her. I felt drawn to her."

"How and when did you first learn that she was actually your aunt?" grilled Jim.

"On March 23rd."

"You seem pretty certain about that."

Eric looked at Ted before answering. "It was the day she went missing."

"Do the residents here go missing very often?" pressed Jim.

"No, of course not!" Eric was becoming irritated with the way Jim was questioning him.

392

"Wouldn't you say it was odd that her estranged brother's body was also found down by the river, less than a mile away from hers?"

"Of course, it was odd," answered Eric.

"And yet you don't remember ever seeing Mark Killingham come here to visit her at Happy Acres, prior to him becoming a resident here himself?"

"Never," interjected Ted again. "And like I said, assuming it was actually him."

"If you keep interrupting, I'm going to have to ask you to go back to your nurse's station," cautioned Jim.

"I probably should do that anyway," agreed Ted as he got up to leave. "Just let me know if you need anything."

"We will," promised Jim.

"Do you have anything for a headache?" called Linda.

"Absolutely. Come with me, young lady," offered Ted as he returned to help her up. "Perhaps her husband would like to come, too?"

"I'll be okay," Linda assured Kevin as she got up to leave with Ted.

"That's fine," agreed Kevin. *As long as it wasn't Eric she was going with.*

"You're welcome to lay down in one of the vacant rooms if you like, too," suggested Ted. "Let's just get you something for that headache first, and then I'll show you where it is."

Ted and Eric then exchanged another look. *Only one room in the place was vacant at the moment and both men knew which one it was. It was Vivian LaMont's old room.*

"Maybe I will take you up on that," decided Linda as she and Ted made their way towards the nurse's station.

"Is that a good idea?" Chip whispered to Jim.

"He seems okay," responded Jim in a soft voice.

Unknown to them, Kevin had overheard their conversation and was having similar thoughts, but then dismissed them. *After all, it wasn't like she had walked off with Eric. Linda would be okay, and Ted seemed trustworthy enough.*

"Where were we?" frowned Jim.

"You were wanting to know if I ever noticed Mark Killingham come here to visit Vivian," reminded Eric with an even gaze.

"That's right," nodded Jim. "So, did you?"

393

"It was my understanding before all this happened that Mark Killingham was already dead," clarified Eric. "I had seen an obituary for him and visited his grave at the Ocean Bluff Cemetery in 2009, while I was on leave."

"When did you first come to know that the man found under the bridge nearby was actually Mark Killingham?"

"I'm sure one of the Seattle police officers must have mentioned it," lied Eric. *He certainly hoped it was true.*

Jim studied Eric carefully for several moments as he considered what he would say next. *Besides Kevin, Linda and the associates at Jim's law firm, only Bill Huong had been aware of the fact that the decedent was actually Mark Killingham.*

"Actually," corrected Eric, "it was Jack Killingham, Jr. that they mentioned. That's right."

Jim continued to study Eric for any sign that he might be lying. *The Seattle PD had originally been under the assumption that the decedent was Jack Killingham, Jr., because of finding a driver's license with that name on it in a pocket of his coat.*

"Are there visitor logs?" asked Jim. "Has anyone looked to see if someone by the name of Killingham ever came here to visit her?"

"Actually, yes," answered Eric. "The policeman who came here from the Seattle PD made copies of all our visitor logs for the past six months, as part of their investigation."

"May we see those logs?"

"Of course," agreed Eric. "Ted has them at the nurse's station."

"I'll go get 'em," offered Chip.

"Thanks," smiled Jim. "Are there any surveillance cameras in use here at Happy Acres?"

"Here?" laughed Eric. "They don't even have computers yet. All their files are still paper."

"Kind of off the grid," commented Jim with a crooked grin. "Just the kind of place two ex-Navy SEALs might come to work where they won't be bothered by the outside world."

"What's your point?" asked Eric as he folded his arms.

"You're not the least bit curious how I knew the two of you served together in that capacity?"

"It's not a secret," replied Eric. *What was Jim getting at?*

"When you spoke on the phone with Chip the other day," continued Jim, "you mentioned to him that you had information about the disappearance of one of your residents. I'm going to assume you were referring to Vivian LaMont, is that correct?"

"Yes."

"Let's have it then," pressed Jim.

"Well," elaborated Eric, "it had become a daily thing for me to stop by Vivian's room for tea each night."

"Really?"

"She was just a lonely old lady, and we hit it off."

"Exactly what did she tell you about herself?" pressed Jim. "Anything about her past?"

"No, not really," lied Eric.

"I've never known a woman *not* to chat with her friends about her past," mentioned Jim with an even gaze. "Especially a friend that she has tea with each day."

"Okay, well, she did mention that she was a widow," offered Eric, "but was always rather vague about it. The things she did talk about were all the cats she used to have, some of the places she'd visited in her travels, that kind of thing."

"Nothing about family, then?"

"No, and nothing about the Killinghams."

"Did she ever mention anything else that might be of interest in solving this case?"

"Not that I can think of."

"So, what was the information you told Chip that you had about her disappearance?" grilled Jim.

"Just that she acted oddly that day," advised Eric. "Like she was afraid of something."

"And she never mentioned to you what or who it was?"

"No."

"Then how does that help us?"

"As you know, we had another resident disappear, too," reminded Eric.

"Go on."

"It was the new guy," continued Eric. "He had actually arrived here that same day, the day that Vivian disappeared."

"The man you knew as Jack Killingham, Jr.?"

"Correct," verified Eric.

395

"Tell me what you knew about him at that time."

"I first learned about him when Marge Billingsly, the day nurse, mentioned to Ted and me that there was a new resident. She said it was some man, but she hadn't even had a chance to make up a file for him yet."

"Did she ever mention his name?"

"Not at that time," lied Eric. "It wasn't until we saw a story on the news about the other body that we realized it was him. That was a couple of days later."

"Is it your opinion, then, that Vivian LaMont might have been afraid of or concerned about Mr. Killingham?" summarized Jim.

"It is now."

"I have a question," interjected Kevin, who had been quiet throughout the interview.

"Sure, what do you want to know?"

"What are your intentions toward my wife?"

"You have nothing to worry about," promised Eric.

"I think we're done for now," mentioned Jim. "I'd like to question Ted now. Would you mind sending him back here?"

"I guess I should go keep an eye on the nurse's station for him," commented Eric as he got up to leave. "Sure, I'll send him back."

"He's lying," Kevin muttered to Jim as they watched Eric leave.

"It's hard to say at this point," differed Jim.

"About his intentions toward Linda," clarified Kevin.

"Unfortunately, that's not a crime," sniggered Jim.

Just then Chip and Ted returned to the kitchen.

"Linda's resting in one of the rooms," volunteered Ted. "She should be fine."

"Here's the visitor log," offered Chip as he handed it to Jim.

"Who's down there with Eric?" Kevin suddenly asked as he thought of Linda. *Would she be safe?*

"No one, why?" asked Ted.

"I need to use the men's room, I'll be right back," mentioned Kevin as he got up to head down the hall. It was his plan to covertly keep an eye on Eric, just to be sure Eric was not attempting to have any inappropriate contact with Linda.

396

The long hallway reminded Kevin of the kind on a cruise ship. Narrow and covered with an overly ornate carpet. Instead of gold fish, this one was decorated with bright floral designs. The framed pictures on its yellow walls were also of flowers. *At least the decor was cheerful.*

Just as Kevin rounded the corner to the central nurse's station, he noticed that no one was there! *Where was Eric? What room was Linda resting in? Suddenly furious, Kevin headed back to the kitchen.*

Unable to let the opportunity slip from his grasp, Eric decided to slip into Vivian's old room where Linda was resting. *He needed to talk with her alone. There were several unresolved issues that they needed to discuss.*

Linda's head was starting to feel better, but she did have a small goose egg on the back of her head where it had hit the floor when she'd fallen.

"Are you okay?" came Eric's voice from the shadows. He was sitting in a chair beside the bed.

Linda set aside the ice bag Ted had given her and started to sit up. Moonlight gently streamed in through a nearby window.

"You really should keep that on your head for a while longer," recommended Eric as he came and sat on the bed beside her.

"Does Kevin know you're here?"

"No," Eric assured her. "I'm at the nurse's station right now, and Ted is down there being questioned. Jim already finished interrogating me, for all the good it did."

"He mustn't find you here," cautioned Linda.

"I just wanted a few moments to talk with you alone," replied Eric. "Why were you so quick to have our marriage annulled? I'd really like to know."

"It wasn't just you joining the military without asking me first," explained Linda. "It was the fact that you were unfaithful to me."

"I'm not making any excuses for what I did, and I don't blame you for hating me," began Eric, "but please hear me out."

"I'm listening."

"When I went out with the guys that night, we'd been drinking."

"I'm well aware of that."

"I was actually passed out in the back room at Philip's house when that woman came back there and got into bed with me."

"And you had no idea she was there?" doubted Linda.

"Not at first. She was just someone that showed up at the party. I never even knew her name."

"Just when was it that you realized you were having sex with someone other than your pregnant wife?" demanded Linda.

"What?"

"Oh, that's right, you didn't know, did you?" fumed Linda.

"You were *pregnant*?" Eric was stunned by the news.

"The trauma of what you did took care of that, though," added Linda. "I ended up miscarrying our child!"

Eric gently took Linda's hand in his and held it. "I am so sorry for what I put you through. Can you ever forgive me?"

Linda suddenly felt herself drawn toward Eric. *Why was he doing this to her? How in the world could she still be attracted to someone who had treated her as badly as he had?*

"Sweetheart, that was a very long time ago, and I know you're happy with Kevin," continued Eric. "All I want now is for you to be happy, and hope that you can somehow find it in your heart to forgive me for what happened." *Oh, how beautiful she still was!*

"In some ways, it's easier for me to forgive the other woman than the fact that you chose the military over me," answered Linda. "The other woman thing I can understand. You were drunk, and things happen. Eventually, we would have worked it out. But the military? What in the world gave you the right to let them just take you away from me like that? Especially when it was something that would affect both of our lives forever?"

"You may dislike the military because you see them as taking me away from you, but it was my choice to join and I don't deny it."

Even in the shadows, Eric could see Linda begin to pout. It was that thing she did with her lower lip when she was upset.

"It was an opportunity," added Eric as he gently stroked the side of her face with the back of his hand. "Most people going into the military don't realize that there is often a price to pay with broken families, divorce, or worse. Young kids come into the service for school or just a job, never thinking that someday they might lose their life. The reality is that people die. Every deployment for a carrier battle group results in at least five to ten people dying."

"Every deployment?" questioned Linda.

"For a variety of reasons," elaborated Eric. "There are accidents, sickness, and sometimes just plain stupidity. Perhaps while visiting a port in a different country they drink too much and get robbed, or stabbed to death for insulting someone. Some are even raped or kidnapped. So many things can happen."

"Why in the world would you want such a life?" grilled Linda.

"I'm trying to help you understand about men willing to do harm on others' behalf. It's about sacrifice. Some people are willing to pay that price. There's a saying that goes, *'All gave some. Some gave all.'* Part of it was about keeping you safe, too."

"Keeping *me* safe?" Linda could feel herself getting angrier by the moment. "I guess that means I was nothing more than some sacrifice you were more than willing to make so you could use it as an excuse to go off and live out your dreams of glory on the battlefield under the guise of keeping your country safe?"

"It wasn't like that at all. You just don't understand."

"Oh, I understand, alright!" snapped Linda. "You were unwilling to include me in your *decision*! Maybe I wasn't willing to sacrifice my husband, my marriage and my child like that! Did you ever stop to think about that, for even a single moment?"

"If only I could go back in time and do things over," lamented Eric as he looked at Linda with his sad brown eyes.

"What would you do differently?" asked Linda as she studied Eric's handsome face.

Meanwhile, in the kitchen, Kevin marched up to Ted and demanded, "Where are they?"

"Where is who?" frowned Ted.

"Eric and Linda," reminded Kevin in a gruff voice. He was in no mood to be toyed with. Then, turning to Jim, "We need to do an immediate, room-by-room search of the entire place, right now!"

"Hold it," objected Ted. "We can't just go barging into people's rooms like that. It's almost nine o'clock at night. Most of the residents would be asleep by now."

"We would need probable cause," reminded Jim.

"I'll give you probable cause," advised Kevin as he walked over to a fire alarm station on the wall and yanked down on the single

399

action T-bar to activate it. Immediately, a shrill alarm began sounding over and over again. Strobe lights also began to flash.

"Oh, boy, now you've done it." Ted shook his head. "Only the Fire Department can deactivate that thing, because of the type of facility we have here."

Jim suddenly began to laugh. Not that it was funny, but just to relieve tension. "Alright. You got your phase one search. You and I can search the rooms while Ted and Chip get the residents to safety."

"I'll get you for this," Chip teasingly threatened Jim.

"Oh, no!" exclaimed Linda upon hearing the fire alarm. "Kevin will find us together like this, and there'll be no convincing him that something wasn't going on."

"You do still go for walks to clear you head, don't you?"

"Yeah, why?"

"Come on," instructed Eric as he grabbed Linda's hand and pulled her up. "I'll take you to the greenhouse. You can tell everyone later that's where you were. You'd never be able to hear the fire alarm from there, anyway."

"What about you?"

"I was in the men's room when I first heard the fire alarm, and then was busy helping people get to safety after that," described Eric. "But, when I noticed you were not in this room, I went looking for you, to make sure you were okay."

"Alright," Linda finally agreed. *It was probably the only way.*

Eric carefully removed the screen from the window to Vivian LaMont's old room. "Hurry!"

After following Eric from the open window, Linda waited while he put the screen back in place.

Eric then grabbed Linda's hand and began skirting the building, behind a row of tall shrubs. Most of the shrubs were either rhododendron or camellia bushes, and all of them had been trimmed at least two feet back from the building by the gardener for ease of access and building maintenance. The cedar chip bark dust through which they were walking was intermingled with mud from recent heavy rains and was difficult to negotiate.

"My new boots!" complained Linda as she struggled to pull one of her stiletto heels from the mire.

400

Without warning, Eric suddenly scooped her up in his arms and began to carry her. The warmth of his powerful arms around her body was almost overwhelming as he effortlessly carried her to the end of the long building. *At least they were hidden from view by the shrubs.*

Eric looked both ways to be sure the coast was clear before dashing across an open segment of lawn and over to a heavily wooded area nearby with Linda still in his arms. *The feel of her shapely body was almost more than he could endure. The formfitting, black leather pants she had chosen to wear didn't help matters much, either.*

"How can you see where you're going?"

"I've worked here for two years now," advised Eric as he hurried toward a huge greenhouse up ahead. Situated around the structure were small area lights, enough to see by without the need for a flashlight. Inside were a series of grow lights that were kept on at all times. Beams of moonlight streaming through the trees provided additional light, as well.

"In here," indicated Eric as he carefully set Linda back down, removed a key from his pocket and unlocked the greenhouse door.

Linda followed him inside. The warmth inside was surprising. Rare tropical flowers, fruit trees, vegetables and other plants filled every corner of the 100-foot structure.

"This is amazing," admired Linda as Eric locked the door again.

"Yeah, it is," agreed Eric as he flirted with Linda. *He just could not help himself.*

"So, this is the greenhouse."

"There are some marble benches over that way," indicated Eric. "Sorry about your boots. We can probably rinse them off at one of the spigots, and they should dry pretty quickly in here."

Linda made no effort to resist as Eric took her hand in his and then put his arm around her. They walked in silence for several minutes, just enjoying their time together as they made their way to one of the white marble benches and sat down.

"How long were you in the service, anyway?"

"I did eight tours of duty, and served in every branch of the military, except the Marines."

"Why not?"

"My focus at that time was on becoming a Navy SEAL," revealed Eric. "I served in Afghanistan, and in the Gulf War and Vietnam before that. But not in the land of porcelain."

"Porcelain?"

"Toilets," interpreted Eric. "Everything out there wants to either sting you, eat you, bite you or kill you, and there are no porcelain toilets. Some people referred to us as the *snake eaters*."

"Did you?"

"Eat snakes?" smiled Eric.

"Yeah."

"Now and then, yes," answered Eric.

"Let's see, four years for each tour, that comes to 32 years," calculated Linda.

"I was in from 1979 until 2012," informed Eric.

"That's 33 years."

"I was so severely injured once that I was in rehab for a year, so that year didn't count."

"Tell me about it." Linda suddenly wanted to know everything about him that she could. *This might be her only chance.*

"Well, to give you a little history first," began Eric. "I was involved in another friendly fire incident prior to that, back in 1991. That was when Ted and I served together in the Gulf War. Two of our men were killed and six others were wounded. Ted and I were among the lucky ones, that time. The whole thing happened when an American Apache attack bird fired on and destroyed one of its own fighting vehicles, as well as an armored personnel carrier during night operations. Ted and I each suffered from some PTSD afterwards and have even attended group therapy sessions together."

"Post-traumatic stress disorder?" gasped Linda. "Talking about this isn't going to bring it on, is it?"

"One never knows."

"What about the time *you* were injured?" pressed Linda. "Only if you can tell me about it."

"That was in Afghanistan," related Eric as he again flirted with Linda. "We had on IR Gear that identified us as friendlies. When the firing started, we even put IR strobes out but we still took on fire."

"IR?"

402

"Infrared," clarified Eric. "Even the planes overhead that were called in for an airstrike didn't fire on us. They waved off and called in that friendlies were being fired on."

Linda could sense that it was becoming difficult for Eric to talk about it so she patiently waited for him to continue.

"The guys on either side of me bought it," continued Eric as his face took on a serious and faraway expression. "I was left for dead, along with them."

"Oh, my God!" exclaimed Linda. "How did they find you?"

"It was Ted," revealed Eric. "He wasn't about to leave the body of his closest buddy behind."

"He thought you were dead when he carried you out?"

"At first, yeah, but I don't remember much about it. I was unconscious most of the time. There was even some amnesia and temporary memory loss after that, followed by a full year of intensive physical therapy and rehab."

"And you still went back out there after that?" Linda could not believe what she was hearing.

"It was my life," replied Eric. "I've tried to help you understand. When you are out there like that, those guys become your family. Nothing else exists. Your loyalty, your allegiance, is to them."

"No, I suppose I never will understand," admitted Linda as she sadly shook her head.

"But, it still took a long while to get things straight again after that," described Eric. "It took even longer to get back in the game, but essentially, I was off the teams. I became a trainer and a mentor. I was still able do everything, but my situational awareness was off. If I'd continued after that, I would only have become a hazard and not an asset to my teammates."

"That was when you finally quit?"

"Actually, I still did some related work after that, but it's not the same as being operational on a Tier 1 Team. Now I'm too old and slow. The young fire eaters will learn all they can from you but they don't suffer old fools trying to relive their glory days."

"Do you ever miss it?"

"Yes, of course. And I miss so many people in my past, but losing two very close friends to a mistake someone made on our own side, that was unforgivable."

"Was there ever someone else besides me?" asked Linda.

"Well, while you were unconscious, I mentioned to Kevin that I finally remarried again in 1979, on Valentine's Day."

"Oh, my goodness, that's the exact same day that Kevin and I were married."

"Yes, that's what he said," nodded Eric. "Unfortunately, Rose and our unborn child were killed when the plane that she was on crashed while flying out to be with me during my first assignment in Okinawa."

"How horrible!" exclaimed Linda as she put a comforting hand on Eric's shoulder. "I can't imagine what that must have been like."

"But in the end, there was someone else," added Eric. "It was in 1992 when I finally settled down again, though we were never actually married. We had a son in 1994."

"Tell me about her."

"If you want to know how she felt, she felt alone even when I was there. The only attention Yosuko got was from my friend the helo pilot. She was with me only because we met first and she felt obligated because of our son. My buddy was an honorable guy, but he loved her. They only got together after I left. He even gave her one last shot with me. I told them that I cared for them both and to have a nice life. Besides, I was still in love with someone else."

"Me?" comprehended Linda.

"Are you surprised?" Eric's longing gaze seemed to pull at the very depth of her being. *She would have to be strong.*

"What about your son, do you ever see him?"

"He lives in Thailand with his mother, and neither of them speak English," related Eric. "The last time I saw Jacob was in 2012."

"What did you do between 2012 and 2021, when you came to work here?" grilled Linda.

"Auto racing, martial arts, scuba diving, skydiving, mountain climbing, and even some treasure hunting."

"Treasure hunting?" laughed Linda. "How could you possibly afford to do all that?"

"There are still some very lucrative shipwrecks, especially off the coast of Somalia," revealed Eric. "Art and antiquities dealers in places like Bahrain and Dubai are always anxious to acquire such things, and will pay quite handsomely for them."

"You were a mercenary?" asked Linda.

"That sounds so ...." began Eric.

"So mercenary-like?" laughed Linda.

"It's called contract work. It pays well, but you develop a lot of the same camaraderie with guys who used to wear the uniform, like you. And you quickly figure out that you know a lot of the same people and were in a lot of the same places, but at different times."

"Wasn't it dangerous?"

"Not for a shooter."

"You were a shooter, too?"

"The correct term is *sniper,*" clarified Eric in a more serious tone.

"Exactly when did you become a hitman for the military?" frowned Linda.

"That was toward the end, when I was in Special Ops," revealed Eric, "though technically I can't talk about it, or even tell you that."

"Of course, you can't," fumed Linda.

"Please try to understand," pleaded Eric. "There are things out there that you have no idea about in your secure little world over here, horrible things and bad people."

Linda pursed her lips as she folded her arms. She was clearly quite upset.

"Linda, there are times when the deed must be done," Eric tried to explain. "Sometimes it is necessary, there's no choice."

"There's always a choice!" exclaimed Linda.

"Not when you've signed a contract with the military," reminded Eric. "After that, they own you."

"You see!" shouted Linda triumphantly as she unexpectedly jabbed Eric in the chest with her index finger several times to make a point. "This is exactly what I was talking about earlier. You were willing to sell yourself to the highest bidder, just so you could live out your dreams of glory on the battlefield, your family be damned."

"Linda, please."

"How does it feel to know you just threw away the life we could have had together to become a murderer?"

"I guess you could look at it like that," agreed Eric, as he gently grabbed Linda's wrist to stop her from jabbing him, "but it's not like that at all. It was NOT something I enjoyed doing – it was dirty but important work."

405

"Then how can you live with it?" demanded Linda.

"Sometimes it isn't easy," admitted Eric. "When we are out there, nothing else exists, not family, nothing else. There is no wife, no child, no past, no future. We must have clear heads and be free from any emotional attachment. Often, that's the only way to make it back."

"That's just not fair."

"But it is the reality of it. It's just us and them, and it's our job to defeat them so our loved ones back home can be safe for yet another day. You tell yourself that if we fight them over there, then maybe Americans won't have to fight them here on American soil."

"You really believe that, don't you?" realized Linda as she sadly shook her head.

"It wasn't always like that for me," mentioned Eric.

"How many people have you killed, anyway?" grilled Linda. "Do you even know?"

"I can't talk about it," answered Eric. "It's classified."

"But do you even *know*?" repeated Linda.

"Of course I do, give or take a couple dozen. Your subconscious remembers every one of them, even the ones you block out of your conscious mind."

"Do you feel any remorse for what you've done?"

"Yes and no. It had to be done. Yes, I feel the weight of it, but I figured if I didn't do it, someone else would have to – and then those images would haunt them. So, it might as well be me."

"So, would *yes* be the innocent bystanders that got taken out while you were busy trying to get the bad guys?" pressed Linda.

"Linda, listen to me," persisted Eric as he gently put his hands on her arms and then forced her to look at him. "I was actually a nurse during my first tour of duty, and my job was to save lives if I could."

"What made you go to the dark side?"

"I don't know," Eric shook his head with frustration. "It was as if everything I touched seemed to die, no matter what I did. As fast as I patched 'em up, more were wounded and dying, right in front of me. I finally wanted a chance to take out the people who did it, to try and make a difference if I could."

"And did you?"

"I like to think so. My next 10 years were spent becoming a Navy SEAL, and getting into DEVGRU. It's not until at least that amount of service and actual combat experience that guys who cut it are even eligible. That means a lot of being shot at during close quarters fighting throughout your entire deployment cycle, and only being accepted after strenuous peer review, that you finally become a part of the team."

"What kind of things did you guys do?" questioned Linda. *She still could not help being curious.* "Your team?"

"Nothing I can really talk about."

"And just who am I going to tell, anyway?" demanded Linda as she folded her arms again. "I was just hoping to try and understand *why* you think it was worth giving up our life together so you could make some big difference!"

After an awkward silence, Eric finally nodded. "Very well, but what I am about to tell you is classified and you cannot share it with anyone, agreed?"

"Of course," promised Linda, more softly.

"During one of our night missions, when we were dropped into hostile territory ...," began Eric.

"Dropped in?" interrupted Linda. "By parachute?"

Eric merely chuckled in response.

"How is that safe?"

"The paratroopers are highly trained before ever being considered for such a mission," described Eric. "The teams practice it over and over again, until they could do it in their sleep."

"What if one of them gets separated from their team?" grilled Linda. "Especially at night like that."

"First of all," explained Eric, "Paratroopers are dropped off using static line jumps over the drop zone."

"That sounds dangerous."

"I guess it could be," agreed Eric, "but all the equipment is rigorously tested first. For example, the chutes are capable of safely handling up to 350 pounds of weight."

"Why so much?" Linda narrowed her eyes.

"Because we usually carry 150 to 180 pounds of gear with us."

"Wouldn't that make you hit the ground even harder than you normally would?"

"Only if the *go bag* failed to release in time."

"Go bag?"

"The main chute is carried on the back of a special harness. The 35-foot chute is designed to fall at a rate of 15 feet per second," elaborated Eric. "A reserve chute, weapons case and *go bag* are carried on the front of the trooper's harness. The *go bag* – which usually contains expensive equipment and extra supplies – is also attached to a 15-foot anchor line while inside the aircraft. When the trooper jumps, the weight of the trooper causes the tie to break once the end of the 15-foot anchor line has been reached. The bag then becomes separated from the jumper and descends independently, though still attached, and is slowed by the trooper's chute as it falls. It usually hits the ground about a hundred feet before the trooper does."

"I didn't realize you had to carry so much," admitted Linda. "I thought 75 pounds was excessive when we used to go backpacking."

"For you, I suppose it was," grinned Eric.

"Go on."

Eric's face took on a serious expression as he continued. "There was this village in Afghanistan. The mission was simple. We were to round up and rescue any civilians first before the bombers came in."

Linda became serious, too. *Would reliving this incident cause Eric to have an episode of PTSD?*

"Everything was quiet – too quiet – as we approached the village. There was some starlight, but there was no moon that night. Just as we reached the perimeter of the main compound where the hostages were being held, the enemy opened fire on us," related Eric.

Linda patiently waited for him to resume his tale.

"Only Ted and I were left after that."

"Oh, my God!" exclaimed Linda. "Your other teammates were all killed?"

Eric barely nodded. It was obvious that he was having trouble keeping his emotions in check. "There was this old woman inside one of the holding cells," remembered Eric. "She was the only hostage left. I can't even remember how many doors we had to kick in before finally finding her. There were bullet holes in most of the walls."

"None of the other hostages was still alive?" Linda was horrified.

"I'm sure most of them died quickly," assumed Eric as he paused to regain control. "After the enemy finally left – or so we thought – it was just us and her. She had to be 90 years old, so I finally just picked her up and carried her."

"With all your gear?"

"I had to ditch most of the gear first," replied Eric. "Anyway, when Ted and I finally got back to the landing zone, the enemy began firing at us again, from behind. Some of them had followed us."

"They didn't capture you, did they?"

"No, they didn't," assured Eric. "But, I had just put the old woman on the copter when I saw Ted go down behind me."

"Ted was *shot?*"

"He took a couple in the shoulder," answered Eric. "That was when I ran back for him, after making sure the old woman was safely on the copter."

"You weren't shot, too, were you?"

"Not that time," replied Eric as he paused to gather his thoughts. *He had never discussed this incident with anyone and was unsure if he could even finish.*

"Ted's obviously still alive," prompted Linda.

Eric swallowed hard and then revealed, "That was when the bird suddenly blew up, right in front of us." Unbidden tears began to stream down his face.

"The helicopter just *blew up?*" gasped Linda as she put a comforting hand on Eric's shoulder. "With the old woman on board?"

"And the pilots and two other men," mumbled Eric.

Linda sadly shook her head. "How did *you* get out of there?"

After several moments, Eric replied, "It was a very long walk."

"What about the enemy?"

"It was either us or them," answered Eric.

"You shot 'em all?"

"There was no choice," responded Eric.

"What about Ted's gunshot wounds?"

"Good thing I was a medic and still had some of my gear."

"How far did you guys have to walk to get out of there after that? Did you have to carry him?"

"Only part of the way, and it was probably 30 miles," guessed Eric. "It was only safe to travel at night, so it took us a while."

"They must have given you a medal for that."

Eric sighed deeply and shook his head. "I knew a lot of guys – highly decorated combat veterans – who had so many medals they

409

would clang together when they walked. You would know they were coming, but none of them cared about any of their citations or medals."

"Didn't anyone find out what you did to save Ted?"

"Of course, but that's not the point," related Eric. "There are just some things so horrible that happen to you over there, that you don't want to bring back any souvenirs. To know the clanging generals was an honor, but once I came to understand them, I tossed every medal and citation I ever received into a fire."

"You *what*?" Linda could not believe it.

"You finally come full circle and realize it's never been about you, but the person next to you, or people who can't help themselves. What I did is what anyone would have done," insisted Eric.

"Burning your *medals*?" argued Linda. "Maybe your family might have wanted them!"

"Sorry," apologized Eric. "I can't go back."

"Can any of the medals be reissued?"

Eric sighed deeply and shook his head. "No, because the ops were classified, so there was only one citation – heavily redacted – and the memory of it. The medals were listed on my DD214, but nothing denoting how, when or where they were awarded, which was enough for me."

"Maybe I might have wanted to have one of them," mentioned Linda. "To remember you by."

"I had pretty much given up all hope of ever seeing you again at that point," reminded Eric. "I think one of my brothers might still have one of my medals, but the others were all destroyed. Sorry."

Linda had become visibly upset.

"Hey, remember that week we spent at Stehekin?" smiled Eric. He was determined to change the subject.

"On Lake Chelan," nodded Linda as she began to smile, too.

It was where she and Eric had spent their honeymoon. The isolated community of Stehekin in northeast Washington was accessible only by boat, air or by hiking over to it on a strenuous cross-country trail. There were no roads to Stehekin from the outside world. The few vehicles within the tiny town had been brought there by ferry at one time or another, along with whatever gas was needed to fuel them. Located near the single gas station was the town's only store. Just beyond that, its single room school house boasted no more

410

than a dozen students at any one time. The simple quality of life there included hunting, fishing, and enjoying the pristine beauty of its untouched wilderness. Several small rental cabins were available to hunters, photographers, writers, honeymooners, or others seeking respite and solitude from the busy influences of the outside world. Stehekin was definitely off the grid.

"Remember that beach by our cabin?" flirted Eric.

Linda felt a twinge of sadness as she thought of it, and how such a perfect memory could never happen again, at least not with Eric.

"Where else could two young people in love run around stark naked, and not have to worry about anyone seeing them?" added Eric with a crooked grin.

Linda then blushed as she thought of the blanket Eric had spread out on the warm sand where they'd made love for hours on end.

"I can still see us there on that beach, in the warm sun," reminisced Eric as he brushed a stray hair from her cheek. "And you're still just as beautiful now as you were then. Even more so."

"That was a long time ago," reminded Linda uncomfortably.

"I'm still very much in love with you," confessed Eric. "And I was such an idiot, to have ever let you go."

"Yes, you were," agreed Linda. "And I still have feelings for you, too, but you must understand. I love Kevin with all my heart and would never leave him. He was there to pick up the broken pieces of my heart after you destroyed my life and left it in ruins."

"I'm so sorry for what happened," Eric apologized again, "and I'll keep telling you that as many times as you need to hear it. Please tell me that you forgive me?"

"Yes, Eric, I forgive you, but I'll never be able to trust you again," admitted Linda. "Don't you see?"

"People can change, you know," pointed out Eric as his warm, penetrating gaze held her captive.

"I've changed, too."

"I sure wish you'd told me about our baby back then," lamented Eric. He was clearly bothered by it.

"Would it have kept you from joining the military?"

"Probably not," admitted Eric. "I was young and stupid. But, perhaps I could have provided for you. I know how hard your life

411

must have been after that, and I am so sorry for what you went through. I'm sure it wasn't easy."

"Kevin and I have miscarried all of our babies, too," revealed Linda. "My life has been no picnic. Besides being sick a lot and haunted by my past, it has been overwhelming at times."

"The past has a way of doing that to a person," agreed Eric. "Still, Kevin is a good man and he must be doing something right. You've been married for 44 years now."

"Yeah, he's a pretty good guy," nodded Linda. "You want to hear something funny?"

"Sure."

"When I first met him, I only agreed to go out with him because he reminded me of you."

"Oh, yeah?" grinned Eric.

"And when I finally agreed to marry him, it was only because he was ineligible to join the military," added Linda. "He has a bad back and flat feet, so they wouldn't take him. Otherwise, he'd probably have gone off and left me, too."

"Linda, I want you to know how sorry I am for what Mark did to you guys, it was inexcusable."

"At least he won't be able to hurt anyone else now."

"Did you really mean it when you said you'd like to shake the hand of the person who finally put him out of the world's misery?" questioned Eric with a raised eyebrow as he extended his hand to her.

Linda slowly began to smile as she and Eric shook hands. She then put her arms around Eric and gave him a hug and a kiss on the cheek. "Thank you so much for what you did! Maybe you were right, sometimes the world does need to be rid of bad people. I'm just sorry that it had to be you, especially with him being your own father."

"Actually, I have no memory of it," related Eric as he put his arms around her, too. "All I have is Ted's word for it. He was an eyewitness."

"How can you have no memory of it?"

"Apparently, I was having a PTSD episode at the time, my first one since 2012."

"What happens now?" questioned Linda. Being in Eric's arms had aroused feelings she did not know she still had. "Are you going to turn yourself in? And what about Ted?"

412

"I'm considering it, but wanted to have a chance to talk with you first," replied Eric. "Ted's lips are sealed unless I tell him otherwise."

Linda merely nodded.

"You can't imagine how I've dreamed of finally seeing you again someday, and of being with you like this," revealed Eric as he gazed with longing into her eyes.

Linda suddenly started to pull away.

"Wait," urged Eric. "Tell me something."

"If I can," agreed Linda, though she was uncomfortable.

"Do you believe in *what if?*"

"Perhaps, why?"

"What will you do someday when Kevin is gone, assuming you outlive him? How will you support yourself?"

"I've never really thought about it much," admitted Linda. "I'm sure I'd get by. We do have life insurance."

"But you have no children," reminded Eric. "Who would be there to care for you when you get old, to help you when you really need it most?"

"Why are you asking me this?"

"Let's just say you do outlive Kevin," continued Eric. "Would you really want to end up old and alone, with no one special to love you or keep you company?"

Linda could feel her breathing become shallow as she tried to force herself to appear calm and to maintain her composure.

"Hypothetically," clarified Eric, "*what if* you do outlive him? Do you think you might be willing to give an old fool a second chance and marry me again?"

Linda suddenly laughed. "What if I were 95 years old by the time that happened?"

"I'd take it," committed Eric. He was quite serious. "I'd take even a day with you, if that's all there was. I love you, Linda."

"There are some bridges that just can't be rebuilt," pointed out Linda. "And that wouldn't be fair to you, either, to spend your life waiting around for *what if* to happen. Suppose Kevin outlives me?"

"What I want most is for *you* to be happy, Linda, even if it is with Kevin. I'm just grateful to be here with you now, for these few moments we have together. Even this is more than I could have dared hope for."

413

Powerless to resist her reawakened feelings for Eric any longer, Linda was just about to let him kiss her.

"There you are!" fumed Kevin from behind them. Ted and Jim were with him, and all three had managed to enter the greenhouse and sneak up on Eric and Linda without being seen or heard.

"It's not what you think," stammered Linda as she and Eric quickly pulled away from one another.

"You want to tell me what's going on?" demanded Kevin. He was angrier than Linda had ever seen him.

"She's right," added Eric. "This is not how it looks."

"You know what, if this is what you two want, then fine!" stormed Kevin. "I'm done." He then turned and walked away.

Linda and Eric exchanged a look of concern. "Linda, I'm so sorry. Perhaps I should go talk to him."

"He'd either kill you or die trying," cautioned Linda. "That's the last thing I need. I'll talk to him."

Eric suddenly pulled Linda close and gave her a long lingering kiss on the mouth. "I will always love you."

"I will always love you, too, but my place is with him. Goodbye, Eric." Linda quickly pulled herself away from Eric and dashed from the greenhouse. Tears were streaming down her cheeks.

Eric's eyes began to water as he watched Linda hurry to catch up with Kevin.

"Wait!" screamed Linda as she ran after Kevin.

Ignoring her at first, Kevin kept walking.

"Kevin, wait!" hollered Linda as she ran even faster to reach him. She was barefooted and had her stiletto boots in one hand.

Kevin finally paused and turned to face her. "I told you already, I'm done."

"YOU are the one that I love! That's what I was just now telling Eric," persisted Linda.

"Why were you alone with him then?" demanded Kevin. *He was well aware that he had arrived in the nick of time.*

"Because there were some unresolved issues we needed to discuss," answered Linda.

"What kind of issues?" fumed Kevin. His nostrils were flaring.

Right at that moment, the sound of a gunshot could be heard. It had been fired from inside the greenhouse.

414

"Oh, no," muttered Linda. "He obviously didn't take it very well when I told him my choice was to be with you!"

"Stay here," commanded Kevin, though not as gruffly as before.

"Not on your life!" snapped Linda as she followed Kevin to the greenhouse.

Once inside, they could see Jim Otterman standing over Eric's body, holding his handgun.

Kevin and Linda both raced over to the scene, surprised to see that Eric was still alive.

"What's going on here?" demanded Kevin.

"Jim tried to arrest him," explained Ted, who had watched the entire thing.

"Why in the world did you have to resist?" demanded Jim as he pressed an icon on his smartwatch. "MIRA, send Life Flight to the greenhouse at Happy Acres Nursing Home immediately."

"Aren't you out of range?" questioned Ted.

"Right away, Jim," came MIRA's voice. Jim's Learjet was parked at Seattle-Tacoma International Airport.

"Satellite relay," explained Jim for Ted and Eric's benefit as he secured the gun in his waistband.

Ted was already kneeling beside Eric. He had just tied a torn shirt sleeve around the wound on Eric's thigh and was keeping pressure on it. "He's lost a lot of blood already."

Kevin and Linda then knelt beside Eric, too, while Jim sat down on the bench to wait.

"I guess your friend Chip is busy herding all the residents back into the building by himself?" asked Eric as he tried to smile.

"Don't try and talk," advised Kevin as he grabbed his half-brother's hand and held it.

"Hey, I'm sorry for even thinking about it," apologized Eric. "She chose the better man, and told me how much she loves you."

Uncontrollable tears began streaming down Linda's cheeks as she grabbed Eric's other hand.

"I want the two of you to have what Vivian left for me," mentioned Eric. "Ted, can you make sure they get it? And anything else I have? I want Kevin and Linda to have it all. The money, everything, okay?"

"Absolutely," promised Ted as he continued to apply pressure to Eric's wound while blood continued to seep through the saturated shirtsleeve.

"Jim, Ted had nothing to do with ... Mark's death," informed Eric. He was starting to lose consciousness. "It was all ... me."

Jim nodded. "Hang in there, help will be here soon."

"Kevin, I ... love you ... both," muttered Eric as he suddenly went limp.

Kevin quickly felt for a pulse and then began administering CPR. He and Linda were both certified, and worked together as a team until it finally became obvious their efforts were in vain.

Jim came close and felt for a pulse. "Again, you guys."

"Eric's got a DNR," explained Ted rather sadly.

"DNR, my butt!" snapped Linda.

"It means *Do Not Resuscitate,*" advised Jim with a deep sigh.

Linda and Kevin each gave Jim a look of disbelief. *Really?*

Kevin suddenly began another round of CPR anyway while Linda assisted him, but still it was of no avail.

"No!" wailed Linda as she suddenly grabbed Eric's upper arms and began shaking his lifeless body. "Eric, wake up!"

"He's gone, sweetheart," advised Kevin as he gently grabbed her arms to stop her.

Ted shook his head as he finally released the pressure on Eric's bandage and reached up to close Eric's eyes with one hand. "Why'd you have to go and get yourself shot like that?"

"Because he wouldn't have wanted to spend the rest of his life confined to a prison cell," muttered Linda. "And because ...," she broke off in midsentence and began to sob again.

Jim then pressed the icon on his smartwatch again. "MIRA, cancel Life Flight. Send the coroner instead."

"Yes, Jim. Right away."

Kevin reached for and continued to hold Eric's lifeless hand as tears began to well up in his eyes. *Goodbye, dear brother.*

Linda then put her arms around Kevin and began to weep on his shoulder. "I love you, Kevin. Please forgive me."

"There's nothing to forgive," advised Kevin as he stood up and pulled Linda up after him. "Come on, let's get out of here."

May 3, 2023

Wednesday morning, at the Killingham Lighthouse Bed and Breakfast, brought with it much of the usual fog that would burn off and be gone by noon. At least Jim hoped so, as he would be conducting the funeral service for Eric Santori that afternoon.

Already, glints of sunlight had begun to peek through the clouds and were reflected against the ocean's massive surface nearby. A slight breeze laced with the smell of eucalyptus and cypress trees was refreshing. Seagulls cawed loudly overhead as they searched the beach below for something to eat. Already, the tide was slowing rising and would continue to do so until reaching its zenith at 4:30 that afternoon. *No wonder the kids would go boogie boarding in the afternoons,* realized Jim as he thought of his former classmates and of their untimely deaths in 1973. *What a tragedy that was.*

Eric's brothers Michael, Justin, Philip, Evan and their families had all traveled to Oceanview to be there for the memorial service, so all of the guest rooms at the lighthouse were currently occupied. Several of Eric's former military friends were there, as well, including Ted, but were staying over at the annex nearby.

Kevin and Linda had prolonged their visit at Jim's insistence and were busy helping Jim and Sheree set up tables and chairs on the beach.

"Make sure they're far enough back," cautioned Jim. "The water usually makes it up to that marker."

"Now you tell us," replied Linda as she and Kevin began moving the chairs over.

"Don't they usually have wakes *following* the funeral service instead of *before*?" questioned Sheree.

"Perhaps I should speak while people are eating," suggested Jim.

"People probably will want to visit with one another while they eat," differed Linda. "Especially his family."

"Say, what ever happened to Jodean?" inquired Kevin.

"That's right," remembered Linda. "Mark did have a sister named Jodean." *The lush!* thought Linda as she recalled how drunk Jodean had been when showing up with Mark and Ms. Flowing Waters during their initial encounter with him at their apartment in Ashton all those years ago.

"There was a half-sister by that name," advised Jim as he paused to consider it, "but she drank herself to death back in the 90s, shortly after Mark cleaned out what little was left in her bank account. Something like $700."

"Who would do something like that to their own sister?" demanded Sheree, who had easily overheard the conversation.

"Mark Killingham," answered Kevin and Linda together as they rolled their eyes.

"Does Ann know about the service today?" Jim suddenly asked.

"Not yet," answered Sheree.

"Perhaps we should let her know," persisted Jim.

"Carolyn said they are flying all the way here, to our little airport," mentioned Sheree. "They should be here any time."

"Just in time for the funeral service?" questioned Linda. "Carolyn ought to like that."

"Where's the urn?" grilled Jim.

"Safe in our room at the lighthouse," advised Kevin. "It arrived first thing this morning."

"What about the caterers?" grilled Jim as he looked at Sheree.

"Jim, relax, everything will be fine," Sheree assured him. *Was Jim really nervous about the funeral service, or just anxious because Carolyn and the others were due to return at any moment?*

"Do we still have that extra room in the attic of the annex available for Carolyn and Sherry to stay in?" questioned Jim.

"Yes, Jim," sighed Sheree. *She knew it!*

"What about the band?" pressed Jim.

"They'll be here," assured Sheree. "You need to calm down."

Kevin gave Jim an odd look. *Why was he making such a big deal about Carolyn returning in front of his wife, anyway?*

"Too much coffee," commented Jim. It was as if he could read Kevin's mind. Jim then shrugged his shoulders. "Sorry."

"Better switch to decaf," added Sheree as she left to go get two more chairs from the pallet of chairs nearby.

"We need a flag!" hollered Jim.

"It's all taken care of. You really need to relax," called Sheree.

"Is he always like this?" grinned Linda as Sheree returned with the chairs. She had not seen Jim behave like this since high school.

418

"Humph," snorted Sheree. Even though she had tried her best to be a good host during the past two weeks, Sheree had never really cared for Linda, especially after the time in high school when Linda had commandeered Lenny Owens as her date for the Harvest Festival Prom their junior year. *Even Carolyn had not deserved to be humiliated like that!*

"Whatever," muttered Linda as she scowled at Sheree. It was obvious that Sheree still did not like her, even after 50 years. Sheree had tried to be hospitable for Jim's sake, but having Linda constantly there was becoming old, especially since Jim had waived Kevin's and Linda's lodging fee.

"Perhaps we should go for a walk," suggested Kevin as he gently put a hand on Linda's arm. He could sense the tension between Linda and Sheree that had been growing since their return from Happy Acres. *It would be a shame to wear out their welcome now, especially when they were already planning on leaving in the morning.*

"Fine," agreed Linda as she shoved the chair she was holding at Jim. "Let us know when you're ready for us."

Jim nodded with understanding. "We'll start at noon."

"We'll be back," advised Kevin as he and Linda began walking down the beach, in the direction of the sealed-off bunker tunnel.

"I see you decided not to wear your stilettos today," teased Kevin as he reached for Linda's hand to hold it.

"One of the heels is broken," mentioned Linda.

"From your little jaunt in the flowerbed at Happy Acres?"

"Why do you always ask me questions you already know the answer to?" frowned Linda.

"I don't know," grinned Kevin. "Just to give you a hard time."

"This is hard enough for me already," advised Linda uncomfortably. It had taken her and Kevin three days as it was to try and make things right between them again. The last thing she needed was to be reminded of every minute detail surrounding the night Eric had been killed. Even now, the thought of being at his memorial service was almost more than she could endure.

"We don't have to stay," Kevin suddenly offered.

"He was your *brother*," reminded Linda.

"Half-brother," corrected Kevin. "It's not as if we were close."

"I wish I could say the same," muttered Linda as she kicked a piece of driftwood from her path on the sand.

"Hey, I'm sorry," apologized Kevin. "It's just that I know how hard this is for you, and whether we stay or leave is your call. I'm fine either way."

A sneaker wave suddenly insinuated itself into their path, getting their shoes wet in the process.

Both Kevin and Linda leaped toward the dry sand, but not before Linda's white tennis shoes were drenched.

"You should wear boots, like me," razzed Kevin as they sat down on the sand so Linda could remove her shoes.

"I may just have to give that some thought," smiled Linda.

"Do you know I love you?" questioned Kevin as he put an arm around Linda and pulled her close.

"I'm so glad," beamed Linda as she suddenly kissed her handsome husband, more passionately than usual. "I love you, too!"

Most of the guests had just finished eating and reminiscing with one another when Carolyn, Sherry, Ann, Susan and Rupert showed up. They were dirty, tired and carrying heavy burlap sacks.

"What happened to your luggage?" questioned Jim as they approached.

"It's over at our little airport," advised Susan with a crooked grin. "Think we might get a bellhop to bring it over here to the lighthouse for us?"

"Very funny," snickered Jim as he hugged each of them. "What's in the burlap sacks?"

"You'll see," grinned Carolyn from behind her.

"So, what's all this?" asked Susan as she nodded toward the crowd of people.

"Welcome back!" greeted Sheree as she rushed over and hugged each of them.

"Yeah, what is all this, anyway?" questioned Carolyn as she motioned toward the tables of guests. "You didn't have to do all this on our account." *It was just like Jim to pull a stunt like that.*

"It's a wake," informed Jim.

"Who died?" frowned Sherry.

"Eric Santori," answered Jim.

"Hello, I'm Eric's friend Ted," greeted a handsome man who had just joined them. He could not take his eyes off of Sherry and was clearly interested in her.

420

"This is Sherry," introduced Jim with a gleam in his eyes.

"That should prove confusing," smiled Ted, who had just met Jim's wife Sheree.

"Hi Ted, nice to meet you," flirted Sherry as she shook his hand. "Jim's wife is the one with two e's in her name. I'm the one with a 'y' in my name, like in the drink."

"I see," grinned Ted as he undressed her with his eyes. "My kind of woman."

Sherry blushed at first but then laughed to be polite. "So, who was Eric Santori, anyway?"

"He was my best friend," advised Ted with a touch of sadness.

"Linda's husband Kevin had a half-brother," volunteered Sheree. "That was him."

"Really?" interjected Ann. "There is no one named Santori in the family tree that I've ever heard of."

"His real name was Eric Killingham," added Sheree.

"Okay, that makes sense," nodded Ann. "You're going to have to tell me all about him."

"That's part of why everyone's still here," advised Jim.

"So, do you think they'd mind if we join you?" asked Rupert. "I'm famished."

"Please, do," urged Jim as he headed for the podium where a microphone had been set up on a stand nearby.

"You heard the man," Rupert flirted with Linda, mostly because she happened to be standing right there and that was just his way. He flirted with all women. His handsome black face, well-built body and flirtatious smile were instantly noticed by every woman on the beach.

"I see you've met *my* husband," Susan mentioned to Linda as she put her arm through Rupert's and led him away from her.

Kevin merely shook his head and smiled.

"What?" demanded Linda. "I was only being friendly."

"Of course, you were," snickered Kevin. "Hey, come here." Kevin then put his arm around Linda and pulled her close as he flirted with her. *He was not about to let her out of his sight again, not anytime soon!*

"Ladies and gentlemen," came the voice of Jim Otterman from the podium. "May I have your attention, please?"

After a few moments, the rippling sound of voices subsided.

421

"We are gathered here today to remember the life of Eric Santori, also known as Eric Killingham. He was many things to many people, and was a very important part of many of our lives. And though I didn't personally know him that well, I respect him and am honored to host this celebration of his life. What I'd like to do now is open this up to anyone who would like to come up and say a few words about him. Ted, how about you?"

"Thanks, Jim," acknowledged Ted as he made his way up to the podium. He was in full military dress, Class A. "It would be my pleasure. As some of you know, Eric and I served four tours of duty together in the military. We killed a lot of bad guys and even got ourselves shot on more than one occasion. But, what I'd like to talk about today is the happy times, and some of the adventures he and I had together."

Ted made eye contact with Kevin and Linda, and then Sherry, before continuing. "During one of our assignments for Special Ops, Eric and I were sent to etiquette school. It was our job that night to look our best, learn impeccable table manners, and to try and remember which fork and spoon went with what." Several members of the audience chuckled at that. "Interestingly, we were stationed in a remote area of the desert where the entire event took place inside a large tent."

"After a few glasses of topnotch champagne that night," continued Ted, "we finally decided to skip out and go have some *real* fun." Ted then grinned. "You can only imagine the look on the face of that four-star general when the outhouse he was using suddenly decided to tip over – with him inside. Understandably, he said some things that would make a sailor blush." Laughter erupted among the listeners.

When it began to subside, Ted went on. "Naturally, we didn't want to get into trouble, so Eric and I decided to practice our Ninja skills. That involved making a clean escape before the local police could arrive."

"Did you manage?" asked a military man from the audience.

"At first, we thought so," answered Ted. "Neither of us knew we could even run that fast, or leap over such high walls with a single bound. But, once we were outside the compound, we made a beeline for a local village several clicks away. Up one alley and down the next we went, leaping over rooftops, and behind buildings. Finally, thinking we were safe, that's when we came face-to-face with the local authorities."

"I remember that!" howled one of the soldiers in the audience.

"Me, too," laughed another as he slapped his knee.

"Would *you* like to tell the story?" asked Ted.

"You're doing fine," encouraged the man.

"That was when Eric and I were finally taken to the nearest base to face the man in charge," described Ted. "Imagine our surprise when it turned out to be the four-star general himself."

Everyone was laughing now, even Linda.

"Unfortunately for him," added Ted, "our Special Ops status granted us certain privileges he hadn't counted on. The man was furious when he called our commanding officer and was told to just let us go."

"You got off scot-free?" grilled Jim from the audience.

"That's about the size of it," grinned Ted. "We were always getting into trouble, though."

"Good thing for your 007 status, then," nodded Jim.

"You could look at it like that," laughed Ted.

"I've got a story," mentioned another man as he got up and came to the podium. "My name is Mike Jackson, and I served two tours of duty with Ted and Eric, most recently in Afghanistan, but our first tour together was in the Philippines."

"Oh yes, I remember that," grinned Ted as he sat down.

"On paydays, some of us would go down to the local tavern and have a few beers," began Mike. "But, one night when we got there, there was no place to sit because the entire town was having their annual celebration of the dead. So, we decided to get some six-packs to go and headed up to an old cemetery on the hill overlooking the town."

Several of the military men chuckled at the memory.

"Naturally, the people there are quite superstitious about cemeteries and avoid going there at night, but many of the younger ones tend to get brave after a few beers during the annual celebration. Imagine their surprise when they got there and saw a *real ghost!*"

Mike began laughing so hard he could hardly talk but finally continued. "The hardest part of the whole deal was trying to explain to our commander that we knew *absolutely nothing* about what had happened to the clean white sheets that were on his bed."

"You didn't?" chuckled Jim.

"The entire town was in such an uproar about seeing ghosts at the cemetery, that a priest was eventually called in to try and exorcise the town," concluded Mike.

"Oh, I got one," spoke up another man as he came to the podium. "I'm Harry Porter, and I served with Eric as a nurse medic during his first tour of duty in Vietnam. That was before both of us went over to the dark side."

Several of the men thought that was funny, but Linda wasn't laughing anymore. She had suddenly become sullen and serious.

"Even in 'Nam, guys will be guys on payday," resumed Harry. "One night we went into this little village to have some drinks when the old bulls decided we should participate in a fighting match so they could bet on us and earn some easy money from the locals."

By that time, Linda was absolutely bristling with anger and had folded her arms.

"It was well known that Eric and I were both accomplished martial artists," advised Harry. "Well, after enough drinks, we were ready to take on anyone. That was when they brought out this gigantic guy, that they had saved for last on purpose. By then, I'd had enough, but Eric decided to try and take him."

"We can leave anytime you like," whispered Kevin to Linda.

"Not on your life," fumed Linda. She wanted to hear every last sordid detail.

"Sadly, for Eric," continued Harry, "the big guy laid him out flat in record time after smashing a beer bottle over his head. There were no rules in those types of bar fights," he added for the benefit of those who were unfamiliar with what he was talking about.

"So, what happened to him?" questioned Kevin from the audience. "I'm Eric's brother Kevin, by the way."

"That was when we realized that both of us needed stitches," elaborated Harry. "So, we managed to make our way to the nearest hospital in town, but were too drunk to find our way inside. So, we decided to stitch each other up, since we both were nurses."

Raucous laughter erupted again from the military guys. When it got back to a dull roar, Harry added, "Eric tried to stitch up a gash in my finger before passing out cold in the flowerbed. The next morning, imagine my surprise when I only had four fingers on that hand."

"Four fingers?" frowned Jim.

424

"Because two of them had been sewn together!" howled Harry as everyone broke out laughing again.

Linda shook her head with embarrassment. *How in the world could Eric have done these things?* Then she heard Harry talking again.

"Good thing we were already at the hospital."

Several more of Eric's former military buddies got up and told stories of escapades and mischief they had gotten into with Eric, including the time Eric had been found passed out naked by the Fountain of St. Peter's Square in Rome the morning after some party he'd gone to while on leave.

Finally, Kevin decided to get up. "Most of you don't know me, but I am Kevin Killingham, and I was Eric's half-brother. I did not have the chance to meet him until recently, but will miss him. Thank you, gentlemen, for a glimpse into his life. I appreciate learning more about him." Kevin then abruptly sat down.

"Let's hear from the band," suggested Jim.

"Wait!" called Michael Santori as he stood up and came to the podium. "I'm Eric's oldest brother Michael. And while I do appreciate hearing about my brother's notorious escapades while he was in the military, you haven't heard from the Santoris yet."

Michael, Justin, Philip and Evan all exchanged mischievous grins with one another.

"Oh, here we go," muttered Linda as she rolled her eyes.

"I'd actually like to hear this," whispered Kevin.

"The first time I met you, Kevin, was when you were just a baby," revealed Michael as he made eye contact with Kevin and then with Linda. "I was only six years old at the time."

Kevin was suddenly uncomfortable being thrust into the limelight but could do nothing about it at the moment.

"Mama was driving Mark Killingham's beat-up old 1948 DeSoto," continued Michael. "It was a sickly seaweed green. I was in the front seat holding baby Eric while Justin, Philip and Evan were in the back seat. Mama was going out to the Johnson Ranch to take Mark his lunch that day."

"I remember that," acknowledged Philip from the audience.

"Me, too," nodded Justin.

Evan merely shook his head in the negative and shrugged his shoulders. He had been too young at the time to recall it.

"That was when we saw this woman walking alongside the road with a huge suitcase, carrying a baby. It seemed odd because it was really hot that day and yet she had a coat on. Kevin, that woman was your mother, and the baby was you."

Kevin merely frowned and waited for Michael to continue.

"Well, after Mama picked you two up, they got to talking about this and that, and suddenly realized that they were both married to the same man. I still remember Mama slamming on the brakes and ordering the rest of us out of the car so she and Bobby Sue could talk alone."

"Did your mother ever tell you about this?" whispered Linda.

"Not a word," confirmed Kevin.

"Once we were back inside the car again," added Michael, "I was right there in the front seat when our mothers decided to do a baby swap before confronting Mark, to see if he would even notice which baby was which."

"And did he?" prompted Kevin, who was now quite invested in learning the outcome of Michael's story about the baby switch.

"No," answered Michael, "but just before that when our mothers were busy juggling babies, I actually got to hold you for a few moments. In fact, that was the *only* time I ever got to hold you, Kevin."

Michael paused to take a drink from the bottle of beer he had with him and then went on.

"Mama told us to wait inside the car, no matter what happened, but of course we rolled down the windows so we could listen to what was going on," elaborated Michael. "It was right after he tossed you onto a bale of hay and grabbed Mama by the hair, that Mark Killingham found himself at the pointed end of Mr. Johnson's pitchfork."

"A very *big* pitchfork," interjected Philip.

"A lot of other stuff was said that we couldn't hear, but I do remember waiting there until the police finally arrived to arrest Mark and took him away. In fact, that was the last time we boys ever saw him."

"Wow," muttered Linda.

"I'm Justin," mentioned the next brother as he took the stand while Michael sat down. "I was only five years old at the time, but will never forget how we drove home that night, packed up everything

426

we had that would fit into that crappy green car, and headed for Bellevue where our grandparents lived."

Justin and his brothers were every bit as handsome as Eric had been and had Linda's full attention.

"It was 37 miles from the Johnson Ranch to Sprague where we lived and another 240 miles from there to Bellevue," described Justin. "Unfortunately, we were only about half way there when we ran out of gas and had to call Grandpa Santori to come and get us."

"When was Mark released from custody?" questioned Jim.

"Who knows," grinned Justin. "But, he probably wasn't too happy when – or if – he ever found his old DeSoto where we left it abandoned on the side of the highway that night."

Everyone in the audience chuckled at that.

"That was also when Mama had our last names changed to Santori," revealed Justin. "The name *Killingham* was never to be spoken in our home again."

"Didn't Mark ever even try to come and see you?" questioned Kevin. He no longer cared that the others were listening to their conversation.

"Actually yes," grinned Justin, "until he came face-to-face with the business end of Grandma Santori's shotgun one night."

Laughter erupted at once. "We could have used someone like her on the team," remarked one of the military men.

"Indeed," nodded Ted as he watched Justin sit down.

"My name is Philip Santori," smiled the next brother as he arrived at the microphone. "That over there is my lovely wife Sally. Our children are all grown and living in Florida with our grandkids, so they were not able to be here today."

Kevin smiled and nodded at Philip.

"I was only 4 years old at the time that all happened," mentioned Philip, "so I don't recall much about it – except that pitchfork!"

Several smiles and chuckles could be seen and heard.

"What I remember most is growing up living in the attic at Santori's Italian Dining," reminisced Philip. "We never went hungry again after that. And, I especially remember some of the pranks my older brothers used to pull on Evan and me."

Michael and Justin grinned and nodded.

427

"In particular, I recall the time they decided to put us onto a piece of plywood they'd found in a dumpster somewhere."

Michael and Justin both began to laugh.

"They actually managed to convince us that it would be like a roller coaster ride, but better," recounted Philip. "We even helped them nail an old piece of carpet to the bottom, so it would glide more easily down the stairs with us on it. Naturally, Mama arrived home just in time to see us sailing directly towards her where she stood at the front door below us."

"Oh my god!" exclaimed Linda.

"Thankfully, Mama managed to jump out of the way, just in the nick of time," elaborated Philip with a mischievous grin.

"What happened to you guys?" questioned Linda.

"Well," continued Phillip, "when the plywood hit the doorjamb, the impact sent us sailing out onto the front porch, but not in time to escape the wrath of Grandma Santori's broom when she found out about it from Mama. If I remember right, she even had to get a new broom after that."

More laughter erupted.

"We Santori boys were just nothing but trouble," interjected Evan from the audience.

"It was when Eric was only 4 years old that Evan and I decided to pull the same stunt on him," continued Philip. "Of course, we were clever enough to make sure no adults were due home at the time and totally got away with it."

"Except, of course, for the unexplainable dent on the inside of the front door after that," reminded Evan from the audience.

"There was that," agreed Philip with a smile as he sat down.

"Yes, those were the days," grinned Evan as he went up to the microphone. "And, as you've probably guessed by now, I'm Evan Santori. Over there is my wife Gina. Sadly, we have no kids, but a lifetime with her is all any man could hope for."

It was obvious how much the two of them were in love as they exchanged a loving glance. Linda's upper lip began to quiver, causing Kevin to put his arm around her and pull her close.

"That's all I could ever hope for myself," whispered Kevin as he kissed Linda on the cheek.

Linda smiled and hugged him back.

"Being only one year older than Eric," continued Evan, "I was probably closer to him than anyone else. My memories include running around the neighborhood with Eric blowing up neighbors' mailboxes with home-made bombs, tossing our mother's favorite Siamese cat over the fence by its tail to the dogs, and putting bananas in the tailpipes of our neighbors' cars. Just the kind of kids anyone would want living on their block, right?" Of course, he was being sarcastic.

Linda could not believe what she was hearing. *Eric had always been kind and gentle to Old Blue, the Siamese cat she'd had at the time of their marriage. How could these things be true?*

There were several snickers and laughs at that. Then one of the military men asked, "What kind of bombs?"

"Well," grinned Evan, "the whole thing involved several stages. The first step, of course, was to kipe a few shotgun shells from Grandma Santori's small weapons cache that she kept in the basement."

"My kinda grandma!" exclaimed Ted.

"And of course, it had to be done in moderation, so we didn't get caught," grinned Evan. "The next step was to take the shells apart, pour out the shot, pry out the wadding, and dump out the gun powder."

"Gun powder?" whispered Linda.

"I used to do the same thing," chuckled Kevin.

Linda gave Kevin a stern look.

"After that," continued Evan, "we'd roll a teased-out cotton ball in it until it was completely saturated with gun powder."

"We used to use strands of hemp from an old rope my dad kept in the garage," mentioned Kevin.

Linda merely shook her head disapprovingly.

"That works," approved Evan. "Well, after that we would tape the bottom of some blown-out eggshells, pour some gas from our Grandpa Santori's fuel canister into 'em, and then insert our wicks."

"How'd you seal 'em off?" questioned Kevin.

"Duct tape."

"Me, too," grinned Kevin.

"Seriously?" whispered Linda. "You didn't?"

"I'm afraid so," confessed Kevin with a crooked smile. "My mom's laying hens were occasionally missing an egg or two."

"Boys will be boys," laughed Evan. "The fun part was when we lit 'em up and tossed 'em into the neighbors' mailboxes."

Linda and several other women present shook their heads with vehement disapproval, including Sheree, Ann, Sherry, Susan, Carolyn and some of the other men's wives.

"The point is," added Evan, "that Eric was always a soldier at heart, even as a boy, though it wasn't until he was out in the battlefield for real that he finally got to blow stuff up for a living."

There were knowing nods among several of the military men.

"I still remember the tour of duty I did with Eric in Vietnam," reminisced Evan. "I had only three weeks to go at the time, so it was devastating to get sent home early when my darned leg got blown off."

Evan then pulled up his pantleg to expose a prosthetic leg.

Linda audibly gasped with surprise. She'd had no idea.

"Good thing Eric didn't step on that landmine with me," added Evan, "or he wouldn't have been able to carry me out of there."

After a moment of silence, Evan continued. "Most of you know already that Eric did eight tours of duty. I'm sure that's something no one else here can say."

"Amen to that," came several voices from the other men.

Kevin remained silent but was clearly troubled.

"Others were not able to serve, through no fault of their own," added Evan as he made eye contact with Kevin. "Those of us who did know you would have done so if you could have."

Kevin swallowed a lump in his throat. *How did Evan know?*

Linda took Kevin's hand and squeezed it. She then leaned close to him and whispered, "Good thing for you, too, or I wouldn't have married you. There was no way I'd ever have gone through that again!"

"Good thing," agreed Kevin as he pulled Linda close again. *He suddenly seemed to understand why that was so important to her.*

"My name is Consuela," mentioned a middle-aged Hispanic woman as she came to the microphone after Evan sat down. "Eric and I worked together at the Happy Acres Nursing Home and Retirement Community for the past two years."

Consuela was trying to fight back tears. "And, I definitely do *not* approve of blowing stuff up!"

The audience began to laugh again. When the commotion subsided, she continued.

"Eric was thoughtful and considerate. He was also a capable nurse, always putting the needs of our residents before his own. More than one of us hoped that someday we might turn his head, but Eric was clearly in love with someone else – someone he knew would never be a part of his life again." She then made eye contact with Linda.

Linda was suddenly uncomfortable again. *Who was this woman, anyway? What did she know?*

Distracted while the other co-workers and friends got up and said their piece, Linda began to think of the night in the greenhouse with Eric, the precious time they had spent together when still alone. Silent tears began to creep down her cheeks.

When everyone was done, Jim got back up. "Some of the guys here have agreed to play some music for us. We are also going to have a 21-gun salute." Jim then motioned for them to proceed.

Suddenly serious, many of the same guys who'd been joking and telling stories about their experiences with Eric grabbed various musical instruments from their cases, assembled themselves beside the platform, and began playing *Taps.*

While they played, seven other soldiers grabbed their rifles from gun cases that had been stashed behind the podium. They quickly assembled themselves together nearby, side by side in a straight line on the sand near the water's edge. Waiting until the music stopped, Ted then commanded, "Firing party, attention. Port arms."

After seeing the remaining military men in the audience suddenly stand and present arms, the audience quickly stood while the honor guard brought their AR-15 service rifles to a 45-degree angle, four inches from their chests. Ted then commanded, "Ready."

The firing squad simultaneously took a step forward with their left feet, aimed their rifles at a 15-degree angle, brought their heads to their rifles as if they were aiming their weapons, and placed their index fingers on their triggers.

"Fire!" yelled Ted.

All seven squad members fired their weapons at once.

"Reset," commanded Ted.

The squad then returned their left feet to attention position, but remained at port arms. As soon as they had snapped back to attention, they grabbed their magazine wells with their non-firing hands, and with their firing hands pulled the charging handle to the rear and released their expended cartridges at the same time.

At Ted's direction, the squad repeated the entire process two more times, firing their weapons and then expending the used cartridges each time.

After the last command of "reset," Ted shouted, "Order-Arms."

When the men had complied, Ted next commanded, "Right-face." The squad turned together as a unit. The middle squad member suddenly handed his weapon to Ted, saluted him, and then fell back from the squad so he could remain behind to pick up the expended cartridges from the sand. Ted saluted back, positioned the rifle that had been handed to him, and then yelled, "Forward-March."

As Ted escorted the rest of the squad back to the podium area, the musicians began playing *Amazing Grace.*

"How come they only fired three rounds?" Linda whispered to Kevin. "Aren't they supposed to do 21?"

"A group of seven soldiers fires off three shots each," Kevin patiently explained. "Seven times three equals 21, which is why it's called a 21-gun salute."

"Okay, that makes sense," nodded Linda.

Those playing musical instruments had meanwhile marched from the beach, up the steps, and toward the lighthouse as they continued to play *Amazing Grace* until finished. With the entire musical group in formation on the bluff above, they next played *The Star Spangled Banner.* The sound echoed across the beach below. Those still on the beach silently stood again and put their hands on their hearts until the song was completed.

Ted and Evan then proceeded to fold the American flag that had been displayed beside the podium. Once the flag was properly folded, they marched over to where Kevin and Linda were seated. Ted handed the flag to Linda, along with a clear plastic bag containing the expended shells, and then gave her a white-gloved salute.

Stunned, Linda's hands shook as she took the folded flag and the bag of used shells from him. *She had not expected this!* Tears began streaming down her cheeks as she sat there holding them.

Evan then pulled a black case from his pocket, opened it, and handed it to Kevin. Inside was a purple heart. "Eric would want you to have this. It was the only one we managed to save from the bonfire that night." Kevin was speechless as he stared at the purple heart before finally accepting it.

Both men then saluted, turned, and marched back over to where the other soldiers were still standing at arms.

Jim was at the podium again. He had picked up the urn in which Eric's ashes were housed. "Kevin and Linda will now accompany me and Eric to the runway. For those who wish to remain, we will shortly be doing a flyover so Eric's ashes can be sprinkled out over the water."

After flying his aging Cessna over the beach with Kevin and Linda inside, Jim then flew out over the water so they could pour out the ashes from Eric's urn onto the water.

"Goodbye Eric," bid Linda as she removed the lid and handed it back to Kevin before tipping the urn to one side by the open window.

"Don't let go of it," advised Jim as he lowered the passenger side of his plane by 15 degrees, to make it easier for Linda.

Eric's ashes slowly began to float out of the urn like gossamer wings, down toward the water. Brilliant colors from the sunset made them appear like a cloud of pink, yellow and purple dust as they went.

"Farewell, brother," added Kevin as they watched the ashes begin to land on the water below.

The military men down on the beach remained in formation and saluted during the entire flyover and sprinkling of Eric's ashes.

Kevin finally took the empty urn from Linda, put its lid back on, and stowed it between his legs on the floor of the back seat. Linda was seated in the front seat next to Jim.

"Hopefully, he'll find some peace now," mentioned Jim as he leveled out the plane and headed back to the tiny airport at Oceanview Academy.

Neither Kevin nor Linda felt like talking and remained silent as Jim began the landing sequence.

Back in the tower room of the lighthouse two hours later, after the remainder of the guests had said their farewells and gone their way, Jim and Sheree had invited Kevin, Linda, Carolyn, Sherry, Ann, Susan and Rupert for a family meeting.

Carolyn and her group were still dirty, even more tired than before the memorial service, and still had heavy burlap sacks with them that were sitting on the floor by their feet. Ann's husband Ted Jensen had retrieved their luggage from Jim's Learjet and put it in their rooms already.

Much to everyone's surprise, Jim's partner Chip had joined them, as well. Both men had their briefcases with them.

"Before we get started," began Jim, "I think everyone knows who Chip and I are, but not everyone knows Kevin and Linda."

Carolyn merely rolled her eyes and folded her arms. She was well aware of who Linda was.

"We know who Linda is," advised Susan with a toss of her head.

"Yes, we know each other," assured Linda uncomfortably.

"I believe Linda has also met my husband Rupert," reminded Susan as she gave Linda a warning glance.

Kevin tried to repress a smile as he observed the social interplay between Linda and her two nemeses from high school.

"Well, Kevin may not know who all of you are," clarified Jim. "Kevin, that is Susan and Carolyn. Susan, of course, was Carolyn's roommate when they attended high school together over there at Oceanview Academy."

Kevin politely smiled and nodded at them. *Had Linda really been as horrible to Carolyn in high school as Jim had described?*

"Carolyn's friend Sherry," continued Jim, "is a filmmaker who makes documentaries."

"How do you do," nodded Sherry.

"And this our daughter Ann, who you met on skype," added Jim as he nodded toward Ann. "She's also the family historian."

"That I am," grinned Ann.

"So, what's this really all about?" questioned Carolyn as she gave Linda a look of disapproval. "Can't this wait until morning?"

Jim merely shook his head in the negative. He was trying with great difficulty to repress a smile.

"Okay, let's have it," insisted Susan. Like Carolyn, all she wanted was a hot shower so she could go and get some rest.

"You bet," agreed Jim. "We can do the quick version now and then go over it again in more detail tomorrow if you prefer."

434

"The quick version of what?" pressed Sherry as she pulled out her notepad. "Do I need to take notes?"

"Only if you like," interjected Chip, who was also being mysterious.

"I'll bet this has to do with how the Santori family fits into our genealogy," guessed Ann.

"Does it involve food?" questioned Rupert.

"After all you just ate?" countermanded Susan.

"Can't blame a guy for trying," grinned Rupert.

"You really must have a hollow leg," chuckled Susan as she flirted with her well-built husband. *It really was incredible that he could eat so much food and never get fat.*

"Kevin, why don't you take a moment to share with us what Vivian LaMont left behind," suggested Jim.

"Aren't you the least bit curious what we have in these burlap sacks?" asked Carolyn as she gave Jim a smug look.

"Hold that thought," instructed Jim. "Kevin?"

Kevin then removed Vivian's diary from a small wooden box and began reading select portions of it to the group. By the time he and Linda had finished relating Vivian's entire tale to them, Susan and Sherry had each begun to nod off to sleep.

"Wake up!" shouted Jim as he shook Susan's arm.

"You're going to have to tell me the rest of that again in the morning," apologized Susan. "Probably after the part where they hopped that train, I think."

"Are you kidding me?" grilled Jim.

"I'm just messing with you," chuckled Susan. "I think I heard everything up until the time Mark and Vivian became lovers, when they were in Seattle."

"Did you get the part about her *murdering* all her husbands?" questioned Jim.

"Yes," laughed Susan. "A very innovative woman."

"Really?" Rupert gave her a strange look.

"I would *never* do anything like that myself, of course," Susan grinned a crooked smile. "I just meant that she was a very clever lady, not to ever get caught for something like that."

"Are you two going to have your name changed to Santori now?" Ann suddenly asked Kevin and Linda.

435

"We could always have it changed back to Smith," teased Kevin.

"Huh?" Ann did not get it.

"That's another long story," Linda assured her.

"I think we'll stick with Killingham," added Kevin as he put his arm around Linda and gave her a hug.

"So, what else is in that box?" asked Carolyn.

"You won't believe this," assured Linda as Kevin opened the box again and removed a solid gold object.

At that same time, Jim removed the solid gold disk from his briefcase that the others already knew about.

"Notice how the scalloped edges of the disk exactly match the rounded edge of Kevin's piece," pointed out Jim.

"It looks just like a giant flower petal," observed Chip.

"It's even got Sumerian writing on it, just like this disk here," added Jim. "I was hoping Rupert might be able to help us out with deciphering it."

Carolyn and the other members of her group each broke out into irrepressible grins as they opened up their burlap sacks. Each of them possessed a solid gold object, almost identical to the one that Kevin had just produced.

"Notice how the writing on this one matches that place right there," pointed out Carolyn as she placed her gold petal in one of the scalloped spots.

"No, I think it goes over there," differed Rupert as he placed his gold petal there and moved hers to another position.

"He's right," agreed Jim as he stared at the pieces with excited amazement. "See how the writing continues from the center disk out onto the petal?"

After Susan, Sherry and Ann had each placed their gold pieces in the designated positions, only two places remained without petals.

"It's a puzzle," frowned Jim.

"No, it's another treasure map," corrected Rupert.

"Can it tell us where the other two pieces are?" grilled Chip.

"They could be anywhere in the world by now," advised Rupert. "We checked the entire village."

"Once we found it," qualified Carolyn.

"Except in the temple," Ann reminded them. "Remember, we didn't go back to that one on the top."

436

"That's right!" confirmed Carolyn. "We didn't."

"Oh, my God!" exclaimed Sherry. "We're not going back?"

"We have to," grinned Carolyn.

"What about that plastic tub of passports at the border?" reminded Sherry. "And the night I spent in jail?"

"What?" frowned Jim.

"There was that," agreed Carolyn. "Still, don't you guys want to know what happened to all the people those passports belonged to?"

"Hold it," commanded Jim. "Back up. Why did Sherry spend a night in jail?"

Sherry looked sheepish as she explained. "You know how they have you put all your stuff through a scanner at the border?"

"Yeah," nodded Jim.

"Well, when we were heading from Peru into Ecuador, I got to chatting with the English-speaking guard there and somehow failed to pick up my passport from the tray," revealed Sherry.

"The same thing almost happened to me," interjected Susan, "but I noticed it right away and went back for it."

"Let her finish," commanded Jim.

"Well," continued Sherry, "it was when we got to the Columbian border that I realized I didn't have it anymore."

"What did you do?" Linda suddenly asked.

"Susan tried to explain to them that it must be back at the other border," elaborated Sherry, "but none of them spoke English."

"Susan speaks Spanish," stated Jim.

"Yes, but the Spanish those people speak is some weird dialect," added Susan as she shook her head.

"Anyway," explained Sherry, "it took these guys about six hours to find someone who could understand her."

Susan shrugged her shoulders. "Nicaraguan accent, Columbian accent, what's the difference, right?"

Jim shook his head with disbelief.

"The guards had big guns that stood guard outside my cement jail cell," described Sherry. "There were rats there, too, and only a hard, wooden stool with a wobbly leg to sit on."

"How horrible!" exclaimed Linda.

"Not too many rats, I hope," grinned Jim, suddenly seeing the humor in the situation.

"Only a couple," replied Sherry. She wasn't smiling.

"So, when we finally did find someone who could understand me," related Susan, "they took us all back to the border at Ecuador – at gunpoint – to see if Sherry's passport was there."

"It obviously was," presumed Jim.

"Along with a huge plastic tub of other passports," interjected Carolyn. "Certainly, they must belong to someone!"

"It is disconcerting to imagine what might have happened to all those other people," agreed Rupert.

"Very sobering, indeed," agreed Ann.

"What about all this gold?" Jim suddenly asked. "How did you ever manage to get that through customs?"

"Even llamas require some food," advised Carolyn with a crooked smile.

"At least none of them were foolish enough to leave their papers behind at the checkpoint," interjected Sherry as she shook her head.

"You traveled with llamas?" Jim seemed surprised.

"For quite a while," confirmed Rupert.

"Anyway," continued Carolyn, "these were the actual feed bags our llamas carried. Mostly filled with alfalfa."

"They never bothered to check them?" queried Jim.

"Not the ones filled with llama beans," revealed Rupert.

"Llama beans?" questioned Linda.

"Llama manure is sometimes called 'llama beans,'" explained Rupert. "It's used as a potassium, nitrogen and phosphorous-rich organic fertilizer in gardens and flowerbeds."

"In other words," interpreted Susan, "it makes good fertilizer."

"Yeah, I get it," snapped Linda.

Jim and several of the others suddenly began to laugh.

"Llama manure is also earth-friendly," added Carolyn. "Florists will pay top dollar for it. Some of the most prestigious florists in the world are based in Ecuador. You should see some of the baby blue flowers they grow."

Linda flushed with embarrassment as her eyes met Carolyn's. *Obviously, Carolyn was trying to remind her of the baby blue corsage incident from high school.*

"It even has the added benefit of being odor-free," snickered Susan. She and Carolyn were both enjoying giving Linda a bad time.

"So, let me get this straight," interrupted Jim, when he finally was able to contain his laughter. "You were posing as manure traders?"

"Organic fertilizer distributors," corrected Rupert.

"Would *you* rifle through a bag of it?" chuckled Carolyn.

"Probably not," agreed Jim with a wicked grin.

"Odor-free?" Linda made a face as she picked up Susan's empty burlap sack and sniffed it.

"That really would make a great documentary," opined Sheree. "You could go down there and find out what happened to all those missing people."

"No thanks," declined Sherry. "I've had enough adventure with these guys to last me a lifetime."

"I'll go," Linda suddenly offered.

"You will not," differed Kevin.

Linda folded her arms with determination.

"Not without me, you're not," added Kevin, more softly. *Perhaps this was just the thing Linda needed to help her get this sudden yearning for adventure out of her system once and for all.*

"You two seriously want to go down there?" scoffed Jim. "After everything we've just been though?"

"Sure, why not?" sighed Kevin. "It does sound like a worthwhile cause. Someone needs to find out what happened to all those missing people."

"Indeed, they do," agreed Carolyn.

"Plus, we might still find those other two gold pieces," pointed out Ann. "We'll need to get some more llamas, of course."

"Not without me, you're not," advised Ted.

"I'll go," agreed Rupert. "If Susan does."

After a long pause, Susan finally nodded her assent.

"Me, too," interjected Chip.

"The more the merrier," smiled Jim.

"It would make an amazing documentary," tempted Carolyn as she gave Sherry a pleading look.

"You couldn't pay me enough," responded Sherry.

"Money's no object," added Carolyn as she glanced at Sherry with determination.

"It does sound like a worthwhile story," opined Sheree.

"We'll see," relented Sherry with a deep sigh.

"I'll double whatever Carolyn pays you," proposed Jim with a wink at Sherry. "It'll be an offer you can't refuse. More than enough to finish producing that new movie you're working on. Trust me."

Made in the USA
Columbia, SC
24 March 2018